Ian Josephs

FORCED
ADOPTION

Lulu.

First Published by Lulu 2008

Second Edition 2009

Copyright © Ian Josephs 2009

ISBN 978-1-4092-6971-7

CONTENTS

PREFACE

This is a very unusual book because I am in effect reproducing my website www.forced-adoption.com in book form, thanks partly to my wife Danielle who nagged me until I got down to writing and producing it. I am doing this so that those concerned who do not possess a computer and those who wish to refer to my advice without having to go online will have an easy opportunity to do so.

There will therefore be quite a few references to websites where I give the link, but not the actual content. The most important and most informative texts however are reproduced in full, so that the content can be read without having to use a computer.

I made this website with two main intentions.

Firstly, to prove to doubters that the family court system is rotten to the core and secondly that it needs the reforms detailed in my 'Detailed Reforms' chapter. Here in the UK, 35000 children a year are being taken into care of which around 600 are newborn babies. A large proportion of these children and also of these babies are taken from parents who have committed no crime and done them no harm but nevertheless, the babies and the children are simply judged to be "at risk" of emotional harm or perhaps to have witnessed domestic violence even though no violence has been perpetrated on the children themselves. In this way, battered women are punished twice because if they report domestic violence, police call in social services who remove their children. Court proceedings are shrouded in secrecy with drastic punishment for those who break the "omerta" of silence. It is planned that certain journalists may be allowed to attend certain family proceedings but the parents will continue to be gagged and will still be unable to protest publicly if their children are taken from them permanently. Until now, once all court proceedings have been concluded, parents have had the right to speak out, but the minister Jack Straw has vowed to close this last chink of freedom and in the name of "privacy" has forbidden them to go public or to reveal any details of court proceedings at all!

Local authorities have until recently been set adoption targets by central government with substantial financial rewards if targets are achieved. Indeed, many have doubled their targets at the expense of mothers who bereft of their children were unable to reveal publicly what happened to them in the secret family courts under pain of punishment and sometimes imprisonment.

Targets have recently been abolished in theory but in practice the savings achieved by adopting children instead of paying around £400 per week per child for fostering are still sufficient incentives for social workers to target children for adoption whenever they can. This is hard for anyone who has not encountered the system to believe, but I think I will have shown in this book that I am not exaggerating these claims.

Secondly and just as important, I hope to offer good advice and help to those in trouble with the family court system. I especially oppose the notion of forced adoption by which I mean the system introduced in 1976 where children who are merely said to be at risk of physical or more often so-called 'emotional harm' sometime in the future, can be taken from loving parents and adopted by strangers. These unfortunate parents are not only legally gagged, they are also forbidden to even look for their child until that child reaches the age of 18, by which time the trail is usually cold. Despite this, more than 200 persons a year are (according to the answer to a parliamentary question) sent to prison for breaking injunctions that often forbid parents to try and contact their own children or for breaking gagging orders that forbid them to tell anyone about the injustices they have suffered in the family courts. Babies are earmarked to be taken at birth while mothers are still pregnant, so claims that children are taken into care only as a last resort just do not stand up to scrutiny. Nothing like this can happen elsewhere in Europe. Only in the UK can parents, who have never committed a crime, be separated permanently from their children against their will.

Lastly, I try to help anybody who asks my advice but I especially appreciate parents who can claim that they have no criminal record, no problem with drugs or alcohol, no crippling learning difficulties and no overwhelming mental problems. Surprisingly, these form the majority of those who telephone me or email me for advice, probably because children who make the best 'adoption material' are white, healthy and happy and come from drug and crime-free families.

Adoption is a money-driven industry where everybody cashes in except the deprived parents, as you will see from the official statistics and newspaper articles I have reproduced in this book.

I am printing this book myself and selling it at cost price, as my purpose is not to make money out of other people's misery but to spread my advice as widely as possible. Each chapter is a separate self-contained unit. For this reason there is a certain amount of repetition where the same material is repeated in more than one chapter. Links and phone numbers are accurate at the time of printing but as time marches on many of them will eventually cease to be operative. Thank you for your kind understanding on this point. Every statistic in this book is backed up by government figures, parliamentary questions or articles from newspapers such as *The Times* and *The Daily Telegraph* who only publish after they have done the necessary research.

Well, I have said enough and I certainly do not want to bore you, so please go on and read the chapters that you think can help you or people you know who need help.

Ian Josephs

1. INTRODUCTION

ABOLISH FORCED ADOPTION!

HELLO!!! LET ME INTRODUCE MYSELF

 My name is IAN JOSEPHS. Social Services have never hurt me, my family, or my friends, but their wicked abuse of power has simply shocked me into action! Many will say that I overstate and exaggerate my case thereby undermining it. I promise you that on the contrary I am understating it as things are now far worse than the public could possibly imagine or accept as credible if I revealed all!

Telephone: 0033 6 26 87 56 84 for free legal advice! Or contact me by email ian@monaco.mc

If you give me a contact phone number and times available to receive a call I can phone you back at my expense.

HOW CAN SOCIAL SERVICES JUSTIFY THE REMOVAL OF BABIES AT BIRTH FOR 'RISK OF EMOTIONAL ABUSE' AND THEIR SUBSEQUENT FORCED ADOPTION BY STRANGERS?

You don't believe this happens? Just read the following *SUNDAY TELEGRAPH* leader article!!

The unnatural justice of secret family courts

Leader article

The Sunday Telegraph, 26 August 2007

The Sunday Telegraph highlights today yet another case in which a mother has been threatened with losing her baby to local authority care. The mother had not shown any sign at all of harming her child, for her baby has not yet been born. The local authority, however, is convinced that there is a possibility that she might harm the child.

To most people, it will seem grotesquely unjust that any child could be removed on such a basis. Northumberland County Council is, however, far from unusual in acting in this way. The courts have endorsed the removal of hundreds of children from their natural parents on the basis that there is a possibility that they might "abuse their child emotionally".

Some of those forcible adoptions are appalling acts of injustice. How can such things happen in Britain? The answer is simple: the courts that enforce the taking away of children from parents on local authority say-so operate in secret. It is illegal to reveal their proceedings, or even their judgments.

"Sunlight is the best disinfectant," insisted US Supreme Court Judge Louis Brandeis. It is because we believe that the only way to improve the decisions made in the family courts is to ensure that they can be scrutinised that The Sunday Telegraph has launched Stop the Secrecy: Open the Family Courts, a campaign to end the ban on reporting any proceedings in the Family Division.

The Government used to recognise the merit in the case for greater openness. But earlier this year, it reversed its commitment to increasing transparency. That was a terrible error.

Children's interests cannot be served by secrecy, for secrecy allows incompetence and injustice to flourish unchecked. We urge the Government to open up the family courts to public scrutiny as soon as possible.

IMPORTANT NEWS: Jack Straw (Lord Chancellor) has announced his intention to change the court rules so as to allow accredited journalists into family courts. This sounds welcome even if few journalists would have time to attend most cases. It is the gagging of parents not the media that is so unjust! It seems certain however that adoption proceedings will still remain secret. The media may be freer but parents who have had their children removed for long term fostering or adoption will still be gagged to the extent that they will still be forbidden to publish their own names or those of their offspring when protesting publicly against a perceived injustice and the probable loss of their children for the rest of their lives. Protest can only be effective when like rape victims parents (and teenage children who wish to express their views) can shed anonymity and campaign under their own names! Worse still the decision in Clayton v Clayton is to be reversed so that aggrieved parents will no longer be free to reveal publicly their own names or those of their children even after all proceedings have finished. One step forward two steps back!

I live and work in Monte Carlo where I own and run a language school. I have an Oxford University law degree but I am not a solicitor or a barrister. So….who am I really? And why do I do what I do?

I am **NOT**, repeat **NOT**, another 'Mother Teresa' and I rarely give to charity (in case I end up paying for the director's Rolls Royce!) but fighting the often **brutal actions of Social Services** is a cause very close to my heart. Social Services have never hurt me, my family or anyone close to me so I have no personal axe to grind but **I HATE THE ABUSE OF POWER** and particularly the way the bullies in Social Services ruthlessly destroy the very families they are supposed to protect. As a matter of principle I never charge a fee and never accept any money whatever for any expenses. Anything a parent tells me is strictly confidential but if parents do want me to involve the press by way of protest I also solemnly undertake that if ever I get offered a fee by a newspaper for introducing a family or writing about parents whose children have been taken then I promise to give 100% of any money received to the family concerned and keep nothing myself. I have no wish to imitate those disgusting people who make money out of the misery of parents who have had their children snatched by Social Services!!

I get two or three new calls from parents nearly every day and advise each one as best I can. Forgive me if I ask you to repeat details and phone numbers each time you telephone or contact me as with around 100 cases going on I need reminding of the basic facts to avoid confusing one similar case with another! I have businesses to run so can only spare the time to fly over to the UK and go to court for parents as a 'McKenzie Friend' (a friend to sit by you and help by suggesting questions that you should ask witnesses and making notes of their replies) in the very worst cases (free of charge) for mothers with no criminal records, drug or alcohol problems who have had their babies snatched at birth by Social Services. This happens more often than you would think!! I will however always find the time to give my advice by email or telephone to **ANY** parent who contacts me concerning a problem they have with the 'SS' (Social Services)!

The public find it hard to believe what is happening to THOUSANDS of parents in the UK.

The following extract from a judgement in the House of Lords confirms that alone in Europe the UK **CONTINUES** to allow and encourage the barbaric practice of taking children from loving and desperate parents and giving them to strangers for closed and secret adoptions without parental consent.

House of Lords - Down Lisburn Health and Social Services Trust .

Baroness Hale of Richmond. Judgement Source: Hansard Lords

34. There is, so far as the parties to this case are aware, no European jurisprudence questioning the principle of freeing for adoption, or indeed compulsory adoption generally. The United Kingdom is unusual amongst members of the Council of Europe in permitting the total severance of family ties without parental consent. (Professor Triseliotis thought that only Portugal and perhaps one other European country allowed this).

It is, of course, the most draconian interference with family life possible.

A secret state is operating in which families are being torn apart
by Camilla Cavendish: Behind the Story
The Times, 20 October 2008

I began writing about parents whose children were being removed by social workers after two chance meetings. One was with a couple who had taken their daughter to A&E with a leg injury, only to have both their children forcibly removed into care and returned only after a legal battle. The other was with a mother whose daughter had said that Daddy, who never lived with them, was touching her in bad places. A psychiatrist who never met them, and was not cross-examined in court, said that she had coached her daughter to lie. She was sent to live with a man her mother thinks is a paedophile.

As I spoke to more parents, patterns emerged which convinced me that these two cases were not aberrations. England and Wales are operating a secret state, where almost any discussion of your case is prevented to protect the 'privacy of the child'. Where courts only need the word of an 'expert' to remove your child. And where some social workers are jumping to wholly erroneous conclusions which tear families apart.

Court of Appeal judges played an important role. Judges such as Justice Judge, Ryder and McFarlane all chose to make public their scathing indictments of local authorities, social workers and/or expert witnesses in individual cases. They made it possible for me to write about those cases.

Sir Mark Potter presided over the High Court this summer, where The Times challenged some reporting restrictions in the case of a man who was jailed for helping his wife to help her son escape from foster care. Sir Mark, in a spirit of openness, released more documents to The Times than we had hoped for — documents that reinforce my belief that that case is a gross miscarriage of justice.

Sir Mark's call for the opening of the family courts to the media is significant. He believes that greater scrutiny will show that the courts generally work well. The argument I have always made is that we should put that to the test. I believe that some social services departments and experts are consistently seeing abuse, especially "emotional harm", where there is none. And that some local authorities are flagrantly ignoring the legal requirement that there should be minimum intervention in family life. We cannot prove that until the courts are opened up.

There is a powerful lobby against openness, made up of those with a vested interest in avoiding scrutiny. Sir Mark's comments today will surely help to shift the power towards those who want to open up the secret state and let the public judge for themselves.

Baby P was 17 months old when he was tortured by his mother's boyfriend in spite of 60 visits by social workers and 3 visits to hospital. It all culminated with a visit from a specialist paediatrician who failed to notice that he had a broken back, 2 finger tips sliced off, several finger nails pulled out, 12 broken ribs and bruises all over his face and body concealed by chocolate. He would still be alive today if someone just once had given him a cursory physical examination but this was not done probably because as usual Social Services etc. were intimidated by this brutal child abuser and his rottweilers and so they left the horrible family alone to look for easier prey mostly among the respectable middle classes.

Most people seem more intent on wreaking vengeance on the murderers of Baby P than preventing the same situation occurring again; may I therefore make a suggestion?

Social Services plead shortage of staff and financial resources as excuses for overlooking torture of children (even after 60 visits to Baby P). In other European countries they take children from parents only if they have been severely physically or sexually abused but in Britain we waste most of our valuable resources fighting cruel cases in secret and costly courts to remove children and even newborn babies at 'risk of emotional harm' and for similar lesser reasons. The parents of Baby P would never have gone to court to fight for his return if he had been taken earlier as parents that violently physically abuse their children avoid courts like the plague!

Physical torture KILLS KILLS KILLS!!!

Emotional abuse does NOT

Poor school attendance does NOT

A cluttered house does NOT

Witnessing domestic violence does NOT

Hostility to the 'professionals' does NOT

A parent with learning problems does NOT

Where therefore should the 'SS' priorities lie?

I'm only asking!!

I would have thought myself it was **MORE IMPORTANT** to concentrate on preventing babies being tortured rather than the more common rush to remove babies **AT BIRTH** from mothers whom some highly paid psychobabble merchants have decided may at some future date emotionally harm their babies! Crystal-ball gazing?

If all the resources of child protection were used to examine thoroughly (looking for visible bruises and burns) say once a month, all those children suspected of having been seriously physically or sexually abused, thousands of children's lives would be saved. At present our resources are wasted fighting in courts to remove happy healthy children from their parents for risk of emotional abuse and similar non life-endangering symptoms.

Only parents that truly love their children fight through the gruelling ritual of the secret family courts and against all common sense they nearly always lose. If they dare to protest publicly more than 200 parents a year are jailed (answer to a parliamentary question) for breaking the 'omertà' wall of secrecy!! If only mothers facing a life sentence by losing children to forced adoption had the right to a hearing by jury most of the present injustices would disappear. In short, what is needed is simply concentration on eradicating physical child abuse and hearings by jury who would rarely take children in other cases such as 'emotional abuse', cluttered dwellings, poor school attendance etc.

The whole collection of judges, lawyers, social workers, and so-called 'experts' giving evidence in secret Family Courts closely resembles one of those fanatical American religious sects! Any hapless parent who contradicts them and declares their innocence of any wrongdoing is 'in denial'! Any suspicion a parent raises that these people are dishonest or untruthful is taken as a sign of paranoia! Any anger or hatred exhibited by parents towards those who have taken their children is 'diagnosed' as having a 'personality disorder' and 'anger management courses' are advised! Nobody can sensibly question religious extremists and fanatics and that is how it is in the secret family courts. The words of social workers and **'EXPERTS'** are always believed in preference to those of the parents. Thousands of children and worse still, newborn babies, are routinely removed to meet government 'adoption targets' on feeble pretexts such as 'risk of emotional abuse'. In the UK this is the greatest and most shocking scandal of our times!

I have sympathy for *Fathers 4 Justice* who are so often wrongfully denied access to their children, but it is still infinitely worse for both parents to lose a child or newborn baby to 'forced adoption' since this nearly always means that they have no idea where the child is to go and usually they never see that child again for the rest of their lives! That is why my main fight is against those wicked people who force weeping parents in court to give up their children for adoption by strangers.

History

This sorry story dates back to the six years 1960-1966 when I was a Kent County Councillor and a mother came to me for help because social workers had taken away her son, Trevor, aged 12 (and of near-genius IQ) because he got bored at school and played truant! She was denied all contact and when I asked where he was and if, as the mother's elected representative, I could at least see him myself I was told to mind my own business! I found him at a special private school (owned by the deputy leader of the Labour Party at the time) that was charging exorbitant fees more than 3 times those charged at **ETON** or **HARROW**! Young Trevor informed me that the boys were paid the sum of one shilling (5p) when required to sleep with any of their 'over affectionate' teachers at this very 'special' children's home! Eventually after acrimonious debates in the Council chamber and a court action he was returned to his mother and I was asked to help many other parents whose children had been removed for absurd reasons.

I applied in court for the discharge of care orders. I called the parents and sometimes the children themselves as witnesses in court against my own Council and I never lost a case so I was not best popular with my colleagues and the social workers! However after 6 years of neglecting my language school (then in Ramsgate) I decided not to stand at the next election as I really had to earn my living and look after my family so I reluctantly gave up the battle for a time.

In 2004 there was suddenly a lot of publicity when it was admitted that thousands of children had been wrongly taken from mothers who had been diagnosed with Munchausen's Syndrome, meaning that mothers who took their children to hospital too often were deliberately hurting them to draw attention to themselves. This was one of the absurd notions of the now discredited Professor Meadows which had no scientific basis that could possibly justify attributing the syndrome to so many unfortunate women. Worse still was his completely unproved theory that two cot deaths in the same family were 70 million to one! Hundreds of women were condemned for murder. Their surviving children and babies born subsequently were taken away and given for adoption by strangers. Only later was it realised that genetic factors made it far more likely for cot deaths to repeat in the same family than elsewhere and odds reduced to about 60 to 1.

These cases were in the Criminal Courts so they got fully reported and this provoked me to write to the *Daily Mail* detailing some of my experiences on Kent County Council all those years ago. They published my letter and I was surprised subsequently to receive several requests from mothers and parents trying to recover - and in some cases just to contact - children snatched from them by Social Services. I am now comfortably off, my 7 children are adult and I am in my seventies, with the time and still with the energy to once again take up the battle with Social Services!

Telegraph View: Child abuse won't be overcome until we define what it is

Ed Balls will fail unless he gives guidance on what social workers should be doing.

Daily Telegraph, 10 January 2009

The horrific accounts of errors and incompetence by social services officials that we publish today will generate outrage and despair: outrage that officials could leave children with parents they know to be violent, criminal and addicted to drugs; and despair that despite the hundreds of inquiries, the hundreds of inspections, despite the repeated promises from the Government that things are getting better, nothing changes. The same mistakes are consistently repeated, with fatal consequences for children.

The persistent failure of social workers to protect children who are in very serious danger is made even more outrageous by the profession's propensity to remove children from parents who are manifestly no danger at all to them. Of the 35,000 children who are taken into care every year on the recommendation of social workers, a large proportion are removed on grounds of "emotional abuse" – a category so broad and ill-defined that it can include both praising your children too much and not praising them enough, or feeding them too many vegetables or too little fresh fruit. It appears that social workers, aware of their inability to intervene in cases where children really are at risk, compensate for that failure by intervening in families where they are obviously safe.

There is no doubt that those two bad practices are connected. The resources of social work departments are, as directors of those departments frequently point out, strictly limited. Time spent investigating parents who do not threaten or endanger the children in their care is time not spent investigating, visiting or intervening in the cases where there is a threat. If genuinely at-risk children are to be protected, resources have to be targeted at cases where parents pose a clear and present danger.

It is, in a literal sense, true that social workers do not know what they are doing. That is not their fault. Government "advice" on what they should do is, quite correctly, centred on ensuring that children are protected from "significant harm". But, in all the many hundreds of pages that both Labour and Conservative governments have issued on when social workers should intervene, the notion of "significant harm" has never been defined in a meaningful and precise way. The result is that it is left to officials to interpret the term as they see fit. And that means "significant harm" has as many interpretations as there are social workers: one can conclude that a child whose parents are violent drug-addicts is not at risk of "significant harm", while another can claim that a parent who "plays too often and too long" with her is so dangerous that the child should be taken into care.

The first step the Government needs to take in order to stop this malpractice is properly to define the notion of "significant harm". That will not prevent fatal misjudgements being made. But it will make those misjudgements less likely. It will save the lives of many children, and also prevent forcible removal from parents who love them and protect them, and who would provide them with a far better start in life than the dismal future that awaits those who are taken into state care. It will also make it possible for the inquiries and inspections that take place after a child dies to say something useful, instead of merely reporting (as they do at present) that "no one was to blame". So long as inspectors do not work with a clear and fixed notion of "significant harm", they are in exactly the same position as social workers: they cannot identify the kinds of practice that they ought to prevent.

Ed Balls, the Children's Secretary, has insisted that he will take steps to end social services' persistent failure to protect seriously at-risk children. He will fail unless he gives clear guidance on what social workers should be doing – and he can only do that by defining the notion of "significant harm." We await his proposals.

The following statistics **REFERRING TO NEWBORN BABIES REMOVED FROM THEIR MOTHERS AT BIRTH** were researched by John Hemming M.P.

Year	Into care	Returned to parents	Adoption
2004	580	90	360
2005	600	100	320
2006	670	70	140

In each case less than 1 in 5 of newborn babies returns to their mothers.

I have expressed it as the situation where if mother stays then you have to toss a coin twice and get heads both times to keep your baby.

The chances are, in fact, worse than that

2. THIS IS THE SITUATION!!

1. There really are **SECRET COURTS** in the UK. 215 MPs of all parties signed the Early Day Motion (EDM) below.

EDM 869
WORKING OF THE CHILDREN ACT 2004 26.10.2005
Pickles, Eric

That this House urges the Government to remove the veil of secrecy from the workings of the Children Act 2004; considers that the closed door policy of the family courts breeds suspicion and a culture of secrecy which does nothing to instil confidence in those using them, which affects not just the courts but the Social Services departments of local authorities; and believes that it is possible to preserve the anonymity of children involved in the proceedings without the cumbersome rules which obstruct parents from receiving advice and support, which in particular works to the disadvantage of parents with special learning difficulty.

2. These courts take children from loving parents who have committed no crime. There are of course parents who brutalise and even torture or kill their children but such parents rarely go to court to recover their children; they stay as far away from courts as they possibly can! Common sense surely tells us that parents who care for their children enough to keep fighting for them in numerous very painful court actions ought to stand a good chance of winning them back. The sad fact is however that although judges often severely criticise Social Services in court they nearly always end up cautiously finding for the local authority and against the emotionally distraught parents. Parents are regularly condemned by 'establishment judges' for neglecting their children, abusing them physically (or more often emotionally) not 'beyond reasonable doubt' but 'on the balance of probabilities'! Lord Denning defined this in *Miller vs. Ministry of Pensions* as 'more probable than not'. Statistically, this means that the judge has at least a 51% chance of

being right and probably at best a 70% chance of being right so at least 30% of all forced adoptions were wrong and families split up on mere 'hearsay' (statements by social workers and other persons, not in court and who could not be questioned). Wicked deeds violating parents' basic human rights!

3. These parents lose their children forever to adoption by strangers. The children adopted are refused access to records of their birth parents or siblings at least until they are 18 and usually for the rest of their lives.

4. Parents are **GAGGED** and regularly sent to prison in secret proceedings if they reveal what went on in court.

Harriet Harman (Minister of State, Department for Constitutional Affairs) Hansard source

My hon. Friend raises an extremely important point, which she has put to me in a written question, so I know what the answer is. Last year something like 200 people were sent to prison by the family courts, which happens in complete privacy and secrecy. The idea that people are sent to prison without any reports of the proceedings makes even more important the work that we are undertaking with the family courts.

5. Establishment judges make decisions to take thousands of babies for risk of possible future emotional abuse.

Extract from *The Times*, Aug 23 2007: "Emotional abuse" has no strict definition in British law. Yet it now accounts for an astounding 21 per cent of all children registered as needing protection, up from 14 per cent in 1997. Last year 6,700 children were put on the child protection register for emotional abuse, compared with only 2,600 for sexual abuse and 5,100 for physical abuse. Both of the latter two categories have been falling steadily. Meanwhile emotional abuse and "neglect" - which replaced the old notion of "grave concern" in 1989 - have been rising. Both are catch-alls. But emotional abuse is especially vague. It covers children who have not been injured, have not complained, and do not come under "emotional neglect".

6. No jury would take babies from mothers because some expert made predictions of their future behaviour.

(Extract from *The Sunday Times*, Nov 18th 2007): A review is still going on of 700 cases in which bogus forensic scientist Gene Morrison gave evidence. Morrison, 48, from Manchester who was sentenced to five years for fraud in February, admitted he pretended to be an expert witness and bought his qualifications on the internet because it "seemed easier" than getting real ones. For many of the genuinely qualified experts, legal work is a lucrative sideline, and if they are perceived to be able to "tailor" their evidence convincingly, the commissions keep flowing in. John Hemming, a Liberal Democrat MP campaigning about the misuse of medical evidence, says fees for a basic written opinion, based on reading through existing files, start at £4,000. If the expert concludes there is a case to answer, they attract court attendance fees as well.

"I have known experts get as much as £28,000 for one report," said Hemming, who is lobbying for experts to be required to produce the scientific publications on which their opinion is based: "Unless we start using evidence-based evidence in court, we will get nowhere."

7. Criminals facing 6+ months in prison can demand a jury; parents losing their children for life cannot.

8. Carefully selected pregnant mothers with vulnerable backgrounds but often with no criminal records or disabilities are told their babies will be taken at birth! Equally carefully selected are the 'expert' psychiatrists and psychologists who regularly 'work' with the family courts and are eager to practice their latest 'psychobabble theories'. They are therefore only too willing to earn their generous fees and diagnose nearly every unfortunate mother presented to them by Social Services with a 'borderline personality disorder' or to report that she 'represents a risk of emotional abuse' to her children. Sometimes they will even diagnose a really hostile mother as 'unfit' to instruct a solicitor! 'The Official Solicitor' is then appointed for her! He will inevitably agree with everything the

local authority demands and will refuse to let the aggrieved mother say a word! The result in nearly all these cases is that babies and quite often all the other children from the same families are taken into care for eventual adoption by strangers.

You still believe in 'psychobabble'? Read this description of the Thud Experiment below and then watch the video here:

http://www.youtube.com/watch?v=hqaptRYjhq4

The Thud Experiment

In 1972, a psychologist named David Rosenhan convinced some of his friends to fake their way into psychiatric wards across the US.

The pseudopatients were to present themselves and say words along these lines: "I am hearing a voice. It is saying thud." Rosenhan specifically chose this complaint because nowhere in psychiatric literature are there any reports of any person hearing a voice that contains such obvious cartoon angst.

Upon further questioning, the eight pseudopatients were to answer honestly, save for name and occupation. They were to feign no other symptoms. Once on the ward, if admitted, they were immediately to say that the voice had disappeared and that they now felt fine. Rosenhan then gave his confederates a lesson in managing medication, how to avoid swallowing it by slipping it under the tongue, so it could later be blurted back to the toilet bowl.

Once in the admissions unit, Rosenhan was led to a small white room. "What is the problem?" a psychiatrist asked.

"I'm hearing a voice," Rosenhan said, and then he said nothing else.

"And what is the voice saying?" the psychiatrist questioned, falling, unbeknown to him, straight into Rosenhan's rabbit hole.

"Thud," Rosenhan said, smugly, I imagine.

"Thud?" the psychiatrist asked. "Did you say thud?"

"Thud," Rosenhan said again.

Rosenhan was led down a long hallway. Across the country, the eight other pseudopatients were also being admitted. Rosenhan must have been scared, exhilarated. He was a journalist, a scientist at the apex, putting his body on the line for knowledge. He was taken to a room and told to undress.

"When will I get out?" we can imagine Rosenhan asked, his voice perhaps rising now, some panic here - what had he done, my God.

"When you are well," a doctor answered, or something to this effect. But he was well: 110 over 80, a pulse of 72, a temperature that hovered in the mid-zone of moderate, homeostatic, a machine well greased. It didn't matter. He was diagnosed with paranoid schizophrenia and kept for many days.

The strange thing was, the other patients seemed to know that Rosenhan was normal, even while the doctors did not. One young man, coming up to Rosenhan in the dayroom, said "You're not crazy. You're a journalist or a professor." Another said, "You're checking up on the hospital."

And then one day, for a reason as arbitrary as his admission, he was discharged.

Rosenhan's paper describing his findings, On Being Sane In Insane Places, was published in Science, where it burst like a bomb on the world of psychiatry.

The experiment was greeted with outrage, and then, at last, a challenge. "All right," said one hospital, its institutional chest all puffed up. "You think we don't know what we're doing? Here's a dare. In the next three months, send as many pseudopatients as you like to our emergency room and we'll detect them. Go ahead."

Now, Rosenhan liked a fight. So he said, "Sure." He said in the next three months he would send an undisclosed number of pseudopatients to this particular hospital, and the staff were to judge, in a sort of experimental reversal, not who was insane, but who was sane. One month passed. Two months passed. At the end of three months, the hospital staff reported to Rosenhan that they had detected, with a high degree of confidence, 41 of Rosenhan's pseudopatients. Rosenhan had, in fact, sent none. Case closed. Match over. Psychiatry hung its head.

9. Local authorities are rewarded by central government for reaching 'adoption targets' hence adoption is prioritised.

10. Fosterers get up to £400 per week per child; special schools up to £7,000 per week per child; adoption agencies, experts & lawyers all cash in lavishly!

SO: What to do?

- Stop the secrecy and the gagging of parents.
- Stop adoptions of children for 'emotional abuse' or for 'risk', and open adoption records to children already adopted.
- Stop judges deciding cases of long-term fostering or adoption, and give juries the final decision. Better still abolish forced adoption altogether!
- Stop excessive rewards for those who live off the misery caused by this wicked system!

This would be a very, very good start!

3. THE GOLDEN RULES!!

Do **PLEASE** remember the Golden Rules: (By all means print this off and keep the copy near at hand if 'SS' approach! Show these rules to your lawyer or social worker to prove that you **KNOW** your rights!)

REMEMBER THESE EVEN IF YOU FORGET EVERYTHING ELSE I HAVE ADVISED!

1. **NEVER** contact Social Services (child protection) for help or advice. Usually you should not report a partner who batters you or even a stranger who sexually assaults your young child, as if you do the 'SS' will as often as not take your children into care (and later for adoption) to 'protect them' from risk! If they have your children and you are fighting to get them back, **NEVER, NEVER** tell social workers how you think you are going to defeat them or what you are going to do next! Remember, without mentioning it to 'them', that even if your children are 'in care' social workers do not have the legal power to stop your children going to a call box to phone you, from going to any public library and emailing you or even meeting you for a meal as long as they return 'home' to the fosterers afterwards!

Care home girl abused by 25 men in 2 years

by Jo Knowsley and Eileen Fairweather

Mail on Sunday, 27 August 2006

A 14-year-old girl placed in a council children's home was prostituted to a group of depraved middle-aged men because staff were powerless to stop her going out. The horrific story of 'Becky' is highlighted in a BBC programme presented by Fiona Bruce this week which reveals how she was sexually abused by 25 men over two years - despite being known to social services and having been placed on the Child Protection Register.

Even when she was put in a children's home - six months after her earliest allegations of abuse - staff allowed her to be used as a prostitute for fear their intervention might infringe her human rights. If the 'SS' cannot prevent a young girl in their care from working as a prostitute then surely they cannot prevent other young people they 'care for' from spending the day with parents if they so choose! Remember also that children of school age have a break so you can call them and speak to them through the railings without trespassing and nobody can stop you except a judge by serving a court injunction on you that will be too late to stop you reminding your children of their real family!

2. Never believe a word 'they' say and always insist they put their promises down in writing. Always be pleasant and polite to social workers, but never forget they are your **ENEMIES!** Remember that they may deliberately try to provoke you into shouting or violence which they will then exaggerate in court leaving you with a criminal record and no children! When they shout at you forget your 'pride' and look very hurt saying "why are you being like this to me?" or "I thought you were so nice until now, please don't bully me!" Be very respectful 'tongue in cheek', but remember **THEY ARE NOT POLICE** so never follow their 'helpful advice' especially if they say your only chance of getting your children back is to split from a partner or parent you love and respect! They will try and turn you against each other as the 'divide and rule' principle makes sure you are confused and demoralised when you lose your case and your children too! Quite often they arrange deliberately awkward contact times with your children. This can result first in the loss of your job and then as a consequence of that, your accommodation also. Object firmly and forcefully in court to their plans and fight hard to keep your job and your house or apartment.

3. **NEVER, NEVER, NEVER** sign any documents they present to you, even if they say "you have to!". Social workers rely on **BLUFF**. In reality they have **NO POWER** and no right to threaten you or give you orders of any kind! Only a **COURT** via an order from a judge can give you orders and you always have the opportunity to contest those orders in court either before or after

they are given to you. No matter what threats or promises they make you can be 100% sure that if you get intimidated into signing they will break their word and expect you to keep yours! So, **DO NOT SIGN**! Answer "yes", "no" or "I don't know" to questions **WITHOUT** further explanations that could be twisted to be used against you! If the 'SS' do not have enough evidence against you do not 'cooperate' by supplying them with what they need, even if they threaten you. If your enemies run out of ammunition, do **NOT** send them over a box of bullets to help them out! Once the 'SS' have applied for a care order, remember their main object is NOT the welfare of the child; it is to WIN their case against you! Disregard any threats that you must "do as they tell you". Be polite and even apologetic when you refuse to obey them!

4. Never, never agree to let your children go into foster care (especially if they say it is **TEMPORARY OR VOLUNTARY**) Never 'agree' the thresholds even if you are advised that this will ensure the return of your children because if you do you will have admitted neglecting or abusing your child and the only question left will be to decide if you have really repented and are capable of 'change'! Usually the answer is no! Sometimes your own lawyer may tell you to agree the thresholds and/or agree to an interim care order otherwise "you will never see your children again!". That is a wicked lie designed to save the lawyers work and to help you **LOSE** your children! Sometimes lawyers will tell you there is no need for you to give evidence as they will speak for you; that way you may find you have lost your children very quickly without being allowed to say a word, so **BEWARE**! Most of the 'legal aid lawyers' in the family courts are rightly known in the trade as **'PROFESSIONAL LOSERS'**!! Many of them pretend to work for you when in fact they are really on the side of the Local Authority. Sack your lawyers and represent yourself if they will not let you speak! Never admit to social workers (who are your **ENEMIES**) that you have been at fault in even the smallest possible way (they certainly will never admit to you that they were ever at fault!). You must never lie in court but you should never, never admit to any fault on your part unless forced to do so by a direct 'yes or no' type question in court. You must never disobey a

court order by taking abroad a child already in care, but if you are pregnant and threatened neither a court nor the 'SS' can stop you leaving the country before the baby is born! Sweden and Ireland are good choices!

5. When possible refuse to be assessed by so called 'experts' (psychiatrists, therapists, psychologists, counsellors, professionals, and the like) unless your children are returned first as otherwise the process will take place in an artificial atmosphere with you as parents emotionally distressed because your children have been taken. Remember that if the 'SS' insist on these assessments their sole purpose is to gather sufficient evidence to help them win their case against you in court! If you talk a lot and do not listen to them they will say you have mental problems or '**PERSONALITY DISORDERS**' so be 'quiet and attentive' during assessments. Try not to answer questions with more than 5 or 6 words (they write down anything unhelpful you may let slip). Try indeed to answer 'yes' or 'no' whenever possible. **NEVER COMPLAIN NEVER EXPLAIN!** Complaints are a waste of time and divert you from the more important task of keeping or recovering your children. Never explain or elaborate when questioned as this only gives extra material to those who wish to discredit you. Never make angry personal attacks on anybody or threaten to sue the 'SS' or police at a later date as it just makes **YOU** sound bad. They may even seize on your resentment as an excuse to diagnose you with **PARANOIA**! Your whole tone must be one of 'sweetness and light' regretting that your children were mistakenly taken and that **THEY** (not you) suffered harm and anguish as a result! Your whole case must be that **YOUR CHILDREN** have suffered harm (not yourself) and that you are taking action for their sake not for your own! If you are accused of 'being unable to work with the professionals', reply that you will work 100% with them if they say their objective is to reunite your family by eventually returning your children, but that it is unfair to expect you to work with anyone whose objective declared to the court is to put your children into care or worse still have them adopted! Remember that the 'SS' often 'brainwash' children in care by telling them that their mother is too ill to care for them or worse still, does not love them or want

them any more, but when they are adopted they will have a lovely new 'forever mummy and daddy'! Make sure you tell the children that wicked people have stolen them for money and that you will never stop fighting to get them back! Whisper in their ears or calmly make the statement in spite of horrified supervisors. Even children as young as three will remember all their lives such a brutal but necessary message. Vital however it is, as it will eventually make a stable adoption impossible to sustain! Your reluctantly adopted children will as a result seek you out and come back to you in the end!

6. Protect yourself against social workers barging uninvited into your home by fitting a small chain inside your front door. This means that if you do not unlatch the chain when you see who is calling that person would have to push the door hard enough to break the chain which would be a 'forced entry' and a criminal offence if committed without a document from the court such as a 'recovery order' specifically allowing entry using reasonable force. Unless they intend to actually arrest someone or have good reason to believe someone in the house is in danger of severe physical harm, police also would have to have a warrant before breaking the chain. Usually they will not have one and would have to convince a judge that a serious crime had been or was about to be committed before one was granted.

7. If Social Services request a look at your medical records (probably to try and find something to discredit you) **ALWAYS** write to any doctor or psychiatrist that has seen you as follows:

"I respectfully request you to keep all my medical notes strictly confidential as I intend to take legal proceedings against **Social Services** and any other persons who might obtain my medical details without my express authorisation".

8. Never write a letter to anyone connected to Social Services as you might include something that could damage your case in the family court. Only accept a solicitor if he/she promises to allow you a free hand to speak in court! You should be asked this simple question in the witness box "Have you anything you would like to say to the court?" Without this promise you may be 'gagged'

and as already explained in Rule 4 you can lose your case without being allowed to say a word!

Represent yourself if you can, but if you really do need the assistance of 'professionals' the contacts further down in this chapter may be useful.

And YES! They really, really do make up false evidence as 'The Times' points out below.............

Blind justice without a name

If social workers really are manufacturing evidence in child abuse cases, their anonymity is assured

by Camilla Cavendish

The Times, 19 October 2006

THIS WEEK Tim and Gina Williams, a Welsh couple, were reunited with their three children. Social workers had whisked them into care two years ago in the wholly erroneous belief that Mr Williams was a paedophile. He had made the fatal mistake of calling social services about an 11-year-old boy he had found half-naked with his daughter. But the tables quickly turned. A doctor claimed to have found evidence of sexual abuse, social workers jumped to conclusions, and the Williamses were prevented from seeing their children except for an hour and a half twice a week. They said that their children never understood what was happening. They thought their parents did not want them. Imagine it, and weep.

The Williamses were saved because an American doctor testified that there was not a shred of evidence of abuse. In a searing judgment, Judge Crispin Masterman has ruled that the children should never have been removed. He criticised social workers for failing to follow the most basic procedures. Yet the doctor and the social workers remain anonymous.

Newport City Council, named as the local authority, has promised a review. This is unusual. In many such cases, even local councillors do not know when their own staff perpetrates miscarriages of justice. In March Mr Justice McFarlane publicly castigated social workers who had removed a nine-year-old girl from her parents for 14 months on the absolutely false pretext that her mother might be suffering from Munchausen's syndrome by proxy (MSbP). The judge found that every one of the 13 assertions made by the social services team leader was "misleading or incomplete or wrong".

But guess what? We will never know who the team leader is. The Tory MP and ex-council leader Sir Paul Beresford, who has called for those involved to be named, has been unable even to find out which local authority was involved. I have a good idea which one it is. But I am willing to bet that even the leader of that council does not know. I am also willing to bet that none of the people involved has even been disciplined.

This is a racket. All other public servants are held accountable for their mistakes. John Hemming, the Liberal Democrat MP, puts it this way: "In a criminal case, where someone can be given a life sentence, police officers are quoted by name as they give evidence. There is no justification for professionals being anonymous when a parent is given an effective life sentence [by losing their child]."

If we do not know their identities, we also cannot tell whether the same people have given misleading evidence in other cases. If the McFarlane case social workers thought they saw MSbP in a woman whose only crime was to have taken her daughter to hospital for stomach pain (I kid you not), how many other times were they visited by similarly delusional visions?

Did Gordon Oliver, the social worker recently jailed for sexually assaulting children over a period of 20 years, ever give evidence in court? What about Martin Thei, the Essex County Council worker who killed himself five years ago after being arrested by police for downloading child porn? One campaign group claims that Thei made many reports that resulted in children being taken into care and/or adopted. The council says that is unlikely but it is not absolutely sure. I have talked to one family in whose case Thei's report was crucial. This has never been reviewed.

The number of calls I receive from parents, some who have lost their children for ever and some who have got them back after dreadful battles, makes me increasingly concerned that social workers and experts are manufacturing evidence; that they are concentrated in certain parts of the country; and that they cover up for each other, because they are convinced that they are right. We are living in a hell of good intentions. We can only root out the bad apples if we can see how they infect the picture.

Anonymity clouds every attempt at justice. Two years ago, after Angela Cannings was cleared of killing her babies, Margaret Hodge, then Children's Minister, announced a review of certain cases where children had been taken into care. But her "review" consisted of asking the same old people in the same old local authorities to question their own original judgments. Only one case was subsequently overturned. That tells us nothing, because Hodge failed utterly to grasp the opportunity to monitor specific councils and witnesses and to see whether there were patterns to their behaviour.

Today, once again, we are in danger of missing an opportunity. For the Government's otherwise excellent consultation on opening up the family courts barely touches on this issue. It concentrates on the anonymity of children and families, and says virtually nothing about the anonymity of professionals. Making more judgments public, as the Government proposes, would clearly be a great step forward. But if we simply get anonymised judgments, such as that of McFarlane, we are not much farther forward in holding fraudsters to account.

Judges currently decide whether to make their judgments public, and whether to name professionals. Very few do, despite guidance from the Court of Appeal (in the McFarlane case, the court even kept secret the identity of the defence counsel). I have no desire to perpetrate witch-hunts: each witness could be given an identity code, if that was felt absolutely necessary to protect their identities, but that would at least enable those of us who want to see justice done track their record.

The debate about child protection and anonymity is always couched in terms of the interests of the child. Those who work in this field have come to believe that a child's privacy is somehow synonymous with their own. But if some people do not understand what real evidence is, should they not be accountable? The oldest law of bureaucracies is "first protect ourselves". How many more cases do there have to be before someone finally kicks down their hiding place?

And YES some people are making a fortune out of the misery of others!

Concern over vulnerable children placed in isolating care homes
by Lucy Ward
The Guardian, 28 March 2007

Councils are paying up to £6,000 a week to place children with extreme and complex needs in "one-person children's homes" without any proof that this will help them.

A report published yesterday by the children's services watchdog found the number of homes caring for only one child is increasing, but questions whether councils have fully considered whether the approach is good for the children concerned.

The homes, in which a child is kept in a private house together with non-resident staff working in shifts, are often located far from the child's home community, despite government guidance stressing the importance of children in care staying in their local area. Children may stay for just a few months or for longer periods of three years or more.

The study, by the Commission for Social Care Inspection (CSCI), says the homes are "extremely expensive" to run, and questions whether children, and the councils who place them there, are getting a good deal.

The CSCI chairwoman, Denise Platt said: "We don't know enough about how children respond to living on their own in these one place children's homes... It may well be convenient for local councils to place children with complex needs in these homes, but the impact on the children who live there is still unclear."

Children living in some of the 166 one-person homes told inspectors they enjoyed more attention from staff and were glad to escape bullying, but also often felt lonely and missed the company of other children.

Inspection reports revealed the homes did worse than larger children's homes in key areas, including support for individual children and the training and competency of staff.

Private providers are able to charge so much for the services because the provision is so scarce, Dame Denise said.

The report says some councils do not use one person homes on principle, while those who do tend not to do so as a first choice. Youngsters being placed usually have complex emotional or behavioural difficulties, learning disabilities and mental health problems, and may be difficult to control.

In some cases the impression was that the care process had not been "thought through", Dame Denise said.

The report also raised concerns that some homes illegally limit children's freedom although they are not officially secure accommodation.

USEFUL CONTACTS:

(If your cause is just these professionals really will be on your side not that of Social Services!)

SOLICITORS:

Sandra Bradley
PRINCIPAL
Bretherton Law
First Floor, Alban Row 27-31 Verulam Road St Albans
Herts AL3 4DG
Tel. 01727 869293 Fax. 01727 853767

William Bache & Co
(best for criminal cases in my opinion)

The Clock Tower, 4 Oakridge Office Park, Whaddon, Salisbury, Wiltshire, SP5 3HT

Tel +44 (0)1722 711719 Fax +44 (0)1722 713370

Email enquiries@williambache.co.uk

BARRISTERS:

Darren Watts

Tanfield Chambers, 2-5 Warwick court, London WC1 5DJ

Tel (0207) 431-5300

Andrew Scott

described by *The Daily Telegraph* as "the people's champion"

Parklane Plowden

www.parklaneplowden.co.uk

Tel: 0844 499 5678

Carol Mcmillan

Westgate Chambers, 64 High Street, Lewes, East Sussex BN7 1XG

Tel: 01273 480510

Dr JOHN FOX

Chambers of Ami Feder, Ground Floor, Lamb Building, Temple, London EC4Y 7AS DX 1038 (Chancery Lane)

Tel: 020 7797 7788 Fax: 020 7353 0535

e-mail: clerks@lambbuilding.co.uk

Out of hours tel: 07721 339232

PSYCHOLOGISTS:

Dr LOWENSTEIN

Tel 02380692621, w www.drludwigfredlowenstein.com

Dr PETER DALE (parent assessor)

Email: info@peterdale.co.uk

Phone from UK: (01424) 424504

Phone international: +44 1424 424504 Fax: 08700 941 477

To sack your solicitor and your barrister just download Form N434! If you do not do this the court will usually send all future correspondence and sometimes vital statements of evidence to your solicitor, even though you have told all concerned that you wish to represent yourself.

N434 - Notice of change of solicitor (Court Service) Download Form N434, Notice of change of solicitor, Court Service Forms, Administrative Court:

http://www.capform.co.uk/fullformlist.asp?Level1=11&Level2=106&Level3=623

A SOCIAL WORKER'S POEM

I am a social worker,
I'm really very nice
I help you loving mothers
And give you good advice!

Your partner has departed
Your income is too low
I'm really very sorry
All your kids will have to go!

Your partner is abusive?
He beats you black and blue?
We'll soon be there to help you
And take your children too!

You have a learning problem
You're really not too clever
We'll get your kids adopted
When can you see them?? **NEVER**!!

Your son is hyperactive?
You need a brief respite
We'll soon take **ALL** your children
Give up the hopeless fight!

Your child was taken into care
So many years ago
If now you have a baby
That too will have to go!

Foster parents love your kids
To get some more they seek,
For each one brings a tidy sum
£400 per week!!

Children's homes are run by us
Where paedophiles abound
Each time we cover up abuse
'The gutter press' come round

'They' said adoptions worked the best
We soon proved that they would
Fathers shout and mothers cry
Their kids are gone for good!

What happens in our special courts?
Our experts they will say
"You're a danger to your children
So we'll take them all away!"

Your children may be healthy,
Happy and well fed
But one day you might hurt them
That's what our experts said

The judges know that we are right
With us they will agree
They dare not risk another course
You have no chance you see!

Our special courts are secret,
So don't you breathe a word
Of what goes on inside those walls
No matter how absurd!

We'll get your kids adopted,
And don't you dare complain!
Or you'll end up in prison
And I won't say that again!

We have adoption targets
They must be met you see
Failure means a reprimand
So spare a thought for me!!!

by IAN JOSEPHS (a very social worker!)

4. USEFUL INFORMATION

At last a **BREAKTHROUGH**!! Read the article below from the '*Law Gazette*'. You can now hit those 'SS' people through their pockets! The more times you go to court the harder they will find it to pay for it all! Fight like a tiger and never give up and like countless other mothers (some of whom I have advised) you can **WIN** and get your children back!

Do not be fooled into cooperating with the 'SS' when you are given their promises or those of your legal aid lawyers that if you go along with the 'SS' everything will be alright! It **WON'T**!! All they want from assessments and psycho-charlatans is more evidence to win their case so do not give it to them! The 'SS' are not police who must be obeyed but they **ARE** your **ENEMIES** as long as their stated intention is to take your children into care or for adoption. When your enemy runs out of ammunition you should never send them a fresh case of bullets for them to fire at you!! Only agree to assessments and psychos if your children are returned to live with you first! Any other assessment or psychiatric examination cannot be normal or natural.

Lastly never get 'conned' into putting your kids into voluntary care because more often than not despite what the *Law Gazette* says you may never see them again. **IF YOU ARE IN THAT SITUATION USE THE LAST PARA OF THE ARTICLE BELOW AS PROOF THAT THEY MUST BE RETURNED TO YOU WHEN YOU ASK!** And the best of luck to you!

Care applications fall sparks safety fears
Law Society Gazette, Aug 21 2008

Just 1,611 applications were made by councils in England and Wales between the beginning of April and the end of July, according to figures from the Children and Family Court Advisory Support Service (Cafcass). This compares with 2,160 in the same period last year and 2,284 between April and July 2006.

Since May, councils have been obliged to foot the bill for child care proceedings as part of a government drive to make the courts entirely self-funding through fees. The move has resulted in a 2,500% hike in costs, with child care proceedings rising from £150 to £4,825.

Anthony Douglas, chief executive of Cafcass, told the Gazette that Section 20 agreements – where children are placed with grandparents or other relatives – 'went up by several hundred' in the same period.

'Care applications have dropped significantly... I am concerned about the drop because it's too large to be complacent about,' he said.

Douglas added that the use of Section 20 agreements – voluntary arrangements between parents and local authorities that do not come under court scrutiny and can be rescinded by the parent at any time – should be kept under review.

As a social worker for 15 years i have seen children taken into care unnecessarily, been ordered to lie in court, had the Dept.'s solicitor reconstruct my witness statement to put parent in a bad light, made to exaggerate a parents problems or blow up a minor incident. I eventually retired on ill health

ian hughes, bridgend, britain

QUESTION THEM!!

Here are 4 important questions that **SHOULD** be answered by Social Services or by Family Court judges but which have so far been systematically ignored!

1. It must surely be the right of parents and anyone else in a democratic country wishing to complain against injustice to go to the media with details of everything that happened to them in the Family Court. Most judges in Family Courts refuse leave to appeal and solicitors always back them up so the idea of appealing when leave has been denied is nearly always a 'non starter'. Parents are at present denied their democratic right to go to the media to get

public and political support followed by possible reform! How can this be justice?

2. Harriet Harman (Minister of State, Department of Constitutional Affairs) said in Parliament: "Last year something like 200 people were sent to prison by the Family Courts, which happens in complete privacy and secrecy."

Surely those who still deny these facts cannot believe she was lying to Parliament! How can imprisonment with no public process be justice?

3. Extract from *The Times*, Aug 23 2007: 'Emotional abuse' has no strict definition in British law. Yet it now accounts for an astounding 21 per cent of all children registered as needing protection, up from 14 per cent in 1997. Last year 6,700 children were put on the child protection register for emotional abuse, compared with only 2,600 for sexual abuse and 5,100 for physical abuse.

How can taking newborn babies for 'risk of emotional abuse' possibly be justified when the effect is to punish parents and abuse their babies not for anything they have done but for something that some hired prophet thinks they might perhaps do in the future? How can this be justice?

4. Any burglar facing a prison sentence of 6 months or more can demand a hearing before a jury so how can it be right or just that parents who risk losing their children for life to 'forced adoption' are denied this option? Juries consider complicated medical evidence in cases such as murder, compensation for injuries, complicated tax laws in cases of fraud and insider dealing. The simple decision whether a mother accused of risk of emotional abuse should keep her newborn baby or not would, I think we must all agree, be more likely to favour the mother if considered by a jury; but records show that such cases nearly always favour the Social Services if decided by a judge. That is probably why juries are banned from the Family Courts but allowed to decide libel cases in other civil courts! To take a newborn baby from its mother and give it away for adoption by strangers is a far far worse punishment for her than any jail sentence as it condemns the mother to a life

sentence and the baby to probable death later in life if it should require a kidney or bone marrow transplant or other medical attention in which a birth family member was needed but could not be located! How can this be justice?

The 4 obvious reforms would be:

1: Remove the gag from parents involved in family court proceedings.

2: Forbid judges in the Family Courts from imprisoning any parent without a public hearing.

3: Abolish 'risk' as a reason for removing children from a sane parent unless in addition to risk it can be clearly shown and proved that such children have already suffered significant physical harm.

4: Any parents facing the possibility that their children could be removed for long-term fostering or adoption without parental consent should have the right to demand that the final decision be made by a jury not a judge. Better still, abolish forced adoption altogether!

Re K D [1998] 1 AC p.812 letter B Lord Templeman stated; 'The best person to bring up a child is the natural parent. It matters not whether the parent is wise or foolish, rich or poor, educated or illiterate, provided the child's moral and physical health are not endangered. Public authorities cannot improve on nature.'

Boy, 5, forced into adoption with gay couple pleads: 'We want to stay with our gran and grandad'

by Jonathan Brocklebank and Michael Seamark

Daily Mail, 29 January 2009

The mother of two children who are being adopted by gay men even though their grandparents want to care for them wept yesterday as she told of her final meeting with her son and daughter.

'I told them, "Listen, Mummy is not going to see you for a while",' she said. Her son replied: 'But Mummy, I want to come and stay with you and Granny and Grandad.'

The row over the future of the five-year-old boy and four-year-old girl intensified yesterday after the Daily Mail revealed details of the heartbreaking case. Their grandparents spent two years fighting for the right to care for the children, whose 26-year-old mother is a recovering heroin addict. She desperately wanted her parents to look after them.

But social workers said their ages – he is 59 and she is 46 – and their health – he has angina and she is diabetic – ruled them out.

The mother told the Mail that she had been ordered to say her goodbyes to the children last August during a trip to Edinburgh Zoo. 'They told me not to cry and be strong so as not to upset the children,' she said. 'How can you tell a mother that when she's never going to see her children again?'

She voiced her anger at the decision to allow her son and daughter to be fostered by a homosexual couple.

'I did not under any circumstances want my children to be placed with gay men. I wanted them to have a mum and a dad.

'They can't be telling me that, within a 60-mile radius, the only people they could find to look after my children were two men.

'I've got nothing against gay people. I've got gay friends, but children need a mum and a dad, not a dad and another dad.

'I'm ashamed of what I've done, especially what I've put mum and dad through because they have been brilliant every step of the way.

'My children deserve so much love and my mum and dad were prepared to give them it, but social work snatched them away.

'They are a mum and dad in a million and I know they would have brought my children up brilliantly.'

The mother also revealed that social workers have asked her to meet the gay couple under their supervision. But she will not see her children – or be allowed to know where they are going to be living.

The Mail revealed yesterday how the grandparents had fought a relentless battle for the right to look after the youngsters after deciding their daughter was unfit to do so.

But they were opposed every step of the way by Edinburgh's social work department, which believed they should go to an adoptive family.

When the grandparents eventually caved in to what they describe as 'bully tactics' by the social workers, the department arranged for the children to be adopted by a gay couple in the Edinburgh area. They had already decided that, whatever the outcome of the battle, the children should not see their mother owing to her unstable lifestyle and history of offences.

Recalling her final, 90-minute meeting with her children, the mother said: 'I was told that this would be the last time. They asked me to pick a place to take them and I decided on the zoo. The social worker was with me and kept saying to me I would have to tell them I was not going to see them any more and that I had to stay strong for their sakes.

'At one point she said that my son was the spitting image of my mum and my daughter looked like her grandad. What kind of thing is that to say at a moment like that, when I'm about to tell them I won't see them again?

'I told them that I loved them and I would write them lots of letters and cards and that they would be going to a new house soon.

'I got really upset and had to keep turning away so that they didn't see me crying. The social worker said, "Just leave it there". Ten minutes later, that was it.'

But the mother still had to help put the children in the social worker's car. 'My son grabbed me tightly on the leg and and would not let me go. It was just absolutely devastating.'

She said that the heartrending last meeting had happened while her parents were still fighting for full parental rights for the brother and sister, who have been staying with foster parents for the last two years pending a decision on their future.

Her parents' last meeting with the children came two months later in October. By then, under mounting pressure from the social work department and concerned about months or years of further disruption to their lives, they had taken the agonising decision to withdraw from the legal fight.

The grandfather, a farm worker, and his wife say the social work department are effectively blackmailing them by telling them they will not see the children again unless they give the new adoptive arrangements their blessing.

Although the family desperately want to reverse the adoption procedure they do not now know how they can. Their previous solicitor has moved to a new job and would-be unable to represent them in her current role. They would also need to reapply for legal aid before taking any action – and time is running out.

The children have already had several meetings with the men who are soon to become their full-time fathers. They are understood to be seeing them for a few hours daily and have recently visited their home. The men are giving them a bedroom each – and the girl's has been decked out with a 'princess' bedspread. The children have also been shown the wellington boots waiting for them at the back door when they want to play outside.

Under the adoption procedure, the children will see more and more of the gay couple, spending occasional nights in their home, until they move in permanently. The social work department will remain in contact with the new parents for the first year of adoption – then, providing there are no serious problems, contact will cease.

Thereafter the only official channel the children's natural family will have for making contact with them would be through an adoption agency. The mother said: 'The social worker told me the kids are getting on really well with them. My daughter had apparently said to the social worker, "Come up and see my princess bed". I just feel totally devastated.

Now they want me to meet the men. Social work phoned me to ask how I was feeling now about them being adopted by a gay couple and if I had calmed down.

'They told me that out of the couples they had on their books they were the ones who were able to cater for their needs best. I find that very hard to believe. I'll have to say that to them when I meet them because it's how I feel, but I don't want the whole thing to become an argument. I will have lots of questions to ask them.'

Councillor Marilyne MacLaren, convener for education, children and families at Edinburgh City Council, said: 'I have been assured that the professional view is that the adoptive couple will provide a safe, secure and loving environment for these children.

'These are always very complex cases but I think it is important to say that the grandparents have been fully involved in discussions about this case over a period of time.'

Social services Stasi should hang their heads in shame
by Amanda Platell
Daily Mail, 29 January 2009

Should proof ever be needed of the scandalous social engineering now so casually carried out by our state, it comes in the case of the loving grandparents of two small children who desperately sought to adopt them but saw them instead placed with a gay couple.

The decision was made to refuse the grandparents the right to raise their own blood relatives and instead give them away to two gay men 'in accordance with who can best meet their needs', according to the social services jargon.

But how can two strangers – gay or straight – best meet the needs of two children abandoned by a drug-addict mother for whom the only constants in their short, difficult lives have been their loving grandparents?

We don't even know what the reasoning behind this perverse decision was, because it was taken in secret, behind the closed doors of a children's court. Those who took part will not be held accountable and we are unable even to identify their victims.

This decision is one of particular cruelty. The decision itself is bad enough, but the grandparents' description of how they were treated give us a chilling insight into the Stasi-like approach of modern social services.

They were told that if they so much as objected to the adoption of the children by the gay couple then they would never be allowed to see the children again.

'You can either accept it,' the grandparents were told by social workers, 'and there's a chance you'll see the children twice a year, or you can take that stance and never see them again.' The Stalinist secret police couldn't have put it better.

Further, the grandparents are not allowed even to know where the children will live, what the gay couple's circumstances are and what kind of a home they will provide for the children. Equally astonishingly, it emerges the youngsters were not given to a gay couple for want of other alternatives: indeed there were several other heterosexual couples desperate and deemed suitable to adopt the children.

But the social workers and the courts opted for the gay men.

As the grandfather in this case says: 'The mother is the cornerstone of any family and the most important person for a young child.' That's hard to argue with. His little granddaughter will no doubt have lots of female role models, gay-speak for women friends, but it's not the same.

A little girl already wary of men, no doubt because in her young life she's witnessed her addict mother being ritually abused by them, will have to turn to one of them one day, when she gets her periods, when she needs her first bra. It's hard enough asking your own mother such things, let alone a gay man.

The only reason given for denying the grandparents the right to adopt their own daughter's children is worries about their age and their health. The 59-year-old grandfather is a farm worker and has angina, his wife, just 46, is being treated for diabetes.

Plenty of people lead normal lives with diabetes – and angina.

And how outrageous to say a woman of 46 is too old to be a mother – particularly when it emerges she is still bringing up children of her own. Who'd have dared to suggest that Cherie Blair was too old – or to suggest it to the countless women who have healthy children in their forties?

When did the State decide to endorse such monstrously cruel social engineering? When did it decide to fly in the face of overwhelming evidence that children's lives are best when they are raised by a mother and father living together – preferably married?

It appears that social services, despite all the evidence to the contrary, still believe that all relationships are equal when it comes to raising children. Indeed, in this case they seem to have decided that a gay relationship is preferable to a couple of opposite sex.

This is simply not true. They are not equal when it comes to the things children need most – commitment and stability. Yet it is regarded as heretical even to state the facts: which are that marriages last longer than cohabiting heterosexual relationships and they both last longer than gay relationships.

Those are the cold, bare truths. It is too soon to know the statistics on same-sex marriages as there has not been enough time to assess the trends and many same sex couples enjoy enduring and truly fulfilling relationships.

But if commitment and stability matter most to children's happiness and success, the least suitable place for them to be raised is by a gay couple. That's not homophobia, that's not bigotry, that's a fact – unpalatable as it might be to the Left consensus.

When you read of such shocking decisions, you can only wonder how any sane judge could put two small children with two men. Are they trying to meet some target they have been set for placing children for adoption with gay couples? Who knows, because shamefully all of this process is conducted in secret.

It also reflects how out of touch the state and the law is now, not just with the traditional family, but with the role of grandparents. Again and again we hear stories of grandparents cut out of their grandchildren's lives after divorce or death and having no recourse to the law.

Grandparents have been written out of the modern liberal family narrative at a time, in reality, when they have never been more needed or more central to the revival of the extended family.

They help out with child care, work around the house, ferry children to after-school classes and even assist with finances.

But against all the evidence social services choose to take two small children away from their natural family and give them up for adoption – to a gay couple.

It beggars belief and seems guaranteed to do only one thing: to give those innocent children the poorest possible start to their lives, the slimmest chance of happiness and the greatest likelihood of anger, bewilderment and failure.

Those who made this decision should hang their heads in shame.

My comments on the recent House of Lords debate concerning identification of sperm or egg donors are as follows:

All the noble Lords and Ladies seem preoccupied with children conceived by sperm donors or egg donors and the rare possibility of siblings adopted by different families meeting by chance at a later date and marrying!

They completely ignore the most flagrant injustices of all, those thousands of babies and young children forcibly adopted against the will of parents who love them and want to keep them.

These babies and young children are then issued with new fake birth certificates by a conniving and deceitful State!

This is how they 'work' it!

'UK Certificates' offers a secure online ordering service for official General Register Office issued adoption certificates for England & Wales.

What Information will I receive?

An adoption certificate is a replacement birth certificate but in an adopted person's new name. It is used by an adopted person for all legal and purposes in place of their original birth certificate. The main difference between the two documents is the addition of court particulars on an adoption certificate.

We will provide an officially certified full version of an original adoption certificate for any event in England & Wales between 1927-present.

We can provide a short version if you prefer, which contains no reference to the fact of adoption.

Your 'fake birth certificate' is ready!

And now for the 'experts'!

So-called 'experts' in the secret Family Courts make crystal-ball type predictions of 'risk of future emotional harm' or 'risk of neglect'. Few families can defend themselves against future 'predictions' so compliant Family Court judges almost inevitably 'go along' with Social Services requests that the children be placed for adoption with strangers! Even when (very rarely) parents are cleared by the courts, once the adoptions have been rushed through they are forbidden to know where their children are or to have any contact with them whether the children want it or not!

A parliamentary question revealed that more than 200 parents a year are secretly jailed for daring to reveal details of those who accused them in court or for contacting their own offspring contrary to a court order. Parents are often forbidden from knowing whether their offspring are alive or dead and if the latter they usually find out a very long time after the deaths occurred.

Children are all too often split up and adopted by different families. This must be contrary to their human rights as all too often they are forbidden to contact their siblings and may not even know of their existence. If many years later a child needs a replacement kidney or bone marrow transplant the birth family records are rarely revealed and very often declared 'lost'. So the unfortunate child whose needs are supposed to be 'paramount' is in fact callously left to die for want of a family donor!

The incredible story of a father who was asked to give one of his organs (probably a kidney) to his son but forbidden to see his child for the rest of his life!

This story appeared in the Daily Mail on the 13rd of November 2008 but I cannot reproduce the original article due to legal reasons, which I hope means that the struggle is still ongoing.

This story kicked off when Hampshire social services rang a quiet and unobtrusive father of three married to a clergywoman. To be precise the photograph in the Mail showed Michael Shergold, his wife Alex and two of his sons Peter and David. The phone call told him that he was the father of another child, already 5 years old, from a previous short relationship with a girl who had handed the son over to foster parents, as she was unable to cope. He was told that the boy was going to be adopted and that he was forbidden to see him, meet him, or even look for him but that the council thought he should know of his existence.

Slowly this man became angry, as he could not understand why the council had waited so long to tell him. In fact, he was for the last 35 years, and still is, a school caretaker for Hampshire council. He was the only person with his surname in the local phonebook so they could easily have found him before. It also seemed nothing short of sadistic to tell him about his son and then forbid him to see him. The council then admitted that all they needed from him as a father was one of his organs as the mother refused to be a donor. He was the only suitable person who could help his son to live as otherwise he would die.

His first reaction was of course to say that he would be delighted to offer a home to his son so that his family would be complete. His wife and his other children, Peter now 17, David 20 and Suzanna 30, were all enthusiastic. They all agreed that they were a very happy and close-knit family, as indeed Peter and David still live at home and Suzanna lives close by. Michael is 55 and has a spacious three-bedroom house in Southampton and his wife Alex is a Pastor with a Pentecostal church in Portsmouth. All children were by his first wife and it was only after they split up that his newly discovered son was conceived. The council dismissed any idea of him having contact with his son let alone welcoming him back into his family as typically they claimed that adoption with strangers was the best option. They said that if he considered himself a good father he should sacrifice his organ for his son and agree not to see him or contact him so that the adoption could go ahead.

After DNA tests confirmed that Michael was the father, Michael and Alex went to court to begin custody proceedings, confident that there was no reason why his son should not be returned to him or at least that he would have immediate contact. The council however opposed the idea in court saying that adoption was the best option though they found nothing whatever wrong with the Shergold family and no reason why they should not take in their 5 year old son. It was simply that the council's plans were for adoption and local authorities do not like their plans to be disrupted. Inexplicably, the judge simply concluded that the local authority and Social Services knew best and once more Michael was asked to donate his organ to his unknown son but still forbidden to even tell him that he had a father at all.

I believe that following this disgraceful decision the father agreed reluctantly to donate the organ even though he was forbidden to meet his son or let him know that he had a father. I believe that this must be contrary to the human rights of the son. To deliberately hide from him that he has a father, to forbid him to meet his father, even if he later finds out that he's got one living, are serious breaches of his human rights to enjoy the benefit of a normal, loving family. I believe that the case is still being pursued through the European courts but alas they have no power to upset a UK adoption. This principle was illustrated in the case of P, C and S versus. UK when a large some of monetary compensation was offered to parents whose baby was wrongly seized at birth for no good reason other than "risk of emotional abuse". The European courts described this process as draconian, fined the UK and awarded a large sum of money to the parents but were powerless to upset the adoption. It is clear that the UK government, issuing fake birth certificates with new fake names to young children so that their true parents cannot trace them, is committing disgusting crimes against innocent children enforcing them to live a lie and concealing from them their own origins. The law should be changed to forbid this horrible practice but until it is, cases like that of the Shergolds will continue to disgrace the British legal system.

Read article here:

http://www.dailymail.co.uk/femail/article-1082379/You-son--organs-How-social-workers-left-man-terrible-moral-dilemma.html

Judges condemn 'foul play' on adoptions

by Rosemary Bennett

The Times, 2 May 2008

Two senior judges have strongly criticised a local authority that forced through the adoption of a baby girl against the wishes of her father.

Lord Justice Thorpe accused East Sussex County Council of being determined to have the child adopted "by means more foul than fair", while Lord Justice Wall accused it of "disgraceful" conduct.

He ordered that copies of their ruling, handed down at the Court of Appeal yesterday, be sent to all family judges and every adoption agency in the country as a warning that the wishes of both parents had to be taken into account in care proceedings.

The case involved a child, known as J-L, who was adopted earlier this year. She was born in November 2006 after a casual relationship between her mother and father, known as MC. He only knew that he had a daughter after the local authority contacted him last summer to tell him care proceedings were under way and asked for a DNA test.

The mother had been living with her baby daughter in a special unit, but had abandoned the baby there. The local authority recommended adoption and placed J-L with foster parents in the meantime.

The father said that he was unable to take part in the initial care proceedings because he was in hospital after a heart attack. When he discovered that adoption plans were well advanced, he went to solicitors who immediately contacted the local authority to try to stop them. However, his intervention through a solicitor's letter was ignored and never recorded formally at subsequent meetings. The local authority then allowed the adoptive parents to begin to look after the baby girl the day before the father's legal case went to court.

A further attempt by him to stop the adoption was blocked by the council using the 2002 Adoption and Children Act. Yesterday's ruling was in response to the father's appeal on grounds of a breach to his human rights.

"The council's failure to answer that letter and subsequent placement on the eve of the hearing give rise to the clearest inference that the council was out to gain its ends by means more foul than fair," Lord Justice Wall said.

"There are many who assert that councils have a secret agenda to establish a high score of children that they have placed for adoption. When such suspicions are rife, a history such as this only serves to fuel public distrust in the good faith of public authority."

People still find it hard to believe that in the UK secret Family Courts are taking thousands of children annually from parents that have never been accused or charged, let alone convicted of any **CRIME**. Yet that is exactly what is happening right now! These children are split up permanently from their grief-stricken families for the rest of their lives. They are then given up for adoption to anonymous strangers so that government adoption targets can be met. Local authorities can then be rewarded by massive extra funding from central government under public service agreements. Just look at this answer to a parliamentary question by the Secretary of State!

Adoption: Standards

Source: House of Commons Hansard
Written Answers for 3 Dec 2003 (pt 4)

Tim Loughton: To ask the Secretary of State for Children, Schools and Families which local authorities have received payments from central Government for achieving adoption target levels; and how much each received in each of the last three years. [151067]

John Healey: I have been asked to reply.

30 local authorities have been rewarded for successfully achieving adoption targets in their local public service agreements (LPSA). The better outcomes and amount of 'performance reward grant' (PRG) each has received over the three years 2004/05 to 2006/07 in relation to their performance in these targets is set out in the following table. In addition, 13 local authorities did not achieve the adoption targets in their local PSA and hence received no PRG for this target. One local authority is still to make a claim

Local PSAs - which are negotiated between local authorities and central Government policy departments, facilitated by the DCLG - have helped to incentivise local authorities and partners to provide better public services to their citizens around priorities for improvement locally. Evaluation shows they have been successful in doing this, with real benefits in improved outcomes for local people and communities.

3 Sep 2007: Column 1703W

Local PSA adoption and placement targets: payments made to date under local PSAs	
Local authority	**Amount of 'reward grant' paid (£)**
Barnsley Metropolitan Borough Council	210,173.00
Blackburn with Darwen	307,367.00
Bristol City Council	307,512.00
Buckinghamshire County Council	526,958.00
Bromley (LB)	499,440.00
Camden (LB)	318,916.50
Cheshire County Council	685,134.00
Doncaster Metropolitan Borough Council	578,333.00
Durham County Council	502,675.00
Enfield (LB)	244,963.00
Essex County Council	2,469,200.00
Gloucestershire County Council	612,209.00
Greenwich (LB)	580,996.00
Halton Borough Council	153,938.00
Hampshire	1,675,619.00
Hounslow (LB)	165,019.00
Kensington and Chelsea (LB)	339,117.00
Kent County Council	2,156,583.00
Lewisham (LB)	602,854.00
Liverpool City Council	347,404.00
Luton Borough Council	400,027.00
Manchester City Council	984,877.00
Merton Borough Council	358,708.00
Northamptonshire	1,119,115.00

County Council	
Sheffield City Council	1,025,000.00
Southwark (LB)	435,242.00
St. Helens Metropolitan Borough Council	83,845.00
Wandsworth (LB)	387,627.00
Warwickshire County Council	231,061.00
York City Council	203,620.00

GOOD NEWS!

Thanks in some small measure to this book and my website and all the others who have campaigned, adoption targets were abandoned on April 1st 2008. The original instruction from the then Prime Minister Tony Blair to increase adoptions by 40% still remains in force however and social workers all know that the way to gain 'Brownie points' with their bosses is to achieve as many adoptions as possible!

Adoption target met

by Hammersmith and Fulham Press Office 10/03/2008

101 children adopted in the last three years

More than 100 children have been adopted in the borough during the last three years, after the Council met a target from central Government target that many experts thought would be unachievable.

The Government target, known as a Local Public Service Agreement (LPSA), challenged the Council to successfully achieve 101 adoptions or secure placements during the last three year period in return for £500,000 of funding.

At the time, the Council felt that the bar was set too high, as in the previous three year period only 71 children had been adopted - a figure that was then considered to be very high.

However, H&F's adoption team swung into action and pulled out all of the stops in order to meet the target.

A TRUE STORY

T'was the night before Christmas, the four children slept
The 'SS' were coming, their mother just wept!
Five burly policemen soon broke down the door
We've come for your children, we must take all four!

The 'SS' have told you 'keep perfectly calm'
Your kids are at risk of emotional harm!
So struggling and kicking and screaming with fright
Four little children went off in the night!

The mother sat weeping, her children were lost
Adoption the target, and don't count the cost!
The welfare of children, that is the thing
And think of the cash that adoption will bring!
Ian Josephs

5. CASHING IN

WHO PROFITS FROM THE ADOPTION RACKET?

- Local Authorities (stars, beacon status, and financial rewards under public service agreements).

- Very highly-paid 'professionals' presume to 'assess' the parenting skills of distraught mothers who have had their children taken into care (around £3,000 per 2-3 hour session).

- 'Legal aid lawyers' (a case in the Family Courts costs an average of £70,000 per day so total legal costs of over £500,000 for one case are not unusual!).

- Therapists, psychiatrists and counsellors who are paid around £3,000 for a few hours work eagerly predict that parents might 'emotionally abuse' their children at some time in the future.

- Tame medical experts somehow always side with Social Services against the parents (they also receive around £3,000 for one afternoon session plus a report).

- Foster parents (up to £400 per week per child plus allowances for Christmas and holidays).

- Special schools charging up to £7,000 per week per child (as shown on TV's Channel 4).

- Adoption and fostering agencies charging up to £18,000 per placement.

http://www.ofsted.gov.uk/reports/pdf/?inspectionNumber=478226&providerCategoryID=8&fileName=\\ey\\SC\\SC_SC060131_20060502.pdf

Here at last is **PROOF** that all concerned in 'child protection' are receiving vast sums of money for work that can at best be described as 'destructive' and at worst 'criminal'. Read the following 8 articles below:

1: Fosterers typically make £400 per week per child!

2: Special children's homes typically make £7,000 per week per child!

3: Lawyers and court costs typically £500,000 per case!

4: Experts typically make £28,000 for a simple report!

5: Adoption agencies make £millions (£18,000 per placement)!

6: Local authorities get £millions hitting adoption targets!

7: Barristers' pay linked to number of court case pages!

8: Barristers average annual earnings of £140,000 for family aid work!

1. Balloons and family fun to promote fostering
Slough Borough Council

Hundreds of balloons will be released from Slough town centre to mark a special event to launch Slough's new fostering Allowance Scheme.

Saturday, July 2 will encourage more people to consider becoming foster parents to local children and see the launch of a new fostering allowance of £400 per week.

Between noon and 4pm, the Town Square will be bustling with activities including face painting and balloon modelling. Football fans should be sure to bring a camera as a David Beckham look-a-like will be ready to pose for photos.

Janet Tomlinson, head of education and children's services at Slough Borough Council, will make a short speech at 1pm before the balloon release.

Team members from Slough's Family Placement Services will be giving out fostering information including the fostering freephone number, car stickers, bookmarks, keyrings, wristbands and balloons.

Janet Tomlinson said: "Fostering offers great challenges and great rewards. Even if you've never thought about it before, why not come down on July 2 to find out more?"

The freephone fostering number is 0800 073 0291.

2. Dispatches: Profiting from children in care
Channel 4, 25 November 2004

In 2004, caring for Britain's most vulnerable children is a multi-million pound industry. Children in care cost the taxpayer over £830 million a year. That's an average of £2,500 per child, per week - more than four times what it would cost to send a child to Eton. Yet many homes are failing to provide children with even a basic standard of care.

In this programme, Dispatches goes undercover to investigate the consequences of the increased privatisation of residential children's homes. The investigation reveals how homes are run by private businessmen charging social services departments enormous and unethical mark-ups on services - many of which aren't even provided. Fees of £7,000 a week are not unusual yet Dispatches finds private children's homes which are failing the children in many respects. Homes often use untrained, and sometimes unvetted, agency staff to look after some of the UK's most at risk youngsters - many of whom have been the victims of abuse, prostitution and drugs.

The current system is failing thousands of children a year. According to a recent report, three in five kids leave care with no qualifications at all. One in five will be homeless after two years and one in three of the current prison population has previously been in care. Tragically, some don't make it at all, with approximately 60 youngsters dying in children's homes every year.

3. Council must pay £500,000 for wrongly taking girl into care

by Clare Dyer

The Guardian, 17 March 2006

The following correction was printed in the Guardian's Corrections and clarifications column, Thursday March 23 2006

(The headline for the article below was misleading. As the story made clear, the £500,000 was the total cost to public funds. The council was ordered to pay the parents £200,000 legal aid costs and will have to meet its own costs. The child would also have been represented and payment of those costs will be met from public funds).

A couple had their family life torn apart when social workers wrongly took their nine-year-old daughter into emergency care without good reason and kept her from her parents for 14 months, a high court judge said yesterday.

Mr Justice McFarlane castigated the social workers for "multiple failings" and criticised the family court magistrates who had granted the emergency order. The costs of the case, payable from public funds, were £500,000, including the parents' legal aid costs of £200,000, which the judge ordered the local council to pay. The judge took the unusual step of making his judgment public after a hearing behind closed doors, although the family, the local authority and the magistrates court are all unnamed.

He laid down guidelines to prevent future miscarriages of justice which are certain to lead social services departments and magistrates courts to re-examine their practices. He said it gave him "absolutely no pleasure to have to record the multiple failings of the local authority in this case".

But to do so was "necessary not only in order to come to a conclusion on the issues in this case, but also in order that lessons may be learned for the future".

He said the girl's mother had sought the help of social services and child health services because her daughter, the couple's only child, was displaying some "modest behavioural difficulties".

Mother and daughter had been referred to the child guidance unit for psychotherapy and the girl had been put on the local child protection register.

The notes of a social services planning meeting read: "No neglect issues. Home and care good. Mother and child have good relationship. Detrimental to move."

But social workers suspected it was a case of Munchausen syndrome by proxy - now called fabricated or induced illness (FII) -a rare form of child abuse in which a mother or carer makes a child ill or fakes illness to get attention. At the end of a case conference on the girl in November 2004, social services received a phone call from a nurse at the local hospital.

They were told that the mother had taken the girl there with stomach pains and was asking to see a doctor after the nurse found nothing wrong. Within hours and without any information from the doctor, social workers were at the magistrates court seeking an emergency protection order allowing the girl to be taken from her parents immediately.

They acted without telling the parents and without seeking any medical opinion to try to confirm their suspicions. The girl had had medical treatment before and no doctor had suggested fabricated illness.

The council's actions were described by the mother's counsel as "outrageous" and "inexcusable" leading, as it did, to "the destruction of this family's ordinary life".

Those descriptions "do not, in my view, overstate the quality of what took place on that day", the judge said. The social services team leader, who had no detailed knowledge of the case, made 13 assertions to the magistrates, of which every one was "misleading or incomplete or wrong".

He ruled that the council had no case to take the girl into care and made her a ward of court "to facilitate the child's return home".

4. The expert as judge and jury
by Lois Rogers
The Sunday Times, 18 November 2007

After a host of miscarriages of justice based on discredited expert witnesses, calls are growing for radical reform of their use in court, writes Lois Rogers

Yet another woman was sent to prison last week, following expert evidence that she had shaken to death a baby in her care. Keran Henderson, a 42-year-old childminder, was said to have killed 11-month-old Maeve Sheppard, by shaking her so violently she was left blind and brain-damaged. The infant died in hospital a few days later.

The case has grim echoes of those of Sally Clark, Angela Cannings and Trupti Patel, all of whom were accused of killing their children only to be found innocent later. Clark, a solicitor, who was released from prison after serving three years, died last March as a result of psychological trauma and alcoholism caused by her ordeal.

At the Court of Appeal, two days after the judgment on Henderson, a retrial was ordered in the case of Barry George, the loner convicted of killing the television personality Jill Dando in 1999 with a single shot to the head. Expert testimony as to the significance of a particle of gunshot matter in his pocket is being challenged.

There has also been the recent conviction of the true killer of schoolgirl Lesley Molseed, 32 years after the event – and after Stefan Kiszko had served 16 years for the sexually motivated killing, even though medical evidence could have pointed out his infertility proved his innocence. Once again the review of the evidence threw a spotlight on the role of expert witnesses, whose testimony is often crucial in criminal cases but can be unreliable.

Our blind faith in scientific opinion makes us reluctant to question pronouncements by "experts", but while the law requires everyone from plumbers to nurses to be trained, registered and checked, there is no such requirement for witnesses who may be pronouncing on matters of life and death in court.

A study by senior barrister Penny Cooper of City University in London, has shown that the majority of lawyers and judges do not bother to check the qualifications of experts they approach to bolster an aspect of their case. She also found a substantial number of the expert witnesses had undergone no training to understand their legal duty.

The disquiet this arouses has led to a clamour for legislation to require expert witnesses to be regulated. But how to do that without calling into question thousands of court decisions will not be an easy task.

There is already acute unease over the proliferation of parents convicted of causing cot deaths, shaking babies to death, or harming them by creating symptoms of fictitious illness.

Henderson, for instance, a mother of two herself, a long-term childminder and stalwart volunteer of her local Beaver Scout group, was sentenced to three years in prison for shaking baby Maeve so violently that she was left with fatal brain damage, despite the fact there was no evidence of any "grip marks" on the child, which would normally be expected to accompany such an action.

Her husband, a former police officer, has said she will appeal and hopes to create a campaign similar to that run by Sally Clark's family, to try to prove his wife's innocence.

Many character witnesses spoke up for Henderson in court and the family has dozens of supporters in their home village of Iver Heath, Buckinghamshire.

Some even believe her prosecution was only pursued because of the successful appeal by Roy Meadow, the expert paediatrician whose evidence led to the conviction of Sally Clark.

Following the Clark case, in which Meadow quoted a completely erroneous statistic suggesting the chances of Clark's babies having died naturally were one in 73m, he was struck off by the General Medical Council (GMC) for misconduct. The Court of Appeal agreed he had acted in good faith.

In the meantime, Alan Williams, the Home Office pathologist who conducted post-mortems on Clark's two infant sons, was less lucky. His appeal against a GMC finding of serious professional misconduct was rejected. Williams was accused of tailoring his diagnoses of the nature of the babies' deaths to fit the police case against Clark.

The GMC is currently hearing a claim of gross professional misconduct against paediatrician Dr David Southall. The council has received evidence alleging that Southall falsified his curriculum vitae.

Southall's evidence has figured highly in at least 50 criminal cases and possibly hundreds of family court cases held in secret, which have led to children being removed from their parents.

Questions of how frequently babies really are shaken to death, and indeed if it is possible to do so, have divided medical opinion for some years. There have, however, been up to 200 convictions annually for related forms of violence against babies and young children.

After Clark, Cannings and Patel, another bizarre case was overturned. Ian and Angela Gay, who had been convicted of poisoning their three-year-old adopted son with salt, were cleared when it was revealed the boy was suffering from a rare, and fatal, congenital abnormality.

Recently, the attorney-general ordered a review of almost 300 criminal convictions and 30,000 family court proceedings where children were taken into care. Only four were referred to the Court of Appeal. This, according to critics, was a function of the way the review was done, with authorities being asked to review their own decisions.

Social workers say the crusade to root out dangerous adults is to some extent a reaction to a previous era of regular criticism of their profession when children were left to die at the hands of their parents. Although some acknowledge the pendulum may now have swung too far, others are furious: "Do people think we spend all our time trying to break up families for no good reason?" said John Coughlan, a joint-president of the Association of Directors of Children's Services. "In comparison with the volume of cases, the number of errors is tiny. We never rely on expert witnesses alone."

Others argue that the opinion of expert witnesses is often the decisive factor. And as we have seen most recently with

Barry George, it is not just child murder cases that have turned on such evidence.

Last year the Home Office took the unprecedented step of holding a disciplinary tribunal against Michael Heath, one of its most senior forensic pathologists: 20 charges against him were upheld. One man was subsequently cleared of murder, and numerous other convictions have been called into question.

A spate of other convictions came from evidence supplied by Paula Lannas, another Home Office forensic specialist who was the subject of a long-delayed disciplinary hearing that collapsed because those investigating her said they had a conflict of interest. Not only has Lannas been deprived of an opportunity to clear her name, but dozens of prisoners who claim they were victims of her errors have been unable to get the evidence reviewed.

Police forensic scientist Peter Ablett, who is now chief executive of the Council for the Registration of Forensic Practitioners, points out there are only three ways to prove a crime: a reliable eyewitness, a confession, or forensics. The advent of DNA technology and other advances in recent years has brought increasing reliance on forensics, yet only about 3,000 of the estimated 8,000 expert witnesses operating are members of the council and signed up to its code of practice.

He said many of those who are not are unaware that their duty is to give impartial evidence to the court, not to bolster the case of their paymaster.

City University's Cooper, who is also a governor of the Expert Witness Institute, was concerned to discover during her research that not only have one in five experts undergone no training to understand this duty, but one in 10 was so arrogant they said they saw no need for it. "There should be a requirement for them to be trained, and there should be rules requiring judges and lawyers to consider their credentials before accepting them as expert witnesses," she said.

Such a provision cannot come soon enough. A review is still going on of 700 cases in which bogus forensic scientist Gene Morrison gave evidence. Morrison, 48, from Manchester who was sentenced to five years for fraud in February, admitted he pretended to be an expert witness and bought his qualifications on the internet because it "seemed easier" than getting real ones.

For many of the genuinely qualified experts, legal work is a lucrative sideline, and if they are perceived to be able to "tailor" their evidence convincingly, the commissions keep flowing in. John Hemming, a Liberal Democrat MP campaigning about the misuse of medical evidence, says fees for a basic written opinion, based on reading through existing files, start at £4,000. If the expert concludes there is a case to answer, they attract court attendance fees as well.

"I have known experts get as much as £28,000 for one report," said Hemming, who is lobbying for experts to be required to produce the scientific publications on which their opinion is based: "Unless we start using evidence-based evidence in court, we will get nowhere."

5. Firms cash in on shortage of foster homes
London Evening Standard, 2 October 2005

LONDON: Private agencies are making millions of pounds out of a critical shortage of foster homes for children. Firms are charging councils on average £800 per child per week, an EVENING STANDARD investigation revealed.

This amounts to £41,600 a year to find suitable homes for the most vulnerable children in society.

One head of social services said: "It is cheaper to send the children to Eton."

London councils are so desperate to hold on to their foster parents that two are offering them free loft conversions - worth up to £30,000 - so they can take in more children. Britain's largest independent agency Foster Care Associates had a £56mn turnover in 2003, the last year for which accounts are available.

Its eight directors - seven of them social workers who set up the company 10 years ago - paid themselves total fees of more than £2.2mn as well as sharing pre-tax profits of almost £900,000.

The directors awarded themselves on average £285,000 each - about 10 times the annual salary of a social worker.

There is an estimated shortage of 10,000 foster carers across the UK. This has driven up the prices charged by the 150 or so independent agencies.

It costs councils between £300 and £400 a week to place children with their own approved foster carers but they cannot meet the demand and have to turn to outside agencies. More difficult children can cost as much as £1,500 per week to place in foster homes.

The problem is especially acute in London, where out of 11,500 fostered children up to one-third are found homes through independent agencies. Many of them are 'dumped' in outlying towns around the capital. A total of 60,000 children are fostered nationally.

A spokesman at the department for education said: "We know there are too many children being placed outside of authorities. We commissioned a report last year looking at how we can reduce that number."

Out of the 11,500 fostered children in London, half of them are teenagers, about 3,000 aged eight to 12 and 2,500 aged under eight.

Children are typically being sent from London boroughs to Kent, miles from their schools and friends. Some 330 problem children from London are being fostered in the Margate area.

This has prompted the Kent child protection committee to compile a report, sent to ministers, warning the town is now at a 'tipping point' and branding the situation 'explosive'.

Paul Fallon, director of social services at Barnet council and spokesman for all London's social services directors, said: "Every penny we spend on one child is a penny we can't spend on another child. If I place a child with Barnet it is £400. But it costs me about double that to place a child in an independent placement.

"It is a sellers' market and that will impact on prices. We are stuck. It is cheaper to send children to Eton."

He estimated that in Barnet about 30 to 40 children - about 10% of the number needing foster care - are unaccompanied child refugees. They have helped to swell numbers of children needing placements, putting added pressure on social services.

A spokeswoman for Richmond council, where private places at £900 cost three times as much as council places, said: "In emergencies we will negotiate with another borough for a temporary foster place, but that's very rare."

The crisis has prompted Barnet council and Hammersmith and Fulham to offer grants of up to £30,000 to foster parents to build loft conversions to house more children. A spokeswoman for Hammersmith and Fulham said the outlay would pay itself back within one to two years even if it creates just one extra fostering place.

Defenders of private agencies point out councils often do not factor hidden staffing costs - such as administration and on-call social workers - into their weekly fees. Private agencies also point out they are often called upon to find placements for the most difficult children. They point out they also provide round-the-clock social worker support as well as educational support and therapy. Not all agencies are profit-making with fostering services carried out by charities such as Barnardo's and NCH.

Marcelle Ibbetson, service development manager at NCH, which also typically charges £800 a week, said: "We don't think local authorities have properly costed the real cost of foster care. Their behind the scenes costs are hidden. What we provide is private placements at the specialist end of the market."

None of the directors of Foster Care Associates was available for comment. But in an interview last year Sally Melbourne, FCA's director for the Yorkshire and Lincolnshire region, said: "The majority of the fee we charge local authorities goes to the carer and on the welfare of the child. We are a business but we make very little profit, last year we made 5% profit."

A spokesman for the company added: "The company specialises in children that are difficult to place. That is not necessarily behaviourally difficult children but it could be kids with five siblings that need to be kept together or from the ethnic minorities that needs to be placed in their own community. We offer a complete support structure including therapy and education, which is why the costing may look more expensive."

6. Written Parliamentary answers

So many times have the 'SS' denied the existence of adoption targets it is worth repeating again that they did exist and that local authorities greatly profited from them!

Source: House of Commons Hansard Written Answers for 3 Dec 2003 (pt 4)

Tim Loughton: To ask the Secretary of State for Children, Schools and Families which local authorities have received payments from central Government for achieving adoption target levels; and how much each received in each of the last three years. [151067]

John Healey: I have been asked to reply.

30 local authorities have been rewarded for successfully achieving adoption targets in their local public service agreements (LPSA). The better outcomes and amount of 'performance reward grant' (PRG) each has received over the three years 2004/05 to 2006/07 in relation to their performance in these targets is set out in the following table. In addition, 13 local authorities did not achieve the adoption targets in their local PSA and hence received no PRG for this target. One local authority is still to make a claim.

Local PSAs - which are negotiated between local authorities and central Government policy departments, facilitated by the DCLG - have helped to incentivise local authorities and partners to provide better public services to their citizens around priorities for improvement locally. Evaluation shows they have been successful in doing this, with real benefits in improved outcomes for local people and communities.

Local PSA adoption and placement targets: payments made to date under local PSAs	
Local authority	Amount of 'reward grant' paid (£)
Barnsley Metropolitan Borough Council	210,173.00
Blackburn with Darwen	307,367.00
Bristol City Council	307,512.00
Buckinghamshire County Council	526,958.00
Bromley (LB)	499,440.00
Camden (LB)	318,916.50
Cheshire County Council	685,134.00
Doncaster Metropolitan Borough Council	578,333.00
Durham County Council	502,675.00
Enfield (LB)	244,963.00
Essex County Council	2,469,200.00
Gloucestershire County Council	612,209.00
Greenwich (LB)	580,996.00
Halton Borough Council	153,938.00
Hampshire	1,675,619.00
Hounslow (LB)	165,019.00
Kensington and Chelsea (LB)	339,117.00
Kent County Council	2,156,583.00
Lewisham (LB)	602,854.00
Liverpool City Council	347,404.00
Luton Borough Council	400,027.00
Manchester City Council	984,877.00

Merton Borough Council	358,708.00
Northamptonshire County Council	1,119,115.00
Sheffield City Council	1,025,000.00
Southwark (LB)	435,242.00
St. Helens Metropolitan Borough Council	83,845.00
Wandsworth (LB)	387,627.00
Warwickshire County Council	231,061.00
York City Council	203,620.00

7. Back to Barristers 'exploiting misery' as fees in family law cases rise 25% in 5 years

Daily Mail, 19 June 2008

Barristers have been making millions of extra pounds from the misery of families and children caught up in the family courts, according to new figures released by ministers yesterday.

Fees paid out of taxpayer-funded legal aid to barristers in family court cases have gone up by almost a third in five years and have now reached nearly £100 million a year, they showed.

And there have been big increases in claims by barristers for obscure special payments that provide 'uplift' and 'bolt-ons' to their basic charges.

Jack Straw's Ministry of Justice lifted a corner of the blanket of official secrecy that surrounds the family courts to disclose that barristers who appear in them can claim bonuses including bizarre 'court bundle payments'.

These give barristers extra money if there are more than 176 pages to their court papers and extra still if there are over 350 pages. Yet another court bundle payment is paid if a barrister carries over 700 pages of papers.

Court bundle payments alone meant taxpayers were charged an extra £8.6million by barristers last year.

8. The Times
19 June 2008

The Bar Council, which represents nearly 15,000 barristers in England and Wales, will announce its proposals in a paper before an all-party meeting of MPs tomorrow. Meanwhile, the Legal Services Commission, which runs the legal aid scheme, has just released figures to show how much barristers are earning from legal aid work.

Crispin Passmore, the commission's policy director for civil legal aid, said that the sum spent on barristers' fees since 2003-04 had risen from £71 million to nearly £100 million.

The number of barristers earning more than £100,000 from family legal aid work had gone up by 14 per cent in the 12 months between mid2005 and mid2006, he added.

"The average annual earnings from family legal aid work is £140,000 – and that doesn't include any privately paid work they might do. So we are not talking about the minimum wage."

Do we get value for money? Well this is what the BBC had to say!

Can children in care avoid prison?
BBC News at bbc.co.uk/news, 15 May 2002

David Akinsanya was raised by the state and in a special BBC Two documentary he asks why so many kids leaving the care system end up in prison.

Government statistics show that 49 per cent of children in care go straight to prison. With 56,000 children in the British care system today, that means 28,000 are set to receive custodial sentences.

David Akinsanya believes the problem lies with the care system itself.

He says the care system is inflexible and does not offer appropriate care to young people.

Research found that 42 per cent of young prostitutes had been in care at some point

The Independent, 14 December 2006

The Government's own research highlights how the care system is not simply a negligent parent but at times probably more dangerous than the family from which some children have been taken. A study commissioned by the Home Office has looked at the link between hard drug use, sex work and various vulnerability factors. The results are astonishing, if not heartbreaking.

Less than 1 per cent of the child population is looked after by the state, but the research found that 42 per cent of young women prostitutes interviewed had been in care at some point in their lives. "This is an extraordinary figure, which demonstrates that looked after children are very vulnerable to involvement in drug use and sexual abuse through prostitution," the report concluded.

Gay foster parents abused young boys

by Nigel Bunyan

The Daily Telegraph, 23 May 2006

A council was condemned yesterday for failing to prevent a paedophile homosexual couple from abusing young boys even after being alerted by one of the victim's parents.

Foster parents Ian Wathey, 40, and Craig Faunch, 32, face long terms in jail after being convicted of molesting and filming eight-year-old twins and two boys aged 14.

The twins were video-taped as they showered together, while one of the older boys was sexually abused by Wathey in his bedroom.

Both men "hurt" him, he told Leeds Crown Court. "I do not like them any more. I want them to go to prison."

Yesterday it emerged that Wakefield council had been warned of possible abuse by the twins' mother, Mrs X.

She had found bathroom photographs of her sons but an inquiry by social workers cleared the paedophiles of wrongdoing and said they had simply been "naive and silly". Police were not called in. Wathey and Faunch had moved on to abusing the two 14-year-olds by the time police arrested them in Pontefract, West Yorks.

The two men began abusing boys within a month of Wakefield social services approving them as foster carers in July 2003.

Outside the court, Mrs X said: "I thought the council would have contacted the police as part of the investigation. . . Maybe if something had been done sooner we would not be here today."

Kitty Ferris, for the council, said applications by the men to become foster carers had been approved "in accordance with statutory requirements and council policy".

She added: "Although correct procedures were carried out at every stage the service has reviewed its internal procedures to identify what lessons should be learned."

Both men were told they faced substantial jail terms and sentencing was adjourned.

Council let known paedophile become foster parent
by Patrick Barnham and Raymond Hainey
The Scotsman, 9 March 2007

A COUNCIL allowed a paedophile to become a foster parent, despite knowing he had been convicted of abusing a young girl, it was revealed yesterday.

William Alexander and his wife, Jessie, were approved as foster carers by Aberdeen City Council in 1993 - 14 years after he had been found guilty of lewd and libidinous behaviour and practices with a youngster.

His conviction - and the fact the local authority knew about it - emerged yesterday after he was convicted of abusing three young girls during the late 1990s. Children's campaigners last night raised questions about how Alexander was permitted to take on the role.

A jury of nine men and six women took just 40 minutes to find Alexander guilty of five counts of lewd and libidinous behaviour and practices at Aberdeen Sheriff Court. Sheriff Colin Harris deferred sentence until next month and Alexander, 57, from Bridge of Don, was released on bail.

Council officials last night defended the decision to allow Alexander to foster. A spokesman said: "Aberdeen City Council was aware of Mr Alexander's previous conviction, but did not consider that it posed a risk to the young person involved."

The spokesman said the couple's registration was suspended in May 2001 after a young person made an allegation of "inappropriate behaviour". They were formally de-registered six months later. He added: "We are aware of the circumstances surrounding the prosecution and conviction of Mr Alexander and have undertaken a complete review of the circumstances surrounding his approval as a foster carer, including reviewing the case files of all the children and young people placed in his care.

"Aberdeen City Council wishes to express its sincere regret at the nature of the offences and the distress this has caused the young women involved."

The trial heard that Alexander abused two 14-year-old girls and one seven-year-old girl between 1995 and 1997.

One of the teenagers was lying in her bed when Alexander entered her room and abused her. The court heard the girl was drunk at the time.

Duncan MacKenzie, prosecuting, told the jury: "She told you in graphic detail what was done to her in the bedroom by the accused and how she felt when that was happening.

"Drunk or not, she was fully aware of what was being done to her and by whom."

Alexander's previous conviction was at Stonehaven Sheriff Court in June 1979, when he was fined £80.

A spokesman for the charity Children 1st last night raised concerns about the council's handling of the case.

He said: "I cannot think of circumstances where it would be appropriate for someone convicted of sexual abuse against children to become a foster carer. You would not expect someone with a conviction of that nature to be approved as a foster carer."

The spokesman said the girls involved would need considerable assistance to help them come to terms with their ordeal. He added: "They will need a lot of support and care to get over this."

Outside court after the trial, Mrs Alexander bundled her husband into a waiting car with a leather jacket draped over his head.

About a dozen of the couple's neighbours lined up outside the court to hurl abuse at Alexander.

One of them, John MacDonald, said: "He got what he deserved at last.

"Those poor girls he molested are scarred for life."

• Social workers in Aberdeen were harshly criticised in the wake of their ineffective supervision of the paedophile Stephen Leisk, who murdered Scott Simpson, nine, in 1997.

A report into that case found that the senior social worker supervising Leisk let himself be conned by the sex offender.

The social worker came under fire over a series of fundamental failings in his supervision of Leisk in the weeks leading up to the boy's murder.

Extract from the Telegraph:

Official figures show that only six per cent of the 60,000 children in care gain five or more A* to C GCSEs and more than a third are not entered for a single GCSE.

Conviction rates for young people in care are three times the rate for other juveniles. One in four girls leaving care is pregnant or already a mother. A recent case which caused outrage involved a 12-year-old living in a children's home in Blackburn who became pregnant while working as a prostitute.

Dismal outcomes are the norm despite the £2.5 billion a year spent looking after them. It costs £100,000 a year to keep a child in a children's home, more than four times the fees at top private schools such as Eton or Winchester.

Fostering can cost up to £30,000 a year, compared with the £7,500 a year that state boarding schools charge parents for accommodation, with the £5,000 cost of education covered by the local authorities.

Harriet Harman (Minister of State, Department for Constitutional Affairs). Hansard

My hon. Friend raises an extremely important point, which she has put to me in a written question, so I know what the answer is. Last year something like 200 people were sent to prison by the family courts, which happens in complete privacy and secrecy. The idea that people are sent to prison without any reports of the proceedings makes even more important the work that we are undertaking with the family courts, and with the important intervention of the Constitutional Affairs Committee, to open them up so that they act in the public interest while maintaining personal privacy.

Only in the **SECRET** Family Courts are punishments (losing their children to long term foster care or worse still, adoption by strangers) imposed on persons (parents) who have neither committed a crime nor even been accused of committing any crime! **THERE IS NO OTHER CASE IN UK LAW WHERE THIS CAN HAPPEN!**

6. HOW TO GET YOUR CHILDREN BACK

Also 'How to keep your children if the 'SS' threaten to take them!!'

The *Daily Mail* headline refers of course to the Social Services appropriately known by all those unfortunate enough to have had 'dealings' with them as the 'SS'!!

There is a wealth of information in this chapter to help you get your children back or to fight in court to keep them if the 'SS' are on the attack! This includes help in drafting a statement for the court (see Your Statement below). You are advised to read **ALL** the legal information in this chapter first however so that hopefully you are better informed before writing it out.

Nearly all the arguments you need to present your case to the court will be found here and you only have to pick out those that apply to and also suit your particular case.

In many courts if you represent yourself you can get technical help with the documents etc. from the PSU (PERSONAL SUPPORT UNIT). In London they are to be found in Room M104, Royal Courts of Justice, The Strand, London. Tel: 0207 9477701/7703 or 4th floor Room 408, First Avenue House, High Holborn, Principal Registry of the Family Division Tel: 0207 9477737.

Remember always that it is a waste of time attacking individual social workers (who investigate themselves) and fosterers who, if they are looking after your children, should be cultivated and made friends with, however much you hate the idea! Make friends with the fosterers and potential adopters if you can meet them, as this way at least you can keep track of where your children are! Attack in court with all your force both the reasons why your baby or your child was taken into care and the system that allowed this to happen!

Parents win right to keep fourth child - but vow to fight for the other three

by Laura Collins

Daily Mail, 1 July 2007

Norfolk couple Mark and Nicky Webster last week finally won their landmark legal fight to keep their fourth child, Brandon, after a false allegation of child abuse robbed them of their three older children.

In what has been described as a "gross miscarriage of justice", the Websters' children were taken away by Social Services and forcibly adopted after a family court hearing that lasted just one day.

Here, the shattered parents tell of their ordeal and their joy at the High Court judgment on their youngest child. But the battle is not over.

The couple have vowed to fight on to clear their names and renew contact with the children they have lost – the siblings 13-month old Brandon has never known.

They had battled for more than a year for this moment and the emotion was almost too much to bear. Last Friday, Mark and Nicky Webster won their fight to keep their infant son, Brandon.

Standing on the steps of the Royal Courts of Justice, factory worker Mark broke down and wept for the three older children he and his wife have already lost to Social Services – almost certainly for ever – after they were accused of child abuse.

Mr Webster, of Cromer in Norfolk, described the judgment as 'partial vindication' but vowed to take the fight to clear their name to the Court of Appeal.

He said: "Of course, we are overjoyed to have Brandon but now let us see the children they stole from us. We've been under scrutiny from Norfolk County Council for the past year and shown we are good parents to Brandon. We were good parents to all our children.

"We've been told adoption is irreversible except under "exceptional circumstances". But we will apply to the Court of Appeal for permission to overturn the care order that led to us being called child abusers and our children being adopted.

"We do want contact with our children (now aged seven, five and nearly four). They're Brandon's brothers and sister and we want them to know each other and know the truth. We would like to make sure they will be told they weren't neglected or abused. They were extremely loved. We want Norfolk to apologise, to acknowledge mistakes were made."

Last night the couple's MP, Liberal Democrat Norman Lamb, said: "I am convinced now that this is a gross miscarriage of justice. We need to have a proper inquiry into how such mistakes can be made. Part of that means addressing the financial incentive that exists for councils to meet adoption targets."

Earlier, the Websters had listened as Mr Justice Holman found "no basis for considering Brandon at any risk of harm and every reason to believe that he is thriving in a caring, loving family".

Yet, in his short life, Brandon has been both the centre of a custody battle and the catalyst for a landmark legal case brought by The Mail on Sunday and the BBC last November to lift a gagging order. Had we not been successful we would not have been able to report any of last week's events.

If ever there were a story in which the danger of the Family Courts' closed-door justice was writ large, it is this. During the four-day hearing, the paucity of the council's original case was laid bare.

Listening to Norfolk's opening statement, Mr Justice Holman said: "The gravity of the situation is obvious. People will say, how could this have happened?"

For, though last week's case was theoretically concerned only with the care of Brandon, it had everything to do with the May 2004 hearing that branded Mark, 34, and Nicky, 27, child abusers.

Their ordeal began in October 2003 when Nicky took their second son (Child B) to hospital with a painful, swollen leg. He was found to have several metaphyseal fractures – a type of break doctors said could be caused only by physical abuse.

A nightmare of council intervention followed. All three children were placed in foster care. Their parents were powerless. Barely six months later, in a hearing lasting just one day, the children were permanently removed and swiftly advertised for adoption.

A year ago last May – with Nicky heavily pregnant and the couple convinced their fourth child would be taken at birth – the Websters fled to Ireland, where Brandon was born. They returned the following month, agreeing to care for him in a Big Brother-style assessment centre. After five exemplary months they were allowed to take him home.

In February this year, at an interim hearing for the proceedings Norfolk County Council was still pursuing, Mr Justice Holman told the council it could not simply cite the May 2004 case as proof of Brandon's risk. It would, he said, have to prove "from scratch" that Child B was abused.

New experts were instructed, the original treating doctors revisited, GP notes thoroughly investigated and witnesses who had never originally been called gave statements.

Then, just days before the hearing, scheduled to last ten days, was to begin, Norfolk dramatically withdrew its care order application. Had Justice Holman simply accepted that, none of what follows would have ever been aired. Instead he decided that would "not do justice to the situation as a whole".

What did emerge was an 'overwhelming' body of medical opinion illuminating the truth about Child B's fractures and the unforgivable extent to which the Webster family had been shattered by the failures of medical professionals, social workers and legal representatives enlisted – at public expense – to protect them and their children.

Tragically, the fractures that Norfolk social workers and doctors branded 'proof' of abuse were shown to be nothing of the sort.

An American expert – known only as Prof P, for legal reasons – was instructed by the Websters. An internationally renowned nutritionist, Prof S, was instructed by the council.

His report was forwarded to an expert radiologist, Dr L, who dramatically reversed an original finding of abuse and recommended the instruction of a further radiological expert, Prof R.

Every one of these eminent specialists was united: Child B's fractures were not evidence of abuse but of bones weakened by scurvy, caused by lack of vitamin C.

Worse, the scurvy was due to the child's "eccentric diet" – almost nothing but soya milk – sanctioned by the family GPs. The Websters' "crime" was to follow medical advice.

Nicky explained: "Our son was lactose-intolerant and had eczema. At a few months he was put on prescription infant soya. But he also wouldn't eat solids. On the very rare occasions he did swallow something he would vomit."

Understandably, the problem – not experienced by her other children – concerned Nicky. She raised it with her health visitor and GP but was told: "He'll eat when he's ready."

Crucially, in February 2003, after a year, the GP stopped the prescriptions for Child B's infant soya. Nicky was told to buy supermarket soya milk. The GP did not give advice about vitamin supplements.

In court, another GP who saw Child B claimed he "would have advised" that orange juice be added to this diet. Nicky denies this was ever said.

From then until his admission to hospital the principal source of Child B's nutrition was soya milk. "Maybe I should have known," Nicky said. "But we're not medical people. We were following advice. We felt we were doing the best for our son.

"Now I can't help holding the GP responsible."

Little wonder. Mark and Nicky were young, inexperienced parents – no different from thousands of others. But they loved their children and the issue of Child B's diet was one Nicky raised repeatedly.

On the very day she took her son to hospital in October 2003 she mentioned it to the dietician, who recorded: "Will be deficient in kcals, iron, vits and minerals."

Later, Nicky wrote pages of questions for her solicitors to investigate. Searching for explanations to the fractures she pointed to her family history of osteogenesis imperfecta (brittle bones) and queried what effect her son's diet might have had on developing bones.

Yet Child B's extraordinary, deficient diet did not feature in the 2004 hearing before Justice Barham. Instead, Norfolk relied "heavily" on a report from a treating paediatrician which described the fractures as "highly specific" to abuse.

That report carried the note: "Not to be used in court proceedings."

Last week Justice Holman said: "It is not difficult to imagine that, later, the paediatrician might say, "I know I put this then but, with hindsight, more information and reflection, I feel differently." '

The key expert witness – jointly instructed – at the 2004 hearing was, according to Justice Holman, "not really the right man".

Positive evidence was finessed out of the picture. Why, for example, was Nicky's health visitor not asked to make a report?

Justice Holman said: "I think if a health visitor says, 'I cannot believe there is non-accidental injury going on here,' that seems evidence I would want to weigh and hear."

Instead, a written statement from the health visitor, read in court last week, revealed how her view was quashed. Asked at a Social Services meeting whether she thought the Webster children should be placed on the 'at risk' register, she said: 'No'.

She explained: "I advised I had no concerns and didn't believe either parent would deliberately harm any of their children.

"Several weeks later there was the suggestion of going for care proceedings in respect of all three children (which) I disagreed with. My superior disagreed with me although she had had no dealings with the children.

"My team leader told me the medical evidence was overwhelming. She told me I should agree with her. I was very upset but felt I had to do what I was instructed."

In the face of such determined pursuit, the Websters could only rely on their legal representation. But today Nicky says: "We were failed in a big way by our lawyers. Days before our final hearing we ended up changing our solicitor."

At that hearing the medical evidence was "all one way" and the Websters' assertion of innocence was termed "denial" – or proof that Mark and Nicky remained incurable abusers.

But when he opened proceedings last Tuesday, Justice Holman posed two questions to Norfolk council: "If all the medical evidence now assembled had been available in May 2004 would Norfolk have sought a finding then that child B was non-accidentally injured?

"And, if they would not have sought (such) a finding, would they have pursued the removal of those children, let alone the adoption?"

The council had always insisted it was "not a single issue" case. Yet the feeble nature of their "other issues" was given short shrift by Justice Holman. Referring to the note that Child A's teeth were very bad, he said: "I don't think children get removed, never mind adopted, for that."

Ultimately, Norfolk failed to answer his opening questions. Yet – just as lawyer George Hawks, who was instrumental in bringing the Websters' case to light, stated last week that recognising the significance of Child B's diet was 'not rocket science' – providing a succinct answer to both questions is hardly a feat of logic.

Unless each eminent physician instructed by the Websters and Norfolk over the past five months were to be discredited or shown to be wrong, the most likely cause of Child B's injuries was scurvy.

But still the Websters await any apology. Still the health professionals who condemned them, the legal professionals who failed them and the social workers who judged them – and ignored those in their own organisation who spoke up for them – are protected by a cloak of anonymity

They all continue to work within the same care services. They all continue to wield the same power they exerted over this family with such devastating consequences.

Mark and Nicky Webster are remarkable in the fortitude they have shown in the past weeks, months, years. Nicky says: "For a while we had to emotionally disconnect from what was going on or we would have just fallen apart.

"In a sense we have Brandon to thank for even getting to this day. But, without the media interest, I have no doubt that Brandon would have been taken at birth and we would have had to fight to get him back. And I don't think we would have managed it.

"Because this was happening in the public eye, we were given the opportunity we never had with the others, to show that we are good parents. The only observation we had then was at contact meetings. Each time that ended with tears."

It is impossible to articulate the impact this has had on Mark and Nicky and on their close, extended family in Cromer, Norfolk. A poignant postscript to this week's events came with the death of Nicky's grandmother, Joyce, at 4am on Friday.

Nicky said: "One of her wishes was to see the children again. I regret we couldn't fulfil that for her. We've lost years with our children, my parents have lost years with their grandchildren and she lost years with her great-grandchildren. That should have been very special."

Mr Justice Holman closed his judgment: "I wish Mr and Mrs Webster and Brandon every possible happiness and fulfilment as a family together in the years to come."

He added: "I'm sorry you've had such a ghastly week. I hope the future's very, very rosy for you." But how can a future be "rosy" when it is bound to such a past? How can a hearing during which a catalogue of errors was exposed end with the conclusion, judicially at least, that no one was to blame?

How can the anonymity of the professionals involved and the secrecy of the Family Courts be defended when this family's story stands as a stark and frightening example of just what can slip through the net, undetected, unscrutinised?

According to Nicky: "The judge was very fair in what he said. But there's no such thing as winning, is there? I would like at least an acknowledgement from Norfolk that mistakes were made.

"We did nothing wrong. We followed the advice we were given. We loved our children. The worst thing about the Family Courts is that it's all behind closed doors. At least this time has been different. Behind closed doors so much goes on that you can't fight against. You request second opinions and you're not always granted them.

"You don't always get the expert you want. You're the only one who knows the truth and it's so hard to convince anyone else that you're telling it. At least now we feel we have gone some way to doing that. But how can it ever really be over for us?

"Now we live with the possibility that, at the age of 18 or whatever, our children will find us and ask, 'Why didn't you fight for us?'

"We want them to know that we fought, that we loved them and that we still love them every bit as much as we love Brandon. They're Brandon's full-siblings and we want for him, and for us, to have some form of contact. They must know the truth. They have a right to know the truth about their history."

Lisa Christensen, Norfolk's director of Children's Service, said: "I welcome the fact that all parties involved in the care of Brandon Webster have agreed a way forward in court."

However, the Websters' requests for an apology were described by both the council and the council-appointed guardian as "inappropriate".

UPDATE 2009 on the WEBSTERS!!

After two years of delays and prevarications from the local authority the Webster's appeal finally got to court. The authority argued that following the two year delay (for which they were largely responsible) the children's best interests were to remain with their "new" families with whom by then they had well and truly bonded. The judge agreed with the local authority despite conceding that the Websters had probably suffered a massive injustice as it seemed on the evidence that the children should never have been removed in the first place!

The judges concluded that they had no powers to overturn an adoption unless it had been obtained by fraud or without the knowledge of the parents, and neither of these conditions existed in the Webster's case. They approved the usual "closed adoption" which meant in effect that these stony-hearted judges deprived the Webster parents and their son baby Brandon of all contact with the three adopted children. Their only hope being that when the children reached the age of 18 they would be curious enough to try and trace their real parents despite their false birth certificates with false names supplied by a conniving and deceitful State !

The Webster family pleaded in vain for at least once a year contact so they would at least know if their children were happy or sad, healthy or ill, even alive or dead but this was ruthlessly denied them. Surely this was a breach of their basic human rights?

Surely also it was baby Brandon's human right to have some contact with his three siblings? Such abuses of family human rights were once again completely ignored by judges to whom such insignificant claims were apparently beneath even their slightest consideration!

YOUR STATEMENT

Begin your statement for the court as follows: (But miss out anything that is not true or anything that just does not apply in your particular case).

I have never neglected or abused my baby/child/children. I have no criminal record (most crimes are wiped clean from police records after periods varying from 6 months to 10 years depending on the crime) and I have never even been charged with a serious crime. I have no problems with alcohol or drugs and no learning difficulties. My husband/wife/partner has a similar record. My child/children have always been happy, well-dressed, clean and have a good attendance record at their schools. Their accommodation is very suitable and has always been kept clean and tidy. My baby/child/children has/have been cruelly abused by the removal from my loving care.

If you have been accused of unreasonable hostility towards social workers, an inability to work with professionals and as a consequence suffering from personality disorder or in need of anger management courses add the following response:

I am and always have been 100% willing to work with professionals performing their statutory duty of trying to reunite families and my family in particular. It is however quite unreasonable to expect me to 'work with' persons whose avowed intent is and always has been to take my baby/child and give him/her away for adoption by complete strangers.

MPs from all parties have signed a motion deploring the taking of children by Social Services in order to meet adoption targets and more than 200 MPs of all parties have signed another motion calling for an end to the secrecy of the Family Courts. Journalists on *The Times, The Telegraph* and *The Daily Mail* plus also highly respected presenters on the BBC and ITV have publicly reached similar conclusions. Please therefore do not accuse me of paranoia, of having a personality disorder or of needing 'anger management courses' just because like these distinguished professionals I too distrust social workers and feel very angry with a so-called Family Court system that has not only abused and split up a family it had a duty to protect and unite but also (and worse) has cruelly deprived my baby/child/children/ of a loving mother/father/ parents.

I wish to appeal (or ask leave to appeal) against the recent decision to make my child(ren) subject to an interim care order/full care order/placement for adoption. I am prevented from doing so because the court/my solicitors refuse to give me a copy of the judgement/my file and my appeal cannot be accepted without proper documentation.

The above is an example of how most statements for the Family Court should begin.

Remember when appealing that it is the previous judgement you must criticise point by point. It is no use just rehashing the evidence unless court procedure was clearly not just unfair but illegal! If, on the other hand, a care order has been in force for at least 6 months, you can ask for it to be discharged due to changed and improved circumstances. This is usually an easier process to initiate than an appeal. Follow this up after you have considered all the information found in this chapter; you can then finally outline your case in your personal statement (preferably after you have finished reading **ALL** the following hints and steps to take). Your task is to prove that the children should be with you, that they will be healthy and happy with you and that they are being abused by their separation from you. Do not waste time and energy attacking individual social workers or solicitors as no matter how bad you make them look it will **NOT** help prove that **YOU** are the right person to have care of the children!

You can however always attack the therapists, psychologists, psychiatrists and other crackpot experts who are hired at vast expense to demolish your character! **ASK THEM IN COURT HOW MUCH THEY HAVE BEEN PAID TO TESTIFY AND TO WRITE THEIR BIASED REPORTS!!** Ask them also how many reports they have written recommending that children be put in care or adopted and how many contrary to Social Services wishes that children should be returned to their parents! Quite often their 'qualifications' are false and bogus and cannot be produced in court! Even more important, usually their own private lives can be exposed when questioned and shown to be in a far worse mess than yours. They are often littered with a series of failed marriages or partnerships with children they never see or who refuse to talk to them! This discredits them from daring to pass judgement on you from giving you any advice about your family! You can in any case point out that these 'money-hungry charlatans' shamefully make their living out of the misery of others. They write long meaningless reports full of psychobabble and pretentious jargon to justify the removal of happy children and worse still newborn babies to meet 'adoption targets'. Often, they pompously predict these children are 'at risk' from 'future emotional abuse' due to events that will probably never happen! Severely abused and physically injured children are **NOT** good adoption material so they are only too often callously left to die!

20 POINTS TO REMEMBER.
SELECT ANY THAT APPLY IN YOUR CASE

(On average two or three will probably apply to you). They are summarised here and explained more fully later.

1. 'SS' cannot stop you leaving the UK if no court order has been made. If you are pregnant and the 'SS' are threatening to take your baby as soon as it is born, your safest option is to leave the UK and take refuge in another European country where benefits are excellent and the regime is sympathetic such as Sweden for example. Even when there is a court order (often made in your absence while you are abroad) the publicity generated by the 'SS' pressurising you to return can still end up with parents, the winners!

There are no longer any frontier controls at the borders between 22 EU countries. This is thanks to the Schengen Agreement which is part of EU law. The Schengen rules remove all internal border controls but put in place effective controls at the external borders of the EU and introduce a common visa policy. The full Schengen members are Austria, Belgium, the Czech Republic, Denmark, Estonia, Finland, France, Germany, Greece, Hungary, Italy, Latvia, Lithuania, Luxembourg, Malta, the Netherlands, Poland, Portugal, Slovakia, Slovenia, Spain, Sweden (but not Ireland and the United Kingdom) plus Iceland and Norway (which are not EU members).

Better still, providing no date for a Family Court hearing has even been fixed, if both parents are later found together with the children in France, Spain, Italy or Portugal the 'SS' can do nothing at all about it!

2. Children in care cannot be prevented by force from afternoon visiting or from telephoning their parents! (Reverse charges if necessary). Also, they can send and receive emails, so **DON'T** lose contact.

If social workers call the police to say a young person of **ANY** age is missing and they believe there is a danger of significant harm they can go to court for a recovery order and the police can take that person back temporarily. They have no power however to stop an immediate return to the parents' home next day and after a few days of going backwards and forwards will nearly always give up! Please note that police sometimes claim that they have a warrant or have authority but have no need to show any documents to support this!

BUT read section 50, subsection 8 of the **Children Act**. They **DO** have to show you written authority!

8) Where a person is authorised as mentioned in subsection (7)(c)—

(a) the authorisation shall identify the recovery order; and

(b) any person claiming to be so authorised shall, if asked to do so, produce some duly authenticated document showing that he is so authorised

Remember that any court document **MUST BE SIGNED** by a judge or a magistrate and usually stamped by the court. **NEVER** be taken in by a false order such as a paper that is waved in your face but not given to you to verify!

If children are under 16 and over 12 they are often classified as 'young persons' and even when in care they cannot be prevented from visiting parents as social workers would risk charges of assault and false imprisonment if physical force was used to stop them.

CHILDREN AND FAMILIES PROCEDURE MANUAL

Section D: Family Proceedings and Protection of Children

JUNE 1999 Page 2 of 4

D10.1 A Recovery Order provides legal powers to help secure the return of a child missing from placement.

D10.1.1 A Recovery Order may only be made in respect of a child who is subject to:-

i) a care order (including interim care order)

ii) an emergency protection order

iii) police protection

D10.1.2 A Court may make a Recovery Order if there is reason to believe that:-

a) the child is unlawfully taken away or kept away from the

person with responsibility for the child's care, or

b) the child has run away or is staying away from the responsible person, or

c) the child is missing

D10.1.3 A Recovery Order requires a person harbouring a child to hand him or her over and a person with information about the child's whereabouts should disclose that information to the Police or a Court. It also empowers a Constable to search named premises.

Section 50(i)

D10.1.4 If a child is missing from placement every effort must initially be made to try and secure the return of the child by agreement. If the person holding or harbouring the child refuses to hand the child over and there is no immediate danger then that person should be notified in writing of the action which the Authority will take if they refuse to comply. If however there is an immediate risk then an application can be made without notice.

D10.1.5 Effect of the Order

i) The Recovery Order must name the child and the person

who has made the application

ii) The Order directs the person holding the child to produce him/her at the request of the authorised person and empowers the authorised person to remove the child.

iii) If any person has information as to the child's whereabouts, he or she is required by the Order to disclose this information if asked to do so by either a Police Officer or Court Officer.

3. Shaken baby syndrome cannot be proved for sure without body bruising or a previous history of injury or abuse (see addendum to the Attorney General's report below).

Addendum to Report

Allegations that a baby has been shaken and consequently injured or even killed are hard to prove but also hard to disprove! Top experts who appeared for both sides in the Louise Woodward case in the USA disagreed with each other and testified in favour of the side that paid them in each case! This does cast doubt on the reliability of highly paid experts who give categoric opinions in court!

The Attorney General called for a review by the best medical and scientific brains in Britain last year and in the addendum to the report paras 14.1 and 14.2 concluded that even when all 3 symptoms were present (known as the triad; being retinal bleeding, subdural bleeding, and brain damage) it would **NOT** be safe to conclude that a baby had been shaken without a previous history of abuse or other injuries such as extensive bruising or broken bones.

Her Majesty's Attorney General. 14 February 2006. ADDENDUM TO REPORT. SHAKEN BABY SYNDROME. On the 21st December 2004 I announced the results of my review ...

www.attorneygeneral.gov.uk/attachments/shaken_baby_syndrom e_review_report.doc

Lords Hansard text for 14 Feb 2006 (60214-04)- Child Protection: Shaken Baby Syndrome. 3.09 pm. The Attorney-General (Lord ... presence of the triad of injuries is consistent with shaken baby syndrome,

...

www.parliament.the-stationery-office.co.uk/pa/ld199697/ldhansrd/pdvn/lds06/text/60214-04.htm -

4. 'Failure of a baby to thrive' can be disproved by comparing progress after removal with that before, and in any case

your own GP is the best person to say you have done all you could. Similarly your own GP is the best person to write a statement saying you have no need to take drugs like Prozac to 'manage your anger' and indeed that you are advised **NOT** to take any drugs against your will, since sometimes you may be ordered to take them by persons with **NO** medical qualifications such as social workers, guardians and even judges!

5. Munchausen Syndrome is a scientifically unproven theory (and now largely discredited) that needs actual proof that some act of the parent has deliberately caused illness or physical harm to the baby or young child. Social workers have no qualifications to make this diagnosis; though they often do!

In recent years, several mothers in the autism community have been accused of Munchausen Syndrome By Proxy (MSBP), in which the mother is thought to be imagining the medical problems in her son/daughter. Former law professor, Dr. Bill Long, wrote a review paper for lawyers and judges on MSBP. Dr. Long's Executive Summary is below.

MUNCHAUSEN SYNDROME BY PROXY ("MSBP")/FACTITIOUS DISORDER BY PROXY ("FDBP"):
A Guide for Judges, Lawyer and Parents
Dr. Bill Long; drbilllong@gmail.com
Executive Summary

For more than 30 years prosecutors, social workers and many mental health professionals have used a diagnosis of MSBP/FDBP as a means of taking children from their caregivers and then, often, bringing charges against the caregiver for abusing the children. At the heart of MSBP/FDBP is the allegation that the caregiver (usually the mother) is either lying about the medical symptoms experienced by the child or has induced real symptoms through poisoning or other injurious actions against the child. Why would the mother/caregiver do such a thing? Those who 'believe in' the diagnosis argue that she does so in order to get attention from the medical community, often for unmet needs in her own life, and become the center of attention in a complex medical drama that she is inducing. Thus, the heart of a MSBP/FDBP allegation is that the mother or child's caregiver is secretly 'working the system' and trying to deceive multiple levels of medical staff as she goes about her nefarious design of injuring and perhaps even killing her child. Because the allegation of MSBP/FDBP relates to child endangerment, it has been a 'hot button' sub-issue in the larger world of child abuse that has been at the fore of American social services and law in the past generation.

It is often difficult for prosecutors to 'prove' that a mother has actually injured her child, especially since so many of the mothers alleged to be 'MSBP/FDBP' 'moms' themselves have medical training, personal charm, apparent solicitude for the child's well-being and the well-being of the medical staff attending the child. Direct evidence (e.g., eyewitness testimony of induced poisons) is hard to come by; circumstantial evidence, too, is often scanty. Thus, the allegation of MSBP/FDPB—that the mother suffers from this 'syndrome'--can be a sort of evidentiary boost for the prosecution when its case might otherwise be weak. By arguing that it is consistent for the sufferer of the 'syndrome' to be an outwardly caring mother, one who eagerly seeks medical advice and affirms the medical staff, prosecutors can leap over a sometimes yawning evidentiary gap and help the state pry the child away from the parents. Then, as is argued in the paper, prosecutors need only refer to vague 'studies' that show that children returned to MSBP/FDBP mothers face a significant likelihood of physical danger and even death at the hands of the caregiver, and courts almost always deprive parents of their child/children. Though child abuse is a significant problem and one that ought to be seriously addressed at all levels of society, the allegation of MSBP/FDBP can function as a evidentiary 'short cut' to help make a prosecutor's case for him/her when direct or circumstantial evidence is lacking.

One of the criteria for MSBP identified in a classic study is that the child's symptoms abate when separated from the perpetrator. This is taken to be a sign that the caregiver induced or fabricated the symptoms. Yet, when the classic article using this definition is examined, one finds that the statistics she provides not only don't support her point but actually lead to the opposite conclusion. Indeed, her evidence points to most cases of worsening of symptoms happening in the hospital. Of course, one could argue that these symptoms were induced by the caregiver in that context, but she does not so argue. In addition, if one thinks about this point for a moment, one would normally expect the child's symptoms to abate when give over to the medical professionals. Perhaps as a result of the flimsiness of this criterion, later papers and definitions of MSBP don't include it as a feature of MSBP.

I argue in the paper that the result of this kind of thinking and action has led to dramatically bad consequences for parents and their children, children who may have medical conditions that are difficult to diagnose and treat. If the mother, for example, denies that she has induced the physical ailment in her child, the state can say, "Ah, a denial is a sure sign that the mother is guilty of being an MSBP/FDBP mother. Thus, we recommend the child be taken away." If, on the other hand, the mother "confesses" to having induced the illness in the child, the child will be taken away because a confession serves as direct evidence of the mother's abuse of the child. Thus, mothers accused of being an "MSBP/FDBP mom" are in a Catch-22 type-of-situation. Shadowy allegations often are enough to take a child away from parents; and denials of abuse protect them no more than a confession.

With this the problem before us, I do two things in the paper: (1) describe the history of the diagnosis of MSBP/FDBP since its inception in 1977 and divide that history into four "sub-periods," so that we can see the nature of the syndrome as it emerged in psychology and was developed in law; and (2) point out a number of vulnerabilities in the diagnosis that my historical discussion has uncovered. Four major difficulties with the diagnosis are: (a) its definition; (b) who is able to diagnose it; (c) who suffers from it (mother or child); and (d) what statistical evidence we have of the phenomenon. I argue that the cumulative effect of these problems is that that courts ought to stop accepting a diagnosis of MSBP/FDBP until they are satisfactorily cleared up. The remainder of this summary states my conclusions on (a)-(d).

First, with respect to definition, I show how the "classic" definition of MSBP in a 1987 article and the psychological definition of FDBP (the "successor" name for it), which appeared in the 1994 DSM-IV, differ in crucial ways. The 1987 article makes the mother's intent and denial crucial to the definition of MSBP, while the 1994 definition focuses more on the induction of symptoms in the child than on caregiver intent. Indeed, in my article, I point to four ways in which the definitions aren't consistent. On top of this is the fact that a new definition was introduced in 2000 as a significant professional group dealing with abused children created yet a third parallel syndrome—"Pediatric Condition Falsification."

Second, the issue of who can diagnose MSBP/FDBP is a subtle one with wide-ranging ramifications. If it is only diagnosable by a mental health professional, then it will be done after suspicions are raised and tests are administered to the one suspected of MSBP. If, however, it is more of a "hypothesis" than a "conclusion," social workers, educators, police, or anyone who might come in contact with a child whom they "suspect" might be a victim of MSBP can "diagnose." But this difference of opinion on who can diagnose goes right to the heart of what MSBP is—a "syndrome" or a "suspicion." The literature, as well as court cases, are confused on this point. A subsidiary point is when such a diagnosis may be made—at the beginning of the relationship between caregiver and professional or only after a process of examination has concluded?

Third, there is the issue of who suffers from MSBP. Most literature today says that it is the caregiver who does, but the classic 1987 article talks about the children being afflicted by MSBP.

Finally, there is disagreement on the statistics for MSBP. How prevalent is it? The early studies talked about its comparative rarity. Indeed, the 1987 study only found 117 cases of it in the previous 22 years of literature review—about 5.3 cases per year. But by the mid-1990s, some articles were claiming that the condition was not rare at all, and that courts, prosecutors, social workers and doctors must be on their guard to "smoke out" some of the hidden ways that this "syndrome" goes unnoticed. Along with great differences on the number of cases of MSBP is the related issue of the treatment of children if they are released back to their "Munchausen home." With almost no foundation, some of the literature claimed that there was about a 20% chance that a child who goes home to Munchausen caregivers is going home to die. But when the 1987 study suggested a much smaller number, even the inventor of the "syndrome," Dr. Roy Meadow, wrote to the publication saying that the 1987 numbers were highly inflated. Thus, we have a major statistical problem on our hands that needs to be resolved before such a diagnosis should be allowed in court.

Finally, it should be noted, the "godfather" of the diagnosis, Dr. Roy Meadow, has now been discredited in his native England for giving expert witness testimony in more than one case where he opined on statistical matters where he was later shown to have no competence, and his opinion contributed to separate jury's finding that two mothers had murdered their children.

Therefore, until these four problems are addressed by those who still support a diagnosis of MSBP/FDBP, I recommend that it should be interred alongside its eponymous ancestor, Karl Friedrich Hieronymus, Freiherr von Munchausen.

6. Smacking that does not leave a mark is no offence. Small bruises and scratches occur during the rough and tumble of ordinary life for nearly all children. Broken bones, cigarette burns, a child's complaints (not anonymous tip-offs!) of sexual abuse, should all be looked at by independent medical experts. It is however very rare that parents who abuse or allow this sort of abuse ever dare to come to court to beg for the return of children they probably detest!

7. 'SS' have a legal obligation to place children with relatives where possible if they have removed them from parents.

The Children Act 1989 clearly states in the following extract:

23.

(4) A person falls within this subsection if he is— (a) a parent of the child;(b) a person who is not a parent of the child

but who has parental responsibility for him; or(c) where the child is in care and there was a residence order in force with respect to him immediately before the care order was made, a person in whose favour the residence order was made.

(5) Where a child is in the care of a local authority, the authority may only allow him to live with a person who falls within subsection (4) in accordance with regulations made by the Secretary of State.

(6) Subject to any regulations made by the Secretary of State for the purposes of this subsection, any local authority looking after a child shall make arrangements to enable him to live with—

(a) a person falling within subsection (4); or

(b) a relative, friend or other person connected with him, unless that would not be reasonably practicable or consistent with his welfare.

(7) Where a local authority provide accommodation for a child whom they are looking after, they shall, subject to the provisions of this Part and so far as is reasonably practicable and consistent with his welfare, secure that—

(a) the accommodation is near his home; and

(b) where the authority are also providing accommodation for a sibling of his, they are accommodated together.

Unfortunately, judges and lawyers ignore the above laws time and time again! In Denmark for example 40% of children in care are placed with relatives but in the UK the figure is only 4%! (evidence given in parliament by Tim Loughton Conservative Shadow Minister for Family Affairs).

8. Despite what your lawyers may say, you are now permitted to consult friends and individual helpers to discuss your case (Children Act 2004, section 62) and even to 'go public' once all court proceedings are finally concluded (Clayton v Clayton). **WARNING!** The government are threatening to pass legislation to overturn this important case!

Talking of lawyers and especially 'legal aid lawyers', the vast majority of these highly paid and highly useless parasites are widely known as 'professional losers'. They simply advise you **NOT** to fight the Social Services and to 'go along' with everything the social workers tell you! For this easy and entirely useless legal advice they charge enormous fees and go home laughing, ready to fleece their next victim!

To sack your solicitor and your barrister just download form N434!

N434 - Notice of change of solicitor (Court Service) Download Form N434, Notice of change of solicitor, Court Service Forms, Administrative Court:

http://www.capform.co.uk/fullformlist.asp?Level1=11&Level2=106&Level3=623

Samantha had 4 children removed after she ejected a rude and nosey social worker from her home (they said she must have a personality disorder!). She and her mother Philomena lost 3 cases in a row and 3 children to adoption when 'represented' so when they threatened to take her new baby as soon as it was born she contacted me and I advised her to represent herself. She did this successfully retaining her new baby and recovering her eldest child even after the 'SS' appealed against her first win but Samantha still beat them again! She or her mother Philomena will advise you and tell you how they did it on 07947468340.

Do not be bluffed by social workers or even your own useless solicitors! If they tell you are not allowed by law to show your documents to anybody else tell them they are years out of date! Section 62, (para 251 explanatory notes) of the Children Act 2004 allows you to show your documents and discuss your case in detail including names with as many individuals as you like! You are however still forbidden to reveal to the press, the public or sections of the public any information that might help identify the children concerned. Tell family, friends, advisers and any other individuals anything you like no matter what bossy social workers and expensive lawyers might tell you!!

See Ministry of Justice Family Procedure Adoption Rules

http://www.justice.gov.uk/family/procrules/index.htm

See also Section 62: Publication of material relating to legal proceedings. Judicial Communications Office News Release:

The Children Act 2004 para 251.   Section 62(1) amends section 97 of the Children Act 1989 to make clear that the publication of material from family proceedings which is intended, or likely, to identify any child as being involved in such proceedings (or the address or school of such a child) is only prohibited in relation to publication of information to the public or any section of the public. This section will make the effect of section 97 less prohibitive by allowing disclosure of such information in certain circumstances. In effect, this means that passing on information identifying, or likely to identify, a child (his school or his address) as being involved in court proceedings to an individual or a number of individuals would not generally be a criminal offence.

27 June 2006

18/06

Clayton -v- Clayton: Summary of Judgment for Media

The Court of Appeal is today handing down its decision in the case of Clayton v Clayton. This may well have widespread repercussions for parents and children, in relation to the identification of children as having been the subject of court proceedings once those proceedings are over. Essentially, the decision concerns the balance between children's right to privacy and their parents' right to freedom of expression under the European Convention on Human Rights.

The Court of Appeal has decided that the prohibition from identifying children which section 97 of the Children Act 1989 provides only applies whilst the proceedings relating to the child in question are in progress. Once the proceedings have concluded, the protection given by the Act comes to an end, the entitlement to anonymity.

The decision above means that once the court proceedings are over you are **FREE** to discuss your case with the press and anyone else you like even if it means that as a result you and/or your children may be identified. **WARNING!** The government are threatening to pass legislation to overturn this important case!

http://www.opsi.gov.uk/ACTS/en2004/04en31-d.htm

9. If your newborn baby is taken the 'SS' have to have an emergency protection order or police protection order and if they cannot show you the document, hang on to your baby by force as they are acting illegally. You have the legal right to continue breast feeding the natural way (not expressing!). This of course gives you the right to much more contact with the baby than otherwise.

10. If 'SS' take your baby and you have never caused it harm and neither you nor your partner have a criminal record you will have a good chance of winning (p, c and s versus UK) by appealing to the Court of Human Rights in Strasbourg (they have an office in the UK) once **ALL** proceedings (including appeals) in UK courts are concluded. Make sure of this last point or your application will be refused.

Strasbourg European Court of Human Rights

Please note that if the 'SS' take your baby or very young child for no very good reason other than for 'risk of emotional abuse' or some similar vague notion, then they are probably just trying to meet their adoption targets and your human rights have certainly been infringed. The decision by the European Court of Human Rights (p, c and s versus UK) was that the action of the UK in taking a baby at birth from a mother that had never been accused of harming it was 'draconian' and merited a large fine and damages to the mother.

If the 'SS' take your newborn baby **QUOTE THIS CASE IN COURT** as a reason for its return to your care. Make it clear that you will appeal on a point of law and if that fails go to the European Court of Human Rights if the judge ignores this case and rules against you.

http://www.nkmr.org/english/p_c_and_s_v_united_kingdom_verdict.htm

(see paragraphs 133,137,and 138)

Quoting Para 133. The Court concludes that the draconian step of removing S. from her mother shortly after birth was not supported by relevant and sufficient reasons and that it cannot be regarded as having been necessary in a democratic society for the purpose of safeguarding S. There has therefore been, in that respect, a breach of the applicant parents' rights under Article 8 of the Convention.

Mothers have the right to breastfeed!

If you are menaced by 'SS' threatening to steal your baby, start breastfeeding **IMMEDIATELY**!! The 'SS' must allow you enough contact to continue and this may give you enough breathing time to defeat their adoption plans!

Precedent
*In the matter of unborn baby M; R (on the application of X and another) v Gloucestershire County Council.

http://www.bailii.org/ew/cases/EWHC/Admin/2003/850.html

Citation: BLD 160403280; [2003] EWHC 850 (Admin).

Hearing Date: 15 April 2003

Court: Administrative Court.

Judge: Munby J.

Abstract.

"Per curiam. If the state, in the guise of a local authority, seeks to remove a baby from his parents at a time when its case against the parents has not yet even been established, then the very least the state can do is to make generous arrangements for contact, those arrangements being driven by the needs of the family and not stunted by lack of resources. Typically, if this is what the parents want, one will be looking to contact most days of the week and for lengthy periods. Local authorities also had to be sensitive to the wishes of a mother who wants to breast-feed, and should make suitable arrangements to enable her to do so, and not merely to bottle-feed expressed breast milk. Nothing less would meet the imperative demands of the European Convention on Human Rights."... Published Date 16/04/2003

This case establishes the right of the mother to breastfeed and is often ignored both by judges and the 'SS' **BECAUSE THE PARENTS ARE NOT AWARE OF THEIR RIGHTS UNDER THIS IMPORTANT CASE**.

11. According to the UN Convention on the Rights of the Child (UNCRC) children old enough to understand the nature of a court have the right to take part and be heard in proceedings that concern them. If you can get your children into court to say they are happy with you and that they want to stay with you, plus your family doctor to say you have always been a good parent you stand a very good chance of winning!

Fight in court to have your children present in person to say that you have always treated them well and that they want to return home and call your own family doctor, who knows your family much better than the weird psychiatrists so often produced by the Social Services. If the allegations made against you by Social Services are false, insist even against ferocious opposition that you cannot have a fair hearing unless your family doctor and any of your children said to have criticised you are present in person. Please understand this above all.

YOUR CHILDREN IN COURT (IF THEY ARE OLD ENOUGH) PLUS YOUR FAMILY DOCTOR OR BETTER STILL AN EXPERT SELECTED BY YOU GIVES YOU AN EXCELLENT CHANCE TO WIN!!

WITHOUT THEM YOU WILL ALMOST CERTAINLY LOSE!

The social workers, the judge and even your own lawyers will usually resist the idea of children appearing in court (suffering emotional harm!) as they prefer to rely on videos where children have been rehearsed and pressurized into saying what they have been told to say.

Your answer must include the following 4 points:

I wish my child to come to court to testify.

A: Children suffer far more from a perhaps permanent separation from their families than from a few hours in court or from any publicity if the 'neighbours' find out!

B: Children who **WANT** to come to court to tell the truth will suffer far more from being forcibly prevented from doing this than from being allowed to do so.

C: There cannot be a fair hearing if my principal witnesses are prevented from giving evidence and therefore I shall appeal if this happens on the grounds that my human rights have been infringed.

D: **Convention on the Rights of the Child Adopted and opened for signature, ratification and accession by** General Assembly resolution 44/25 of 20 November 1989 entry into force 2 September 1990, in accordance with article 49.

Article 12 of the United Nations Convention on the Rights of the Child gives a parent the legal right to call their children in judicial proceedings as quoted below.

Article 12 (child's right to participate in decision making)

1. Parties shall assure to the child who is capable of forming his or her own views the right to express those views freely in all matters affecting the child, the views of the child being given due weight in accordance with the age and maturity of the child.

2. For this purpose, the child shall in particular be provided
the opportunity to be heard in any judicial and administrative
proceedings affecting the child, either directly, or through a
representative or an appropriate body, in a manner consistent
with the procedural rules of national law

Any claim that this clause is satisfied by the appointment of a 'guardian' or 'independent solicitor' to represent the children's views by stating in court an opinion diametrically opposed to that of the children concerned should be exposed as the sham that it is: Simply a device to keep the children's true opinions and desires from reaching the court and as such, a clear breach of the spirit of the convention.

In Mabon v. Mabon [2005] 2 FLR 1011, the Court of Appeal considered Rule 9.2A and the older line of authorities in the light of Article 12 of the United Nations Convention on the Rights of the Child 1989, and Article 8 of the ECHR. The court acknowledged the greater appreciation and weight which must now be attached to the child's autonomy and consequential right to participate fully in the decision-making process that fundamentally affects his life. It held that

"in the case of articulate teenagers…. the right to freedom
of expression and participation outweighed the paternalistic
judgment of welfare."[paragraph 28].

However, if direct participation would lead to a risk of harm that the child was incapable of comprehending, then a judge could find that sufficient understanding had not been demonstrated. Judges must equally be alive to the risk of emotional harm that might arise from denying the child knowledge of and participation in the continuing proceedings [para.29].

UK LIFTS RESERVATIONS ON THE UN CONVENTION ON THE RIGHTS OF THE CHILD (UNCRC)

Department for Children, Schools and Families

(http://www.dcsf.gov.uk)

22 September 2008

Jacqui Smith, Jack Straw and Ed Balls today announced that the UK Government is removing two reservations, relating to immigration and children in custody with adults, on the UN Convention on the Rights of the Child (UNCRC).

The Government will now also ratify the Optional Protocol on the Sale of Children, Child Prostitution and Child Pornography by the end of the year.

The news comes ahead of the UK's appearance at the UN this week (23/24 September) where it will set out its commitment to the Convention and update it on progress on children's wellbeing

So if lawyers say UK law does not incorporate the convention the above proves them wrong!

12. Never sign any documents or undertakings and never agree that the 'thresholds' of abuse or neglect have been reached. If your solicitor 'agreed the thresholds' on your behalf this amounted to an admission that you abused or neglected your child or put it at risk. Make it clear on appeal that you did **NOT** agree to this at all but were prevented from saying so in court by your own solicitor or better still by the judge telling you to sit down! You are entitled to receive a judgement so that if you wish to appeal or ask for a discharge of an interim care order, a final care order or an adoption placement, you have a valid excuse for the delay. You state that you are 'out of time' simply because you have been refused a judgement and therefore cannot know the grounds against which you are appealing!

13. RISK = future danger and 'experts' make gypsy-like predictions that are really just guesses that can never be proved. These so-called 'experts' are not infallible. Professors Meadows,

Southall and Dr Marietta Higgs have all been discredited and in the Louise Woodward case the top experts in the country violently disagreed in a shaken baby case and each testified for the side that paid them! 'SS' ignore experts who do not agreé with them and only produce experts in court that will help their case!

14. You do not suffer from a 'personality disorder' just because you distrust social workers as many distinguished MPs, journalists and broadcasters think the same as you but do not face the same accusation!

15. If your house was 'cluttered' or untidy the 'SS' should have helped you tidy up or at least warned you to do so rather than take your children without giving you a chance.

16. Emotional abuse = expecting too much of your child, or treating the child with contempt and without love. This can and should be disputed if you apply the legal definition specified later in this book. Usually the accusation of 'risk of emotional abuse' is so vague that it cannot possibly be covered by the official definition given by the Department of Health.

Your statement should say: "There is no evidence to show that my children ever have suffered or risk suffering emotional abuse as defined below by the Department of Health".

'Emotional abuse is the persistent emotional ill-treatment of a child such as to cause severe and persistent adverse effects on the child's emotional development. It may involve conveying to children that they are worthless or unloved, inadequate, or valued only insofar as they meet the needs of another person. It may feature age or developmentally inappropriate expectations being imposed on children. It may involve causing children frequently to feel frightened or in danger, or the exploitation or corruption of children. Some level of emotional abuse is involved in all types of ill treatment of a child, though it may occur alone'. (Department of Health et al, 1999, p.5-6)

17. If school attendance was bad you should at least have received a written warning from the school or from 'SS' before your children were removed!

18. Remember that social workers **ARE NOT POLICE** and cannot give you orders or forbid you to tell your children that you love them, miss them and are fighting to get them back! It is absolutely essential that you blurt out "I love you and want you back but wicked child stealers have kidnapped you and these horrible thieves are stopping you from coming home!" Say this or words to that effect before anyone can stop you as 'SS' nearly always tell children "Mummy does not love you or want you any more" and the children **MUST** know the truth. Only a court can legally give you orders so do not be bluffed into signing documents or obeying orders from the 'SS'!

19. Social Workers have a statutory duty to try and keep families together not split them up, so they should be asked in court just what attempts they made to keep **YOUR** family together before taking the baby or the children!

QUOTE THE "HUMAN RIGHTS ACT" section 8:

Article 8: Right to Respect for Private and Family Life

1. Everyone has the right to respect for his private and family life, his home and his correspondence.

2. There shall be no interference by a public authority with the exercise of this right except such as is in accordance with the law and is necessary in a democratic society in the interests of national security, public safety or the economic well-being of the country, for the prevention of disorder or crime, for the protection of health or morals, or for the protection of the rights and freedoms of others.

Article 8 guarantees respect for four things: a person's private life, family life, home and correspondence.

This guarantee applies also to the rights of grandparents, siblings, aunts, uncles and cousins to remain in contact with each other contrary to the forced adoption of a child by adopters whose names and locations are kept secret!

20. **YOU MUST BE ALLOWED TO SPEAK IN COURT AND TO SAY ALL YOU WANT TO SAY, CALL ALL THE WITNESSES YOU WANT TO CALL AND MAKE ALL THE POINTS AND ARGUMENTS YOU WANT TO MAKE!** Sack any solicitor or barrister that refuses you these very elementary legal rights OR worse still who advises you to surrender and go along with everything the 'SS' demand. You do not need a lawyer to earn easy money by arranging your surrender. If you represent yourself then at least you won't be gagged! You will at least have a chance to win!

QUOTE ARTICLE 6 of the HUMAN RIGHTS ACT!
ARTICLE 6
RIGHT TO A FAIR TRIAL

1. In the determination of his civil rights and obligations or of any criminal charge against him, everyone is entitled to a fair and public hearing within a reasonable time by an independent and impartial tribunal established by law. Judgement shall be pronounced publicly but the press and public may be excluded from all or part of the trial in the interest of morals, public order or national security in a democratic society, where the interests of juveniles or the protection of the private life of the parties so require, or to the extent strictly necessary in the opinion of the court in special circumstances where publicity would prejudice the interests of justice.

2. Everyone charged with a criminal offence shall be presumed innocent until proved guilty according to law.

3. Everyone charged with a criminal offence has the following minimum rights:

(a) to be informed promptly, in a language which he understands and in detail, of the nature and cause of the accusation against him;

(b) to have adequate time and facilities for the preparation of his defence;

(c) to defend himself in person or through legal assistance of his own choosing or, if he has not sufficient means to pay for legal assistance, to be given it free when the interests of justice so require;

(d) to examine or have examined witnesses against him and to obtain the attendance and examination of witnesses on his behalf under the same conditions as witnesses against him;

(e) to have the free assistance of an interpreter if he cannot understand or speak the language used in court.

Many of the above points will probably apply in **YOUR** case and if they do you are advised to include them in your statement.

IF YOU EMAIL (ian@monaco.mc) ME THE STATEMENT YOU HAVE COMPOSED I WILL ALWAYS READ IT AND SUGGEST POSSIBLE IMPROVEMENTS!

You can also phone me to discuss it on 0033626875684.

Remember that if you need transcripts from a previous case you can get at least one free!

Practice Memorandum No. 4 - Transcripts at Public Expense (PDF 16KB) 31 December 2004

Sets out when a transcript of an oral hearing before a Commissioner will be provided at public expense.

Transcripts at public expense

11.1 Where the lower court or the appeal court is satisfied that an unrepresented appellant is in such poor financial circumstances that the cost of a transcript would be an excessive burden, the court may certify that the cost of obtaining one official transcript should be borne at public expense. 11.2 In the case of a request for an official transcript of evidence or proceedings to be paid for at public expense, the court must also be satisfied that there are reasonable grounds for appeal. Whenever possible a request for a transcript at public expense should be made to the lower court when asking for permission to appeal. Transcripts of evidence are not generally needed for an application for permission to appeal.

11.3 If you wish to ask the court for transcripts at public expense and you did not ask the lower court or your request was refused you should contact the appeal court immediately. Civil Appeals Office 30 June 2004.

THIS IS THE QUESTION YOU SHOULD ASK EVERY SOCIAL WORKER WHO ENTERS THE WITNESS BOX!!

The various Children Acts all say that every effort should be made to keep children with their birth families.

CAN YOU PLEASE DESCRIBE IN DETAIL ANY EFFORTS YOU MADE TO KEEP MY CHILDREN WITH ME??

IF YOU ARE REPRESENTED INSIST THAT YOUR BARRISTER PROMISES TO ASK YOU THE FOLLOWING QUESTION WHEN YOU ARE IN THE WITNESS BOX!

HAVE YOU ANYTHING YOU WOULD LIKE TO SAY TO THE COURT?

This question makes sure that you have a chance to say everything you like and the opportunity to put across all the important points that would otherwise get left out!

In court, above all be brief! Your two special words in court when questioned by 'SS' lawyers (or by the 'SS' at case meetings or by therapists, psychologists etc.) must be 'YES' and 'NO'. If you are pressed to explain further, do not elaborate or try to explain your answers with more than 9 or 10 words as only things you let slip that can count against you will be noted and anything favourable will be discarded and forgotten! Never think that if you 'admit' some small fault that it will make your story more credible.

It will not, it will simply help the 'SS' to keep your children so admit **NOTHING** voluntarily; keep firm in the simple and forceful assertion that the children need love and care and you are the best person to give it! Above all stress that **THEY** are the victims of 'SS' abuse not you, as it is their welfare that is paramount not yours!

As already stated in the Introduction chapter, children of all ages even those under 12 aged 7 or 8 for example can go to any phone box and call parents using reverse charges if they are quietly told how to do this:

Dial 100 from any private phone or public call box and you will be offered 4 options (choices). Choose Option 4 and ask the operator for a call transferring the charges. The operator will then ask you for your name and the number you are calling (this must be to a fixed line not a mobile). Your mother or father will then say ok they accept the call and no money is needed from the child who is calling!

If there is no court order Section 34 forbidding contact they can always meet you for an afternoon or so and it would be an assault for social workers to physically stop them!

The important thing is firstly to keep in touch with your children telling them you still love them and are fighting the wicked social workers who kidnapped them (social workers have absolutely NO legal right to censor your conversation). You should then take positive steps to recover them and welcome them back home.

Allegations that a baby has been shaken and consequently injured or even killed are hard to prove but also hard to disprove! Top experts who appeared for both sides in the Louise Woodward case in the USA disagreed with each other and testified in favour of the side that paid them in each case! This does cast doubt on the reliability of highly paid experts who give categoric opinions in court!

The Attorney General called for a review by the best medical and scientific brains in Britain last year and in the addendum to the report paras 14.1 and 14.2 concluded that even when all 3 symptoms were present (known as the triad; being retinal bleeding, subdural bleeding, and brain damage) it would

NOT be safe to conclude that a baby had been shaken without a previous history of abuse or other injuries such as extensive bruising or broken bones.

FORCED ADOPTION: The weak point!

Take a look at the articles in the complete Convention to see which of them 'SS' have broken in their dealings with you! Remember that brothers and sisters and newborn babies all have a Human Right to enjoy face to face contact with each other even after being adopted into different families. Remember to tell any older child with whom you still do have contact who is capable of understanding the situation to go to a solicitor to demand visits to a sibling who has been adopted and consequently that child when old enough to speak and understand can let you know all about the baby or child you lost so that eventually you can contact them yourself and tell them who you are and who they are!

One mother I have been helping succeeded in persuading the court in Strasbourg to take up her case! The whole affair is still very much ongoing and despite delays initiated by the 'SS' we are hopeful eventually of a satisfactory conclusion. She is willing to talk to other parents whose children have (like hers) been wrongly put in the 'care' of Social Services. She will explain the steps she took after her baby and her other children were brutally snatched even though she was never accused of harming them. The lawyers acting for the 'SS' were so worried when Sharon asked the judge for a copy of the judgement in the family court, that their barrister shouted out across the court room "Don't give her anything she's contacted Strasbourg!" Sharon's home number is 0151 295 2268. Or try her mobile 07877316250.

A second mother had her baby ruthlessly 'confiscated' at birth because her husband was merely 'suspected' nearly 10 years previously of injuring one of his children from a previous marriage and who contracted cerebral palsy. Both children were left in the joint care of their father and his ex-wife so the 'SS' were not too concerned at the time. The second wife's new baby however was, the 'SS' said, "ideal for adoption" and though she was herself blameless, she was judged too supportive of her husband!

They persuaded the European Court of Human Rights to take up their case in Strasbourg and will explain how they did it to you and other parents. Just contact them at Tel: 02084823019.

Your Rights: The Human Rights Act: European Court of Human Rights ... F-67075 Strasbourg Cedex France Fax: 00 33 3 88 41 27 30 When it has received your letter the ECHR will send you one of its application forms to complete. ...

- http://www.yourrights.org.uk/.../european-court-of-human-rights/european-court-of-human-rights.shtml

- http://www.pfc.org.uk/legal/echrtext.htm

Important please note: A 'sympathetic' Social Services complaints officer brought up in care thought this might be worth sharing.

When writing complaints it is a good idea to write as little as possible in the complaint! He recommends writing something like...

Your name/address/date etc

I wish to make a complaint about the Local Authority's failure to consult with me regarding my child's medical treatment (for example).

I also make this complaint under section 26, Children Act and request assistance to write this.

Yours sincerely etc

He says they are then obliged to visit you, take the details, write your complaint and give it to you to check before signing.

That way not only do you get help to write the complaint but you don't 'show your hand' before the investigation begins.

He said "never give them all the evidence until you see the independent investigator."

If you have a serious complaint against the police I advise you to go directly to the Independent Police Complaints Commission and follow the procedure outlined below.

IPCC Independent police complaints commission

How to make a complaint

There are many ways you can make your complaint, you can make a complaint directly to the police force concerned, through the IPCC or another advice organisation. Whatever the route, all complaints, by law, must be forwarded to the 'appropriate authority' for consideration.

You can make your complaint:

You can complete an online complaint form

You can download a complaint form or we can send a form to you.

Via the IPCC by phone, email, post, fax, minicom.

To any police force by phone, email, post, fax or in person

By contacting any local Citizens Advice Bureau, Youth Offending Team, Racial Equality Council, Probation Service or Neighbourhood Warden. They can give information about what to do next. A solicitor or MP can make a complaint on your behalf.

If you would like someone to act on your behalf (perhaps a relative or friend) please provide their details and your written permission separate to your complaint.

What you should include in your complaint:

As well as your full contact details, please try to provide the following information;

WHO? Which police force is your complaint about?

WHERE? Where did the incident/s happen that led to your complaint?

WHEN? When did the incident/s happen that led to your complaint?

WHAT? Please describe the circumstances that have led to you feeling the police have treated you badly.

Please include details of:

Who was involved

What was said and done

Any other people who witnessed the incident

If there was any damage or injury

Details of any witnesses

We also need your consent for us to pass the details of your complaint to the police force concerned for consideration.

See also: www.adviceguide.org.uk the site of the Citizen's Advice Bureau gives a lot of information including the following:

Police powers of entry
When can the police enter and search

Police can enter premises without a warrant in a number of different situations. Examples include:

deal with a breach of the peace or prevent it

enforce an arrest warrant

arrest a person in connection with certain offences

recapture someone who has escaped from custody

save life or prevent serious damage to property.

Apart from when they are preventing serious injury to life or property, the police must have reasonable grounds for believing that the person they are looking for is on the premises.

If the police do arrest you, they can also enter and search any premises where you were during or immediately before the arrest. They can search only for evidence relating to the offence for which you have been arrested, and they must have reasonable grounds for believing there is evidence there. They can also search any premises occupied by someone who is under arrest for certain serious offences. Again, the police officer who carries out the search must have reasonable grounds for suspecting that there is evidence on the premises relating to the offence or a similar offence.

In other circumstances, the police must have a search warrant before they can enter the premises. They should enter property at a reasonable hour unless this would frustrate their search. When the occupier is present, the police must ask for permission to search the property – again, unless it would frustrate the search to do this.

When they are carrying out a search police officers must:

identify themselves and - if they are not in uniform - show their warrant card, and

explain why they want to search, the rights of the occupier and whether the search is made with a search warrant or not.

If the police have a warrant, they can force entry if:

the occupier has refused entry, or

it is impossible to communicate with the occupier, or

the occupier is absent, or

the premises are unoccupied, or

they have reasonable grounds for believing that if they do not force entry it would hinder the search, or someone would be placed in danger.

When can the police seize property

Police should only seize goods if they have reasonable grounds for believing that:

they have been obtained illegally; or

they are evidence in relation to an offence.

In either of these cases, they must also have reasonable grounds for believing that it is necessary to seize the goods to prevent them being lost, stolen or destroyed.

7. DETAILED REFORMS

We must reform Family Courts and Family Law. The *Sunday Times* will tell you why:

Secret courts that steal our children

by Stuart Wavell

Sunday Times, 6 July 2003

Kafkaesque children's courts sitting in private are playing God with the families that come before them, writes Stuart Wavell.

They sound like a chilling legacy from the bad old days of the Soviet Union — secret courts that have taken thousands of children from their families and put them into foster homes or farmed them out for adoption. There can be no appeal nor legal redress for most traumatised families. Lone judges, sitting without a jury, sever loved ones from each other on the word of omniscient medical "experts". Any parent foolhardy enough to protest to the press risks dire penalties.

Yet this is the Kafkaesque nature of Family Courts in England and Wales — an iceberg of civil litigation that lies submerged beneath a few high-profile criminal cases that hit the headlines. In a blaze of publicity last month, the pharmacist Trupti Patel was found not guilty of murdering her three babies. Earlier this year the solicitor Sally Clark was freed from jail after being wrongly convicted of killing her two baby sons.

Both cases cast doubt on the credibility of Professor Sir Roy Meadow as an expert medical witness — now under investigation by the General Medical Council — but the joyful outcomes partly reflected the high standard of proof required in criminal cases.

By contrast, Family Courts do not demand that a doctor's diagnosis of child abuse should be beyond reasonable doubt, but rather on the balance of probability. The courts' culture of secrecy, sternly policed with the commendable aim of protecting children's identities, has had the unintended effect of shielding experts' flawed deductions from public scrutiny or comment. As a result, an unseen and unheard process of winnowing children from their parents is taking place, largely on the say-so of doctors whom they have often never met.

According to Beverley Beech, chairwoman of the Association for Improvements in the Maternity Services: "It is, I believe, an underestimate to say hundreds of children have been taken away from their families. It must now run into thousands. I have seen with my own eyes newborn babies seized from their mothers in maternity wards."

Statistics suggest that each year thousands of families undergo the ordeal of having to prove their innocence against false accusations of child abuse. According to government figures in 1997, there were 160,000 reports of child abuse in England and Wales, of which 120,000 were ruled false. Of the remaining 40,000 cases, 25,000 were put on the "at risk" register, but the number of people pursued through the courts and separated from their children is unknown.

The main instrument of the final processing is the family court. When a child has died, and in other serious cases, a criminal prosecution may be pursued.

William and Michelle Carter (not their real names) lost their four children in 1999 on the sole evidence of Meadow at a family court; the elder two, aged 17 and 14, are in foster care and the younger ones, aged eight and six, have been adopted.

The family's future was decided at the family division of the High Court in London, the largest branch of the system and the scene of a protest last week by angry parents, many of whom have had children taken from them on Meadow's evidence.

Most cases are heard in county courts, presided over by specialist district judges. Children, supposedly protected by hearings in camera, do not appear in person but are usually represented by an independent social worker.

The Carters' nightmare had begun nearly a year earlier, when their youngest daughter, then 16 months old, fell ill and was taken to hospital where she suffered multiple heart attacks and a stroke.

Although she made a full recovery, six months later social services contacted the Carters to say a urine sample taken from the girl had shown traces of a powerful drug. Police dismissed the case after the Carters explained that one of the tablets prescribed to their eldest daughter to stop her wetting the bed must have fallen on the floor and been accidentally swallowed by the infant.

However, the Carters ended up in a family court where Meadow concluded that the girl had been poisoned by her mother while the latter was suffering from Munchausen's syndrome by proxy — the condition coined by Meadow in 1977 for women who hurt children to draw attention to themselves.

The next day the children were taken away. The Carters' were told to go home and forget they ever had four children. That night Michelle attempted suicide. "We were hung, drawn and quartered by Meadow," says William. "He never backed up his diagnosis with evidence. Why was a paediatrician giving evidence on toxicology?" The best the couple can hope for is eventually to get their elder two children returned to them. "Unfortunately," adds Carter, "it's too late for the younger two."

Cases involving Meadow may just be the tip of the iceberg. To stop more such miscarriages, Carter would like to see several changes to family courts, notably a bench of three judges instead of one and the proceedings open to media coverage — while protecting children's identities by the same process as applies in the criminal courts.

Recently social services asked him to stop talking to the press. "They are threatening me with contempt of court, but I have done nothing to identify the children. We know we have done nothing wrong."

Such threats are not uncommon; a family court's punishment can be draconian. Last month Mark Harris won a 10-year fight to gain full access to his three daughters. But for picketing the homes of judges who had denied him and other desperate fathers access to their children, he was sentenced to 10 months in prison for contempt of court.

Marilyn Stowe, a Leeds family solicitor, says that protection of children is the Family Courts' paramount concern. "But if any injustice occurs, the fallout is that it's very hard to make it public. And the court relies so heavily on the evidence of independent experts."

Technically, there is a mechanism for appeal, but the grounds are so narrowly defined that few people succeed. "You've got to show effectively that the judge has exercised his discretion wrongly and made a mistake," says Stowe.

Some commentators on the Patel case suggested that the more sensitive Family Courts would be a better place to deal with a suspected mother, rather than putting her through a public ordeal.

However, "sensitive" is not an epithet Mark and Karen Haynes would apply to their harrowing experience of a family court. In essence, the unexplained death of their son in hospital and Karen's subsequent pregnancy resulted in an order that led to their newborn daughter being seized 20 minutes after coming into the world.

"There was an adversarial element to the court proceedings," says Mark. "Compared to a criminal court, the family court was a little less formal, but it was very much a point-scoring game between barristers."

Once again, Meadow's opinion — that Karen Haynes had smothered her son — was believed by the judge, even though seven experts disagreed. And, once again, the couple were told to keep their mouths shut. To their dismay, the person appointed to represent their daughter's best interests urged her speedy adoption, on the basis that before the age of two she would forget her parents.

"The guardian wasn't independent: she was singing from the same hymn sheet as the other social workers," Mark Haynes complains. He, too, wants the Family Courts' secrecy removed and the introduction of their own independent medical advisers.

One of the vaunted advantages of Family Courts is that, unlike their criminal counterparts, they do not seek to blame or punish, but rather to create the best upbringing for the child. However, the consequences of their decisions can be life sentences of misery.

Many parents are effectively found guilty without a trial and cannot erase the stigma. Even those exonerated of any wrongdoing find it difficult to shake off the bureaucratic repercussions.

When Rioch Edwards-Brown satisfied a judge that her son's shaking fit was caused by a difficult premature birth, she thought that was the end of the matter. "The judge said, 'Go home and start your life all over again'," she recalls.

However, when she took her son to hospital for a check-up she discovered her case remained on file. "I thought everything was done and dusted. It turned out I had been cleared by the court but not by the system."

Every visit to the hospital triggered a follow-up call by the home visitor. She discovered she represented a potential threat to her son until he was 18 and could not bring herself to play with him until he was 7½ in March, when she won her seven-year, £50,000 battle to have the records amended.

Edwards-Brown believes many shortcomings would be solved by a diagnostic protocol she has dubbed Riordan's Law. She wants babies with potential "violent shaking" injuries to be seen by brain, eye and bone specialists within 24 hours of hospital admission and reviewed after 14 days.

"Everything starts and stops with the doctors, who don't have to prove their findings," says Edwards-Brown. "That's where we need to concentrate."

All names have been changed

Family Court Judges who order forced adoptions are themselves criminals who should **ALL GO TO PRISON** for a very long time!!

Websters' MP: Stop cash for adoptions

by Laura Collins

Mail on Sunday, 7 July 2007

The MP of a couple who lost three of their children because of a false abuse claim has called for an end to Government adoption targets.

Liberal Democrat Norman Lamb said the targets, introduced by Tony Blair, 'provide a perverse incentive', with councils winning cash rewards if a specified number of children are adopted.

Mr Lamb, who also wants family court proceedings to be opened up, has applied for a Commons adjournment debate over the tragedy of Mark and Nicky Webster.

Their three eldest children were taken from them by Norfolk County Council because one had a fracture that doctors said could only have been caused by physical abuse.

But later, four eminent specialists found that the boy was lactose-intolerant, would not take solids, and was probably suffering from scurvy, which would have made his bones brittle and liable to break.

These experts gave this evidence for Mark, 34, and Nicky, 26, from Cromer, when they won a landmark court fight to keep their fourth child, 13-month-old Brandon.

The Websters are fighting on for the right to have contact with their lost children, who are with separate families, but have been advised that the adoption order is irreversible.

Their story could only be told after The Mail on Sunday and BBC won a ruling allowing the media to report a family court case for the first time.

North Norfolk MP Mr Lamb said: "Theirs was an appalling miscarriage of justice and part of any proper discussion must mean rethinking social services' adoption targets."

The financial incentives were introduced in 2000 in an attempt to see adoptions rise by 50 per cent. The number of babies taken into council care in England before being adopted has risen from 970 in 1996 to 2,120 last year.

Mr Lamb said: "It ought not to be a factor that taking children into adoption means the social services bringing in money from the Government.

"I'm sure that when these annual targets were set, they were done so with the best of intentions.

"But it brings a financial motivation into a process which just should not be influenced in that way."

The Mail on Sunday has learned that a county council, which cannot be named for legal reasons, has won an injunction preventing ITV's Jeremy Kyle Show from featuring a mother whose five children, all under six, are being adopted forcibly.

Social workers and others from the family and adoption authorities etc. rarely debate the merits or otherwise of the Family Courts, the Social Services and adoptions without parental consent. When on those rare occasions they do comment, they always decry their critics as irresponsible, dangerous and guilty of slandering devoted public servants. They **NEVER** answer the points made in the argument! I therefore invite someone from Social Services, the courts, or from government, to comment on the following:

1. Parents whose children have been taken are 'gagged' from protesting publicly and cannot reveal any details of what they might regard as unfair treatment in the Family Court. The fundamental right to protest against a perceived injustice is thus completely undermined.

2. Children are often removed because some 'professional' decides that they are 'at risk'. Parents therefore lose their children not for anything they have done but for something someone else thinks they might do at some time in the future!! Who can defend themselves against a mere prophecy that labels them guilty until proved innocent?

3. Adoption targets do exist and several are published by local authorities on the internet showing the financial rewards for achieving them (often millions of pounds). Fosterers are often paid

£400/£500 per week per child and 'special schools' charge as much as £6,000 per week per child (10 times the fees for Princes William and Harry at Eton!). Adoption agencies (often owned by social workers or ex-workers) charge around £18,000 per placement, Experts charge £3000/£4000 for a report on a parent, and lawyers fees + court charges can range from £30,000 to as much as £500,000 depending on the length of the case! Everybody 'cashes in' except for the parents and their children!

4. Family Court judges nearly always 'play it safe' and 'go along with Social Services' treating them like police in the sense that when a parent's evidence conflicts with that of a social worker the latter is nearly always believed. A jury would never take a child for adoption for 'risk of emotional abuse', 'failing to appreciate a child's emotional needs' or 'unable to protect a child from witnessing domestic (often only verbal) violence'. Even more certainly a jury would never take a newborn baby for adoption merely because there were unproved suspicions of violence in the father's past, or because another child or newborn baby had previously been taken in completely different circumstances and maybe with a different partner/father. If a burglar facing a possible 6 months jail sentence has the legal right to demand a jury so should parents facing a 'life sentence' when they lose their children to adoption by anonymous strangers!

5. At 'contact sessions' parents are in most cases forbidden to mention court proceedings or even that they long for their children's return. Telephone conversations are usually similarly restricted and even forbidden altogether leaving vulnerable children to wonder why their parents do not want them back. The cancelling or reducing of contact sessions is often used as a 'weapon' to threaten parents who do not cooperate or who too actively oppose the care plans of the local authority. All this smacks of George Orwell's worst nightmares!

6. Too often innocent parents who do not confess their supposed errors and repent are labelled non-cooperative and 'in denial'. If mothers are upset when their babies are 'confiscated' they are 'over emotional'. If parents are hostile to social workers who take their children they need 'anger management courses' and must

suffer from 'personality disorders' and if they dare to criticise the powerful forces leagued against them they are labelled 'paranoid'!

Maybe some 'establishment figure' could comment on these points instead of just deploring critics and calling them ill-informed and dangerous!

The forces of secrecy are prevailing
by Camilla Cavendish
The Times, 29 March 2007

Last week a High Court judge denounced the "nightmare" suffered by a couple who were wrongly accused of harming their baby son. They were separated from that child for 12 months, the first and formative year of his life. During that time the mother became pregnant again but had an abortion, because she could not bear to risk the authorities taking that child too. So those who rushed to judgment ruined four lives.

"This is not a case," said Mr. Justice Ryder, "where there is no smoke without fire. This is a case where a family court and the expert who advised it got it wrong." The consultant neurologist, Wellesley Forbes, was "too absolute" in blaming the parents. Two courts refused to let the parents seek a second medical opinion. The appeal court finally agreed to call a paediatric neurologist, who found that the injury had been caused before birth.

Mr. Justice Ryder described a doctor who "strayed from the role of expert into the role of decision maker" and a family court judge who "failed to detect that that was what had happened". Even more shocking is that we would know nothing had Mr. Justice Ryder not chosen to make his judgment public.

Oldham Council, which brought this case against this couple, opposes the Government's proposals to open up the Family Courts to scrutiny. No surprise. Oldham's response to the Government's consultation is that open courts could worsen "an already upsetting experience" for children. But who will be more upset by transparency, children or sloppy professionals? What is most upsetting about the Family Courts is that they can pass an effective life sentence, the permanent removal of a child from its parents, on the word of an "expert", with no criminal conviction and no accountability. The Family Courts operate in secret. Secrecy is a gift to the incompetent and the corrupt.

County court judges, family lawyers, doctors, children's charities and councils are massing to block reform. This was predictable. Harriet Harman, the Constitutional Affairs Minister, still has a strong hand to play as her reforms were recommended by the Constitutional Affairs Select Committee. But a new and unexpected obstacle has thundered into her path: her boss. It is becoming clear that Lord Falconer of Thoroton, the Lord Chancellor, is a staunch ally of the forces of conservatism. He is deeply uncomfortable about letting the press and public into Family Courts. As a lawyer married to a county court judge, he is being heavily lobbied by his profession.

In a little-noticed but important speech last week, Lord Falconer left little doubt where he stands. He explained his extraordinary recent decision to limit the Freedom of Information Act by saying that it had become "a research arm of the media". He went on to make the breathtaking claim that children had made it "crystal clear" that they did not want journalists in Family Courts. That is a bizarre interpretation of the consultation findings: a third of children agreed that the media should be allowed into Family Courts automatically, with a majority agreeing that the decision should be up to the people involved in the case. One can only conclude that he was expressing his own view, not that of children.

That is not to dismiss the genuine concerns about how to protect children. Of course they should not be named, or be at risk of being tracked down by abusive parents. Of course some journalists may seek to breach their privacy for a headline. But other countries have found ways to resolve this, including strong sanctions for breaching reporting restrictions. Many options are being debated. This is not the real issue.

The opponents of openness claim that their concern is the "welfare of the child". Yet the true interests of the child lie in protecting him or her from a miscarriage of justice. At the moment we are simply protecting the professionals. The Royal College of Paediatricians fears that doctors will not give evidence if they can be named. But the Chief Medical Officer has found that 80 per cent of paediatricians have never been expert witnesses, not because of adverse publicity but because they have never been asked. The lawyers say, in effect: "Trust us." But the few cases made public reveal errors by judges who were confident that their reasoning would never be read by anyone.

Lord Falconer says that striking the balance between privacy and open justice "may well involve allowing the press or the public in only where the judge expressly agrees as an exception". That would be the death knell of these reforms, a blatant attempt to preserve the status quo. Judges are free to publicise their judgments now. But few do.

It seems that Lord Falconer may not be content only to scupper the Harman reforms and turn the clock back on freedom of information. He is also considering giving magistrates discretion to close their courts. Is that really his solution to the anomaly of Family Courts being secret and all others open: more secrecy?

Ms Harman will not stop yet. But she needs the legal profession to understand that more openness is the only way to ensure that justice is done, and is seen to be done. In Oldham, the only reason the parents of that baby boy have got him back is because of the courage and tenacity of their defence lawyers in pursuing a second medical opinion.

They are the heroes. Is it not better that we should know them? Is it not better that we should know if Dr Forbes has been criticised by other judges in the past? In the dark, we cannot see whether patterns of injustice exist. We cannot help the victims. The Lord Chancellor cannot believe that secrecy serves justice. He cannot.

Time and again we hear about the merits of either admitting or excluding the media from proceedings in the Family Courts. This is in practical terms irrelevant as journalists would seldom bother to sit through days of tedious hearings even if they could! The important reform needed is to end the gagging of parents and other parties to the case and to allow them the very fundamental right to protest against injustices.

In 2006 statistics from the newly-formed 'Department for Children, Schools and Families' show that 4,160 children under 5 were taken into care and 2,490 of these were rushed into adoption! The financial rewards given by central government to local authorities under public service agreements for those who meet or exceed their 'adoption targets' have caused an unprecedented stampede to adoption. It has also caused misery to thousands of loving parents who will never see their children again and who face jail if they reveal details of their ordeal to the public!

There has been no case on record of a parent succeeding in court in retrieving children against opposition from Social Services and subsequently killing or severely harming them. If any such case had existed it would have been in the criminal court, well publicised in the press, and widely quoted as a warning by Social Services. The only case frequently quoted by social workers to justify removing children they consider 'at risk' is that of Victoria Climbé who was in fact in care and killed by her 'carers' not her parents! There have however been literally thousands of cases of children put into care despite opposition from parents who have subsequently been sexually abused, physically damaged, or even killed when in 'care'.

Scandal of children's homes abuse payouts
by Moira Sharkey and Phillip Nifield
South Wales Echo, 2 October 2006
www.icWales.co.uk

More than 160 adults who claim they were abused in a sex scandal that rocked children's homes in South Wales have been paid a total of £3m in compensation.

Around £1m of this has been paid to former residents of homes or approved schools in Cardiff and the Vale of Glamorgan, an Echo investigation has revealed.

The compensation was paid out following Operation Goldfinch, a police inquiry into claims of abuse of children in care including approved schools and residential homes 20 and 30 years ago.

Many of the claims were made by solicitors as part of a group litigation.

The figures have not been made public before but were revealed after an 18-month investigation and a series of Freedom of Information Act requests made by the Echo, Cardiff councillor Jayne Cowan and a former social services manager.

Official figures from South Wales Police show 79 people were arrested or interviewed and 30 were charged during Operation Goldfinch. The offences included indecent assault, child cruelty and actual bodily harm.

Of these, a total of 17 people were convicted.

Carol Floris, advice and support manager of Voices From Care Cymru, believes compensation was an important part of the healing process for many of the alleged victims.

Goldfinch detectives spoke to former residents of children's' homes and approved schools, some of which are now closed. They asked whether the people, now adults, had been abused when they were young.

The inquiry became highly controversial for its method of 'trawling' for witnesses and evidence. In 2002, the Home Affairs select committee pointed out that it and similar operations run by more than 30 police forces across England and Wales ran the 'unusually high' risk of causing miscarriages of justice. One reason for concern was the opportunity to apply for compensation.

In response to an inquiry made by Coun Jayne Cowan, it was revealed that £2,927,800 was paid to 162 claimants across South Wales.

Chief Legal officer for Cardiff council Kate Berry said in a statement that 186 claims were dealt with under a group litigation which is understood to be more widely known as the South Wales Class Action. She confirmed that none of the staff involved in the litigation were still working with children in Cardiff.

In a separate Freedom of Information request it was found that around £1m had been paid out to claims of abuse in council homes in Cardiff and the Vale of Glamorgan.

These included Penhill, Taff Vale, John Kane, Suffolk House and Crosslands, Cardiff and Sully and Bryn y Don, Dinas Powys.

Coun. Cowan added: 'These figures, which it took the council more than six months to produce, to my knowledge have never been made public before. As far as I am aware, they were not even seen in confidential council reports. I believe this should be a matter brought before the full council.

'The scale of the bill being paid out is alarming. Something of this importance should not be kept secret. The public have a right to know the impact of this scandal which should never happen again.'

Newport City Council confirmed it had paid out £717,000 to 44 claimants. Swansea paid out more than £340,000 to 35 claimants. Rhondda Cynon Taf County Borough Council has paid out almost £250,000 to 16 claimants.

The allegations related to homes including Bryn y Don in Dinas Powys, Neath Farm in Neath/Port Talbot, Preswylfa in Bridgend, Silverbrook in Church Village, Suffolk Place in Cardiff Boverton and Sully Assessment Centre.

The latest figures provided under a Freedom of Information request show no compensation has been paid out in relation to allegations of abuse against former teacher John Owen. Nine cases for compensation are being processed. Owen, 49, committed suicide in 2001 before he could face trial on charges of indecent assault.

The Clywch inquiry led by Children's Commissioner Peter Clarke found that Owen who worked at Ysgol Gyfun Rhydfelen for 17 years, had abused pupils for more than two decades. No compensation claims were dealt with by Caerphilly, Merthyr Tydfil or Vale of Glamorgan councils. All the compensation has been paid through the public purse and councils' insurers.

60,000 children in care 'betrayed' as three out of four fail at school
Daily Mail, 18 Sep 2006

The shameful betrayal of more than 60,000 children caught in the state care system is exposed today in a damning new report.

It shows that just a quarter of children in care manage to leave school with as much as a single qualification.

And those who are brought up by the state have no more than a 100 to one chance of going to university.

Instead of education, the report found a care home system where the rule is that "the boys do crime, the girls do sex."

The report by leading writer Harriet Sergeant, serialised in the Daily Mail today, points to a system in which half of the 6,000 young people who leave state care every year to make their own lives are unemployed within two years. It found:

• A quarter of girls in care have been pregnant by the time they leave and half are single mothers within two years.

• Half of all prisoners under the age of 25 have been through the care system.

• A third of the homeless are people who were brought up in state care.

• Only 60 out of 6,000 young people leaving care each year goes to university.

• The Government's target for young people as a whole is that half of them should go to university.

The analysis of the Dickensian brew of official indifference and everyday squalor and violence that haunts the lives of thousands of children in care comes as ministers prepare a Green Paper intended to improve their educational chances.

The plans to be published next month are expected to include new rules to ensure children with foster parents or living in care homes always get their first choice of school, and an ambitious pilot scheme to send children in care to state or independent boarding schools.

But the Green Paper - it will be the fifth major initiative in just five years aimed at improving the pitiful state of the care system - is likely to prove a sticking plaster rather than a solution, the new report suggests.

The report, to be published in full by the Centre for Policy Studies think tank, points to a world in which children trapped in the care system where they are moved rapidly from foster home to foster home without thought for their welfare, where many may have been through as many as 10 schools before they leave care, and where children's homes are rife with violence and indiscipline.

Miss Sergeant said: "Over-stretched, badly organised, lacking direction and a clear sense of priorities,the current approach to looking after neglected children is patently inadequate.

"The full scale of this failure is rarely exposed in public, with ministers and social services chiefs preferring to drown out any argument with blizzards of statistics and paper policies.

"But the raw experience of those taken into the system points to an expensive disaster which is storing up more problems for the future."

Her report said that the care system costs the taxpayer £2.5 billion a year, or more than £40,000 for each child.

The cost of looking after those who stay in children's homes is far higher than the boarding fees of the most expensive public schools.

Since 2000 the Government has passed a Children (Leaving Care) Act meant to improve the chances of those leaving care; it has appointed a Children's Commissioner to look after their rights; put through an Adoption Act intended to find permanent new families for more of them; and passed the 2004 Children's Act which requires new monitoring and safeguards which have cost each local council an average of £832,000.

At the same time the Government and major charities have campaigned ceaselessly for children's rights.

New legal curbs on parents' powers to smack and constant charity advertising about violence against children has developed sensitivity to the point where last week six detectives were assigned to investigate a public horseplay between Cherie Blair and a teenager.

But Miss Sergeant found that little of this has made any difference to the lives of children in care.

She identified a series of intractable difficulties in the system.

Among them is the rights culture that has meant children are subjected to repeated attempts to re-unite them with parents who are incapable of looking after them.

The report said that social workers interpret the Human Rights Act as saying that parents must have the right to form a relationship with their children.

But, she found, even social workers think this is "a crazy system".

The report cites children distressed and traumatised by the experience of meeting violent and drug-addicted parents who in reality have no hope of ever reclaiming custody of their children.

The rights of children also mean discipline is absent and violence among residents common in children's homes.

Miss Sergeant said: "Care homes have no means of controlling their charges. They are unable to keep young people safe in the home or to stop them wandering off."

One worker told her: "Young people are very up on their rights." Rights culture, she found, has developed to the point where children in care homes have the right to refuse to go to the doctor or dentist. As a result, many of them have bad teeth.

Her report exposed the frequent moves to which children are exposed when in foster care: often for reasons of social services policy, or because a social worker doesn't like the foster parents, or because a child is sent back to inadequate natural parents, or to save money with a cheaper placement.

Many children are torn from loving homes with highly destructive effects on their lives.

The report also investigates the chaos in children's homes, where untrained and frequently-changing staff keep uncertain watch on very troubled children, at a cost of up to £6,500 a week for each one - a sum which spent otherwise would be enough to pay for a place at Eton, a full-time personal mentor, and intensive psychotherapy.

System 'failing children in care'
BBC News at bbc.co.uk/news, 23 Aug 2006

Children in care are written off by the education system, with nearly eight out of 10 gaining no qualifications, children's charity Barnardo's says.

Its Failed by the System report assesses the experiences of the 80,000 children looked after by councils.

A survey of 66 children found they had multiple placements and school changes, which Barnardo's says is common.

The government said reforms within its education White Paper would help cared-for children reach their potential.

'Cycle of disadvantage'

Barnardo's chief executive Martin Narey said: "The cycle of disadvantage that haunts these children as they grow up shows no sign of being broken as they enter adulthood.

"Our report shows that many looked-after children have both academic potential and the desire to work hard and would have liked to succeed in education but the state, as a parent, fails them terribly.

"Dreadful GCSE results compound the disadvantages they face and commit them to unemployment and long-term disadvantage."

Barnardo's claimed multiple care home and foster care placements, repeated school changes, exclusion and insufficient support all contributed to a cycle of disadvantage.

Findings of the report included:

* More than half reported being bullied at school as a direct result of being in care.

* Four out of 10 said no-one had attended their school parents' evenings.

* Nearly half said no-one went to sports days or other school events.

* The number of care placements young people had lived in varied between one and 30 - half had been in more than four placements.

* More than half were not currently in employment, training or education.

Almost half the group had attended six or more schools and 11% had attended more than 10.

Barnardo's said an NOP poll of 500 parents of children who took their GCSEs this year illustrated the contrast between experiences.

This found that 58% had never moved home, 96% had attended their child's parents' evenings and just 6% were expecting their child to leave school with no qualifications.

Designated teachers

Barnardo's works with 120,000 children, young people and their families at more than 370 projects in the UK.

The charity has called for designated teacher posts to be created at all schools to help vulnerable children.

It also wants staff to be taught how the care system works and for bullying policies to take into account those in care.

A Department for Education and Skills spokesman said the government recognised that children in care underachieved significantly and that they needed to be put in schools that met their needs.

He said regulations were already in place to ensure looked-after children were the main priority for school admissions.

The spokesman added that the Education and Inspections Bill would give local authorities the power to direct schools to admit a child outside the normal admissions round.

He said: "This will form a key part of a wider package of reforms to be published in our forthcoming green paper, which will be designed to help ensure looked-after children realise their fullest potential."

One third of the prison population was brought up 'in care'. Worse still, children forcibly removed from their mothers and brought up in care often fall pregnant at a very early age. When this happens they run a very real risk of having not just the first baby but every new baby removed at birth for adoption each time they too in their turn become mothers.

All the above surely makes a case for at least a presumption that any parent willing to spend day after day in various intimidating courts, begging for the return of their children should be granted their wish unless overwhelming evidence is produced to show why this should not be done.

Parents or carers who brutally mistreat children do not go to court to fight for their return, so those who do go should, if possible, be given the benefit of any doubt rather than the contrary, as is now the case.

A malevolent judge threatened to send a mother and father **TO PRISON** if they went to the press or did anything that could betray the identity of their baby stolen at birth by social workers because they did not like her father!

HYPOCRITICAL SOCIAL WORKERS THEN ADVERTISED in the *Daily Mirror* to millions of readers offering no less than 10 unfortunate little victims **FOR ADOPTION BY STRANGERS** rather like pedigree dogs!! (See below)

Note the 'whites only' racial discrimination of these hypocrites!!

Crystal is nearly 3 and is a clever, lively, cheerful and inquisitive little girl. She likes swimming, reading and doing puzzles. We are looking for adopters from a White background to provide these children with a caring environment. If you would like to find out more about these children please contact.......

The following extract from a judgement in the House of Lords confirms that alone in Europe the UK **CONTINUES** to allow and encourage the barbaric practice of taking children from loving and desperate parents and giving them to strangers for closed and secret adoptions without parental consent.

House of Lords - Down Lisburn Health and Social Services Trust.
Baroness Hale of Richmond. Judgement

34. There is, so far as the parties to this case are aware, no European jurisprudence questioning the principle of freeing for adoption, or indeed compulsory adoption generally. The United Kingdom is unusual amongst members of the Council of Europe in permitting the total severance of family ties without parental consent. (Professor Triseliotis thought that only Portugal and perhaps one other European country allowed this.) It is, of course, the most draconian interference with family life possible.

Social workers in 'child protection' are now reviled throughout the land as 'childsnatchers' **TAKING CHILDREN FROM PARENTS WHO HAVE NOT BEEN ACCUSED OR CONVICTED OF ANY CRIME WHATSOEVER!** Instead of 'helpers' they are known as bullies who intimidate single mothers and whose main intent is meeting 'adoption targets', not keeping families together. For this image to change vital reforms are needed:

In brief,

1: Abolish the Family Court secrecy that gags parents who wish to complain.

2: Abolish 'emotional harm' and 'risk' as justifications for putting children into care.

3: Abolish 'forced adoption' if a parent opposes an adoption in court.

4: Abolish decisions by Family Court judges to take babies and young children into care (let juries decide).

5: Abolish the power of Social Services to regulate and control contact between parents and children, to censor their conversation or to restrict phone calls. The court must control the frequency of contacts.

6: Abolish the restriction preventing a lay advisor from presenting a case for parents refused legal aid.

7: Abolish hearsay evidence in Family Courts and require witnesses to stick to facts without 'speculation'.

8: Abolish the removal of children for non life-threatening forms of neglect such as absences from school or unsanitary dwellings unless a written warning has been served and the situation has not been remedied.

These reforms would stop most of the present injustices.

Read more detailed reforms below together with the reasons for them and the proof that they are necessary.

FAMILY LAW REFORMS

1. SECRECY

More than 200 MPs have called for the abolition of all secrecy in Family Courts:

EDM 869 Source: PIMS
WORKING OF THE CHILDREN ACT 2004 26.10.2005

Pickles, Eric

That this House urges the Government to remove the veil of secrecy from the workings of the Children Act 2004; considers that the closed door policy of the family courts breeds suspicion and a culture of secrecy which does nothing to instil confidence in those using them, which affects not just the courts but the social services departments of local authorities; and believes that it is possible to preserve the anonymity of children involved in the proceedings without the cumbersome rules which obstruct parents from receiving advice and support, which in particular works to the disadvantage of parents with special learning difficulty.

There should be no gagging orders on parents who should be free, like rape victims, to waive anonymity and go to the press with their history, their identities and their complaints (including details of the court proceedings, the witnesses who testified and the judgement) if they believe their children have been unjustly taken. These children are routinely advertised for adoption like pedigree dogs by Social Services in magazines 'Adoption UK' etc., and on the internet www.uk-kids.org.uk etc. and even in *The Daily Mirror*! All with full colour photos, first names and birth dates, allowing easy identification by the neighbours! The secrecy exists to gag protesting parents, not to protect the identity of the children and should be scrapped! Also abolition of 'jail with no public hearing' (a parliamentary question revealed that more than 200 persons were sent to prison in secret last year by Family Courts!).

2. HARM & RISK

The notion of 'emotional harm' is a vague concept impossible to either prove or disprove and should be scrapped.

Most important of all however is **'RISK'**. Parents and children are split up and in effect punished, not because of anything they have done, but only for what the 'professionals' think someone might do in the future! Perfectly happy and healthy children are declared to be at risk of harm at some time in the future by social workers and hired 'experts' (psychologists, therapists, psychiatrists and the like!) who base their opinions very largely on the reports from social workers, which are always so thoughtfully provided for them!

Any experts that are consulted should start 'with a clean sheet', unbiased by reports favourable or otherwise from social workers, expert 'colleagues' or other outside sources. Parents are asked how they can possibly know better than these highly qualified (and very highly paid!) professionals! In fact the answer is both simple and financial. In the Louise Woodward case for example, top experts disagreed about a possibly shaken baby but each expert gave evidence for the side that paid them!!

Some supposedly 'top experts' like Professor Meadows, Professor Southall and Dr Marietta Higgs caused literally hundreds of children to be legally kidnapped on evidence based on their crackpot theories that have now been thoroughly discredited! In any case, the experts hired by Social Services always tend to take the side of their Social Services or Family Court paymasters so children and worse still, newborn babies, are then sent for adoption. This is said to avoid any more risk from parents who are naturally angry and upset that their children have been removed and who can then be declared to be emotionally unstable. A result as unjust as it is absurd! Would any genuinely loving mother be able to remain calm and cooperative with those who had taken her children or worse still, her newborn baby?

On the continent in France, Spain, Italy etc. children are only taken from parents if they have suffered severe physical harm. The concepts of 'emotional harm' and 'future risk' quite rightly do not exist there! Children from these countries are only taken if a parent has committed or at least been charged with a **CRIME** against their child. '**NO CRIME NO CARE ORDER**' should be the rule also in the UK. The simple fact that 'other children from the same mother have previously been taken into care' should no longer be considered an adequate reason for removing children, and **ESPECIALLY NEW BORN BABIES** from parents. Circumstances can and often do change, and it is wicked to ignore such changes. To take a baby from a mother of sound mind who has never in any way caused it harm must be a **CRIME** (as an article in *The Times* clearly states). Every completely blameless mother in the UK is now at risk of having her baby taken at birth because the father has merely been 'suspected' (not charged or convicted) of some violent incident in his distant past.

Family Courts are the B-side of the law
by Camilla Cavendish
The Times, 26 December 2006

What a strange, fumbling kind of justice system it is that condemns a woman as an unfit mother for the heinous crime of trusting her husband. Yet this is what seems to have happened in a recent case that I feel compelled to write about, even though legal restrictions force me to leave out much of the detail.

The nub of the case is this. A woman, let us call her Janie, gave birth to her first and only child a year ago. That baby was taken away from her and subsequently put up for adoption. Not because of her own failure to care for the baby — her own love and care never seem to have been in question. No. She has lost her baby because of a suspicion that her husband John may have injured another child in his previous marriage almost ten years ago.

The suspicion was no more than that. John was never charged with anything, let alone convicted. Social workers were never sufficiently worried to take that first child into care. Since his divorce John has shared custody of that child perfectly amicably with his ex-wife. Yet the same local authority which left the first child with him has forbidden him to see this new baby. And his new wife, despite having nothing to do with the first case, may never see her baby again.

Unless this case is overruled in the European Court of Human Rights (ECHR) in Strasbourg, where it is now heading, it will set a peculiar precedent. For it implies that any British mother could be penalised for choosing a partner to whom the State has taken a dislike: penalised with the loss of the thing that is most precious to her in the world.

It cannot be this simple, you are thinking. Well, not quite. The child of the first marriage is disabled, and did seem to have suffered an injury — I am not permitted to say more. But no one knows how. Both John and his first wife have always protested their innocence. They had a second child who came to no harm. No court will ever truly know whether John was innocent. But the fact is that he was never found guilty. For the local authority to leave him alone with a child that it thought he had harmed, and to take away another that had not been harmed, is utterly hypocritical. No court should be able to punish you for a crime you may commit, when there is no evidence.

It should, surely, be a crime to remove a newborn baby from a mother who has never harmed it.

For that in itself is a form of abuse. Yet the secret State often chooses to abuse the children itself, rather than let them run the risk of staying put. They are at least alive, it calculates, even if it is a diminished kind of alive, deprived of the mother bond. And too often, it strikes the wrong balance. In 2002, the ECHR ruled against the British Government for removing a new baby from its mother in hospital and refusing even to let her cuddle it under supervision, when there was no evidence that the baby faced a serious risk at that time. The judgment came too late, though. The baby had already been adopted.

This is what Janie fears. The ECHR has agreed to hear her appeal and to consider whether the English court ruling breached Janie and John's right to family life, to freedom of opinion and to freedom of expression. That is quite a ticket. But even if the ECHR finds in Janie's favour, it may be too late. The local authority is already seeking families to adopt her baby. Her only hope is that prospective adopters will be put off by knowing of her appeal.

Any lawyer will tell you that Family Courts are the B-side of the legal system. The majority of judgments will never be read outside the courtroom. Perhaps judges fear the consequences if they do not support social services and social services are later proved right. They seem to start from the assumption that children are de facto wards of court who need protection from their parents.

Even then, Janie's case seems extraordinary. Certainly the parents are not the brightest people in the world. They are not perfect. But the more I learn about it, the more I believe that Janie and John's biggest mistakes were emotional. Janie seems to have been very co-operative. However, John has been irritable, even aggressive, which would support the view that he has a violent nature. But can you really convict on that basis? Which of us could control our temper if faced with losing a child to a bunch of hypocrites? In a Hollywood movie, anger is a natural reaction to injustice. In an English suburb, defiance makes you guilty. The legal system wants "remorse". But how can you show remorse for something you haven't done?

Until this case I had tended to be sceptical about the claims that the Government's targets for adoption were leading to miscarriages of justice. I still feel that ministers were right to want to speed up adoption and to release more children more quickly from the hell of care. But I have now started to take more seriously the argument that these targets have created a perverse incentive for local authorities to take more babies into care. Babies are, after all, more attractive to prospective adopters than older children and therefore an easy way to reach those targets. In Janie and John's case, you do have to wonder why the authorities have rushed to take away a healthy baby, when they did not take away a disabled one.

Janie's case seems to me to make a strong argument for introducing juries. Why is a burglar facing six months in jail allowed to ask for a jury trial, but a mother facing the irretrievable loss of her only child is not? Mistakes will always be made when the ordinary, imperfect citizen is judged by the imperfect and powerful. Personally, I would rather face 12 men good and true.

The parents asked judge Munby to stop any adoption of their daughter until a verdict had been given by the European Court in Strasbourg. Exceptionally Judge Munby published his refusal for all to see!

The perpetrators should be punished!

Babies 'removed to meet targets'
by Brian Wheeler
BBC News at bbc.co.uk/news, 26 January 2007

Babies are being removed from their parents so that councils can meet adoption targets, MPs have claimed.

The MPs fear a rise in the number of young children being taken into care in England and Wales is linked to pressure on councils to increase adoption rates.

Lib Dem MP John Hemming, who has tabled a Commons motion on the issue, said it was a "national scandal".

The government said the courts decided on care cases but there had to be evidence a child was being harmed.

A spokesman for the Department for Education said there were "no targets relating to the numbers of children coming into care".

But Mr Hemming argued that social services departments are under pressure to meet targets set by government on children in care being adopted. In an Early Day Motion, with cross-party support from 12 MPs, he warns of "increasing numbers of babies being taken into care, not for the safety of the infant, but because they are easy to get adopted".

In 2000, ministers set a target of a 50% increase in the number of children in local authority being adopted by March 2006.

According to the latest available figures, the number of "looked after" children being adopted had gone up from 2,700 in 2000 to 3,700 in 2004, an increase of 37.7%.

The biggest rise was in the one to four-year-old age range.

'Scandal'

These figures would be "laudable" if it meant children were being rescued from a life in care, said Mr Hemming.

But he said he had evidence from people who had contacted him, prevented from publication by contempt of court laws, that children were being separated from parents without proper grounds.

And he called on the government to reveal "how many of the children that are adopted would otherwise have remained with their birth parents".

Mr Hemming pointed to figures showing an increase in the number of children aged under one being taken into care.

"A thousand kids a year are being taken off their birth parents just to satisfy targets. It is a national scandal," said the Lib Dem MP.

Transparency

He said children were increasingly placed under "care orders" - where they remain with their birth parents but are kept under supervision by social workers - rather than with foster parents.

And this supervision meant some social workers were "gradually taking them away from the parents, step by step, and giving them to someone else," the Birmingham Yardley MP said.

He called for more transparency in the proceedings of Family Courts and an independent watchdog to scrutinise the work of social services departments.

In a statement, the Department for Education said: "The law is clear - children should live with their parents wherever possible and, when necessary, families should be given extra support to help keep them together.

"The decision to take a child into care is never an easy one, and it is a decision that is taken by the courts."

'Best interests'

The statement went on: "In every case where a child is taken into care on a care order, the courts will have considered the evidence and taken the view that the child has been significantly harmed, or would be if they were not taken into care.

"The final decision on adoption rests with the courts and before a court makes such an important decision it must be convinced on the basis of the evidence that this is the best way to meet the child's needs on a long-term basis.

"There are no government targets relating to the numbers of children coming into care. The decision to bring a child into care must be made on the basis of their best interests."

The British Association for Adoption and Fostering (BAAF) said it was "dangerous" to suggest children were being taken into care unnecessarily.

Chief executive David Holmes said: "Children come into care for many reasons including parental abuse and neglect. The rise in the numbers of young children coming into care may be explained by a variety of factors including a rise in parental substance misuse."

He pointed out that the decision to take a child into care was scrutinised by an independent children's guardian and the courts. Adoption is scrutinised by the guardian, the courts and an adoption panel.

Mr Holmes added: "If birth parents believe they have had their child taken into care unfairly, they should lodge a formal complaint with their local authority. I believe that this is rare. I certainly do not believe children are systematically being taken into care to meet adoption targets."

3. JURIES

Decisions in contested cases in Family Courts **THAT INVOLVE LONG-TERM FOSTER CARE OR ADOPTION** must be decided by jury. Any burglar or other criminal facing a possible 6 months or more in prison has the right to demand a jury so why not a parent facing the loss of a child to adoption? In effect a life sentence! A jury would be less likely to 'rubberstamp' demands of Social Services than 'establishment judges', who inevitably take what they often describe as 'the safe option' and agree with highly-paid experts who foretell that children are at risk of emotional harm! It is very rare that any judge will restore children or babies to parents against opposition in court from Social Services. **THESE JUDGES ARE THE REAL VILLAINS AS THEIR JUSTICE SHOULD PROTECT THE WEAK NOT OPPRESS THEM.** I believe (like *The Times* article 'Family Courts are the b-side of the law' above) that these establishment judges commit a wicked crime every time they condone the taking of newborn babies from sane mothers that have never caused their babies harm. At Nuremburg after World War II the Nazi judges were condemned to prison as criminals and many of our Family Court judges deserve the same fate. Most of the decisions that now divide children from loving parents would be decided quite differently by a jury! This would soon reduce the number of cases brought by Social Services before the courts!

4. CONTACT

Telephone contact must never be forbidden between parents and children. Letters and conversations between parents and children must **NEVER** be censored or restricted by the Social Services' 'thought police'. Frequency of contact visits between parents and children in care should be decided specifically by a court and **NOT** left to the discretion of Social Services who sometimes use their discretion as a weapon to subdue 'difficult' parents.

5. NEGLECT

Parents accused of neglect that has not endangered the life of the child (absences from school, dirty or cluttered house etc.) should be given a written warning to put matters right, and a chance to do so before children can be taken.

6. ADOPTION

The Government's own research in 2001 already showed 'concern that the needs of the children were being overlooked because of the struggle to meet adoption targets'. **Our top priority should be the abolition of forced adoption** i.e. when a parent who has not been convicted of any crime that might affect the child, opposes adoption in the Family Court. **Also, all adopted children should retain their original birth certificate so they know who their birth parents are!** It is a wicked deed when the State conspires to conceal from adopted children the identity of their own parents by faking a new but false certificate of birth!

Adoption targets and large government rewards for achieving those targets (under public service agreements) should be scrapped. Kent got £21million(!), fosterers get as much as £400 per child per week, Special Schools up to £7,000/week per child, adoption agencies around £18,000/placement, lawyers as much as £50,000 per case, 'experts' up to £4,000 for a 3-hour interview with a parent. Without these rewards, social workers and others might be more motivated to keeping families together instead of splitting them up! Over 60,000 children are in care and more than 3,000/year are adopted, of which over 700/year are taken after hearings contested by distraught parents who nearly always lose! These figures are extremely disturbing. 20 MPs from all parties have signed early day motion 626 deploring the way social workers take babies and young children into care **NOT** for the benefit of the child but to meet the adoption targets set by the Government.

LOCAL AUTHORITY ADOPTION TARGETS
15.01.2007
EDM 626 Source: PIMS
Hemming, John MP

That this House notes that local authorities and their staff are incentivised to ensure that children are adopted; is concerned about increasing numbers of babies being taken into care, not for the safety of the infant, but because they are easy to get adopted; and calls urgently for effective scrutiny of care proceedings to stop this from happening.

7. WITNESSES

So-called 'experts' and 'professionals' should no longer be allowed to make 'prophecies' and 'risk assessments' in court but should confine themselves to what has happened not what might happen! It is incredible that in the UK families are ruthlessly split up **NOT** for events that have happened but for events that so called 'experts' think one day might happen! As already stated the Louise Woodward case demonstrated the fallibility of 'professionals' when the most distinguished experts in the country disagreed about a 'shaken baby' case. 'Experts' that are selected by Social Services or by 'the court' unsurprisingly almost always end up deciding that the hapless parents are 'in denial', suffer from 'paranoia' or have a 'personality disorder'. Many journalists from *The Times, The Telegraph* and the *Daily Mail,* broadcasters of programmes like 'The Real Story' and thousands of other people see social workers as 'child snatchers' rather than kindly helpers devoted to the public good! No more forecasts of 'risk' from hired experts should be considered in Family Courts. Parents are rarely allowed by their lawyers to call their own 'experts' and if they represent themselves they cannot afford to. **Parents who risk losing their children to adoption on the word of a medical expert should ALWAYS have the right to a second opinion by an expert of their own choice**. Most legal aid lawyers are widely known as 'professional losers' because they collect large fees for simply advising parents to give up the fight. They almost never win cases in the civil Family Courts as they rarely call all the witnesses and often forbid parents to say anything in court at all!! Parents should be able to testify and to call their children, their family doctor, and other family members as witnesses. According to the UN Convention on the Rights of the Child (to which the UK subscribes) children capable of understanding the nature of a court have the right to testify in proceedings that involve them and the right to an undisturbed family life, including contact with their siblings. These rights are normally completely disregarded by the secret UK Family Courts. Both parents' human rights and their children's rights should be respected at all times. Hearsay and recorded or video material should no longer be allowed as evidence in Family Courts.

8. EMERGENCY PROTECTION ORDERS

These must be abolished as parents have no opportunity to oppose them or defend themselves. The police have authority (police protection) to remove children they believe to be in danger and they alone should decide if any immediate danger really exists.

9. ADVISOR

A McKenzie Friend should be allowed to present the parents' case and cross-examine witnesses. This clause is doubly important when parents have been refused or are not eligible for legal aid. Such a person would usually stand a better chance of winning a case for parents than most of 'the legal aid lawyers' (**PROFESSIONAL LOSERS**) who collect huge fees for advising hapless parents not to fight Social Services but to go along with everything they say. Parents have no need for lawyers to do that, but how those legal sharks must laugh as they cash in! Parents who represent themselves and who wish to appeal should be supplied by the court with a copy of the judgement within 7 days so that they can put the appeal into court before expiration of the time limit.

10. ACCESS

A parent who loses custody of children to an ex-wife, ex-husband or ex-partner should have an enforceable right to such contact as the court awards. If such contact is denied or persistently prevented by one parent the court should warn the offending parent that if there is any more refusal to obey a court order for contact then the court will transfer custody to the parent who has been deprived.

FREE LEGAL ADVICE: ian@monaco.mc TEL: 0033626875684.

If you ring me, IAN JOSEPHS, from a fixed phone (not a mobile) and you give me the number I will ring you straight back at my own expense! If you have no phone at home any public phone box will do.

Here are the 10 reforms advocated by Camilla Cavendish in *The Times*:

I believe that wholesale reforms are needed, which can be summed up in ten points:

1. Open family courts to the press in all but exceptional circumstances (as recommended by the Constitutional Affairs Select Committee).

2. Let any parent or carer accused of abuse call any witnesses they need in their defence. At the moment, they are routinely refused permission to do so.

3. Give automatic permission for parents who are refused legal aid to get a lay adviser to help them present their case. This is routinely refused.

4. Remove the restrictions that prevent families from talking about their case (as recommended by the Constitutional Affairs Select Committee).

5. Review the definition of "emotional abuse" across local authorities, to make sure that it cannot become a catch-all for overzealous officials.

6. Provide an automatic right for parents to receive copies of case conference notes and all evidence used against them in court, just as they would in a criminal trial.

7. Create an independent body to oversee the actions of social services, with proper sanctions. If that body is to be the General Social Care Council, make it easier for parents to go directly to that body rather than having to face delays from the local authority.

8. Let children in care waive their right to privacy if they wish to speak out. For gagging children is surely not consistent with promoting their welfare.

9. Restructure CAFCASS, the Family Court Advisory Service, from being an organisation that reports on the parents to the courts to one that actively promotes the parenting needs of children. The primary focus should cease to be assisting the court process. It should be diverting parents away from contested hearings into the making of parenting plans.

10. Review the recent legal aid cut-backs that are deterring lawyers from taking on these complex family cases. It is quite

wrong that desperate parents are unable to find a lawyer to help them in their time of need.

Lord Denning was one of the greatest British judges in living memory. He condemned the secrecy of children's courts in the following words:

> Every court should be open to every subject of the Queen.
>
> I think it is one of the essentials of justice being done in the community. Every judge, in a sense, is on trial to see that he does his job properly. Reporters are there, representing the public, to see that magistrates and judges behave themselves. Children's courts should also be open. Names should be kept out but the public should know what happens to the child and proceedings should never be conducted behind closed doors......
>
> Somehow I believe, in the words of Jeremy Bentham, that in the darkness of secrecy all sorts of things can go wrong.

And if things are really done in public you can see that the judge does behave himself, the newspapers can comment on it if he/she misbehaves; it keeps everyone in order".

There is one special reason why reform progress is slow!!

Following the epidemic of false allegations made against innocent and vulnerable parents and their children, one puzzle has continued to dominate:

1. Why, when in many cases there is documentary evidence that social workers and others have presented perjured evidence to the Family Courts, has no prosecution followed?

2. Why have the police not proceeded with the charges they have informed parents they were going to bring? This includes the CID.

3. Why when there has been documented evidence recorded by the social workers themselves, identifying social workers as being engaged in child abuse, has no prosecution followed?

This has been going on for a number of years and recently it has been getting more blatant.

There has to be a reason for this! And although one might not discover the complete reason for such activity, one might be expected to discover some significant component driving the epidemic of false allegations.

We know that social workers have established de facto immunity for themselves in the Family Courts. But why and how?

Could this be a contributory reason for the failure of the police to prosecute those engaged in perjury and other offences in the Family Court?

Could this be the reason for the huge explosion of children taken into care and then adopted?

Consider the following:

This is the current list of MPs and MSPs (Scottish) who were previously social workers or worked for Social Services (this list is not complete):

1 Tessa Jowell MP. Minister. (Lab)

2 Beverly Hughes MP. (Lab)

3 Margaret Hodge MP. (Lab)

4 Rachael Squire MP (Deceased) (Lab)

5 Jane Kennedy MP (Lab)

6 John Austin MP (Lab)

7 Paul Goggins MP.(Home Office Minister)

8 Hilton Dawson MP (Lab) (left Parliament)

9 Meg Munn MP (Lab)

10 Hilary Armstrong MP (Lab)

11 Hewell Williams MP (Lab)

12 Julie Morgan MP (Lab)

13 Dan Norris MP (Lab)

14 Jenny Willot MP (Lib Dem)

15 Anthony Steen MP (Con)

16 Madeline Moon MP (Lab)

17 Sian James MP (Lab)

18 Cathie Jamieson MSP

19 Shiona Baird MSP

20 Scott Barrie MSP

21 Margaret Curran, MSP. Glasgow, Labour, former social worker.

22 Trish Godman, MSP. West Renfrewshire, Labour, former social worker.

23 Jonathan Shaw MP who assists Ruth Kelly as her PPS - he was a social worker for Kent CC.

24 Ann Coffey MP who was a social worker in fostering and adoption.

25 Mike Wood MP was not only a social worker but chair of Kirklees Social Services Committee before being an MP.

26 Sylvia Heal MP was a social worker.

27 Baroness Pitkeathley, (Lab) House of Lords.

There are others. Who are they? There are further ex-social workers in the House of Lords.

It has been noticeable that social workers who have been identified being involved in/the perpetrators of perjured evidence in Family Court proceedings or involved in physical abuse against children are seldom prosecuted by the police, despite there being plenty of supporting evidence and documentation.

- So we ask ourselves; who is in charge of the police force who is so reluctant to investigate these Family Court cases?

ANSWER: The Home Office

- And who is the Minister at the Home Office responsible for offences against children?

ANSWER: Paul Goggins (No. 7)

- So what's this chap's previous employment?

ANSWER: Social worker for 15 years

- And where specifically was Paul Goggins employed ?

ANSWER: National Childrens Homes (NCH)

- So why isn't any action being taken against those social workers involved in the Rochdale ritual satanic abuse case? (In this case, the BBC broadcast a programme documenting the recorded evidence against social workers involved in perjured statements and actual physical abuse).

ANSWER: NCH is the leading child protection organisation promoting the idea that ritual satanic abuse exists in this country. Even though there is no evidence that it happens.

CONCLUSION:

The House of Commons has ever so quietly replaced Eton and Harrow with social workers. No wonder there is all the smoke and mirrors involved in protecting the delinquent and dysfunctional social workers who have been involved in the False Allegation Industry. Their activities are rife in the Family Courts!

Some of the social workers are also involved with the adoption and fostering agencies. So the conveyor belt is fully manned, front and back!

No wonder they are concerned about continuing the secrecy of the Family Courts!

Enquiries are currently perusing leads to follow up social workers who have foster care agency and/or adoption agency connections. This is presently under way.

The huge number of social workers now in Parliament cannot be compared with lawyers or others, simply because social workers are limited to one employer...the State.

Lawyers and doctors traverse a wide area within their disciplines. They function as lawyers and doctors in the private or the public sector.

Social workers are definitely and only State employees, with a particular esprit de corps. They are now (and have been since New Labour came to power) in a very ascendant role, making policy that is unmistakably interventionist and prescriptive.

Could the immunity now accorded to social workers engaged in perjury and other offences committed in the Family Courts be the direct consequence of the influence of the huge number of ex-social workers now in Parliament?

8. SAD TALES

British justice: a family ruined. A chilling example of our secret State where a mother and child are forced into hiding by Camilla Cavendish

The Times, 21 February 2008

Last autumn a small English congregation was rocked by the news that two of its parishioners had fled abroad. A 56-year-old man had helped his pregnant wife to flee from social workers, who had already taken her son into care and were threatening to seize their baby.

Most people had no idea why. For the process that led this couple to such a desperate act was entirely secret. The local authority had warned the mother not to talk to her friends or even her MP. The judge who heard the arguments from social services sat in secret. The open-minded social workers who had initially been assigned to sort out a custody battle between the woman and her previous husband were replaced by others who seemed determined to build a guilty case against her. That is how the secret State operates. A monumental injustice has been perpetrated in this quiet corner of England; our laws are being used to try to cover it up.

I will call this couple Hugh and Sarah. Neither they nor their families have ever been in trouble with the law, as far as I know. Sarah's only fault seems to have been to suffer through a violent and volatile first marriage, which produced a son. When the marriage ended, the boy was taken into temporary foster care for a few months - as a by-product of the marriage breakdown and against her will - while she "sorted her life out" and found them a new home. But even as she cleared every hurdle set by the court, social workers dreamt up new ones. The months dragged by. A psychologist said the boy was suffering terribly in care and was desperate to come home. Sarah's mother and sister, both respected professionals with good incomes, apparently offered to foster or adopt him. The local authority did not even deign to reply.

For a long time, Sarah and her family seem to have played along. At every new hearing they thought that common sense would prevail. But it didn't. The court appeared to blame her for not ending her marriage more quickly, which had put strain on the boy, while social workers seemed to insist that she now build a good relationship with the man she had left. Eventually, she came to believe that the local authority intended to have her son adopted. She also seems to have feared that they would take away her new baby, Hugh's baby, when it was born. One night in September they fled the country with the little boy. When Hugh returned a few days later, to keep his business going and his staff in jobs, he was arrested.

Many people would think this man a hero. Instead, he received a far longer sentence - 16 months for abduction - than many muggers. This kind of sentence might be justified, perhaps, to set an example to others. But the irony of this exemplary sentence is that no one was ever supposed to know the details. (I am treading a legal tightrope writing about it at all.) How could a secret sentence for a secret crime deter anyone?

Sarah's baby has now been born, in hiding. I am told that the language from social services has become hysterical. But if the State was genuinely concerned for these two children, it would have put "wanted" pictures up in every newspaper in Europe.

It won't do that, of course, because to name the woman and her children would be to tear a hole in the fabric of the secret State, a hole we could all see through. I would be able to tell you her side of the story, the child's side of the story. I would be able to tell you every vindictive twist of this saga. And the local authority knows perfectly well how it would look. So silence is maintained.

And very effective it is too. The impotence is the worst thing. The way that perfectly decent individuals are gagged and unable to defend themselves undermines a fundamental principle of British law. I have a court order on my desk that threatens all the main actors in this case with dire consequences if they talk about it to anyone.

Can that really be the way we run justice in a country that was the fount of the rule of law? At the heart of this story is a little boy who was wrenched from the mother he loves, bundled around in foster care and never told why, when she appears to have been perfectly capable of looking after him. When she had relatives who were perfectly capable of doing so. In the meantime, he was becoming more and more troubled and unhappy. To find safety and love, that little boy has had to leave England.

What does that say about our country? The public funds the judges, the courts, the social workers. It deserves to know what they do. That does not mean vilifying all social workers, or defending every parent. But it does mean ending the presumption of guilt that infects so many family court hearings. It does mean asking why certain local authorities seem unable to let go of children whose parents have resolved their difficulties. It does mean knowing how social workers could have got away with failing to return this particular boy, after his mother had met all the criteria set by a judge at the beginning. It is simply unacceptable that social services have put themselves above the law.

We need these people to be named, and to hear in their words what happened. We need to open up the family courts. We need to tear down the wall of secrecy that has forced a decent woman to live as a fugitive, to save her little boy from a life with strangers, used like a pawn in a game of vengeance. Even if the local authority were to drop its case, it is hard to see how Sarah could ever trust them enough to return. At home, for their God-fearing congregation, the question is simple: what justice can ever be done behind closed doors? And in whose name?

Jailed: The man who helped his wife flee abroad as social workers threatened to take their baby

by Fiona Barton

Daily Mail, 7 February 2008

A father is in jail and his wife is in hiding abroad with her children after he helped them flee the country to escape social services, it emerged yesterday.

The businessman's wife was heavily pregnant with their first child - and was terrified the baby would be taken at birth by social workers - when he drove his family to Dover, and then on to Paris.

She had a second reason for fleeing - she believed her eight-year-old son from a previous marriage was to be adopted against her wishes.

Her 56-year-old husband was arrested on his return to Britain, and later jailed for 16 months for abducting the eight-year-old, known as Child S.

The boy's mother, who is a professional woman in her 40s but cannot be identified for legal reasons, has since given birth prematurely to a girl and is struggling to cope far from friends and family.

Her plight raises further disturbing questions about the secret family courts which only last week were in the spotlight when social workers illegally snatched a newborn baby from its mother.

Such cases are shrouded in the heaviest secrecy - with families threatened with jail if they discuss their fears that their children are being removed unjustly.

But the story of the father and his family in hiding can be revealed for the first time because he appealed in a criminal case - which can be reported - begging for his 16-month jail sentence to be reduced.

His plea to the High Court was dismissed and the father, who has never seen his baby daughter, was led away in tears.

A teacher friend of the father was also in tears.

The friend said: "This isn't justice. They are a law-abiding family with respect for the police, but putting him in prison for protecting his family makes the law an ass. What good does it serve?"

The three appeal judges were told yesterday how Child S's parents had separated in 2004 after a volatile and violent marriage.

The mother claims she was told the boy would be taken into temporary foster care until she "sorted her life out".

But when she asked for his return, social services refused.

After months of legal battles, a family court judge sided with the council's plan to put the boy up for enforced adoption. By this time, the mother was pregnant.

A friend said: "She was led to believe by social services she would have no chance of keeping the child she was carrying, which is outrageous. She was in despair."

According to papers before the appeal court, she then made contact with her son at school last September and whispered instructions to him through the playground fence.

In the early hours, Child S "crept out" of his foster home to meet his mother and stepfather and the escape plan was under way.

The mother left a note which claimed: "We had to go." The court was told that detectives believed the mother and children were in Spain or France.

Dismissing the appeal, Mr Justice Bennett acknowledged the "powerful emotions" involved, but said: "Such proceedings taken by a local authority must be respected by parents.

"Those who act must expect a prison sentence because a real punishment is called for and to deter others who might be subject to the same pressures."

The judge expressed his disbelief that the father did not know the whereabouts of his wife.

The father - who has adult children from a previous marriage - is being destroyed by prison, a friend said outside court.

She added: "He is absolutely shell-shocked by the actions of the courts. Basically, they have said you are not allowed to be human in your responses.

"What parent wouldn't act to stop their child being taken from them? He has aged ten years and gone grey with the worry of it all."

Free the 'Grandfather One'

Is it really in the public interest that a grandparent is jailed for not avoiding his grandson?

by Camilla Cavendish

The Times, 13 December 2007

Two MPs have put down an early day motion in the House of Commons to bring attention to what they believe is a miscarriage of justice. It notes that a man named Charles Roy Taylor has been sent to prison for 20 months for being in contact with his step grandson. It "wonders if this is a good use of scarce prison resources; and calls for the Secretary of State for Justice to consider whether he should be released for Christmas". Jack Straw no doubt has bigger things on his mind. And no story like this is ever as simple as it looks. But it deserves attention.

Charles Roy Taylor is a 71-year-old with a heart condition. He knew that a jail sentence was the penalty he might pay if he did not take steps to avoid his step grandson. But this seems desperately unfair. The teenager, whom we shall call John, has been in care since his mother died of an overdose. He has been phoning his grandparents and running away to see them for some time. In the end, social services became concerned that the grandparents were "undermining the care plan" by continuing to see John. It does not appear to be clear to the grandparents what the care plan is. But it does not seem to include them, even though they could presumably be John's first port of call when he leaves the care system at 18.

It is not the local authority's fault that this child had a difficult childhood. In taking responsibility for him, social workers were doing their best. Neither he nor his grandparents sound like the easiest people to deal with. But as in so many cases of this kind, bitterness between the family and the authorities appears to have escalated into a ludicrous situation, which simply cannot be in the best interests of the child.

After a great deal of argy-bargy that I cannot go into for legal reasons, Mr Taylor last year gave an undertaking not to communicate with John until he was 18. But asking a man not to pick up the phone to a child, not to take him in when he turns up at the front door, is a harsh demand. It is tantamount to asking him to deny that the child exists, when what that child may need most is attention.

In stalking cases, when Person A is ordered to avoid Person B, it is usually at the explicit request of Person B, who fears assault. In this case, Person B was apparently desperate to see his grandparents. He seems to see them as his best hope. So in whose interests was such an order? If he has broken his undertaking, Mr Taylor has surely been responding as humanely as most of us would. A jail sentence seems wholly disproportionate.

When I first learnt of this case I felt that there must be more to it. That perhaps the grandparents were suspected of abuse. I can find no evidence of any such allegation. Indeed, the authorities initially seemed happy to leave them in contact with John. What appears to have happened is that the exchanges between the family and social workers became increasingly bitter, all of whom no doubt believed themselves to be in the right.

The council cannot comment on individual cases. It will say only that "Mr Taylor was sentenced by the High Court after he breached a court order". It cannot comment on John's treatment in care. John seems unhappy. He has apparently asked to be discharged. But his voice can only be heard within the system, a system he seems determined to rebel against.

There is a growing campaign on the internet to release Mr Taylor. This has two parts. The first is that a 20-month jail sentence is preposterous when the prisons are so overcrowded that dangerous criminals are being released early. The second is that Mr Taylor was allegedly committed to jail in a "secret court". This seems unlikely. But it is an allegation that is made frequently. Legally, you cannot send someone to jail in a secret court. In practice, it is questionable whether a judge sitting in a family court from which press and public are excluded, who declares the court open for a few minutes to pronounce sentence, is really "open".

This matters, because the view of the legal profession increasingly seems to be that the less we know the better. The justification for keeping family courts closed, despite the recommendations of the Commons Constitutional Affairs Select Committee, is to protect children's privacy. Yet this argument is no longer confined to the family courts. It is increasingly being trotted out in criminal cases too.

In the past month, one court has ruled that the defendants in a witchcraft trial, who were alleged to have done unspeakable things to children, could not be named in case this led to the identification of their victims. Another court banned publication of anything about a mother accused of poisoning her child with salt, in case the information affected her surviving child. The Times has recently succeeded in overturning yet another ruling, that a man who pleaded guilty to making indecent images of children could not be named in case his relatives might suffer. The Court of Appeal found that the man should be named, and that the attempts to restrict the proceedings were invalid.

The law must not become a secret process. Some lawyers seem convinced that the media want to identify vulnerable children, but it is always possible to write these stories without doing so. Seeing that justice is done is a fundamental part of law.

What is sad is that our elaborate system of child protection, which is designed to put children first, has sometimes become a way of avoiding accountability. The two MPs are right to ask whose interests Mr Taylor's jailing serves. Presumably, the last thing John wants is for his grandfather to be in jail. They are both victims of a system that asks us to take on trust that it knows best. But prison is surely the wrong place for Charles Roy Taylor.

How social workers took away our children for 11 months without a shred of evidence

by Sue Reid

Daily Mail, 9 May 2008

Enjoying the sunshine at a park near their home, the Aston family cling closely to each other as if to make sure they will never be prised apart again. Jodie, a bubbly ten-year-old, entwines her arms around her brother, Luke, who was 12 last Thursday, while both children smile fondly at their parents, Craig and Donna.

Yet the happy scene is full of poignancy. Until very recently, this Yorkshire couple were trapped in what a High Court judge described this week as "every parent's nightmare".

For an interminable 11 months, Jodie and Luke were removed from their home because their parents faced accusations from doctors of the most hideous crime imaginable: sexually molesting their own daughter.

They were permitted to visit their children only under strict supervision, for just three hours a week. All letters which they sent to Jodie and Luke were vetted by social workers - making them feel like criminals.

What's more, they were cruelly ordered not to say "I love you" to either boy or girl. Throughout this ordeal, the couple always protested their innocence and were relieved beyond belief. When Mr Justice Holman cleared them of any wrong doing. He ordered the children's return, insisting that his ruling be made public so lessons are learned by doctors, social workers and lawyers working in the child protection service.

In a landmark judgment, he warned that even two decades after the infamous Cleveland child abuse scandal, parents are still being wrongly accused of molesting their sons and daughters.

The Cleveland controversy was Britain's biggest and first mass child abuse scare.

In 1987, 121 children were taken into state care in North-East England over five months after abuse was diagnosed on the basis of physical examinations carried out by a controversial paediatrician called Marietta Higgs.

The parents were often wrongly condemned - just like the Astons today - without their children being listened to or their family background being taken into account.

The doctors in the Eighties had relied on the discredited sign called Reflex Anal Dilatation (RAD), said to indicate sexual abuse.

Last year, the controversial sign was condemned as unreliable by the Government's chief medical officer, Sir Liam Donaldson, who admitted that its use had led to mistakes in Cleveland.

Everyone hoped the lessons had been learnt from Cleveland. But now the shocking extent of young Jodie Aston's ordeal is becoming clear, it seems that is tragically not the case.

Mr Justice Holman said it was inevitable that Jodie was now "emotionally damaged" by her experiences.

After the private hearing at Leeds High Court, he said: "Unless there is clear diagnostic evidence of abuse (for example, the presence of semen or a foreign body internally), purely medical assessments and opinions should not be allowed to predominate. Even 20 years after Cleveland, I wonder if the lessons have fully been learned." The importance of this judgment cannot be overstated. Jodie's father, a 33-year-old railway signals' engineer, courageously agreed to talk for the first time about the case.

He said: "I hope the judge's words will rein in doctors, and help other parents accused of sexually abusing their children without any real proof." What happened to the Aston family seems incredible in 21st-century England. They are now seeking legal advice in the hope that the General Medical Council, the doctors' disciplinary body, will investigate their case.

Yesterday, Leeds' Safeguarding Children's Board launched a review into Jodie's case, saying "all relevant, accurate facts" must be taken into account in future child abuse inquiries.

Officials said it was too early to reveal how many other children have been taken into care or even adopted, as a result of suspected sexual abuse over recent years.

However, the Mail is aware of two other families in the city who have had their children removed, largely on the basis of the RAD testing technique, yet who insist they are entirely innocent.

The Astons' nightmare began when they took Jodie, then aged eight, to Leeds General Infirmary's casualty department on a Monday evening in August 2005. She had scraped her groin on a small wall while playing with friends.

She was examined by doctors in Leeds at least eight times. Photographs and videos - later shown in court - were taken of her naked body again and again.

The girl was referred to the community paediatrics department at the city's St James's University Hospital on the following Thursday. Nothing was found to be amiss after an intimate examination. But two months later, Jodie was changing into her pyjamas after school when her mother saw a spot of blood on her pants.

Jodie, who was prone to eczema and had visible raw splits in the skin of her hands and arms, was again taken to casualty before being referred for a second time to the paediatrics unit at St James's.

The hospital has a busy child protection team, overseen by the respected paediatric consultant Dr Christopher Hobbs.

Significantly, he is an original pioneer of the RAD technique in this country. In June 1986, just a year before the Cleveland controversy broke, Dr Hobbs and his colleague Jane Wynne introduced young Marietta Higgs to this new way of diagnosing child molestation during a Leeds' medical conference.

By looking at and probing a child's bottom, the paediatricians claimed they could see if there was reflex anal dilatation and - therefore - abuse.

Dr Higgs enthusiastically embraced the technique, provoking the Cleveland crisis.

However, 80 per cent of the "victims" were later returned to their parents because they had not been hurt at all.

Since then, the nagging doubts about the technique have grown. Today, it is well-known that RAD can appear normally and spontaneously in any child.

According to some paediatricians - notably an expert named Professor Astrid Hegar from America, where RAD has been abandoned in some states - half of all children who have not been sexually abused show the same "tell-tale" sign when their bottoms are examined.

That means, of course, that almost any family taking their child to hospital or the doctor's surgery can be accused of child abuse.

Yet in Britain, many child doctors - including Dr Hobbs - rely on the technique as an important piece of many pieces in the jigsaw of diagnosing child abuse.

Even before 1987 - at the height of the Cleveland crisis - both Hobbs and Wynne were discovering high numbers of child sex abuse cases in Leeds by using RAD.

According to the doctors' research, published in the medical journal The Lancet, 94 boys and 243 girls were diagnosed as sexual abuse victims in a previous two-year period. The paper - still quoted in medical literature - says that eight in ten of the boys, and a quarter of the girls, had "anal signs".

Astonishingly, in half of all cases, the abusers were deemed to be the children's natural father and - even more bizarrely - five per cent were women. A quarter of the Leeds adults involved were convicted by the courts. The two doctors wrote at the time: "Sexual abuse is emerging as a major child and mental health problem." So it was against this background - in a city whose medical establishments were at the centre of the RAD debate - that Jodie Aston was taken by her mother to hospital. It was the first of many visits and, during one, on November 24, 2005, she met Dr Hobbs.

Although he did not physically examine Jodie, at the end of the appointment he and a fellow paediatrician said that they suspected child abuse. It was a terrible moment for Jodie's mother, Donna.

She says today: "I couldn't believe it. I began to cry. I walked out of there not knowing what to think. Jodie saw that I was quiet, and thought she had done something wrong. I waited in the car park for Craig to come and pick us up.

"I asked Jodie if her Daddy had done anything to her. She said "no" and I believed her. But when I got in the car, Craig saw that I had been crying. He asked me what was wrong and I just mumbled something about child abuse because I didn't want to upset Jodie." At home, after the children had gone to bed, Donna had to ask her husband a question that no wife should have to. Craig said he had not touched his daughter.

"I was being accused of something worse than murder," Craig said this week.

"From that point, we began to watch the children like hawks.

"We did not allow them even to go to the shops nearby. Luke said we were treating them like babies," added Donna, 34. However, the family remained under suspicion. Donna was told by the authorities that she was also considered the potential abuser of her daughter.

The following March, Jodie faced another assessment with Dr Hobbs. Just a few weeks earlier, she had again come home with a small blood spot on her pants.

This time, the paediatrician conducted a physical examination, which included RAD. He wrote in his report afterwards: "I feel that the time has come for me to involve social services, because I am concerned about the possibility that she may have been sexually abused."

The family were trapped. The doctors ignored Donna's suggestion that eczema might be the cause of the blood spots. Meanwhile, social workers began visiting the family regularly.

Overwhelmed with worry, Craig and Donna were advised to get an independent second medical opinion on Jodie's condition. Therefore, their GP arranged for a doctor called Ruth Skelton to examine their daughter. This proved to be a disastrous move.

Dr Skelton had been trained by Dr Hobbs. As Mr Justice Holman commented in his judgment: "In my view, the selection of her was deeply regrettable. Dr Skelton lacked the complete independence that is required for a second opinion in these sorts of circumstances.

"She was being asked to review the previous opinion of someone who was a more senior colleague, then working daily at the same hospital, and who had been her own teacher."

It emerged that Dr Skelton had discussed Jodie's case with Dr Hobbs before the so-called independent examination took place in March last year.

Dr Skelton concluded that she could spot RAD. According to her report, she said that Jodie had "been sexually abused chronically, over a long period, both anally and probably vaginally . . . I feel that this child is not protected at all at present." Both Jodie and her elder brother, Luke, were taken away from the parents the same day. It was arranged that they would live with their maternal grandparents, aged 77 and 78, three miles away from their home in Armley, a suburb of Leeds. Donna still finds it hard to relate the story as she sits with the children and Craig in the family's neat sitting room.

She says: "The social workers came at 9.30am to tell us they wanted to remove Jodie and Luke. It was a Thursday. Jodie and Luke were at school. They never came home for almost a year.

"I packed a few things for the first night: toothbrushes, pyjamas, a big bear toy that was Jodie's favourite. Then I had to come home alone.

"Craig was in a worse state than me. I thought he was going to harm himself. We woke up in night crying. We hugged each other because it was as if the children were dead."

This week, she said: "There were more tears, but we had to cope for the sake of the children. On Christmas Day last year, we were only allowed to see them for one hour." Yet the family's fortunes were changing.

Craig's lawyers had instructed the American paediatrician, Professor Hegar, to give her views. She has examined 40,000 children for suspected abuse during a 28-year career. She believes that a family's history - and a host of other factors - are vital when deciding if a child has been molested.

Professor Hegar studied the medical reports and photographs of Jodie. She said: "I believe that the medical examiners in this case have relied heavily on Reflex Anal Dilatation as diagnostic of sexual abuse.

"This is a common finding in up to 49 per cent of children who have not been abused. There is no research ... that supports the use of RAD as a sensitive or specific finding for sexual abuse."

Professor Hegar also suggested that dermatologists should examine Jodie to find another cause of her bleeding. One skin expert diagnosed that a small split in her skin, caused by eczema, may have produced the suspect spots of blood on Jodie's underwear.

Her crucial views were also heard by video link during the hearing into Jodie's case. Afterwards, Mr Justice Holman said Donna and Craig Aston are intelligent, responsible parents.

During the hearing, he met both their "bright and well-mannered" children, giving them chocolate biscuits and talking to them for nearly an hour.

Jodie told him that no one had touched her at home, or at primary school. Her brother Luke declared, quite spontaneously, that it was "all a big mistake".

He added: "We have got the best mum and dad. Why would they abuse my little sister?"

Both of the Aston children said they loved their parents dearly and only wanted to go home. Now, at last, thanks to an enlightened judge, they have finally got their wish.

But how many other families who suffered similarly disgraceful misdiagnoses, more than 20 years after it had been presumed the lessons of Cleveland had been learnt, are still fighting to clear their names?

My baby had cancer but social workers falsely accused me of child abuse and took all three of my children

by Sue Reid

Daily Mail, 22 February 2008

One November afternoon at just after two o'clock, Louise Mason stood in a hospital ward and kissed her 11-week- old baby goodbye.

She had dressed the little girl with care, packing a suitcase of tiny clothes and soft toys. Inside, she had placed a handwritten letter to the foster parents who would look after her in the future.

On that day five years ago, Louise felt as though her heart would burst.

"I wrote down everything about my daughter," she told me this week.

"I said she had colicky attacks at six in the evening, and should be rocked until she slept. I said she needed to be coaxed to take her milk."

After writing that sad note, the young mother from Northampton was forced to hand over the baby girl to social workers, who carried her off to her new home.

Louise, 32, then returned to her house, with its empty cot, in the seaside city of Derry, Northern Ireland. It must have been one of the loneliest journeys of her life.

The baby girl - now aged five - has never been returned to this wholly innocent mother who, because she was wrongly accused of harming her baby, also subsequently had two other children taken away from her.

This week, though, a High Court revealed there had been a terrible miscarriage of justice, and ordered that Louise must be reunited with all her children.

Furthermore, the judge, Mr Justice Gillon - in an age where children are removed from their parents by family courts sitting in secret - took the extremely unusual step of allowing Louise to be named, and for the tragic details of her case to become public.

In a statement he said: "The workings of the family justice system in this case are matters of public interest, and do merit public discussion. Public confidence in the process is necessary, and the emergence of the changing circumstances of this case merits an open discussion."

He went on to list the extraordinary catalogue of events which began when, worried out of her mind, Louise took her sickly month- old baby daughter to her GP, begging for help.

These shocking details shed light on a family justice system normally hidden from view.

Of course, there are parents who harm their children and deserve the full punishment of the law.

But in the family courts, thousands of children are removed from their parents to adoption or foster care in deeply dubious hearings which never become public.

If anyone speaks about the details - to a neighbour, to a friend, to a relative - they are in contempt of court.

Crucially, the courts' culture of secrecy means that if a social worker lies, or fabricates notes, or a doctor makes a mistake, then no one finds out, and there is no retribution.

It is only because Louise was charged with a criminal offence in an open and public court - like other innocent mothers wrongly accused of infanticide, such as Angela Cannings and the late Sally Clark - that her harrowing story can be heard.

Louise was born in Northampton, the youngest of three. Her father had a plastering business, and her mother raised a close, caring family.

By the time she was in her 20s, Louise was running a successful restaurant. A few years later, she met her boyfriend, who came from Derry, and the couple had a baby. They moved to Northern Ireland to set up home.

Louise says now: "I came here in 2001, thinking Derry was the perfect place for children to grow up."

The couple had a second baby - another girl, born a healthy 7lb. But then she and her partner split up, leaving Louise a single mother.

"I was quite able to cope with the toddler and the baby, who was very placid," explains Louise. "I was a full-time mother and proud of it."

Then came the bombshell. One Saturday, when the baby was just four weeks old, Louise noticed that she was looking very ill, as though she was about to collapse.

In fact, it is now known that without medical care she would have died within an hour.

"I rushed my daughter around to our local doctor, who immediately rang the Derry hospital. I hurried there with this little bundle in my arms.

"The baby was taken off me in the children's ward. I next saw her five hours later, at 7pm.

"One of the doctors then sat me down and said: 'It is touch and go'" The team mentioned right away that it might be cancer. I remember that as though it were yesterday," says Louise, crying this week at the memory.

"The next morning, they again said cancer was suspected."

A day later, on the Sunday, the baby was taken by ambulance to the Royal Belfast hospital 60 miles away. She had a blood transfusion and tests. By the Tuesday, three days after the emergency admission, Louise was hoping that she would get a proper diagnosis.

But further investigation had showed that the left kidney and the area around it was swollen, and among medical staff there was a wide variety of opinion about the cause. Before long, doctors became highly suspicious that this was, in fact, caused by an injury.

Louise was called into a room and confronted by a doctor.

"He asked me if I had done anything to hurt my baby. He said he had called the social services and the police. I promised him I had done nothing to my child."

Her words fell on deaf ears. Back home, her elder daughter, who was being cared for by a neighbour, was collected by social workers and taken into foster care.

Yet still the trusting Louise thought it would all be sorted out in a few days. How wrong she was.

Seven weeks later, on November 15, 2002, the police contacted her.

"They asked me to attend the police station for an interview under caution. They said I was suspected of grievous bodily harm with intent."

The interview dragged on. At lunchtime, Louise was put in a cell. She was distraught.

"I was frozen with fright," she recalls.

"I kept telling them that there was no bruising or redness found on the baby, so how could I have hurt her?"

Four days later, worse news followed: her baby daughter was to be taken into foster care, too.

At the hospital, she was told by social workers to get the 11-week-old baby she was accused of harming ready. Her fingers trembling, Louise dressed her baby and kissed her goodbye.

From then on, she was allowed to see her children at a special supervised centre for only four-and-a-half hours a week.

They were delivered to the centre from their foster homes by social workers, and then taken away again.

"The eldest one could remember me," says Louise, "but I had hardly had a chance to bond with the new baby before she was taken from me."

All the time, Louise faced a barrage of accusations. The authorities claimed that she was a potential killer.

A leading member of the social work team told her: "I do not think you are safe to be left in a room alone with any boy or girl."

In January 2004 - a little over year later - a formal application to take the children into care was made in the family division of the Northern Ireland High Court in Belfast.

The medical evidence given by five doctors from the hospitals was damning. They said Louise had deliberately hurt the baby girl with great force.

"It was then that they began to make noises about adoption,' says Louise. 'My legal team were fighting hard, but it was a battle we could not win because we did not have the medical evidence." The children remained with their foster parents.

That autumn, Louise was brought before a criminal court in Derry facing two charges of causing grievous bodily harm to the baby girl.

It was only then that anyone listened to her.

In an emotional outburst, she blurted out to the jury that she wanted to take a lie detector test to prove that she had done nothing wrong. It was the turning point. The jury believed her, and in November 2004 she was acquitted of the charges. However, her children remained in care.

Meanwhile, the story of the mother begging for a lie detector test was reported in the local Press. By chance, the consultant radiologist who had treated Louise's baby girl at the local hospital on the very first day she was brought in, read the article and was appalled.

He remembered the case and the wide divergence of medical opinion, yet had never known that Louise was under suspicion or that she was to have been prosecuted. He was convinced then that the child was suffering from a rare form of cancer of the left kidney, called neuroblastoma, which could have caused the bleeding.

Dr D - as he was called in Mr Justice Gillon's judgment this week - contacted Louise's solicitor and offered to help clear her name.

"It was a miracle," Louise told me.

"That doctor was my guardian angel. The last years have been very hard for me. I was pilloried. It felt like torture having my children taken from me."

Even though she had been acquitted, the social workers appeared to ignore the verdict.

But Dr D told Louise's solicitor that he was struck by the "power" of her request to the jury to have a lie detector test.

He offered to help, suggesting that a team of independent paediatricians, including experts on kidneys, cancer and non-accidental injury, should be asked to give their own opinions on the findings of the five hospital doctors.

Significantly, the independent experts thought that the baby's internal bleeding had occurred naturally. And when their testimony was produced by Louise's lawyers at a Court of Appeal hearing, the judges quashed the family court rulings.

As a result, in June last year the Foyle Health and Social Services Trust, which covers Derry, said it no longer intended to pursue their action to keep Louise's children in care or have them adopted. It was an almighty climb-down.

By then, however, another tragedy had happened on the say-so of the social workers.

In 2005, a year after she had been acquitted, Louise had became pregnant for a third time.

She is reluctant to talk about the father, or name him, although they are no longer together - but at Christmas time, when she was heavily pregnant, the social workers called and told her they planned to take the latest addition away from her at birth.

"I couldn't believe my ears," says Louise.

"I had been declared not guilty in a criminal court - yet they still had both my children and were wanting my new baby. It was torture."

The baby was born early in 2006. True to their word, Louise had just given birth and was trying to breastfeed when the social workers arrived at Altnagelvin Hospital, Derry.

The nurses, on the instructions of the social workers, took the newborn baby away to safety in another ward while Louise's solicitor remonstrated with them that it was cruel to do such a thing.

It was five hours before the baby was returned to Louise in the maternity unit.

Ten days later, when she was about to leave hospital, the social workers returned and seized the child, placing the baby with foster parents.

Only recently - following the collapse of the Social Services Trust case - has Louise been given back the baby, and her eldest child, too.

She has missed a whole chunk of their early years.

But perhaps the saddest thing of all is that the little girl who was so sick as a baby may never return home again. She has known no mother or father apart from her foster parents, and has bonded with them very closely.

Although she has now recovered - significantly, it was a form of cancer that can go into remission of its own accord, without the need for surgery or chemotherapy - her left kidney does not function normally.

But she is happy with the couple whom she calls her Mummy and Daddy.

Recently, as part of a phased plan to reunite her permanently with her natural family, she came back to stay with Louise for a night.

"She cried terribly for her foster parents all the evening - it made us all unhappy," says Louise, sadly.

"She knows me, but will only call me Mummy Louise. It breaks me into pieces.

"She may never come home and live with me again because she wants to be with the only people she has ever recognised as her parents. It may be cruel to take her back now."

It is, by any standards, a tragic indictment of the child protection system.

What do our MPs who represent us in Parliament think about all this?

Prime Minister Responds on Adoption

Source: Hansard

Q6. [163661] John Hemming (Birmingham, Yardley) (LD): In England in 2006, 4,160 children under five were taken into care and more than 60 per cent of them - 2,490 - were adopted. However, in Scotland 574 left care and 373, roughly 64 per cent., went home to their parents. Can the Prime Minister explain why in England children under five who leave care get adopted, while in Scotland they go home to their parents?

The Prime Minister: Social work legislation in the two countries is, of course, different. I shall look at the figures that the hon. Gentleman has put before me. But as is known, we have made strenuous efforts to try to ensure that children in difficulty are given the proper upbringing, whether that is by returning to their parents or, where it is essential, by being fostered or adopted. I will continue to look at the matter, but the hon. Gentleman has to understand that social work practice in the two countries is different.

This does go to the nub of the issue. What is so different between parents in England and parents in Scotland that means that it is 'essential' for under 5s to get adopted in England, but they can go home to their parents in Scotland?

Early Day Motions

EDMs are motions in Parliament. Normally they don't get debated. However, they are a sort of petition signed only by Members of Parliament. You can ask your MP to sign an EDM. You need to say which number EDM it is. MPs who are members of the government cannot sign EDMs, but you can ask them to write a letter to the minister in support of the EDM.

EDM 124 (Source: PIMS)

That this House notes that local authorities and their staff are incentivised to ensure that children are adopted; is concerned about increasing numbers of babies being taken into care, not for the safety of the infant, but because they are easy to get adopted; and calls urgently for effective scrutiny of care proceedings to stop this from happening.

EDM125 (Source: PIMS)

That this House believes that mothers should be encouraged to breastfeed as this is in the interests of the long-term health of babies; recognises that for newborn babies this means breastfeeding on demand; further believes that newborn babies in care should also be breastfed on demand where this does not result in any risk to the baby; and calls for the Government to introduce guidelines to ensure that facilities are provided to ensure that newborn babies can be breastfed on demand.

EDM 126 (Source: PIMS)

That this House notes the comments of a senior social worker that meetings have been held during which solicitors acting for parents have discussed how to undermine the cases of their clients; further notes that there are many odd cases in which solicitors fail to oppose care proceedings or accept that the section 31 threshold has been met notwithstanding the opposition of their clients; recognises that reporting and obtaining the investigation of such behaviour outwith parliamentary proceedings remains a contempt of court for hon. Members; and asks the Solicitors Regulatory Authority to review the implementation of the new solicitors' code of conduct and how this relates to conflicts of interest in the Family Court.

To sack your solicitor and your barrister just download form N434!

N434 - Notice of change of solicitor (Court Service) Download Form N434, Notice of change of solicitor, Court Service Forms, Administrative Court:

http://www.capform.co.uk/fullformlist.asp?Level1=11&Level2=106&Level3=623

Local solicitors and barristers often already enjoy a close and friendly 'working relationship' with the local authority. These legal aid lawyers are widely known in the trade as **PROFESSIONAL LOSERS!'** and justifiably so as they make a point of losing every single case they undertake when opposing Social Services! You cannot win if you have 'enemies in your own camp' so if your lawyers start conceding every point to the opposition and stop you from saying anything in your own defence then be brave! Get rid of them!

In many courts if you represent yourself you can get technical help with documents etc. from the PSU (PERSONAL SUPPORT UNIT). In London they are to be found in room M104, Royal Courts of Justice, the Strand, Tel. 02079477701/7703 or 4th floor Room 408, First Avenue House, High Holburn, Principal Registry of the Family Division, Tel 02079477737.

EDM127 (Source: PIMS)

That this House regrets the Government's proposals to retain secrecy within the family courts; believes that this secrecy permeates bad practice throughout the whole system of children services; feels that it is possible to protect the identity of the child while allowing parents to talk and seek advice publicly about their treatment in the family courts, and that professional witnesses should be uniquely identified to monitor consistency; further believes that every case should have an anonymised judgement handed to the parents that they can discuss publicly; and calls on the Government to recognise that there are very serious problems in the system that have been postponed rather than resolved by the limited proposals contained within the consultation document.

EDM128 (Source: PIMS)

That this House notes that in an email dated 24th October 2000, John Radford, Doncaster's then Director of Public Health, described the issue of research on babies by Dr David Southall at Doncaster Hospital in the late 1980s as `potentially a hot potato as to my recall the intervention resulted in increased deaths and didn't have proper consent'; expresses concern that the details of this research and its outcomes have been covered up by the health authorities; expresses particular concern that the research protocol specifically required that no action be taken to prevent cot death in the children selected until sufficient data had been collected; notes that the inquiry into CNEP ignored CNEP in Doncaster; and calls for a public inquiry into this and other research managed by Dr Southall to identify why the checks and balances in the system failed.

EDM129 (Source: PIMS)

That this House notes that it is common practice for a firm of solicitors to perform outsourced work for a local authority and also to represent parents when parties in cases against the same local authority; notes and is surprised that this conflict of interest is acceptable under the professional conduct rules; understands that some parents would be surprised to find that this is the case; and calls for the Law Society to require that parents be asked to confirm in writing that they recognise that the firm they are instructing is conflicted in this way as part of the client engagement process.

EDM130 (Source: PIMS)

That this House notes that from time to time the advice given by an expert appointed by one party to a court case is used to permit the exclusion of capacity of a further party to that case and then the Official Solicitor is brought in to act on behalf of the latter party; believes that it is an unacceptable conflict of interest; and calls, notwithstanding the duty of experts to the court, for the Government to introduce legislation to prevent this from occurring.

Don't just take my word for the rest of my allegations. Please read the following articles from the *Daily Mail* and the *Sunday Telegraph* as they very accurately depict the mounting and highly-justified public disquiet over the secret Family Courts and the 'adoption industry'.

Courts won't reveal rulings in adoption cases
by Ben Leapman
Sunday Telegraph, 8 August 2007

Pauline Goodwin's baby was taken from her but she was denied a copy of the judgment. The court service has now apologised

Family Courts are refusing to tell mothers why their babies are being taken away and put up for forced adoption.

Two mothers have told The Sunday Telegraph that their pain at losing their children was made worse by not knowing the grounds on which judges took the decisions.

Both women had their requests for copies of the judgments turned down repeatedly. As a result, they were prevented from launching legal battles to win their babies back, because appeals cannot be lodged without -written judgments.

Critics claimed that the cases are an extreme example of the secrecy that runs throughout the family court system. Earlier this summer, the Government abandoned plans to open up hearings to the media.

John Hemming, the Liberal Democrat MP and chairman of Justice for Families, said: "It seems quite strange that somebody can have their child removed and adopted, and the system will not give reasons.

"This arises from the secrecy of proceedings and the fact that people are allowed to misbehave professionally in the Family Courts without any fear of sanctions against them."

The cases are the latest in a series highlighted by this newspaper which have raised concerns about the workings of the Family Courts and social services.

It included a professional couple who had their daughter taken away because the mother has a history of mental illness and the father was "confrontational" towards social workers, while another couple were told they cannot have their two daughters back despite being cleared of allegations of abuse.

Last year, 2,120 babies were taken for adoption before their first birthday, almost three times as many as a decade ago. Adoptions leapt after councils were offered cash incentives to increase the number.

One of the latest cases involved Pauline Goodwin, 39, from Merseyside, who suffered a breakdown after her marriage ended. As she struggled to cope, her baby girl, born in 2005, was taken away by social services at birth.

At a court hearing in June last year, held at a time when she was temporarily homeless, Judge Wallwork ruled at Liverpool Family Court that the baby should remain in foster care.

The mother says she was told that despite the outcome of the case, the judgment would not be critical of her. However, in the 14 months since the hearing, her repeated requests to obtain a copy of the judgment have proved fruitless. She has been told by social workers that her daughter has now been adopted.

She said: "They had my baby adopted, then they said they make no findings against me, but they won't give me the court order. I need the judgment because I want to lodge an appeal. It's supposed to be within 28 days but it has been more than 12 months.

"If they give me the transcripts I can prove the whole thing was wrong, and my baby wouldn't be where she is now, she would be with me."

Sharon Harkness, 37, also from Merseyside, won the first round of her courtroom battle when social workers tried to take her baby son away. In August 2005, at the High Court in London, Mr Justice Holman turned down a bid by a local authority to take the boy, then only three months old, into foster care.

However, at Liverpool Family Court in November, Judge Roddy reversed the earlier decision and granted the council a care order. The baby was removed from his family and is now living with prospective adoptive parents.

In the intervening 21 months, repeated requests by Mrs Harkness for a written judgment have been refused or ignored. She said: "It's within my rights to at least see the kind of care order they've put my son on. It's like they've taken my baby and forgotten to give me the receipt."

At one point she tried to go to the European Court of Human Rights in Strasbourg, only to be told that the court could not consider her case because she had no written judgment on which to base it.

At the end of last week, after The Sunday Telegraph took up the cases with the Judicial Communications Office in London, officials issued an apology within hours and finally pledged that both women would receive the vital documents within days.

In Miss Goodwin's case, a spokesman said: "Her Majesty's Court Service would like to apologise that in this case, the transcripts were not provided as requested. There appears to have been a breakdown in communications. The transcription company will prepare the transcripts next week and once they are approved by the judge, the court will send them out."

Regarding Mrs Harkness, the spokesman said: "There was an ambiguity in the original order which had not been corrected and caused a delay in the process. The transcript has now been produced and is with the judge, prior to being sent to the family next week."

Pauline (story and photo above) has learned a lot during her 3 year struggle with the 'SS'. She now helps and advises other parents in distress and also organises demonstrations. Contact: 07859080258.

My baby will be taken from me the moment it's born
by Helen Weathers
Daily Mail, 6 September 2007

The daughter of teachers and with a glittering academic future, Fran was delighted when she became pregnant. But social services discovered the illness she thought she'd put behind her - and will confiscate her daughter when she is born...

Fran Lyon is due to give birth to her first child - a daughter she has already named Molly - on January 3. But the prospect, far from being one of joyous anticipation, fills her with a dread that keeps her awake at night.

It's not because Fran doesn't want the child. She does. Desperately. And not because she is frightened of the pain of labour. She is prepared for that.

It is what happens afterwards that fuels Fran's anxiety. And there can be no preparation for that pain.

For within 30 minutes of birth, barring any medical complications, Molly will be handed by doctors to social workers. They have instructions to take away Fran's newborn baby and place her in foster care.

The 22-year-old will then be transferred from the maternity wing to a gynaecological ward, because Northumberland Council has decided that Fran - who has never harmed anyone in her life - is potentially a risk to other mothers and their babies.

Fran has no idea if she will be able to touch her baby, even for a minute, before leaving hospital alone, or if she will ever get her daughter back. Her biggest fear is that she won't, and that Molly will be put up for adoption.

'It is incredibly upsetting not knowing if I will be allowed even to hold my baby,' says Fran, a charity worker. 'Until social services became involved in my life, I was having a normal pregnancy and was full of excitement.

'They have taken away what should be the most precious time in my life - and I will never get that back. I'm already in love with my baby. I can feel her moving, I talk to her. I've bought her baby books and clothes. You just can't undo that attachment.'

Fran is an intelligent and articulate woman. She has nine A-starred GCSEs, five grade A A-levels and is in the third year of a neuroscience degree at Edinburgh University - which she is completing at home in Hexham, Northumberland.

However, what concerns Hexham Children's Services, which is part of Northumberland Council, is Fran's medical history.

Having had a difficult relationship with her parents, who are teachers in good state schools, from the age of 15, she started self harming. Fran spent three years - on and off - in psychiatric hospitals.

Her problems appear to have begun when she was raped by an acquaintance at the age of 14. Diagnosed with a borderline personality disorder, she was discharged from a therapeutic facility in 2002, where she had spent 13 months, and spent nine months as an outpatient.

Today, she needs no medication and, according to her former psychiatrist, Dr Stella Newrith, 'has made a significant recovery to the point where her difficulties are indistinguishable from those of much of the general population'.

In a letter to Northumberland Council, Dr Newrith, who treated Fran for a year when she was 16 and has known her for many years, stated: 'There has never been any clinical evidence to suggest that Fran would put herself or others at risk, and there is certainly no evidence to suggest she would put a child at risk of emotional, physical or sexual harm.'

Furthermore, she said: 'I would view the removal of Fran's baby as an extraordinarily heavy-handed gesture. It is also my professional opinion that doing so would be an infringement of Fran's human rights, as it would be much the same as removing a child from someone from the general population.'

Yet on August 16, a child protection case conference recommended that Fran's baby should be taken away at birth - a decision based in part on the contents of a letter from consultant paediatrician Dr Martin Ward Platt, who has never met Fran and could not be present at the meeting.

In his letter, Dr Ward Platt states that 'even in the absence of psychological assessment, if the professionals were concerned on the evidence available that [this woman] probably does fabricate or induce illness, there would be no option but to put the baby into foster care at birth pending a post-natal forensic psychological assessment'.

However, he warned that it was necessary first to establish as far as possible whether or not Fran does suffer from this illness - something Fran claims they have failed to do.

Fran has never been diagnosed with this condition, yet she has nevertheless been deemed by Northumberland Council as someone likely to suffer from Munchausen's Syndrome by Proxy, a controversial and unproven condition in which a parent - usually the mother - makes up or induces an illness in her child to draw attention to herself.

And so, unless a judicial review next week rules in Fran's favour, her baby Molly will almost certainly be taken away at birth.

'I can understand why they might have concerns about my past, but the speed with which they have come to this conclusion, despite the evidence of my own psychiatrist, is terrifying,' she says.

'I was at the case conference and it lasted just ten minutes.

'This letter from Dr Ward Platt was given to me just five minutes before the meeting started, and when it was produced, the chairman said there was no point - in the light of what this letter stated - even considering the other evidence which I wanted to present, which was letters of support from psychiatrists.

'I think they simply panicked, and when people panic they make, in my opinion, bad judgments. I left that meeting numb with shock. I'd had absolutely no time to digest the letter or argue my case, and I was so horrified at what they'd said that I just couldn't even begin to respond to it.

'I have never harmed anyone in my life. I have no criminal convictions. I believe I can be a good mother to Molly - but they are not even prepared to give me a chance to prove that.

'I have offered to stay in a mother and baby unit after Molly's birth for as long as they want, and to be monitored. I would be prepared to stay there for 18 years if it meant I could be with my baby. But that, it seems, is not even an option.'

Fran's case is far from unusual. Two thousands babies under one year old were taken from their parents last year by social services - three times the number ten years ago. Critics believe councils are doing this to help meet government adoption 'targets'.

Liberal Democrat MP John Hemming, chairman of the Justice for Families campaign group, certainly thinks so.

'How can it be in the child's best interests to take a baby away from its mother at birth? The reason why they do it is because it's much harder to take away a baby the longer it spends with its mother, and a healthy newborn baby is so much easier to find adoptive parents for.

'It is estimated that 97 per cent of babies taken away from their mothers at birth, on the basis that the mothers are 'capable of emotional abuse', are never returned to them - and that is simply scandalous.

'Of course, there are cases where it is right to do so, but the whole public family law system is corrupt because of the secrecy which surrounds it. Decisions are based on opinion and conjecture, rather than fact and evidence.

'What does Fran's case tell us? That no woman who has been raped or had mental health problems can be allowed to have a baby, even years later?

'What could be more traumatic than for a mother to have her baby taken away at birth? It's monstrous. That, in itself, can cause mental health problems, which is then used by social services against the mother as a reason not to return the baby. It becomes a self-fulfilling prophesy.

'There has been a massive increase in younger babies being taken into care, before there is even any evidence of harm - and you have to ask why that is.'

Despite her own troubled past, Fran Lyon is convinced she can be a good parent, and is desperate to prove that. From the start, she has been open and honest with social workers about her medical history, but she feels this has been used against her.

Although she describes her childhood as 'difficult', she refuses to elaborate, other than to say that she is close to her mother and younger brother, but has no contact with her father.

The catalyst for her severe mental health problems was, she says, the rape she suffered when she was 14.

She told police that she was attacked while working as a Saturday volunteer in a charity shop in Northampton, when the shop's founder - a middle-aged man - drove her to an empty warehouse supposedly to pick up supplies for the shop.

When Fran reported the rape, he was interviewed by police. Three more women claiming they, too, had been attacked came forward and agreed to testify against him. However, in 2001 the man killed himself before the Crown Prosecution Service could decide whether to proceed.

'After the rape, I became clinically depressed,' says Fran. 'I lost a huge amount of weight and was admitted to a psychiatric hospital after trying to kill myself with an overdose of tablets. It wasn't a cry for help; I wanted to die because of what he had done to me.'

She spent the next three years, on and off, in residential psychiatric hospitals in Oxford, Nottingham and London after being diagnosed with a borderline personality disorder, in her case characterised by self-harming, instability and suicidal tendencies.

For the final 13 months, Fran went to a therapeutic residential clinic, where she attended individual psychotherapy sessions and group analysis before being discharged as an outpatient.

By the time she was 18, she appeared to have put her problems behind her.

She started to flourish, taking five A-levels at Orpington College in Kent and applying to study neuroscience at Edinburgh University.

At the same time, she worked for two mental health charities, Borderline and Personality Plus. It was through that job, two years ago, that she met the man who is the father of Molly.

'Of course, I was worried when I fell pregnant. I wondered how we would cope as a couple, because we weren't living together,' says Fran.

'But once that wore off, I was excited. I would go shopping with my mum to baby departments, buying books and looking at prams.'

But a few weeks ago, all normality ended. Social services suddenly became involved when Fran phoned the police after what she describes as a 'disturbing incident' with her partner. Fran's relationship with him ended immediately.

'The case was referred to social services and I was interviewed by two social workers, who said from the beginning that they would have to look at the whole family, not just one person in isolation,' says Fran.

'At that first meeting, they asked about my concerns regarding the baby's father, but then it became clear through their questions that their investigation was centred on me. I have never made a secret of my mental health problems. I felt I had nothing to hide.'

Fran was co- operative, she says, because she naively thought children's services would offer her help and support. She was stunned when she received a letter informing her that a child protection case conference would be held on August 16.

'That's when I became frightened and thought for the first time: "Are they going to take my baby away from me?"

'I couldn't believe how everything had happened so quickly. When you are up against a big system such as social services, it is very easy to feel overrun and overwhelmed.'

Realising the seriousness of the situation, Fran instructed a solicitor and contacted her former psychiatrist, Dr Stella Newrith, who offered her full support.

A second psychiatrist, who Fran knew through her charity work, offered a character reference stating: 'I have no doubt that her diligence and capacity, particularly in dealing with complex emotional situations, will stand her in good stead for the rigours of parenthood.'

Yet these testimonials, Fran says, were never even read out at the conference after Dr Ward Platt's letter was produced.

Northumberland Council insists that two highly experienced doctors - another consultant paediatrician and a medical consultant - attended the case conference.

Neither they, nor anyone else present - including Fran solicitor - made any objection. Feeling stunned and intimidated by what she had heard, she felt unable to speak out.

Everything she wanted to say will now be heard - with the help of a new solicitor who specialises in such cases - at appeal.

According to MP John Hemming, Fran should win her case; but there is no guarantee that she will. Both he and Fran are particularly concerned that last week social workers contacted the psychiatrist who provided a character reference for Fran. They believe this was done with the intention of 'pressurising' the witness into withdrawing his support, and undermining Fran's appeal.

It was seemingly suggested by a social worker to the doctor in question that Fran had given incorrect details about her health to hospital staff: in short, doubt was cast on the reality of an ectopic pregnancy Fran suffered on Christmas Eve two years ago.

'Is it ethical for social workers to go behind my back and speak to my witnesses, discussing my private confidential medical history and suggesting to them that I might have made things up?' says Fran.

'I did have an ectopic pregnancy, and I have the scars to prove that I had abdominal surgery.' Mr Hemming goes further, describing such behaviour as akin to witness nobbling. He also claims it is not uncommon for social workers to pressurise witnesses - a punishable practice in the criminal courts.

'There is a culture in which the end is seen to justify the means, and sometimes the means employed would not be tolerated in any other court of law,' he says. 'Yet if anyone tries to speak out, they are guilty of contempt of court. The whole family court system, because of the secrecy which surrounds it, is vulnerable to bad practice. Social workers are under pressure not to lose cases.' Northumberland Council, while legally prevented from speaking about individual cases, insists there is nothing sinister in their actions.

A spokeswoman said it was the court which would make the ultimate decision, after hearing legal representation from both sides. 'Safeguarding children is our top priority,' said a spokeswoman. 'We speak to all sides without bias or pressure. 'We would welcome a review of the family court arrangements, and support transparency, as long as this is in the best interests of the children.

'Safeguarding arrangements have been praised as good following a rigorous inspection by a number of Government departments. It was specifically noted that "good action was taken to enable parents to keep their children safe in the home and the community. Our duty to safeguard children is our only motivation, and we strive to keep children with their families wherever possible, or extended families if that is not possible.

'We do not have numerical targets for adoption; nor have we received any financial rewards in relation to adoption figures.'

As for Fran, the final four months of her pregnancy are filled with stress and uncertainty, and the nagging terror that her worst nightmare will become a reality and her baby daughter will be snatched away from her. 'Some days I feel positive,' she says quietly.

'But others I feel totally overwhelmed. All I am asking for is a chance to prove that I will be a good mother.'

Sadly, that wish may not be granted her.

AND THEN? Fran flees the country, see the link below!

·   **IMPORTANT!** The miserable wretch who was chairman of the so-called 'Case Conference' that lasted 15 minutes should be dismissed in disgrace. His name is **BOB HILL** and he should never be allowed near any case conference ever again!

Councils making millions in incentives after snatching record numbers of babies for adoption

by Sue Reid

Daily Mail, 2 July 2007

Councils are being offered bonuses of millions of pounds if they meet controversial State adoption targets.

Confidential figures obtained by the Daily Mail show that £36million in 'reward grants' has been promised to English councils in an attempt by Labour to increase adoptions of children by 50 per cent.

The money-earning targets were introduced by Tony Blair in 2000 and were intended to lift more older children out of the care system.

But critics say it is the most 'adoptable' babies and children under four who are being removed in the biggest numbers.

Court battle: Mark and Nicky Webster won the fight to keep little Brandon

More than 900 newborn babies are now being taken from their mothers each year, a 300 per cent increase in little more than a decade

The number of children aged between a week and a month removed from their parents has risen to 1,300 annually, a rise of 141 per cent in the same time.

In the past two weeks alone, eight newborn babies have been taken from their mothers at hospitals in Newcastle and North Tyneside.

The number is so high there are not enough foster parents in the area. One baby - thought to be the ninth taken from its parents - is being cared for in a special hospital unit because there is no foster home available.

Liberal Democrat MP John Hemming has demanded an explanation.

He said: "We are seeing a massive increase in the forced removal of newborns. Babies are being taken before they can even be breastfed. Social workers are seizing very young children on the flimsiest of excuses and giving them to other families.

"This smacks of social engineering on a grand scale. The offer of monetary rewards for meeting the targets has created a frenzy among social workers. There are council targets for recycling rubbish and now targets for recycling children."

Figures prepared by the Department for Local Government and Community Cohesion show that two councils - Essex and Kent - were offered more than £2million over three years to encourage additional adoptions.

Four others - Norfolk, Gloucestershire, Cheshire and Hampshire - were promised £1million in extra funds.

Critics say very young children are specifically selected - even before birth - by social workers to get the bonuses. It is believed that 1,000 each year are wrongly taken from their parents.

Last week a court ruled that a couple whose first three children were taken for adoption should keep their fourth, now a year old

Abuse allegations against Mark and Nicky Webster turned out to be false. But they will never see their three lost children again because adoptions are irreversible.

Despite the cash inducements, adoptions of older children - the very ones who were meant to be helped - have dropped dramatically.

The number of over-sevens adopted in England has fallen from 100 in 1996 to 50 last year out of a total of 5,400 adoptions.

Beverley Beech, of the Association for Improvements in the Maternity Services - a body which advises new mothers - said: "The Government is denying that social workers are targeting babies for adoption.

"But the desperate calls on our helpline from pregnant women who have already been told by social workers, for no good reason, that they will lose their babies immediately they are born, or from mothers of new babies taken for adoption, prove these denials are not true."

Campaigners also want an opening up of family courts, where adoptions are overseen in utmost secrecy. Parents are warned that if they tell anyone - even their closest family - what goes on they could face prison for contempt of court.

Family law solicitor Sarah Harman, the sister of Labour deputy leader Harriet Harman, said: "It's not the welfare of the child that is being protected - it's the welfare of social workers".

North Tyneside Council said last night: "In the past few weeks steps have been taken to protect six babies at serious risk of significant harm. In all cases the mothers have frequent contact with their babies and are encouraged to breastfeed."

Newcastle Council confirmed that two babies had been removed during the same period.

MP bids to lift secrecy in family courts
By Ben Leapman and Andrew Alderson
The Sunday Telegraph, 7 July 2007

A legal bid to lift the secrecy surrounding children taken from parents and put up for adoption has been launched by an MP.

John Hemming claims to have details of 90 cases where mistakes were made in family courts, whose hearings are held behind closed doors.

He has applied to the High Court for permission to pass details to watchdogs -- including the General Medical Council, Solicitors' Regulatory Authority and the Bar Council. If turned down, he is threatening to disclose the information in the Commons under Parliamentary privilege.

Mr. Hemming, the Liberal Democrat MP for Birmingham Yardley, said: "We know that there are cases where children are wrongly removed from their parents and put up for adoption. This, however, is far more common than people think. It is important for an MP to be able to speak about injustice."

The Sunday Telegraph revealed last week that judges, senior lawyers and politicians have relaunched attempts to open up family court proceedings to more scrutiny - even though Lord Falconer seemed to have crushed the move less than three weeks ago, shortly before stepping down as Lord Chancellor.

Campaigners said they have renewed hopes of bringing about change under Gordon Brown's Government.

The current law means reporters or members of the public cannot attend family court hearings, see documents, review evidence or obtain copies of judgments.

Last week's article led to a huge response from readers. One, who wrote in anonymously, said a female relative took her daughter into hospital only to be accused of abusing the girl.

The accusation led to a second child, born weeks later, being taken into care almost at birth. The mother was cleared of abuse but the children have not been returned because they are "settled".

Sarah Harman, sister of Harriet, the Labour Party deputy leader, and others formed Families Action for Court Transparency and Openness (Facto) three years ago in an attempt to open up the Family Courts system.

Other leading figures have backed the campaign, including Lord Justice Wall, a senior Court of Appeal judge. He believes that allowing the media to report proceedings would help rebut accusations that the family justice system was secretive. "I find it unacceptable that conscientious magistrates and judges should be accused of administering 'secret justice'."

Family Courts in England and Wales hear 400,000 cases a year, mostly divorces and child custody cases. However, in some 20,000 cases a year, local councils apply to remove children from parents on the grounds that they are abusive of neglectful.

Concerns over secrecy were heightened two weeks ago by the case of the Webster family from Cromer, Norfolk. Mark Webster, 34, and wife, Nicky, 26, were told they could keep their fourth child Brandon, aged 13 months.

The couple fled to Ireland to have him after claiming they were wrongly accused of child abuse and had their first three children taken into care four years ago and later adopted.

Norfolk county council withdrew proceedings to take Brandon into care after conceding that injuries to one of the couple's other children might have been caused by vitamin deficiencies. The authority said it no longer relied on evidence which suggested that leg fractures were caused by abuse.

New figures show that more than half of all children taken into care below the age of five end up being adopted.

Critics claim that targets set by Tony Blair to increase the number of adoptions, intended to cut the number of children languishing in foster care, have given social workers a perverse incentive to seize more children, a claim strongly disputed by the British Association for Adoption and Fostering.

The Government's priority is to increase the number of children adopted from care while not compromising the quality and stability of adoptive placements. The most effective measure of performance is to deliver adoptive placements that last and that are properly supported....................

Adopters want BABIES or Toddlers not older children!

LOTS OF MONEY TO BE MADE BY ADOPTION AGENCIES TOO!! Local authorities that do not snatch enough children to meet their 'adoption targets' get into trouble!

SEE THIS ARTICLE FROM THE TELEGRAPH!

'Shaming' policy on adoption attacked
by Nicole Martin
Daily Telegraph, 19 June 2001

THE Government's decision to highlight eight local councils with poor adoption records was criticised yesterday.

John Hutton, the health minister, named the councils in Barnet, Lambeth, Slough, Newham, Peterborough, Coventry, Northamptonshire and Torbay as targets for a new adoption task force. But adoption agencies and social services said the "naming and shaming" approach could be detrimental to the 5,000 children waiting to be adopted in Britain.

Felicity Collier, chief executive of the British Agencies for Adoption and Fostering, said that the policy could worsen the recruitment shortage in social services, where a fifth of posts remain vacant. She said: "What really concerns me is that if I was an adopter and I lived in one of the areas that the Department of Health announces is lagging behind the pack, adoption might look unappealing."

Moira Gibb, president elect of the Association of Directors of Social Services, welcomed the task force but doubted the effectiveness of identifying authorities.

Mr Hutton denied that the Government was "naming and shaming". He said: "There is a steady rise in adoptions. But we have to keep the momentum going. The task force will help by identifying barriers to change and supporting those councils that need help."

9. YOU CAN WIN IF YOU FIGHT

I try to help parents who are desperately trying to recover or at least make contact either with their children or worse still, with 'newborn babies' snatched by Social Services from mothers that have never caused them harm. Those social workers who snatch, and those lawyers, 'experts' and especially the **'ESTABLISHMENT JUDGES'** who combine to help them should all be sent to prison for **'CRIMES AGAINST HUMANITY'** for a very long time! I will explain and justify this later on. They can be beaten, but only if you fight from start to finish as the following shows!

June 22 2007

Dear Ian,

THANK YOU SO MUCH

You would not believe it but social services actually want <u>nothing</u> to do with us!

Para 49 in the case outline they actually said " Should the Court deem it in Tess's best interest to be rehabilitated to her parents care, the local Authority do not feel that this is a case where they are able to share parental responsibility with the parents or to carry out their duties under an interim care order effectively due to the **lack of co-operation from the parents.**

The social worker actually CONGRATULATED me saying that Andy and I were unique! She said "you have fought your corner and fought it well."

This was because of <u>your</u> advise. Fight like a tiger you said, well it would appear that they are no match for Tigers Ian!

THANK YOU once again.

Sue, Andy and Family

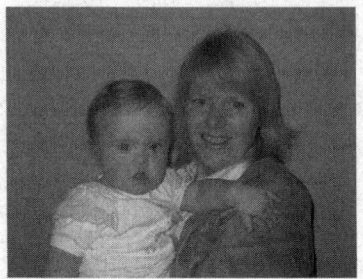

Sue & Tess

Sarah and Ian Walton are Pleased to Announce the Arrival of their new Baby Girl

Baby Emily Arrived AT 22:07pm on The 31st July 2008!

She Weighed in At 7 pound and 3 ounces.

Thank you to all the staff at the private hospital at ?????????

Special Thanks to our friends for keeping it quiet!

Baby Emily Is In Hiding Now and Will Not Be Registered, So Shw Will Never Be Found By the Social Services. So Keep You're Kidnapping Hands Away. You're Not Having Her!

Here Is A Photo Of Our Beautiful Baby:

From Catherine Sara

----- Original Message -----

To: ian josephs

Sent: Saturday, August 04, 2007 6:26 AM

Dear Ian,

I am posting this as asked by members whom you have worked day and night to help in every way possible.

I know you are very modest and expect nothing in return for all your help.

Day and night you answer the call.

If only all Social Workers, Lawyers, Judges, etc were as dedicated to the higher good as you are,

Then oh what a world we would have of happiness and joy and light for ALL OF US.

May your light shine ever brighter and may all our lights shine like beacons until all our lights touch and spread to cover

OUR MOTHER ....EARTH.

THE ONE MOTHER WE ALL SHARE.

Thank you Ian.

We salute you. 😊😊😊

All it takes for evil to succeed is that good people do nothing.

----- Original Message -----

To: ian@monaco.mc

Sent: Saturday, August 04, 2007 1:03 AM

Hi Ian, Dave and myself would like you to know all the mothers and people we have spoken too. All agree that you are one of the few genuien persons we all know. I dont think you quite realise the hope and the determination that you give to us when we feel like giving up you have a certain power that gives us all insperation to keep fighting you are very special to us all, and we won't forget you I will still be contacting you when this is all over with. I will even bring Connor to see you and tell him of all your support and insperation that you gave to us I will tell him you are the main man the one we first found when you was snatched from our arms.

Know this Ian because it is the truth when I say to you that you live up to more than our exspectations your an angle a bright light in a very dark wicked world showing everyone the truth about the ss,lawyers, and the evil judges we were all lost until you showed us the way to fight.

Sharon xx

Dear Ian

I thought I should just write to you to advise you that after great effort on my part and after following the excellent advice you gave me I can now report that my daughter has been returned to my care.

I cannot thank you enough for the advice you gave me and which I took. It was from your advice that I decided to stand up for myself and sought advice from another solicitor who was willing to give me her assurance that she would fight my case every step of the way.

Needless to say I had my day in court and although the final hearing is still to happen in July 08 my daughter has been returned to me and the care plan is for reunification. Thank you so much. Please keep up the good work. If you would like the name of the solicitor I used I would be happy to pass it on to you so that others may take advantage of having good legal representation in court.

Kind regards and God bless you.

Mandy Price

----- Original Message -----
To: ian@monaco.mc
Subject: supervision order

Hellow Ian,

Thank you for all your advice,it really helped, fight like a tiger you said, and that is exactly what we did and our children are back.

Nancy

Baby 'snatched' from mother minutes after birth is ordered BACK into foster care

by David Wilkes

Daily Mail, 2 February 2008

A mother who had her baby son taken illegally by social workers wept yesterday as a court ordered he should be put in care after all.

The 18-year-old, who cannot be identified for legal reasons, broke down in tears and had to be supported by two relatives as she received the devastating news.

It has been a three-day rollercoaster for the young mother. Her son, known as Baby G for legal reasons, was snatched from her in hospital by social services two hours after birth.

Family courts decide on children's lives behind closed doors

Then the infant was returned to her later that day after a High Court judge ruled the officials had acted illegally because they did not have a court order.

Yesterday, after a further hearing before the Family Proceedings Court over two days, district judge Richard Inglis upheld an application by Nottingham council for an interim care order.

The mother attended the behind closed doors hearing yesterday but did not give evidence.

"It has been a thoroughly traumatic few days for her and she is devastated and drained," a friend said afterwards.

The case highlights the lack of transparency in the family courts, with the reasons behind the decision will not be revealed to the public.

Liberal Democrat MP John Hemming, who campaigns for greater openness in the system, said: "If they are going to take such draconian action as to separate a newborn baby from its mother, they should be willing to justify it in the open.

"What worries me most about these types of cases is they do not explain what they are doing or why.

"There are other options, like a mother and child foster placement or an assessment centre so that they do not have to be separated.

"But they almost seem to revel in separating newborn children from their mothers in this country."

Baby G was born in hospital in Nottingham at 2am on Wednesday and social services took him around 4am. His mother, who has mental health problems, has just left local authority care.

The baby was taken after staff at the hospital were shown a "birth plan" that was prepared by social workers.

The plan said the mother, who had a troubled childhood, was to be separated from the child, and no contact would be allowed without supervision by social workers.

Mr Justice Munby made an order in the High Court in London that the baby should be returned to his mother, which he duly was.

In his ruling, he said that "on the face of it" social services officials had acted unlawfully because they had not obtained a court order.

Giving his decision at the Family Proceedings Court in Nottingham yesterday, Judge Inglis said: "The court has decided that the welfare of G requires that he lives in local authority foster care on an interim basis.

"His mother will have frequent periods of contact with him.

"When further inquiries have been made the court expects to be in a better position later this year to make a decision about who should care for G."

Afterwards, Nottingham council said that the interim care order "enables the council to provide appropriate protection for the baby, whilst continuing to support the mother, who is also our concern".

It added: "The council and a range of other partner agencies had enough concern for the baby's welfare during the pregnancy to believe that action would be needed to protect the baby when it was born."

The decision was made at a case conference in December 2007 at which the mother and her legal representative were present, the council said.

"The law does not allow application for a court order before birth. The protection plan made in advance included the intention to apply for a care order immediately following the birth of this baby."

Margaret McGlade, chairman of Nottingham's safeguarding children board, said there will be a review of "the communications between all parties, particularly following the baby's birth to see if there are any lessons to be learned".

Last night the mother's solicitors, Bhatia Best, said they are considering a renewed application to the High Court under the European Convention on Human Rights.

JUSTICE IN SECRET

THEY are the most secret courts in Britain, making fundamental decisions about more than a million lives each year.

The Family Courts sit without jury or public scrutiny to hear cases of adoption and care proceedings brought by councils. The reason given is the protection of youngsters' confidentiality.

The Adoption Act 1976 prevents the courts admitting anyone who is not an officer of the court, one of the parties, lawyers or witnesses.

Families who believe they may lose their children because of a miscarriage of justice are prevented by law from making any part of their case public.

However, high-profile cases, Government adoption targets and public unease about enforced adoptions mean the rules are now being re-examined.

If you 'cooperate' when the 'SS' make threats, they will at once class you as 'easy meat' and you will soon be 'lost!' The only chance you have of winning is to ignore threats and 'fight like a tiger'! Always be the opposite in character to the type they say you are! If they say you are aggressive be very quiet, and if they say you are too feeble to control your children start acting assertively but never tell them what you intend to do next!

In many courts if you represent yourself you can get technical help with documents etc. from the PSU (PERSONAL SUPPORT UNIT). In London they are to be found in Room M104, Royal Courts of Justice, the Strand, Tel 02079477701/7703 or 4th floor Room 408, First Avenue House, High Holburn, Principal Registry of the Family Division, Tel 02079477737.

10. HOW TO FACE THE 'SS'!

NEVER, NEVER cringe and obey social workers who are hostile or disrespectful, no matter how many threats they make to "take your children" or "cut off your contact". You, like every human being, have a right to be treated at all times with kindness and respect and you should say so, frequently if necessary! Threats that in effect amount to moral blackmail should always be greeted with polite amazement that those whose duty is to help families should shout and issue threats! Always apologise very politely for doing what **YOU** think right and never get so worried by their threats that you feel forced to give in and obey!! Always meet social workers on an 'equal footing' so that only one of them can meet you if you are alone and if two of them come together, insist you have a friend or other family member present so you are **NEVER OUTNUMBERED**. Their threats are bluff as even if you do everything they say, they will long before then have made up their minds to take your children and/or cut your contact anyway. So if you do obey them, they will (after thanking you for making their task so easy) graciously let you 'wave goodbye' to your precious children!

BEWARE and **REFUSE** if they decide to make an unannounced 'home visit' or worse still ask you to take your children to the hospital for a 'check-up' on a Friday afternoon! In the latter case they will keep you waiting until 5 or 6pm and then snatch your children when it is too late for you to get legal help or advice before Monday! They have no legal power (only the courts have that) so if they dare to threaten you instead of helping you, **NEVER** give in to their outrageous blackmail, and **NEVER**, obey **ANY** of the loathsome creatures who dare to behave as described above!

Some critics of the 'SS' in an attempt to seem reasonable and moderate claim that "there are many excellent social workers in 'child protection' but also there are a minority who do not behave as they should". This to put it politely is an understatement of staggering timidity! Are there any excellent members of the Ku

Klux Klan? How about suicide bombers? Were there any nice people in the Spanish Inquisition, the Gestapo, Stalin's KGB, or Murder Incorporated? Any worthwhile and sincerely motivated social workers who join the 'child protection service' do not stay long once they see what goes on. Once they realise what they have to do they either transfer out of 'child protection' into a different section or if that is not possible, rather than continue the criminal kidnapping of newborn babies they **RESIGN**!! That is why the 'SS' are constantly advertising for new recruits. Nearly all of those who still remain 'in the service' taking babies from sane mothers who have never caused those babies to suffer any harm are quite simply '**SCUM**'!

If the worst happens and your children are snatched by force, try and ruin the 'SS' adoption plans! **DO NOT LET POLICE OR SOCIAL WORKERS IN YOUR HOUSE TO REMOVE CHILDREN UNLESS THEY SHOW YOU A COURT ORDER**. Make sure your children cling on to you until the 'SS' rip them away by force! Shout and cry that wicked people are stealing them. Cuddle those poor children telling them that "Mummy loves them" and will try to get them back! Any children aged 4 or more will remember this for the rest of their lives and will not believe the 'SS' who will later tell them that "their Mummy does not want them" and soon they will have a new "for ever Mummy and Daddy!" It is worth upsetting your beloved children briefly to make sure that always in the future they will remember you loved them and wanted to keep them from the 'child stealers!'

What if your child is badly neglected or injured whilst 'in care' of fosterers? Well, take photographs of the bruises then go to a magistrate and just like the 'SS' ask for an 'emergency protection order' emphasising that fosterers must surely be subject to the same laws as birth parents! Follow up by taking your photos to the police demanding a prosecution failing which your photos will go to the local press! Fight like a tiger and you can win your children back!

After all, even *The Guardian*, the social worker's favourite newspaper (earning vast sums from hundreds of 'SS' adverts for jobs) is getting worried about adoptions.

Unfit to be a mother?

In the 60s, many women were forced to give up their illegitmate babies. Everyone now agrees that was a shocking practice. But a recent rise in the number of newborns up for adoption suggests we have found new reasons - or excuses - to take children from their parents. Kate Hilpern investigates

The Guardian, 15 January 2008

Laura was about to give birth in hospital when the authorities arrived to take her baby. "The doctor just handed her over and that was that," she says. "All I wanted was to die," she adds, barely audible. Laura had been in a violent marriage. She left her husband when she was pregnant, but went on to have a breakdown. She says she had recovered by the time social services got involved, but they encouraged her to sign papers consenting to the adoption of her unborn baby. She refused. They insisted. She still refused. They said they would take the baby anyway.

Laura's daughter was initially cared for by foster carers and she was allowed to visit five days a week, although there was no opportunity to breastfeed. Once the adopters had been identified, the meetings were reduced to one day a week at a time and finally she was offered a "goodbye visit".

"My life will never be the same again," she says. "Somewhere out there is my baby and I don't know where. You can't explain the psychological effects of something like that. It's beyond words. It's beyond anything."

Government statistics show that 1,300 babies under a month old are now being taken into care and subsequently adopted, compared with 500 in 1997. Campaigners, including members of the legal establishment, academics, an MP and even some social workers themselves, are worried that we are returning to the draconian attitude of the 1960s, when society was more eager to whisk babies away for adoption than support mothers in keeping their children. Today's social workers, they say, are rushing cases through to hit the government's adoption targets just as social workers decades ago hurried to fulfil the dreams of childless couples waiting in the wings.

Others view the increase in baby adoptions as positive. Far better that children begin life in a loving adoptive family than risk multiple placements in and out of the care system, they argue. When you consider that the key reasons for today's babies being removed are drug and alcohol abuse and domestic violence, this is clearly a danger. Then there's the Victoria Climbié case, where a little girl suffered horrific abuse and died under the noses of social workers - evidence that a rule of optimism can lead to fatal results. "There are likely to be more children living unsafely in the community who should be in care than the other way round," says Anthony Douglas, chief executive of Cafcass (Children and Family Court Advisory and Support Service). "Only Poland and Italy take fewer children into care in Europe than we do. The UK public service is not a serial child-snatcher."

So which argument stands up? Are we repeating the mistakes of the past, or does the growth in baby adoptions demonstrate that we have learned from previous errors of judgment? And is there a "third way" - an alternative to adoption that is kinder to all concerned?

Adoption was first introduced in the UK in 1926. For the next 50 years it was used almost exclusively to avoid the stigma of illegitimacy. Half a million unmarried mothers had little choice (some would argue none) but to relinquish their babies, especially during the "sexual revolution" of the 1960s when adoption reached an all-time high. Many have experienced an unending grief. Even those who have had reunions with their adult offspring bear scars from the missing years.

"It ruined my life," says Padmini Staple, 58, co-chair of the Natural Parents Network. "I got pregnant at 16 and you can call it 'relinquishing' or 'giving up my baby' or whatever you like, but I had absolutely no say in the matter. Nobody ever suggested any alternative. When I had my son later on, I had postnatal depression and continue to suffer from depression to this day.

Even though I'm now in touch with my daughter and I'm trained as a counsellor, I still have periods when I enter a huge black hole. I've talked to so many women like me. They've all been affected."

By the mid-70s, contraception, changing attitudes to illegitimacy and welfare benefits for single parents meant the number of babies adopted dropped drastically. Adoption shifted from being a service for childless couples to a service for children needing families. Indeed, baby adoptions in the past three decades have been set in a context not of morals, but of child protection. But perhaps even more alarming than the recent increase in newborn adoptions itself is the uncomfortably large minority of women who are claiming their babies are being taken with insufficient evidence of wrongdoing.

Lucinda, 40, is among them. "I started to drink quite heavily when I lost both my parents in quick succession," she admits. "It came to social services' attention two weeks into my daughter's life because someone reported me. I completely understand their need to get involved, but what I don't understand is why they took my baby away even when I'd turned my life around."

Lucinda says that a 14-week assessment in a mother-and-baby unit culminated in a recommendation that she should keep her baby, albeit with support - including the proposal that social services should pay for her to continue seeing the psychologist at the unit. "The support didn't happen and the psychologist didn't happen, so I paid to see her myself. I also paid to go into rehab for three months. But my baby was taken anyway and as the care plan stands, she'll be adopted. I'm willing to do anything, including having a supervision order placed on me for a year. But it seems that once a local authority has made up its mind about adoption, they are like a dog with a bone."

Lucinda believes that if the adoption goes through, her pain will be similar to the mothers of the 60s. "I just hope that by then we will have woken up to the horror of what's happening now in the same way that we did after that period. But it will be too late for me."

Probably the most notorious recent case is that of Fran Lyon, 22, who was told last year by social services that her baby could be taken into care 15 minutes after it was born, with no chance to breastfeed. According to Lyon, who has since fled the country, the only reason was because, like many young girls, she had mental health problems as a teenager that are now "completely behind me". Her lawyer, Bill Bache, has described the practice of removing babies from such women as "a very sinister trend".

John Hemming, Liberal Democrat MP for Birmingham Yardley and chairman of the Justice for Families group, is campaigning for a public inquiry. "We are getting three or four new cases referred to us each day," he says.

Like many people, Hemming believes the main problem is the adoption targets introduced by the government in 2000 to try to reduce the number of children in long-term residential care. "What you wind up with is social workers under pressure to achieve these targets. They know older children are harder to place, so they find babies. I know of one children's services department that acted to prevent a mother moving from her local authority area to another so that they could get the baby to meet their own targets."

Hemming says the moral panic following Victoria Climbié is also significant. "It means social workers are finding it difficult to pull back legal proceedings as they develop. It also means that when parents ask for help from the system, the system is turning on them."

Social worker Rachel Bramble agrees. "Much of the reason why babies are taken into care quickly is due to reactionary systems that have been created by a government that fears the press coverage of a child death and so has become overcautious," she says. "Vast amounts of local-authority money are consequently spent on looking after children and care proceedings compared with supporting families - even though there is much said about supporting families."

Bramble became so appalled by the system that she left her social services job three years ago. In one case she dealt with, she says she suggested to the local authority solicitors that they could perhaps apply for temporary parental responsibility for a period of six months so that they could still be involved with the family but without care proceedings. "But they just looked at me astonished that I had suggested such a thing," she says.

Gina Gibb, 44, says she was refused the opportunity to even be assessed in a mother- and-baby unit. "I was fine when my first son was born, just a bit of baby blues. But when I had my second child, I had postnatal depression. After my third baby, I wound up with mental health problems. A social worker came to the house and said, 'Whatever you need, I'll help.' But she never came again until I had what's called a psychotic episode. Being pushed to crisis point was bad enough, but I was then accused of neglect and was told that if I didn't get better within a certain timescale, they would take my baby, which they did."

Gibb's mother rang the community heath service and finally Gina received some support. "I fought to get my baby back in court and won. But without that help that I had to seek out myself, I probably wouldn't have my children now. Yet I've had another baby since and I've proved I'm a good mum to all my children." Gibb now does charity work to try to change the way mothers are treated by social services.

As you might expect, local authorities are quick to deny wrongdoing, although not always. Chris Smith, 40, says he received a written apology from his local authority when his two young sons were adopted, but because adoption is legally irreversible he has been told he will never get them back. "They'd been living with my ex-partner, but she had some emotional problems. When it became clear she couldn't keep them, I said I would like to care for them, but social services said that I would fail to meet my children's emotional needs. They said that what levied against me quite extensively was my dishonesty about the fact that I have a half-brother and half-sister. They said I never told them about these half-siblings, whereas in fact they had been informed. Obviously this small issue wouldn't make a difference as to whether I could care for my children, but they felt it was proof that I was an untrustworthy individual."

Later Chris attended a family assessment centre and they too concluded that he was not capable of meeting his children's emotional needs. "A significant part of this was back to the dishonesty issue about my half-siblings. They said that I was clearly involved in a fight with the local authority and if I got my children back, I wouldn't be able to work with them."

A friend of Chris's happened to be a senior manager for social services. She had helped Chris write a letter of complaint during the process and an independent investigation ensued. "My solicitor asked for a copy of the findings but was refused. We finally got it after we'd lost the children and still didn't have the evidence in time to go back on appeal. That's when I got my letter of apology."

The impact has been unbearable, he says. "My mum died at 53 from a short, sharp illness and I thought nothing could ever be worse. On a scale of one to 10, that scores one and this scores 11."

Campaigners say that where parents are not together, fathers are all too often overlooked as potential carers. But being male is not the only thing going against parents such as Smith, says family law solicitor Sarah Harman. She believes that the time limit on appeals also leaves many parents unable to challenge adoptions effectively.

She adds: "I think there is a rather unhealthy relationship between some experts and some local authorities and the judiciary. Local authorities know that if they instruct Dr X, they'll say this mother has no hope of turning her life around and that the judge will accept it. Because of the secrecy of the family courts, which means nothing that goes on in them can be shared with the outside world, such practice is not scrutinised. There is no western democracy that has such family-court secrecy as we do."

Harman has a further worry: "I've dealt with lots of cases where adoption was a good thing but I've also dealt with cases where I've been very frightened about the way the court process works. It goes like this - a child's been injured, parents can't explain why, parents must be responsible, child goes for adoption. What's particularly scary is that it happens much more to families who are disadvantaged. Family courts always say they don't go in for social engineering but I think judges do sometimes think, 'This is a single mother, something's not right in the household, the child would be better off somewhere else,' and off the child goes."

Yvonne Coulter, 35, believes she is a victim of just this. Eighteen years ago, her six-month-old baby Tammy fell while playing in her baby bouncer. When she was at the hospital, Yvonne was told that if she left the hospital with Tammy, she would be charged with kidnapping her daughter. "I was astounded. I'd never had anything to do with social services before," she says.

Following three years of legal battles, Coulter claims it was proved beyond doubt that she was a good mother. "But by the time the case wound up in court, it was too late. The judge told me, 'Miss Coulter, if I return your daughter home to you, you will be a stranger to her.' So Tammy was adopted."

The following year, as she lay naked with her legs in stirrups giving birth to her son, Coulter says a male social worker walked in the labour suite and tried to hand a safety order to take this baby too. "Medical staff had to ask him to leave three times. It went to court and I won this time, but my family was never complete. It felt like my life was permanently on hold. My sleeping was horrendous and every special occasion - Christmas, Mother's Day, Tammy's birthday - was terrible."

In 2006, when Tammy was 17, she sought out her natural mother. Within a matter of months, Tammy moved in with her. Together, they are taking legal action against Derbyshire social services and are campaigning to stop babies being removed unfairly. "I am very angry and upset that both of us had the right to family life taken away for no good reason. It's like it was generations ago," says Tammy.

Not all adoptees feel aggrieved that they were removed from their families as babies. Annabel, 45, was taken at nine months old. "Today, it would be called neglect. My mother would leave me in the cot when she went to work and come back at lunchtime to feed me. I honestly don't think she meant to harm me. She was young and naive. To my knowledge she was never offered any support, but I actually think it was better to remove me. In fact, I think I should have been removed even earlier than I was. I say that even though I was placed in an adoptive family with problems and even though I know my natural parents now. If a child might be at risk, the sooner the better."

Patsy, an adoptive mother of a nine-year-old girl who was removed at four years old, agrees. "My daughter should have been taken years earlier than she was. It's not that I don't feel dreadful for her birth mother. I do. But at the end of the day, she is a year behind at school and her self-esteem is not what it could be because her care was lacking for so long. We're lucky because she's a survivor, but some children are not and the damage could be irreparable."

The evidence is not just anecdotal. Research shows that when there is a view that a return to the birth parents should be the first choice of a care plan, it can lead to delay for many babies, says Julie Selwyn, director of the Hadley Centre for Adoption and Foster Care Studies at Bristol University. Delay, she continues, is damaging, not least in terms of forming attachments, educational outcomes and self-esteem. "We studied 120 children who entered the care system in the early 1990s and by far the best outcomes were for children adopted young," says Selwyn, who adds that her research also identified a significant increase in the number of mothers abusing drugs and alcohol to the extent that they were unable to meet the needs of their babies.

David Holmes, chief executive of the British Association of Adoption and Fostering (BAAF), says that we should be praising social workers for bringing more babies into the care system. "The adoption targets came about because a government-led review found that adoption was being used as a last resort and children were being allowed to drift in care. If social workers are picking up cases more quickly and working faster to get children into the care system, should we be criticising them? It's naive to suggest that every birth parent can turn their life around."

The government says the increase in the number of babies being removed from parents should therefore not be viewed negatively. "In fact, statistics show that the number of children aged one to four coming into the care system has reduced by the same amount," says a spokesperson for the Department for Children, Schools and Families. "This means that children who would have come into care anyway are simply coming in earlier than in the past."

John Coughlan, joint president of the Association of Directors of Children's Services, shares the view that neither adoption targets nor the Climbié case have caused social services to break up families unnecessarily. "What I do accept is that there probably has been a heightened risk awareness of protection of younger children post-Climbié, and I also think the new adoption targets have focused attention on those families where there is a better-than-average chance you'll end up in permanency planning for the child. But knowing what we know about moving children sooner rather than later, and knowing what we know about the prospects of finding a permanent placement for a child over a certain age, this is surely a good thing."

He adds that local authorities aren't able to comment on individual cases, which leaves the press only ever able to tell one side of the story. "The reality is that the average adoption case takes two and a half years of vigorous assessment and challenging, with a wide range of professionals involved, with judges making the final decision. John Hemming's conspiracy theory just doesn't stand up against such a process."

The system isn't foolproof, admits Anthony Douglas of Cafcass. "It's not like shoplifting cases where there is clear-cut evidence, not usually, anyway. It's more like the McCanns' case where you have the whole 'Did they? Didn't they?' argument, while in other cases it's more about risk of harm than actual harm. In the end, you have to remember that parents don't always tell the truth and you have to work on a balance of probabilities. What's the alternative? It is unacceptable to take undue risks with children's safety."

But although he believes the whole idea of social workers taking babies to meet adoption targets is a "conspiracy theory running away with itself", he does believe there are ways of increasing the percentage of accurately diagnosed cases - notably, better training and mainstreaming of expert witnesses and more specialist family judges and specialist family solicitors.

Other improvements are already in the pipeline. This April, stricter controls on the cases local authorities bring before a family court come into force. Meanwhile, the Ministry of Justice is to pilot a new scheme aimed at opening up proceedings of the family courts, where more information will be given in cases with a significant public interest.

The first family drug and alcohol court in the UK also starts work this month. The court, based on a model that has proved successful in the US in helping parents fight addictions and keeping families together, has been launched by district judge Nicholas Crichton. Having seen mothers lose child after child to care through addiction problems (one had 14 babies removed), he has long been campaigning for this £1.34m initiative in London, which will allow judges to follow their own cases through, offering parents early intensive intervention by experts, as well as support from mentor mums who have weaned themselves off drugs and got their children back.

One of the mentor mums, Sharon Simms, 36, had three children removed by social workers, the youngest just days after she was born, due to her addiction to crack cocaine and alcohol. She credits the Maya treatment centre in London for turning her life around. Project manager Angela Wells says: "When I was a senior social worker, there was utter pessimism about the ability of substance-misusing mothers to be good parents and the culture was to remove babies at birth. So I left to come to this project, which has a clear remit of working with mothers in a therapeutic way, with a parenting programme run alongside. We work with women for up to six months residentially and support continues in the community afterwards. Sadly, the project is currently unique, yet we are managing to help mothers keep their children and be good mums."

Other projects, such as the charity Addaction's Breaking the Cycle in London and the Liverpool Women's Hospital in Merseyside, offer support to substance-using mothers in the community. Sue Wilson, a midwife at the latter, says: "These women tend to be labelled as bad parents unable to change, whereas we've had many success stories." But again, such projects are rare.

Perhaps the most wide-reaching "third way" - although still not common - is "concurrent planning". Carol Homden, chief executive of Coram, a charity aiming to improve chances for children, explains: "If a child is under two and the court is deciding on their future, then concurrent planning means that they are placed with a foster family who will go on to adopt them should the court decide not to keep the birth family together. But the overriding aim is for the baby to be returned to the parents' care, in which case the concurrent carer has the satisfaction of knowing they gave these children love and security when they needed it."

In the end, only time will tell whether drug and alcohol abuse, along with domestic violence, have become "the new illegitimacy", in terms of a stigma that attracts the removal of babies rather than much-needed support; or whether support in the majority of cases is simply too optimistic, robbing children of a right to a stable upbringing elsewhere. In the meantime, Cathy Ashley, chief executive of the Family Rights Group, hopes the debate continues to gather momentum so that complacency itself doesn't become the driving force. "Besides capital punishment, the worst thing you can do to a human being is remove their child. If the state is going to do that, it needs to be the very, very last resort".

· Some names have been changed

NEVER, NEVER lose contact with your young children, just read the paragraphs below!! Send them your phone number buried in the middle of a cd, written on a doll, written in invisible ink on a seemingly innocent postcard or simply whispered in their ears at a suitable moment.

Alternatively if your name is Jane for example, register an easy email address (e.g.) mumjane@hotmail.com. Any child old enough to send an email will then be able to contact you no matter where you are or where they are! If the child has no easy access to a computer, then a visit for 'study purposes' to any public library will also allow free use of one of their computers to send emails free of charge!

If, on the other hand, your baby or toddler is being snatched, insist on breastfeeding a baby as this gives you extra contact.

Citation: BLD 160403280; [2003] EWHC 850 (Admin).

Hearing Date: 15 April 2003

Court: Administrative Court.

Judge: Munby J.

Abstract.

"Per curiam. If the state, in the guise of a local authority, seeks to remove a baby from his parents at a time when its case against the parents has not yet even been established, then the very least the state can do is to make generous arrangements for contact, those arrangements being driven by the needs of the family and not stunted by lack of resources. Typically, if this is what the parents want, one will be looking to contact most days of the week and for lengthy periods. Local authorities also had to be sensitive to the wishes of a mother who wants to breast-feed, and should make suitable arrangements to enable her to do so, and not merely to bottle-feed expressed breast milk. Nothing less would meet the imperative demands of the European Convention on Human Rights."...

Published Date

16/04/2003

This case establishes the right of the mother to breastfeed, and is often ignored both by 'SS' and judges!

Fight for parents, grandparents, aunts, uncles and cousins all to have contact under the Human Rights Act (see chapter 'How to Get Your Children Back).

Children of all ages even those as young as 6 or 7 years old for example, can go to any public phone box and call parents reverse charges if they are quietly told how to do this, explained as follows:

Dial 100 from any private phone or public call box and you will be offered 4 options (choices) Choose Option 4 which asks if you want to speak to an operator. You then ask the operator for a call reversing the charges. The operator will then ask you for your name and the number you are calling (this must be to a fixed line not a mobile). Your mother or father will then say ok they accept the call and no money is needed from you, the child who is calling!

If your children are still with you or at least in contact get them to practice telephoning you reverse charge so that if the worst does happen and they are removed then contact is **NEVER** lost!! Remember also that if no court order forbids you expressly and specifically from contacting the children there is nothing to stop you seeing them when they come out of school (even nursery school!).

Remember that all children 'in care' have 'personal education plans' that the 'SS' are supposed to share with you. If you know where the school is you know where your child is! Ask the local education authorities (**NOT** the 'SS'!) for a copy of these plans and ask also to be put on their mailing list so you can continue to follow your children's progress even after they have been snatched! If you are not sure how to do this, call Pauline, a mother who knows how to 'play the system' on 07956371132.

PERSONAL EDUCATION PLAN FOR YOUNG PEOPLE IN PUBLIC CARE - Guidance for Completion

Responsibilities

Social Workers will have the responsibility for initiating the planning process and integrating it with the Care Plan

Designated teachers must ensure that each child in Public Care has a PEP and will have responsibility for completing and monitoring it

Completing the PEP (SCS81) – before the meeting

Sections 1, 2, 3 and 4 will be completed by the Social Worker.

The Plan should then be sent to the designated teacher and a time and venue agreed for an initial meeting·

Whom to invite – the Social Worker should normally invite the foster carer or residential key worker and parents, unless there are significant reasons why one or other parent should not attend, following the same guidance and rationale for LAC reviews. In exceptional circumstances other interested adults could be invited, but care should be taken to keep the number of adults to a minimum.

The designated teacher will then select the most appropriate member of staff to complete the Plan and attend the meeting.

Prior to the meeting, consideration should be given to the young person's strengths, achievements and ambitions. The young person's views are central to this section and they should be given support to express them.

Prior to the meeting, consideration should also be given to the young person's priority educational needs/actions, which should be specific and time-related. The PEP should make connections with, but not duplicate, other plans. Where specific targets have been identified in pre-existing plans, these can be incorporated into the PEP.

Completing the PEP – detailed notes

Section 5   This can be completed before the meeting, by the designated teacher.

If you know the school, you know how to contact your children when they come out! If 'SS' have already cut your contact, you can **STILL** meet your children when they come out from school unless a court order or injunction expressly forbids you to do so - in which case send a relative or friend!

Above all do not lose heart if the 'SS' decide to snatch your babies or your children. Because it is so important, let me repeat what I said earlier! Social workers are **NOT** police! They have no authority to give you orders and most of their threats are **PURE**

BLUFF!! Disregard their threats to 'take your children' or if they already have them, to 'stop contact' if you do not obey their orders. If they have reached the stage of threatening you **THEY HAVE ALREADY MADE UP THEIR MINDS**. If you obey them it will just make their task easier. They will break their word and take your children, or stop your contact later even if you have 'cooperated' by doing everything they ask! They will then just regard you with contempt as a 'pushover' and you will lose your children for good! You have no need to obey these petty tyrants unless they have a court order! Nevertheless, I beg you, please do not let arrogant social workers provoke you into anger or violence so they can later claim you were 'unstable'. Do however continually remind them that their duty is to help keep families together not split them up. Politely insist that they always treat you with respect and dignity and that they do **NOT** make angry threats! Do not get angry with them, show instead that **YOU** control the situation and please do not get flustered or even the slightest bit worried if they 'lose their cool' and get angry with you! Quietly oppose them in your home, fight them hard in the courts and never, never give up! Believe me, in the end you **CAN WIN**!!

JUST LOOK AGAIN AND REMEMBER THE RISK A YOUNG GIRL RUNS WHEN TAKEN INTO 'CARE'!

Sunday Mail August 27 2006 - Care home girl abused by 25 men in 2 years - A 14-year-old girl placed in a council children's home was prostituted to a group of depraved middle-aged men because staff were powerless to stop her going out. The horrific story of 'Becky' is highlighted in a BBC programme presented by Fiona Bruce this week which reveals how she was sexually abused by 25 men over two years - despite being known to social services and having been placed on the Child Protection Register.

Even when she was put in a children's home - six months after her earliest allegations of abuse -staff allowed her to be used as a prostitute for fear their intervention might infringe her human rights.

7 children 'may be buried at Jersey care home'
By Caroline Gammell in St Martin, Jersey
Daily Telegraph, 26 February 2008

The bodies of at least seven children may be buried at a former care home in what police fear is one of the worst instances of child abuse in Britain.

The remains of a skeleton were discovered on Saturday under the concrete floor of Haut de la Garenne in Jersey.

Specialist teams using sniffer dogs and radar equipment flown in from the mainland have identified at least six other locations at the site where bodies are suspected to have been concealed.

Murder detectives now believe they have uncovered the first physical evidence of a child abuse scandal that could rank among the worst ever at a British institution.

Last night there were claims that decades of abuse at the children's home had been covered up for many years by Jersey officials. Police fear the abuse - sexual, physical and psychological - could date back as far as the 1940s and '50s. They are now scouring records of missing children.

When the inquiry was made public last November, more than 140 people came forward to tell of their harrowing experiences.

Victims claimed they had been savagely beaten, indecently assaulted and raped by staff. There were accounts of children being punched in the head, flogged with canes and kept in solitary confinement.

The NSPCC received four times more calls over this inquiry than any other previous appeal.

Three former residents told police that children they knew at Haut de la Garenne had disappeared.

As a result, police teams began searching the large brick building - now a youth hostel - last Tuesday.

The investigation was prompted by police officers who realised that several former employees at the home were being investigated over alleged child abuse.

Deputy Chief Officer Lenny Harper, who is leading the investigation, said the testimonies of former residents could not be ignored.

Mr Harper said a dog specialising in tracing human remains picked up a scent in a corridor on the ground floor.

When officers dug up the concrete, they found the partial remains, believed to be a skull, fragments of fabric, a button and what they thought could be a hair clasp.

Scientists will take several days to identify the gender and DNA evidence may be too decomposed. However, the body is thought to be of a child, aged 11 to 15, dating from the 1980s.

Mr Harper said the dog had identified another six areas where bodies could have been buried at the property.

The findings seemed to be corroborated by the radar equipment. Searches are expected to last another two weeks.

"There are six other areas, half inside and half outside," he said. "Some of the areas may be linked."

When asked about the number of bodies he expected to find, he said: "There could be six or more, but it could be higher than that, depending on what happens over the next few days.

"The radar has tended to show that where the dog has picked up the scent of something, there appears to be some sort of disturbance under the ground, either holes or gaps - disturbed earth."

Police also want to re-examine bones found on the property five years ago which, when discovered, were assumed to be from an animal.

However, they cannot currently be traced, he said.

The latest finding follows a series of scandals during the 1990s.

An inquiry was held in 1990 into abuse at children's care homes in Staffordshire, dubbed the Pin Down scandal after the rooms the youngsters were locked in for weeks.

In 1996, an inquiry looked into allegations of hundreds of cases of abuse in care homes in Clwyd and Gwynedd, Wales, between 1974 and 1990.

In 1997, the NSPCC completed an inquiry into a council home in Sunderland called Witherwack House.

The inquiry named 23 men and women who had physically and sexually assaulted children during the 1970s and 1980s.

However, the Jersey case involves allegations of abuse of a horrifying new level. The former children's home was founded in 1850 as a Victorian establishment for boys.

Towards the end of the 20th century, it catered for 60 children at a time and girls were introduced.

Haut de la Garenne closed in 1986 and lay empty for almost two decades.

During this time, the property was used as the police station for the television detective series Bergerac.

In 2004, it was turned into a 100-bed youth hostel.

Several local inhabitants recalled that the children mainly stayed inside Haut de la Garenne.

A farmer, who did not want to be named, said: "People have been surprised. We didn't think that was going on here."

Jersey's Chief Minister, Senator Frank Walker, said he was determined that "whoever committed this outrage should be swiftly found and brought to justice".

Social Services do **NOT** have the power they pretend to have over you and your children! They rely almost entirely on threats and on **BLUFF**!! If they admit they have no power to stop a 14 year old in their care from working as a prostitute for 2 years, they certainly cannot stop children in care from phoning their parents, meeting them or visiting them for a meal as long as they return to the fosterers or care home afterwards!

Do not be bluffed by social workers or even your own useless solicitors! If they tell you are not allowed by law to show your documents to anybody else tell them they are years out of date! Section 62, (Para 251 explanatory notes) of the Children Act 2004 allows you to show your documents and discuss your case in detail including names with as many individuals as you like! You are however still forbidden to reveal to the press, the public or sections of the public any information that might help identify the children concerned. Tell family, friends, advisers, and any other individuals anything you like no matter what bossy social workers and expensive lawyers might tell you!!

Section 62: Publication of material relating to legal proceedings

The Children Act 2004 (Para 251 explanatory notes) Section 62(1) amends section 97 of the Children Act 1989 to make clear that the publication of material from family proceedings which is intended, or likely, to identify any child as being involved in such proceedings (or the address or school of such a child) is only prohibited in relation to publication of information to the public or any section of the public. This section will make the effect of section 97 less prohibitive by allowing disclosure of such information in certain circumstances. In effect, this means that passing on information identifying, or likely to identify, a child (his school or his address) as being involved in court proceedings to an individual or a number of individuals would not generally be a criminal offence.

Legal aid lawyers in the Family Courts are for good reason known in the trade as 'professional losers'. Most of them collect a hefty fee for advising you not to resist Social Services, but to go along with all they say! Often they tell you there is no need for you to go to court at all and if you do go they refuse to let you speak whilst they agree to surrender to the care orders and/or adoption placements demanded by the 'SS'! So my advice is, if your solicitor or barrister stops you speaking in court or advises abject surrender to 'SS' demands, sack them and **REPRESENT YOURSELF**!! At least then you will be able to put your own point of view to the court and will be able to ask awkward questions of social workers and their so called 'experts'.

To sack your solicitor and your barrister just download form N434!

N434 - Notice of change of solicitor (Court Service) Download Form N434, Notice of change of solicitor, Court Service Forms, Administrative Court:

http://www.capform.co.uk/fullformlist.asp?Level1=11&Level2=106&Level3=623

Don't believe me? Look at this early day motion at present before parliament.

EDM 2021 SOLICITORS AND THE FAMILY COURT PROCESSES
http://edmi.parliament.uk/EDMi/EDMDetails.aspx?EDMID=33888&SESSION=885

That this House notes the comments of a senior social worker that meetings have been held during which solicitors acting for parents have discussed how to undermine the cases of their clients; further notes that there are many odd cases in which solicitors fail to oppose care proceedings or accept that the section 31 threshold has been met notwithstanding the opposition of their clients; recognises that reporting and obtaining the investigation of such behaviour outwith parliamentary proceedings remains a contempt of court for hon. Members; and asks the Solicitors Regulatory Authority to review the implementation of the new solicitors' code of conduct and how this relates to conflicts of interest in the Family Court.

Several single mothers I have advised had lawyers who lost every case for them but when later they represented themselves they **WON**!! Some of them are quite willing to help you and explain by phone how they did it! Here are just 3 of many:

Samantha Walsh 07947468240 or 02086591901,

Samantha Jackson 07514099583

Lonia, 07707333804 or Lonia29@yahoo.com

Ian thanks for your help we was just given our kids back during our contact session

thanks for your help again

----- Original Message -----

From: ian@monaco.mc

To: Daniel Braddick

Sent: Monday, June 25, 2007 6:48 PM

Links to web sites dealing with similar issues include:

www.fassit.co.uk

www.stopinjusticenow.com

www.paroc.org.uk

www.unity-injustice.com

www.uktrackers.co.uk

www.parentsagainstinjustice.org.uk

www.pafaa.org.uk

The chapter '**How to Get your Children Back**' tells you in easy steps exactly how to write a convincing statement for the court using a very simple template plus the points that are applicable in your case. Please use these aids and also all the other information in this book to give yourself the confidence, the morale, and the fighting spirit to make sure you have the best possible chance of success in the family courts! As to how to tackle social workers and the like.....also remember '**The 8 Golden Rules**'.

These will show you the best way to deal not only with social workers, but also with health visitors, 'experts', therapists, psychologists, psychiatrists, 'professionals', 'Mystic Meg' and in effect the complete unholy rabble of bossy social service bureaucrats and money-hungry charlatans!

Who are these people really?

The whole collection of judges, lawyers, social workers, and so-called 'experts' giving evidence in secret Family Courts closely resembles one of those fanatical American religious sects! Any hapless parent that contradicts them and declares their innocence of any wrongdoing is 'in denial'! Any suspicion a parent raises that these people are dishonest or untruthful is taken as a sign of paranoia! Any anger or hatred exhibited by parents towards those who have taken their children is 'diagnosed' as having a 'personality disorder' and 'anger management courses' are advised! Nobody can sensibly question religious extremists and fanatics and that is how it is in the secret Family Courts. The words of social workers and **'EXPERTS'** are always believed in preference to those of the parents. Thousands of children and worse still, new born babies, are routinely removed to meet government 'adoption targets' on feeble pretexts such as 'risk of emotional abuse'. In the UK this is the greatest and most shocking scandal of our times!

Just look at this motion raised in Parliament and an announcement by the Borough of Bromley!!

FAMILY COURTS (No. 2)

17.07.2007

Lamb, Norman

That this House notes the growing concerns over miscarriages of justice in family courts in cases where children have been removed from families and adopted; believes that financial payments to social services authorities to meet adoption targets introduce an unacceptable, perverse incentive in complex cases; further notes that cases are heard and decided in secret without any public scrutiny; notes that the Government brought forward proposals last year to open up family courts; regrets that the Government has announced that it will not now proceed with these proposals; and calls for a public inquiry to examine the system in its entirety and to make recommendations for reform so as to secure the best interests of children and justice for innocent parents

Public Service Agreement - Adoption

The London Borough of Bromley and the Government made a Local Public Service Agreement (LPSA) for the three years, April 2002 to March 2005, to further improve services to local people. Adoption was one of thirteen service areas to be awarded extra funding - £93,000 over the three years - to meet or exceed the Government's target of improving the numbers of children adopted from public care by 50%. Where a service area is successful in meeting the agreed target the Council will receive £0.5 million in additional funding.

What did this mean for us in Bromley?

In 2004/05 18 children needed to be adopted from care to meet the agreed target.

To achieve these targets we had to recruit more adopters to meet the needs of the increased numbers of children requiring adoptive families. This was to be achieved through additional recruitment by the Bromley Adoption Team and through membership of the Adoption South East Consortium (consisting of five other local authorities).

THE OBVIOUS CONCLUSION: After 17 children have been successfully adopted in Bromley, if your child is 18th in line to be considered, your precious child will also be very, very precious to Bromley as it will be worth £500,000 to the Borough to make sure he/she is adopted!!

YOU ARE NOT ALONE!!

Key adoption targets missed (Official government papers)

The government has missed its key targets on adoption, despite making them a priority area for action for councils more than three years ago.

The government's overarching target, included in the Priorities and Planning Framework 2003-6, was to increase adoptions by 50% by 2006 from 1999 levels.

However, the latest figures show that just 3,700 children were adopted in the year ending 31 March 2006 – a 34 per cent increase since 1999 and a 3 per cent fall on last year's figures.

More than 60,000 children are 'in care' of the State. Thousands of these have been taken from loving parents not for anything that has happened to them, but because 'experts' said one day something might happen. As a result, every year, thousands of children and newborn babies have been ordered by secret Family Courts (no public admitted) to be removed to avoid future risk of physical, or more often 'emotional abuse' (a vague accusation impossible to disprove). Unlike any other court parents have to prove their innocence against accusations and worse still predictions by 'professionals' and 'experts'. If they fail to do this (and usually they do fail to disprove these forecasts) they lose their children.

More than 700 babies and young children are taken every year from the few parents who manage to pluck up the courage to go to court and fight! Once there they despairingly beg stern unbending family court judges to let them keep their own children. The judges in the secret Family Courts however inevitably respond by threatening parents with prison if they reveal to anybody details of proceedings. The identity of the children must be protected at all costs they say with an intimidating judicial frown! They follow up this stricture by authorising Social Services to advertise the unfortunate babies and toddlers as 'adoption candidates' in magazines like 'Adoption UK' and on the internet on sites such as http://www.uk-kids.org.uk/ like pedigree dogs, with large colour photographs, first names, dates of birth and character descriptions for easy identification by 'the neighbours'. These children are finally given away via 'forced adoption' to anonymous strangers for the rest of their lives.

MOST OF THESE FAMILY COURT JUDGES SHOULD BE SENT TO PRISON themselves to pay for their crimes but in fact a parliamentary question recently revealed that these renegade family judges regularly send more than 200 people a year to prison in strict secrecy with no public hearing at all! The judges are the real criminals not the hapless and helpless parents! All this is happening in the UK right now!! Read on for details and proof.

A typical mother who successfully challenged Social Services is happy to support anyone who has had their children taken away! Just ring Lonia at: 07707333804 or email: lonia29@yahoo.com.

Every story, every legal quotation, and every statistic I quote has been carefully checked and verified from official government published figures, acts of parliament, published judgements from actual cases and articles in reputable newspapers such as *The Times* or TV programmes such as 'The Real Story'.

In 1926 the first 'Adoption Act' was passed legalising the concept of adoption in the UK. Parental consent could be dispensed with if those parents could not be found, had abandoned the child or who were plainly mentally incapable. This dispensation happened very rarely. The vast majority of adoptions concerned mothers who were not married and who were persuaded by parents to give up their babies to avoid the 'terrible disgrace' that this was at the time.

In 1976 the second 'Adoption Act' was passed allowing secret Family Courts to order the adoption of children and even newborn babies against the express wishes of their parents. A barbaric measure unique in Europe that was to cause more misery to both parents and children in the UK than any other laws passed in the last 2 or 3 hundred years! Since then 'Acts' have been passed in 1989 and 2002 that have facilitated and speeded up this appalling forced adoption process. In the year 2000 Tony Blair called for a

40% increase in adoptions (supposedly to stop children languishing in care) and targets were set for local authorities throughout the UK. As a result of all this, record numbers of loving parents have seen their children and especially newborn babies (the best adoption material) literally stolen to fuel the adoption industry.

How social services can seize our children
by Cassandra Jardine
The Daily Telegraph, 30 August 2005

It is scant solace, but parents whose children have been taken from them by social services on what they consider insufficient grounds now know that they are not the only ones. Over the year since I first described the plight of Emma and Martin, and looked into Essex's child protection and adoption procedures, scarcely a day has gone by without a distraught parent bringing another case to my attention.

These parents cannot understand why seemingly minor or passing problems have become magnified or distorted by social services. Time and again, rather than investigate and observe - or support and rehabilitate - the chosen solution has been to take a child, and often then that child's siblings, into care.

A major factor seems to be the Government's target, set in 2000, for a 40 per cent increase in adoptions. The motive was to take children off the care register but, like many well-meant initiatives, it has had undesirable consequences. The target has encouraged social services departments to achieve Beacon status by arranging the adoption of easy-to-adopt children - young, healthy and white - rather than strive to find permanent homes for older children, or those from ethnic minorities, or those with disabilities.

Again and again, I have heard parents say that social workers seem to make an instant judgment about their fitness as parents and then assemble the evidence to support that decision. One woman sobbed down the phone from South Wales that she had been accused of neglecting her children because one of them was underweight; even those of her children without dietary problems have been taken from her. A cluster of women from Sheffield contacted me about the high-handed behaviour of social services: one had had her two children taken because she had left them with a 12-year-old while shopping; another had had her younger children taken because her eldest had mental health problems; a third because she and her partner had been arguing. From the Isle of Wight, I heard from a woman whose three-year-old cowered whenever the doorbell rang because twice she had been taken into care by social services on the basis of inaccurate information.

The pattern of these cases became all too familiar. An initial incident brought a family to the attention of social services. Sometimes it was the parents' backgrounds: they might have been in care themselves, have a police record, or just a low IQ. In other cases, they had been denounced to social services by a vindictive ex-partner or relative. Still others had been drawn to social services' attention by an incident that appeared suspicious to a doctor or child protection officer.

In several cases, behavioural issues due to autism had been blamed on bad parenting. In every case, the parents felt that minds were set against them before they had been able to assemble a defence.

These parents often told me that their loss felt like a bereavement, but worse because there was no closure. They had to struggle with the guilt of feeling that somehow they had brought this situation upon themselves, and the frustration of not seeing any way to clear their names. As they wandered the streets hoping to catch a glimpse of a lost child whom they feared might have changed beyond recognition, they felt anger against a system that allowed professionals to act before they knew the facts.

Some of these parents may be failing to disclose pertinent information, of course; but in every case they are desperate to be allowed to care for their own children. Those who have made mistakes, been in bad relationships or had mental or physical health problems clearly want to be allowed a second chance. Yet, in their children's "best interests", secure, loving attachments had been severed and children placed in the cold limbo of state care.

There, many of them seemed to be receiving far worse physical treatment - not to mention emotional deprivation.

Often the parents had tried asking social services for a review of their cases, but their letters, and those of their MPs, routinely received brief responses saying that the matter had been investigated internally by the social services department in question and that the local authority's actions had been found to be above reproach. Many felt that their complaints hardened attitudes against them.

In frustration, many have turned to the police hoping to bring their grievances into the criminal courts. Parents feel they have strong cases: they have documentary evidence of distorted reports, refusal to share vital documents and failure to follow procedures. A group of such parents in Essex who went to the police found that initially they received an interested response. Inevitably, when investigations stall, they suspect collusion between social services and the police. They have no proof, but, unless their complaints are investigated, they will always harbour such suspicions.

There is, however, one case that has got further. A couple whose child has been forcibly put up for adoption after what they consider to be a false accusation by an aggrieved ex-wife have been to the Independent Police Complaints Commission. The Crown Prosecution Service is now looking at 11 complaints against 13 police officers ranging from unlawful arrest, imprisonment and harassment to refusal to accept the parents' alibi.

"If this comes to court," says the father, "the social workers concerned will be named and will not be able to hide behind the mantle of secrecy that protects them in the family courts."

On other levels there has been progress over the past year. Following one case that I brought to light - involving a family in which a mother was deemed to have too low an IQ to care for her children - other newspapers have taken up the cudgels. The vulnerability of the low IQ group to interference from social services is now better understood and the mental health charities are making a stand against this practice. There is also wider recognition that the policy of increased adoption needs looking at.

Such moves are positive. But what is really needed is an independent body overseeing the actions of social services which would operate like the Independent Police Complaints Commission. Until we have such a body, social services will be able to carry on acting as they feel best - which may not be, whatever they say, in the best interests of children.

In France, Spain and other continental countries Social Services only remove children from their families if there is clear evidence of physical or sexual abuse suffered by children at the hands of other family members.

'Emotional abuse' as a concept is simply unknown and so is using the threat of 'risk' as an excuse to take children from their families and give them to strangers. Compulsory adoption of children taken from parents who are begging in court to keep them is practically unknown in Continental Europe where this cruel and abusive UK practice is regarded as little short of horrific!

In the UK (and also North America) the 'SS' ask compliant judges in **SECRET** Family Courts to authorise the (often permanent) removal of children whom they consider to be merely 'at risk' of either 'physical abuse' or that ever so vague concept 'emotional abuse'. Most of our Family Court judges should themselves **BE SENT TO PRISON** for these crimes against humanity! **OUR** Social Workers, like gypsies, claim to foresee the future and based on their forecasts (often backed up by highly paid 'experts' boasting the same gift of foresight) children and even newborn babies are brutally removed and given for adoption to strangers, thus avoiding this 'risk'. Parents who are naturally angry and upset when their children have been taken are often declared to be emotionally unstable. Such parents of course cannot defend themselves against these expert 'forecasts'. Criminals are punished for crimes they have committed whilst UK parents (and their children) are punished (often for life) for faults that Social Services believe that they might commit in the future!! **NO WONDER IN**

EUROPE THEY THINK OUR SOCIAL SERVICES ARE COMPLETELY CRAZY!!

In the UK even perfect mothers are at risk of having their babies snatched at birth. Social Services only have to find some allegedly violent incident in the past of the baby's father and the mother loses her baby to the adoption industry even when in many cases she knew nothing of these allegations when she fell pregnant. More often than not the father was never charged by the police, let alone convicted of any offence. Hard to believe? Well this happens far more often than you would think! It means in effect that **EVERY MOTHER IN THE UK** is at risk of having their newborn baby 'confiscated' by the 'SS' if the father has some episode in his past that maybe the mother knew nothing about when the baby was conceived!

A couple I helped recently had their baby removed the same day it was born! The distraught mother was told that she was blameless but that her partner, the baby's father some years previously had been accused by his ex wife of violence towards her in a custody dispute! No charges were ever brought by anyone but this unproved accusation was enough for the horrified mother to see her baby taken by Social Services with a view to adoption. After several court cases a second baby was born and threatened with the same fate so the useless lawyers were sacked and the couple represented themselves with such success that both babies were eventually returned to their care under a supervision order (which is still being contested!).

Fight every step of the way and you can win! Submit and you are doomed!

JOANNA will tell you how she and her partner got their babies back and will advise you by telephone: 07724056999 or by email joanna_06@blueyonder.co.uk

No wonder that social workers in 'child protection' are now perceived **NOT** as protectors but as child snatchers who break up the very families they are mandated to cosset and preserve. They are now trained to show no pity and no remorse when they take babies at birth from mothers that have never harmed them. Social

Services are unfortunately thoroughly obsessed by an urgent need to meet government adoption targets and reap financial rewards. This need supersedes all traces of pity or compassion. Adoption is 'big business' and very profitable for those who do not hesitate to deal in a murky industry where children are just a 'commodity'!

'Legal aid lawyers' who often work closely with Social Services are waiting, only too ready to 'represent' bereft parents and urge them to 'cooperate' with the 'SS' and all will be well. Alas it almost never is.....

Talking of 'legal aid lawyers', the vast majority of these highly paid and highly useless parasites are widely known as 'professional losers'. They simply advise you **NOT** to fight the Social Services and to 'go along' with everything the social workers tell you! For this easy and entirely useless legal advice they charge enormous fees and go home laughing, ready to fleece their next victim!

Ring Pauline on 0151 475 6007 for her opinion of her solicitor who, faced with her determination to fight for her children, actually promised in turn to fight too. He verbally guaranteed that he would stop care orders from being put on her children at the appointed half day hearing. "They haven't got nearly enough" he said! What happened next?

Of course he never even turned up in court (he sent his clerk!). He had promised that the 'SS' witnesses would be rigorously cross examined in court and that witness summonses would force them to attend. In fact they did not come. The guardian sent a written statement and the 'SS' barrister himself 'reported' the support worker's opinions to the judge. No cross examination was possible but the judge believed their slanderous hearsay rather than the mother who had testified in person on oath and who also had produced an excellent 'psychological' report on herself from the court appointed 'expert' which described her parenting skills as first class. Pauline alas did not like or respect her social worker and for this alone, believe it or not, she lost the last 2 of her 6 children! She has no criminal record, no problems with alcohol or drugs, no learning difficulties, has a university degree and an intense repugnance for social workers (personality disorder?) who in turn cannot understand why anyone should dislike them! They were as usual vindictive towards her because (as the judge put it) of her 'inability to work with professionals'. Her newborn baby has been taken for adoption and her 6 children split up from her and from each other.

She has wisely decided to represent herself on appeal! She also wishes to form a support group for parents who have had their children 'snatched' by Social Services so ring 01514756007 for mutual support.

Samantha had 4 children removed after she ejected a rude and nosey social worker from her home (they said she must have a personality disorder!). She and her mother Philomena lost 3 cases in a row and 3 children to adoption when 'represented' so when the 'SS' threatened to take her new baby as soon as it was born she contacted me and I advised her to represent herself. She did this successfully retaining her new baby and recovering her eldest child even after the 'SS' appealed against her first win; but Samantha still beat them again! She or her mother Philomena will advise you and tell you how they did it on 0794 746 8340.

Battered women (and sometimes men too!) are now too frightened to notify the police. Not because they fear a partner's reprisals, but because the police inevitably inform Social Services who arrive not to help but to confiscate their children! Also parents with mild learning difficulties, parents who let their houses get dirty (or even merely untidy on just one occasion), parents who take their child to the doctor or to hospital 'too often', parents whose children are too often 'late for school', parents whose children suffer minor injuries from an accident where police are either not involved or who bring no charges whatever and even parents whose only fault is that they dare to insult or show disrespect to social workers, all run the risk of seeing their children and even their newborn babies, snatched to meet the adoption targets .

As stated earlier, more than 200 MPs think the secrecy is very wrong!

http://edmi.parliament.uk/EDMi/EDMDetails.aspx?ED
MID=29194&SESSION=875

The Daily Telegraph quotes "Often, concern for a child's welfare can turn into a battle between parents and social workers. Whether innocent, guilty or just struggling, parents are afraid when social services become involved in their lives. Bill Bache, Angela Cannings' solicitor, says parents view social services as 'the Gestapo' and social workers know it. "Our image is of trendies in sandals who snatch babies," says one Essex child service manager.

University of Bristol research showed that at least 50% of parents with learning difficulties have their children snatched for fostering or adoption by social services! http://news.bbc.co.uk/1/hi/uk/4752887.stm . Eric Pickles M.P exposed in Parliament one appalling case where the mother was "slightly slow" and the father perfectly normal. They successfully brought up one child for three years but when a second baby was born 'SS' seized both children for adoption on the grounds that even though they admitted that both children were healthy, happy and well clothed nevertheless their welfare was paramount and they would be more likely to fulfil their potential with a more prosperous and better educated adoptive family!

What did Felicity Collier (former head of BAAF the official adoption association) say in *The Guardian* in her very typical 'defence' of the SS in this shocking case?

The Guardian article quoted Felicity Collier as follows: The campaign in question was a series of articles claiming that over-zealous social workers in Essex were snatching children from families because the parents had learning disabilities. Collier is still furious about it. "The case of the parents who weren't bright enough had full judgments and it was clear that there were many reasons, and that this decision was not taken lightly," she says. "The fact is that there are people with learning disabilities that are fine parents, but there are also those for whom looking after their children is very difficult."

Please note that Felicity Collier never at any time gave **ANY SPECIFIC EXAMPLES** of the children suffering in any way when living with their parents. No denial that the eldest child was healthy and happy for 3 years in their care. Just an indignant claim that the seizure of the children was "justified", with no reasons why. The judgement published on the Essex Council said exactly the same! The judge concluded that the parents could no longer cope but he never said why, which made it impossible for the parents to defend themselves since nothing specific was ever alleged against them!

Yes, it's true that hundreds of parents physically abuse their children but it's also true that **THOUSANDS** of foster parents, step parents, adoptive parents and yes, even social workers themselves working in children's homes do exactly the same! All deserve to be punished when detected, but in fact most of the cases **CONTESTED** by parents in the Family Courts concern either 'emotional abuse' or worse still 'risk of future harm' the two latest 'excuses' to take babies and young children from their parents and give them to complete strangers to meet adoption targets! As far as I know there is no recorded case where parents recovered their children in court against opposition from Social Services and subsequently abused or injured them. Surely this indicates that mothers who come weeping into the Family Courts begging for the return of their children should be given the benefit of any doubt?

11. STEPS TO TAKE

1. If your children have been taken into care indefinitely or even 'temporarily' do not be bamboozled or fooled by social workers or by legal aid lawyers!! In cases such as these Social Services are not there to help you, they are your **WORST ENEMIES**!! Whatever they suggest is usually not to help you or your children, but to make sure you lose any case you are pursuing to recover them. You must oppose any suggestions in or out of court that your children would benefit from a period in care otherwise at a later hearing the judge can and probably will say that you have already admitted that your children would be better off in care than with you. The decision will usually confirm that opinion and you will probably lose them for good.

Above all **NEVER NEVER NEVER** agree that the thresholds have been reached! They may tell you that this is the only way to get your children back. In fact if you agree that the thresholds of abuse or neglect have been reached you are in effect already admitting that you are a child abuser and the only question left for the final hearing to decide is whether or not you can confess all the errors of your ways and reform! Usually of course the decision is "no" and your children are lost (often for good). The interim care orders normally only last one month and the only reason for that is to allow parents to challenge the orders each time they expire. That therefore is exactly what you should do!

DIVIDE AND RULE is another 'SS' tactic. When social workers tell you that if only you split from your partner you will keep your children, **DO NOT BELIEVE THEM**! Unless to your knowledge your partner is a violent or sexual abuser of children **STAY TOGETHER**! Once you are apart in court represented by two (often opposing) lawyers it is child's play for 'SS' to win their case and take your children.

2. Do **NOT** fall for any suggestion that you engage a local legal aid solicitor with 'experience' of dealing with care problems, especially those who are highly recommended by a helpful social

worker! I advise that you represent yourself if possible. Samantha is a young 25 year old mother of 5 children whom I have helped and she began with legal aid lawyers who lost every case by not putting up a real fight and as a consequence she lost 3 of her children to adoption. At this point she decided to represent herself and defeated attempts by Social Services to steal her newborn baby and her eldest son. The fact is that her lawyers had a 100% **FAILURE RATE** in each of several court actions but Samantha, acting for herself, has had 100% SUCCESS in each court hearing where she represented herself! She is willing to advise any other young single mother as to how she did it. Samantha's phone number is 07984373141.

If you do get legal aid, use a solicitor who lives well out of the area from which the children were taken and if possible from a completely different county. Search Google 'family law solicitor Manchester' (or whichever nearby but - not too near - town you choose). There are many other ways of contacting a solicitor outlined at the end of this section. Select someone who will promise to fight Social Services all the way and allow you to speak your mind in court. Do not bankrupt yourself by paying huge fees to private lawyers who will take you for every penny and leave you with financial worries to add to your family problems.

3. Most of the legal aid solicitors are a bunch of professional **LOSERS**. They can certainly afford to be! An average case can cost at least £500,000 when all the legal fees on both sides are added up! When they represent parents begging for Social Services to return their precious children they lose nearly every case they take on because they rarely call the witnesses that can help and they practically never challenge anything the Social Services say because they work closely with these people and want more business from them. These so called lawyers will usually advise you to plead guilty if you are accused of abuse or neglect as this saves them a lot of trouble. The less time they take over your court case and the fewer witnesses' expenses they have to pay the more money they make while their friends the social workers applaud as you lose your case. Luckily there are a few exceptions as the following article from *The Daily Telegraph* shows!!

'The Barrister Andrew Scott is drawing plaudits for clearing the name of parents'

by Cassandra Jardine

Telegraph Magazine, 11 February 2006

The Barrister Andrew Scott is drawing plaudits for clearing the name of parents who have been accused of harming their children. The secret of his success? Twelve years experience as a nurse.

Andrew Scott has spent the morning at the Royal Courts of Justice. In front of two judges, he has been arguing that a couple whose children have been put up for adoption should be allowed to appeal. Knowing how much it means to them, he has hardly slept all weekend. It is more than a year since the children were taken, on the grounds that the mother is too slow-witted to care for them. One piece of evidence against her is that she took too long to brush her teeth when a child needed attention. Another is that when her toddler fell over, she did not pick her up. At the time, she says, it didn't seem necessary. Although it is lunchtime and the parents and their lawyers are sitting in a cafe, Scott is not eating. He failed in his efforts and his attention is entirely focused on the dignified but bereft parents. Despite being a large man with a bullet head, his manner is exceptionally gentle. 'You must take care of each other,' he says, giving the mother a hug. 'We will keep fighting.'

As the couple leaves the cafe for their home - a place of unused toys and photographs of absent children - Scott looks despairing. There seems no way to overturn the judgment. An appeal will only be granted if there is new evidence,' he says. 'Judges won't want to look again at the original evidence, even if it is flawed. It's the same in all these cases: the legal system likes finality, a settled view of the facts.'

Their solicitor, Bill Bache, reassures Scott that the failure is not his fault, but he doesn't accept it, 'I always think, "Was I eloquent enough? Were my tactics right?"' Although he speaks as if used to defeat, that is not so. He has been a qualified barrister for just over a year, but already Scott has battled so successfully on behalf of parents accused of harming - or potentially harming

- their children that he has gained a reputation as a white knight. 'My greatest victory,' he says, 'was in the case of a mother accused of poisoning her child with epilepsy drugs. [Secrecy rules prevent the individuals being identified.] I was able to show that the child had a defective liver, so that what looked like an overdose was not.'

And his proudest moment? He smiles as he recalls the inquest into the death of three-month-old Toby Woods, whose mother, Donna Hanson, was arrested in January 2000 on suspicion of smothering him, 10 months after his brother had died in similar circumstances. Scott was able to show that, when not in his mother's care, Toby had spontaneously stopped breathing and that these episodes had been observed by nurses who hadn't recorded them and did not mention them in their written statements. Scott insisted on cross-examining the nurses and the crucial details emerged. The jury duly found, in September 2004, that the child had died of natural causes.

As Hanson left the court,' Scott remembers, with a catch in his voice, 'the jury formed a guard of honour. As she walked through, they said how sorry they were. It was a John Grisham moment.'

The rash of cases in which parents have been wrongfully imprisoned or had their children taken from them is one of the great scandals of our time, even though no one knows how many cases pass through the family courts each year (there are no published figures). Unlike criminal courts, family courts are not open to scrutiny and the standard of proof is lower: judgments are made on 'balance of probabilities' rather than having to be 'beyond reasonable doubt'. Strict rules on secrecy prevent parents from discussing their cases or questioning expert opinions, and journalists are not allowed to report proceedings. Best known are the cases of Sally Clark and Angela Cannings. After being imprisoned for murdering their children, their verdicts were overturned in the Court of Appeal when Professor Sir Roy Meadow's evidence against them was shown to be statistical rubbish. Prof Meadow's view was that two cot deaths in the same family were suspicious, while three inevitably meant murder. In fact, there is a strong genetic component to Sudden Infant Death Syndrome, making the chances of more than one occurring in the same family about 200 to one, rather than

Meadow's estimation of 73 million to one. Yet despite Meadow being struck off the medical register last summer, hundreds (possibly thousands) of families' lives are still being destroyed by a system that requires defendants to prove what is often impossible: their innocence.

'You can get a lot from a textbook, but it is no substitute for experience. Barristers often have no medical knowledge, so they believe what doctors say when they should be challenging them'

Following a review of 88 cases in which parents were imprisoned for shaking their babies to death, the Attorney General, Lord Goldsmith, is expected to announce this month that only four convictions merit reinvestigation

'It's disappointing,' Scott says. 'The individuals concerned will be heartbroken.

Hundreds of families' lives are still being destroyed by a system that requires defendants to prove their Innocence

'I expect it is because the Attorney General is only looking at the evidence given at trial. Sally Clark and Angela Cannings were able to overturn their convictions because they brought in new evidence'

Though 37 years old, Scott is not yet one of the well-known names of human-rights law, but he is a late entrant to the bar. A school failure from a council house in Newcastle, a potential Labour Party candidate and a former trade-union official, he is gaining respect because he seems to have the knack of unlocking these cases.

He has the rare advantage among barristers of having worked as a nurse for 12 years. When defending parents who have been branded shakers, poisoners and smotherers of their own babies, he has to work out how else the death could have occurred. His medical knowledge means that he can spot a flaw in a theory that expert witnesses have presented as fact. He can also come up with an alternative explanation. His other asset is his common touch. 'It's just like being a nurse,' he says. 'You often have to break bad news to people. How you do it has a bearing on how well they cope.'

This approach is not just humane, it is important to his success. As Michael Mansfield pointed out to him when Scott acted as his junior on his first case in March 2004 (the case was that of Mark Latta, accused of shaking his 10-week-old baby to death), parents may instinctively know the errors in the prosecution case - but unless they are asked, they may not say.

These qualities all brought Scott to the attention of Bill Bache, the solicitor who handled Angela Cannings's successful appeal, even before he had finished his pupilage at the bar. Since then, Bache - who describes Scott as 'brilliant' - has channelled so many cases his way that the dining-room of his Teesside home is buried under legal papers relating to cases that cover the whole range of allegations commonly made against parents.

It is exhausting work, for the parents are distraught. They know they have done nothing wrong and yet their lives have been ruined. Their surviving children have been taken from them and, in their own 'best interests', been placed with foster parents or put up for adoption. The parents fear not only for themselves, but also for their children, who may be emotionally scarred for life.

Scott is eager to do what he can for them because he is horrified by what goes on. 'I don't think the public appreciates how low the threshold is,' he says. 'When children are taken from their parents, it is not because there is a certainty of future harm or even that, on the balance of probabilities, those children could be harmed.

It is enough that there is the possibility of future harm. If there is a 70 per cent risk of a child being harmed and every child with that risk is taken into care then, in 100 such cases, 30 children will be taken from families where they would come to no harm. Sometimes, I wonder whether it is the children who are being protected or the social workers' careers.

'I have two daughters, aged 12 and 10. They could fall downstairs. All children could come to harm. I leave it to my wife to decide when they should go to the doctor, yet I see parents criticised for not taking children to the doctor when something turns out to be wrong. If, however, they take them to the doctor too often they can be accused I of having

Munchausen Syndrome by Proxy, or | Factitious or Induced Illness, as it is now called.

I've seen reports saying the child had crisps and a sandwich for lunch and "the parents didn't intervene when the child ate the crisps first".

My children might not have eaten the sandwich at all. Does that make me incompetent? There seems to be a lack of common sense. The raison d'etre of the 1989 Children Act is that families should be kept together, but the state acts too quickly to remove children. There seems to be a feeling that the child would be better off with a new family. Since Labour came to power, there has been a shift - a concern not just about the physical wellbeing of a child but about better development outcomes when they are adults. There's an unspoken fear that children from poor backgrounds are being freed up for middle-class adopters.'

Scott was born in Skelton, Cleveland, the son of a redundant foundry man who took a degree in politics and history; his mother was a nurse. At school Scott's intellect stood out sufficiently for the deputy head to tell him that he ought to be a barrister, but although he loved watching Crown Court he was more interested in snooker than exams. Instead, he followed his mother into nursing.

It was only when he won a battle with his union he became interested in law. Representing himself, he did such a good job that the union's barrister offered his congratulations and Unison offered to sponsor Scott while he did a part-time law degree at the University of Teesside. It took five years, working as a nurse and studying at weekends and in the evening, but in 2001 he was awarded not only a first-class degree but also three prizes.

His interview to read for the bar at Gray's Inn, however, could have proved unsettling. 'What does your wife do?' he was asked.

'She's a dinner lady,' he replied.

'How charming,' the interviewer remarked.

But Scott is not chippy. 'They wanted to know if I could stand up for myself,' he says, 'so I said: "You haven't got a problem with that, have you?" *

He was then asked about his outside interests, to which he replied that he was a member of the Magic Circle, but would not tell them if he sawed his wife in half unless defence counsel was present. He was given the top scholarship and when he had finished his studies at Northumbria University, he came top in crime and fifth overall.

Even so, finding a pupillage was hard. Eighty-six sets of chambers rejected him and he was about to give up when he was asked for an interview at Doughty Street, a prestigious radical set dedicated to carrying out the words carved into the stone of the Old Bailey: 'Defend the children of the poor'. Despite arriving 'covered in bird shit and Coca-Cola', he was one of four out of 350 applicants to be offered a place. He spent his gap year as an official with the NASUWT teaching union.

Robin Oppenheim, his first pupil master, is a distinguished medical-negligence specialist. Before Scott's six months with him was up, he got his first break. In March 2004 Gill Evans, a criminal barrister and his second pupil master, asked if he could help with the medical evidence in the trial of Mark Latta. 'Having worked as an aesthetic nurse, I worked out that a laryngeal spasm could have caused the baby to stop breathing. I told the silk who was leading the case - Tony Jennings from Matrix [Cherie Booth's chambers] - about the mode of death and he won the case.'

Scott sees himself as the conduit between legal and medical experts. Although many barristers acquire a knowledge of medicine, they are often better at 'talking the talk' than understanding the fundamentals.

'You can get a lot from a textbook,' he says, 'but it is no substitute for experience. Barristers working on medical negligence and child-care cases often have no medical knowledge, so they believe what the doctors say is correct when they should be challenging them. Judges can only base decisions on the evidence put before them.'

Doctors are often viewed as the villains in cases of false allegations against parents. When Prof Meadow was shown to have made a mistake in the case of Sally Clark, it undermined public confidence in the profession. If such an eminent paediatrician could be so wrong, many other parents could have been wrongfully accused on the basis of doctors' over-bold pronouncements. It can appear that doctors are too ready to act as expert witnesses in return for handsome fees, too eager to believe fashionable ideas about wicked parents.

Having worked with hospital doctors for many years, Scott is not so cynical. 'They don't set out to deceive,' he says. 'The role of the medical expert is very difficult to undertake, but there are things that aren't explicable by the science that we know, and experts often fail to tell the court when they speculating, or giving a opinion outside their area of knowledge. My experience in a clinical setting is that they are never sure. They say, "It could be this. It could be that." Yet in court they present a theory as a certainty even though the issue is so important - the irrevocable loss of a child.

'When I was working in a hospital I saw parents being accused of having Munchausen's and I questioned that diagnosis. We have to be sensible. Parents do kill and harm their children. Fact. But I am concerned that those doctors who challenge their peers are seen as mavericks. The hospital is the consultants' domain, but the courtroom is my domain and I can question them.'

Following Angela Cannings's successful appeal two years ago, it looked as if many similar cases would quickly be reviewed and further such cases would be halted. But change is slow in coming.

Each case has to be argued on its own merits, with the lawyers having to find grounds for appeal. Having been involved in a large number of these, Scott can suggest some reforms that might at least make injustices less likely to happen in future. He starts with the law: if barristers lack the specialist knowledge to challenge doctors, he would make sure they were trained.

'After all, nurses now get training in legal matters. Why shouldn't lawyers? Judges should be regularly retrained, too - they already are for rape cases.'

Having seen how social workers' subjective reports can lead to parents losing their children, he would introduce trial by jury in such cases. 'Juries are the best mechanism we have for detecting dishonesty,' he believes.

'I wonder whether its children that are being protected, or social workers' careers'

He would also establish specialist regional social-services departments to deal with children at risk, where experienced workers would review such cases and introduce an element of consistency - as it stands, a family's chances of staying together seem to depend on where they live: some local authorities will give them the benefit of the doubt, others (perhaps fearful of Victoria Climbie on their patch) err on the side of caution. He would also pay social workers more: 'The better ones shouldn't have to move into management to get higher pay,' he says. 'And there needs to be a public body to discipline them for the protection of the public.'

Most of all, he would change the way they operate. 'If social workers were brought in to assist families and got to know them, they would be able to assess risk better than if they are expected to take immediate action.

Families need more support: I was a great believer in the welfare state when I was a nurse on £20,000 a year and a trade-union official on £38,000; as a barrister, I earned £89,000 in my first year, doing legal-aid work, and I still believe in the welfare state. I would bring back National Service, not just in the Army but in the police, social services and across the board.'

One day, perhaps, if he becomes an MP (he put himself forward for Mo Mowlam's Redcar constituency in 2001), Scott may effect such changes, but he is in no hurry to leave the law. He loves it with a late starter's passion and is keen to work all hours, often pro bono, to assist victims of injustice. Later this month, he is bringing an appeal for a couple (who cannot be named) who were thought to have poisoned their youngest child.

Two children were adopted; two put in care. Even though Prof Meadow's evidence was pivotal, Scott has had to go to the High Court to fight for them to have their fostered son back. The higher up the legal system you go, the braver the judges,' he hopes.

Soon after, he is involved in the appeals of Ian and Angela Gay, a Worcestershire couple imprisoned for force-feeding salt to a child they were planning to adopt. Without wanting to reveal his evidence, Scott is confident that he knows what really caused the child's death.

He has another salt-poisoning case to fight on behalf of a terrified mother, and he is going to the Criminal Cases Review Commission for a father accused of smothering his child. He is also handling an appeal for a father accused of shaking his child to death. As in many cases of sudden infant death, the true cause may be gastro-oesophageal reflux: many children who spit up constantly stop breathing suddenly. After that, he is representing a local authority in a child-protection case: 'It's important to act for the other side, too,' he says.

Each of these cases involves many boxes of documents. 'It's daunting,' he says, 'but I often find that the first piece of paper says it all. The doctors haven't considered an obvious medical possibility.'

4. Unlike social workers, the Clerks in the court are nearly always very helpful if you file an application to get your children back yourself. Even if you are not used to court proceedings, at least you can call your own witnesses and unless there is some special reason to the contrary **ALWAYS ALWAYS** call the family doctor and the children themselves. This usually makes the difference between winning and losing.

The most difficult accusation to deal with is when 'SS' pay enormous sums of money to 'experts' i.e. therapists, psychiatrists, psychologists and medical specialists, who will dutifully support 'SS' (with reports comprising 20 or more pages of meaningless jargon) in their dire forecasts that your children (or even newborn babies) are at great risk of 'emotional abuse'. These reports avoid like the plague pointing out specific faults in your parenting that you could possibly rectify. Instead they ramble on about your 'state of mind', your unreasonable hostility to dedicated social workers (who have literally kidnapped your children!), amounting to paranoia and personality disorder; and of course your emotional instability (sometimes suicidal). Incredibly, it seems to surprise them that desperate mothers who have lost their children show these symptoms and they then claim that it proves their instability and unsuitability as parents!

Happy, healthy, well-dressed and well-fed your children may be, but these accusations by experts predicting the future like gypsies gazing into crystal balls are difficult to refute and are usually enough to lose you your children to adoption by complete strangers! Sometimes a distraught mother fighting for her children against the opinion of medical 'experts' called by Social Services will be questioned by the judge. "Do you think the experts are all wrong?", he will ask. A good answer is that experts tend to side with those who pay them. Professor Meadows, Professor Southall, and Dr Marietta Higgs are three supposedly 'top experts' in their fields paid by Social Services for supporting the legal kidnapping of literally hundreds of children through evidence based on crackpot theories that have now all been thoroughly discredited! Even more respectable experts can be 'suspect'. In the Louise Woodward case in the USA for example some of the most eminent experts in the country appeared for opposing sides and disagreed on the evidence. Parents in Family Courts usually have to submit to evidence from experts called by Social Services or by the court and are either not allowed to call their own experts or cannot afford to do so. Social Services call only those experts who agree with them! If exceptionally they stumble on one who disagrees that expert is simply not called and is quietly replaced with someone more amenable! No experts can understand the needs of a child like its natural mother no matter how many degrees in psychology they have, especially if their motivation for their testimony is at least partly financial!

There is however another good argument to use against these money hungry charlatans. Their rambling accusations seldom fall within the official definition of emotional abuse as specified by the Ministry of health.

You should get copies of your 'SS' files to see if anything 'inaccurate' (to put it politely) has been recorded against you.

5. The social workers often rely on winning their cases on 'hearsay'. This means that they tell you what the children have said

to them (sometimes on video) and what neighbours and other people have said without ever producing them in court. They say they do this in order to spare the children the ordeal of appearing in court when in fact it is to stop you asking awkward questions which may show up any lies that have been told or pressure that has been put on young children to make them criticise their parents or parent. Often the children desperately want to come to court to tell the truth but are prevented by Social Services.

6. If you represent yourself, the judge should give you a lot of help. You also have the right to have a friend to sit by you and help you by suggesting questions that you should ask witnesses and making notes of their replies. This is called a McKenzie Friend (parents' lay advisor) after the first person who established this right. Mention that you will require such a friend when you make your application to the court naming him or her if possible at the time.

7. If the children are old enough you should try to get them to telephone you reverse charges when no one is watching them so you can keep proper contact with them. You can also discreetly give them mobile phones equipped with sim cards so you can contact them. Unfortunately most social workers, once the children are in care will do everything they can to break contact with you and will even stop you talking about the case with them during those rare closely supervised visits that they allow. It is important that you let your children know that you have not abandoned them and that you want them back at home. You have the right to say what you like to your own children so do not let them stop you with a lot of bluff. If the phones are confiscated children can still go to any public call box (usually there is at least one available in every school), dial 100, choose option 4 and ask for charges to be paid by their parents!

Grandparents and any other relations you can think of should be persuaded to apply for regular contact and to receive them for home visits. Such applications should be made to the court. If lawyers are used they should not come from the same county as the one from which the children were taken.

8. Contact must be fought for before, during and after any court proceedings. As a rule 'SS' will gradually reduce contact between parents and children that have been 'selected' for foster care or adoption on the grounds that there is a risk that the placements with foster parents or prospective adoptive parents might be undermined.

It is vital that phone contact at least be kept up with older children, and all children must know their parents still love them and want them back. 'SS' will almost certainly have told them the contrary! Any mother who has never harmed her children and has been served with a section 34 forbidding her any contact at all with the children to whom she gave birth should defy the order at least once!! Go to their school and meet them as they come out and if they are guarded in an enclosed area tell some of the other children to let your children know that you are trying to see them. Jailing a blameless mother for loving and trying to see her children one last time would give 'SS' and the courts such bad publicity that they would be unlikely to risk such extreme measures!

If you do not know where your children are fostered and you know the name and district but not the address, then first look in the phone book and then the voters list available in the library. Brothers and sisters have the human right to keep in contact and if this is denied them go to court to protest the illegality of this! When they are in contact you only need one to tell you where all the others are! If your child is about to be freed for adoption and the adopters are put in a separate court so you cannot see them or identify them persuade a friend to hang about the corridor tables outside the court room looking busy but ready to follow the adopters to find out who they are and where they live! Do everything you possibly can to avoid losing contact altogether.

9. If you are a parent who is denied proper access by the other parent, try and arrange for the right to take your children for half the school holiday periods or at least once a year so that you have exclusive contact for a short but continuous period rather than frequent contact for only a few hours at a time. Keep applying to the court for this, however often and however many applications it takes to succeed. The point is that if you have the right to take

them on holiday or at least to live with you for a specified period and you go to fetch them, you are not kidnapping them and they will probably be anxious to go with you.

If a parent flouts a court order for contact with the other parent then that parent should as a last resort apply for a care order to the court so that care and custody is transferred to the parent aggrieved. Just the threat of this happening can sometimes ensure that both parents have the contact that the court has awarded.

10. Never shout and get angry with social workers; always be very quiet, calm, and polite, no matter how much they try to provoke you into showing 'character instability'. Nevertheless take **NO NOTICE** of any advice or instructions that they try to give you, and above all **NEVER** sign anything they place before you!! Apologise profusely each time for "doing what is best in the interests of your children" and smile sweetly **WITHOUT** getting angry or above all violent. You can serve your interests much better by making repeated court applications for return of your children from care, refusing to sign adoption papers when this is proposed, and repeatedly asking for more contact for your children from grandparents, aunts, uncles, cousins and their own brothers and sisters (if they have been split up) by numerous court applications that you and your relations make individually by filling in simple forms with the help of one of the Clerks at the court. Your one advantage over the Social Services is that you are concerned only with your own children while they have any number of cases to deal with so that if you keep dragging them into court, supported by solicitors and barristers who cost them money, they will give up and return your children as often as not.

This is one tactic I employed for mothers who came to me for help when I was an active member of Kent County Council years ago and was known for helping parents recover their children from the clutches of social services. Until they changed the law so that only those with parental responsibility could apply to the court, for the discharge of a care order I was able to apply in person and so effectively represent these parents against my own county council. I never lost a case. These tactics worked better than any other so take no notice of lawyers and social workers who tell you to cooperate with 'nice social workers' because in fact you and all the close relatives you can persuade to help you should make their life as difficult as possible by repeating court applications for better access and you the parent must keep applying to have the children returned to you for every reason you can think of until they just get fed up. They have no right to stop you talking to your children about how much you want them back as the judge never restricts your conversation and only Social Services do this by bluffing you when they have no right to do so. Tell your children to keep on asking to go home until they are allowed to do so.

To whoever needs the information needed to challenge Social Services:

Myth 1: "Family Court secrecy protects the identity of the children".

Reality: In fact social services advertise these same children for adoption on many websites such as http://www.uk-kids.org.uk/ and in magazines such as 'Adoption UK' giving first names, photographs, birth dates and characteristics. Essex council has also featured a complete judgement concerning the children featured in *The Daily Mail* on their website for all to see. In other words the councils can break secrecy but parents risk prison if they do the same.

What the secrecy does do effectively is to stop aggrieved parents going to the press or revealing their names (like rape victims can do if they wish). The courts also often issue gagging orders stopping all discussion as indeed they did to Barry Aspinell even though he was an Essex Councillor trying to help a constituent.

Myth 2: Social workers pathetically repeat "damned if we do and damned if we don't" as an excuse for their actions.

Reality: They get damned because they avoid the violent type of parents and carers who torture their children as they are afraid for their own safety and feel damaged children might be hard to foster or adopt and they therefore prefer to take the easier option of targeting happy healthy children whose mothers have low income or low IQs (as pointed out by the *Daily Mail* and the *Daily Telegraph*). Rather like some police who prefer to target motorists with a defective rear light rather than go after armed robbers. Social workers often point to the large numbers of children in voluntary care but do not mention that many of these were given up to care because parents were promised that if they cooperated by agreeing to this the children would be returned in 2 or 3 months. Of course this promise is too often broken. Parents are frequently horrified to see these same children advertised for adoption (often when subject only to interim care orders and before the court has made any decision on their futures). When these same parents lose their children for good to the 'adoption industry' they feel betrayed both by social workers and their own lawyers who have inevitably advised these parents to cooperate with Social Services when they affirm that 'temporary care' is the best option .

Myth 3: Social workers, judges, foster carers and heads of special schools all do what they can to reunite children with their parents.

Reality: In 2000, Tony Blair called for a 40% increase in adoptions. Margaret Hodge fixed targets for local authorities giving beacon status and stars and even large financial rewards (Kent got £21 million pounds for hitting 10 out of 12 targets under a public service agreement) to those councils who were successful. Most social workers are therefore motivated to take children into care with a view to adoption to meet their targets. Government research papers have publicly confirmed this. Judges have admitted in court that it is safer to 'go along with social services' rather than take any risks and that is why parents almost never win their children back.

As for foster parents who are lucky enough to live in Slough, they get a tax free allowance of £400 per week per child so a fosterer with 3 or 4 children is very well off indeed and is not likely to encourage the children to return home.

Private special schools according to channel 4 charge the council up to £7,000 per week per child so they too prefer to keep the status quo.

Myth 4 "The welfare of the children is paramount"

Reality: This phrase of course does not say who is to decide what the best interests of the children are. Social workers trying to meet their targets soon translate this principle into "the children's welfare is best served if we win our case" and they try to win at all costs. Judges, as I have said, freely admit that they take the safe route of going along with Social Services when their evidence conflicts with that of the parents. Mothers who come weeping into court to try and recover their children are not usually the type of person who would abuse or neglect their children. They should therefore usually win and get their children returned but they nearly always lose. Even worse **CONTACT** between mothers and children is gradually reduced (and used as a weapon if mothers are 'difficult'), phone calls are forbidden and grandparents, aunts and uncles are frequently stopped completely from any form of contact. Criminals actually in prison are allowed phone calls and family visits but this is very often denied to parents and grandparents seeking contact with children in care or worse still 'on track for adoption'.

Myth 5: The British legal system is widely admired throughout the world and the Family Courts are fair and highly respected in other countries.

Reality: The European Court of Human Rights in the case of P, C, and S, vs. United Kingdom condemned as draconian the action of the UK Family Court when they followed their usual custom of taking a baby from the mother at birth because on a previous occasion one of her children had been taken into care many years earlier. The UK was fined but the child was already adopted. The essential difference between British social workers and those in Latin countries for example is that in France, Italy or Spain children are only removed from their parents if they have suffered severe physical harm. In the UK however children are taken not because they have actually suffered physical harm but rather some very ill defined sort of 'emotional harm' or more often because so called 'experts' (using a crystal ball?) decide that there is a risk that children might suffer 'physical' or far more often 'emotional' harm at some date in the future.

It is impossible for parents to prove that their children will not suffer emotional harm in the future when these experts swear to the contrary so the unfortunate parents nearly always lose.

http://www.dfes.gov.uk/adoption/adoptionreforms/CLA bulletin2003-04final1.pdf (see page12 tableB)

If Social Services are starting care proceedings against you, they may not tell you about it until you receive a notice from the court through the post telling you when the first hearing is. If you do not feel able to represent yourself you **MUST** get immediate legal advice. You **MUST** get a solicitor who is a member of the Law Society Children's Panel and specialises in family care work. The solicitor will act on your behalf and may instruct a barrister to represent you in court. You can get legal advice on solicitors from:

- Government booklet from the Legal Services Commission explaining Parents and Carers Legal Rights in Care Proceedings. http://www.clsdirect.org.uk/documents/leaflet29e.pdf

- Your Local Citizens Advice Bureau http://www.citizensadvice.org.uk/

- FASO www.false-allegations.org.uk 0870 241 6650 Mon - Fri 6pm - 12pm

- The Law society of England and Wales www.lawsociety.org.uk Tel: 0207 242 1222

- The Law Society Information Line www.solicitors-online.com Tel: 0870 606 6575

- or you can get limited Free Initial Advice by Email from firms of Solicitors listed below.

Only employ a solicitor who will promise to fight Social Services fiercely, call your witnesses and above all allow you to say your piece in court! Maybe you can persuade one of the sources above to put you in touch with one of those named below!

To sack your solicitor and your barrister just download form N434!

N434 - Notice of change of solicitor (Court Service) Download Form N434, Notice of change of solicitor, Court Service Forms, Administrative Court:

http://www.capform.co.uk/fullformlist.asp?Level1=11&Level2=106&Level3=623

Solicitors and barristers who fight for their clients:

SOLICITORS:
Sandra Bradley
PRINCIPAL
Bretherton Law
First Floor, Alban Row 27-31 Verulam Road St Albans
Herts AL3 4DG
Tel. 01727 869293 Fax. 01727 853767

William Bache & Co
(best for criminal cases in my opinion)
The Clock Tower, 4 Oakridge Office Park, Whaddon, Salisbury, Wiltshire, SP5 3HT
Tel +44 (0)1722 711719 Fax +44 (0)1722 713370
e-mail: enquiries@williambache.co.uk

BARRISTERS:
Darren Watts
Tanfield Chambers, 2-5 Warwick court, London WC1 5DJ
Tel (0207) 431-5300

Andrew Scott

described by *The Daily Telegraph* as "the people's champion"

Parklane Plowden

www.parklaneplowden.co.uk

Tel: 0844 499 5678

Carol Mcmillan

Westgate Chambers, 64 High Street, Lewes, East Sussex BN7 1XG

Tel: 01273 480510

Dr John Fox

Chambers of Ami Feder, Ground Floor, Lamb Building, Temple, London EC4Y 7AS DX 1038 (Chancery Lane)

Tel: 020 7797 7788 Fax: 020 7353 0535

e-mail: clerks@lambbuilding.co.uk

Out of hours tel: 07721 339232

PSYCHOLOGISTS:

Dr Lowenstein

Tel 02380692621, www.drludwigfredlowenstein.com

Dr Peter Dale (parent assessor)

e-mail: info@peterdale.co.uk

Phone from UK: (01424) 424504

Phone international: +44 1424 424504 Fax: 08700 941 477

Yes it is difficult to get hold of 'the best' but search Google for the name you have selected, or consult the law society so that even if your first choice is not available their office may be able to recommend someone sincere in your area who is willing to act for you!

Crusading Journalists in the family courts:

- Camilla Cavendish (The Times)
- Cassandra Jardine (The Telegraph)
- Melissa Kite (The Telegraph)
- Stuart Wavell (Sunday Times)
- Nick Cohen (The Observer)
- John Sweeney (Channel 4)
- Fiona Barton (Daily Mail)
- Denise Robertson (tv)

MP's who are 'on your side'

- Eric Pickles
- Anne Widdecombe
- John Hemming

DO NOT BE INTIMIDATED INTO SILENCE BY THREATS FROM SOCIAL SERVICES!!!!

You can make public your own name, your child's identity, and all the circumstances of their removal, as long as you do **NOT** reveal anything to the press or public at large that happened in the Family Court or any documents used in the court, or the name of any witness called by the court.

http://www.fathercare.org/munby19-3-04.htm

(See paras 81 and 82 especially 82 (v))

Since that case para 251 Section 62 of the Children Act 2004 now allows you to show all documents and discuss **EVERYTHING** with family, friends, advisors and any number of

INDIVIDUALS! Only the press and 'sections' (groups) of the public are still not covered by the new exemptions.

I can only finish my advice by repeating that you and your relations should file repeated court actions by the dozen, as many and as often as possible. Never give up!

Good luck to all of you!

Ian Josephs (Free Legal Advice)

ian@monaco.mc

Phone me at 0033 6 26 87 56 84

If you ring me from a fixed phone (not a mobile) and you give me the number I will ring you straight back at my expense! If you have no phone at home any public phone box will do.

DON'T LOSE HEART IF YOUR LEGAL AID SHYSTERS LET YOU DOWN! You can represent yourself! The list of forms below shows you what you need whether you are appealing against a care or 'freeing for adoption' order, asking for a discharge from care or asking for more and better contact. If you are not sure, ask the staff at the court to help you. They are actually paid specifically to do this but they don't make it too obvious! Sometimes you might run into an initial fee of around £100 maximum but providing you don't employ more lawyers that should be the lot! **DON'T GIVE IN!!**

To find out the address of your local Family Court in England or Wales (or to order the forms below by telephone) see this website :

www.hmcourts-service.gov.uk

If you require assistance with obtaining a court order, you should see a solicitor or call in to your local Citizens Advice Bureau. Please click on a link below. This will show a link to your chosen form and links to related guidance. Alternatively, if you click on the form format your form will open for viewing online.

LIST OF LEAFLETS FOR APPLICATIONS TO THE FAMILY COURTS. www.hmcourts-service.gov.uk

Description Forms/Leaflets

Adoption

A4   Application For Revocation Of An Order Freeing A Child For Adoption

A5   Application For Substitution Of One Adoption Agency For Another

A50 Application for a placement order Section 22 Adoption and Children Act 2002.

A51 Application for variation of a placement order Section 23 Adoption and Children Act 2002.

A52 Application for revocation of a placement order Section 24 Adoption and Children Act 2002.

A53 Application for a contact order Section 26 Adoption and Children Act 2002

A54 Application for variation or revocation of a contact order Section 27(1)(b) Adoption and Children Act 2002.

A55 Application for permission to change a child's surname Section 28 Adoption and Children Act 2002.

A56 Application for permission to remove a child from the United Kingdom Section 28 Adoption and Children Act 2002.

A57 Application for a recovery order Section 41 Adoption and Children Act 2002.

A58 Application for an adoption order Section 46 Adoption and Children Act 2002.

A59 Application for a Convention adoption order Section 46 Adoption and Children Act 2002.

A60 Application for an adoption order (excluding a Convention adoption order) where the child is habitually resident outside the British Islands and is brought into the United Kingdom for the purposes of adoption Section 46 Adoption and Children Act 2002.

A61 Application for an order for parental responsibility prior to adoption abroad Section 84 Adoption and Children Act 2002.

A62 Application for a direction under section 88(1) of the Adoption and Children Act 2002.

A63 Application for an order to annul a Convention adoption or Convention adoption order or for an overseas adoption or determination under section 91 to cease to be valid Section 89 Adoption and Children Act 2002.

A64 Application to receive information from court records Section 60(4) Adoption and Children Act 2002.

A65 Confidential information.

FP1 Application under Part 10 of the Family Procedure (Adoption) Rules 2005.

FP2 Application notice Part 9 of the Family Procedure (Adoption) Rules 2005.

FP3 Application for injunction (General form).

FP5 Acknowledgment of service Application under Part 10 of the Family Procedure (Adoption) Rules.

FP6 Certificate of service.

FP8 Notice of change of solicitor.

FP9 Certificate of suitability of litigation friend.

FP25 Witness Summons.

A20 Adoption - A Guide to Court Users.

A20(1) President's Intercountry Supplement

A20B President's Adoption Guidelines Booklet (Adoption Proceedings - A New Approach)

A50 Notes   Application for a Placement Order (Form A50) Notes on completing the form.

A51 Notes   Application for variation of a placement order (Form A51) Notes on completing the form.

A52 Notes   Application for revocation of a placement order (Form 52) Notes on completing the form.

A53 Notes   Application for a contact order under section 26 of the Adoption and Children Act 2002 (Form A53) Notes on completing the form.

A54 Notes   Application for variation or revocation of a contact order made under section 26 of the Adoption and Children Act 2002 (Form A54) Notes on completing the form.

A55 Notes   Application for permission to change a child's surname (Form A55) Notes on completing the form.

A56 Notes   Application for permission to remove a child from the United Kingdom (Form A56) Notes on completing the form.

A57 Notes

Application for a recovery order (Form A57) Notes on completing the form.

A58 Notes   Application for an adoption order (Form A58) Notes on completing the form.

A59 Notes   Application for a Convention adoption order (Form A59) Notes on completing the form.

A60 Notes   Application for an adoption order (excluding a Convention adoption order) where the child is habitually resident outside the British Islands and is brought into the United Kingdom for the purposes of adoption (Form A60) Notes on completing the form.

A61 Notes   Application for an order for parental responsibility prior to adoption abroad (Form A61) Notes on completing the form.

A62 Notes   Application for a direction under section 88(1) of the Adoption and Children Act 2002 (Form A62) Notes on completing the form.

A63 Notes   Application for an order to annul a Convention adoption or Convention adoption order or for an overseas adoption or determination under section 91 to cease to be valid (Form A63) Notes on completing the form.

FP1A   Application under Part 10 of the Family Procedure (Adoption) Rules 2005 Notes for applicant on completing the application (Form FP1).

FP1B   Application under Part 10 of the Family Procedure (Adoption) Rules 2005 Notes for respondent.

A21   Intercountry Adoption;

12. THE TIMES CAMPAIGN

The Times Online Family Justice Campaign 2008

In July 2008 *The Times* newspaper launched its campaign to open up the Family Courts and make Social Services more accountable for the removal of children from their families. Read the articles below.

Family justice: the secret state that steals our children

Every year thousands of children are taken from their parents, largely on the say-so of 'experts'. It is a secret and sometimes unjust process and the system must change

by Camilla Cavendish

The Times, 6 July 2008

Two weeks ago I got a phone call from a woman I hadn't seen for four years. She was calling to tell me that she was moving abroad, unable to bear the pain of living in the same country as the daughter she is no longer allowed to see. "I wanted to thank you," she said, "for being the only person who ever gave me a fair hearing." I was seized with guilt. This woman had asked for my help, and I had utterly failed her. Her story had been just so incredible. She described a world where courts need no criminal conviction to remove your child, only the word of a psychiatrist or doctor, and can deny you the chance to call any expert in your defence. A world that uses the "welfare of the child" to gag you from discussing your case. Where even if you prove yourself innocent on appeal, your children may already have been adopted: in which case you will never be allowed to contact them again. A world which had treated her so badly, this rather pretty and utterly normal young woman, that she was sincerely thanking me just for listening.

It had taken three calls from this lady and her boyfriend, a clean-cut army bloke, before I had agreed to go down to their provincial semi. We sat in their front room with the curtains drawn while they got out box after box of papers. And I got my first inkling of what it is like to go through the door into the secret state.

This particular case had started, as many do, with a custody battle. The mother had started to worry about her ex-partner's behaviour during his visits to their daughter. She approached social services to ask if they could supervise his visits. When the child then told a teacher that her father had touched her in bad places, the police were called. They filmed the child repeating the allegations. The upshot? A psychologist who watched the film but never met the mother, father or daughter wrote a report alleging that the mother had coached the daughter to lie. He never appeared in court, and was never crossexamined. Yet the court, encouraged by social workers, accepted his view. The judge ordered that the daughter should go to live with her father - a man the mother was convinced was an abuser.

My bitter regret, now, is that I did so little about that case. At the time I couldn't help wondering if there was not more to it than the mother had let on. And there may well have been. But today, I'm not so sure. Because so many elements of her story fit patterns that I have since heard again and again. The reliance on experts who have never met the accused. The stormtrooper behaviour of some social workers. The legal aid solicitors acting for parents who are always in a rush. This mother was plunged into a world of acronyms and organisations that she knew nothing about. She was always on the back foot. Having been the person who reached for help from the system, she became its victim.

The tale niggled away at me. I started asking questions. Soon after this encounter I met Denise and Nigel Clarkson, who had lost both their daughters after one sustained an unexplained injury, and who fought like tigers to get them back. Through the Eaton Foundation, which they founded, I met American doctors and radiologists who were challenging many of the assumptions made by British doctors who were diagnosing abuse from so-called "shaken baby syndrome" and certain tiny bone fractures.

I began to write about cases where judges were speaking out publicly about the failings of social services. In early 2006, Mr Justice Ryder denounced Oldham Council for taking a baby away from his parents because of a doctor who "strayed from the role of expert into the role of decision-maker" and a family court judge who "failed to detect that that was what had happened". Two courts refused to let the parents seek a second medical opinion. It was a year, the most formative year of that child's life, before the Court of Appeal allowed them to call a neurologist who proved that the injury was caused before birth. We know of that blunder only because the judge involved chose to make his judgment public. Few judges do.

The stories began to pour in. People left messages on my answering machine saying that the system was rotten but that they dared not speak out, because they had managed to get their children back. Some had taken a sick child to hospital, only to be accused of physical abuse. Some had been accused of "emotional abuse", a category that has no definition in British law but which has jumped 50 per cent in the past ten years as a reason for taking children into care. Quite a number had complained about their local authority, for letting them down over special-needs education, for example, only to find themselves in turn accused of neglect. One woman in Sheffield sobbed that her two autistic sons had been robbed of their mother, as well as the care they needed, because she was accused of making up their symptoms.

Some parents complained about social workers and hospitals refusing to give them copies of any papers or X-rays in their cases, which they needed to mount appeals. Every single one felt that the system was set against them before they could even assemble a defence. Some had real problems: violent ex-partners or unreliable new ones, low IQ, brushes with drugs in the past. Many had never been known to social services or the police before. All were desperate to be given the chance to prove that they were good parents, some begging the local authority to install CCTV cameras in their homes.

Many alleged that their children were treated far worse in care: unloved, not allowed to do homework, some with a new bruise almost every time they came for supervised contact, bruises that were never explained.

Since local authorities generally would not talk to me, citing confidentiality, I still had only part of the picture. Was there really a problem, or were these people all lying? I looked for figures. Were particular local authorities taking above-average numbers of children into care, for example? How many of these proceedings were contested? How many mothers were being accused of having Munchausen's Syndrome by Proxy, a psychiatric disorder that is supposed to be rare but seemed to be cropping up too often in my conversations? I would call the Home Office, which would refer me to the Lord Chancellor's Department, which would refer me to the various incarnations of the Education Department, which would usually refer me back to the Home Office. Many of my questions were met with the answer that the data was "not held centrally". This whole area started to look more and more like a hole inside government that ministers were simply not interested in.

Telling the stories was fiendishly difficult. First there was the legal requirement to avoid publishing anything that might even indirectly lead to the identification of the child involved. This is understandable, but it means that what journalists can write is sometimes so thin, so patchy that it is hard to ask anyone to believe us - because the most pertinent facts are often very distinctive. It also means that we can never humanise stories with photos, of the kind that helped to secure the freedom of Angela Cannings and Sally Clark. This is despite the fact that children can be pictured and named in adoption magazines, even while their frantic parents are trying to mount an appeal to get them back. Secondly, there were often additional reporting restrictions. Some of these were sought by local authorities as soon as I called them to try to get their sides of the stories. Some of these orders were so badly drafted that our lawyers simply could not tell what we could say. Some bore no relation to the draft that we had been sent before the hearing. It costs money to fight such orders, money that local media may not have and nationals are reluctant to commit.

The more often my articles were spiked or denuded of interesting detail, the more incensed I became. I began to feel that we, the liberal press, were part of a conspiracy of silence against people who had no voice. Worse, their children had no voice.

Some of these children were being told that they were in care because their parents no longer wanted them. As soon as a care order is made, the local authority controls all communications between parents and children. In many cases contact is gradually reduced, sometimes from a few hours a week to an hour or so a month, at which point social workers can return to court and claim that the child no longer has a strong bond with his family. Such tactics are unbearable. Clearly there must be some protection for authorities that work in extremely tough territory. Social workers are lambasted as often for failing to protect children from danger as for misjudging the innocent.

The problem is when laws that are meant to protect professionals from malicious allegations become an armoury against truth. There are good reasons why it is illegal to name a child involved in family court proceedings. Family law cases are fraught enough, without publicity adding to children's suffering. But it is quite wrong that laws framed to protect child privacy are being used to protect the professionals. Two years ago, when the children taken into care by Rochdale Council in the fabricated "satanic abuse" scandal left care and publicly attacked the council for removing them, the council argued that it would be wrong to name the social workers because that would breach the children's privacy - even though the children were desperate to speak out the minute they were free.

It does not have to be like this. The media cannot name the victim in rape cases. But we do report the evidence. Family courts, which operate in camera, have a lower standard of proof than criminal courts. They "convict" on a balance of probabilities, rather than beyond a reasonable doubt. A lower threshold is thought acceptable because civil courts cannot send people to jail. But to lose your children, and for them to lose you, because a court finds that abuse is a "probability", is a life sentence of another kind. This makes it even more vital that the system is accountable. Yet I cannot think of another area of public life that operates with so little scrutiny.

The main piece of legislation governing child protection is the 1989 Children Act. The Act was passed in the wake of the Cleveland scandal, in which allegations of sexual abuse by two consultant paediatricians at one hospital led to 121 children being removed from their homes. The Act clearly states that there should be "minimum intervention in family life" and that a court order should be made only if "it can be shown that this is better for the child than not making an order".

Yet some parts of the country seem to have strayed a long way from that. This year, the education watchdog Ofsted became the regulator for Cafcass, the Children and Family Court Advisory and Support Service that provides guardians ad litem for children in care cases. Ofsted's first two reports so far have been devastating. "Inspectors could not find evidence," Ofsted says, "about how service managers satisfy themselves that family court advisers are reaching sound conclusions in order to make the right recommendations to courts about children's lives". It found that "most reports contain recommendations to the court that fail to take account of a key principle of the Children Act that there should be minimum state intervention in family life". There is much more in similar vein. The hapless state of Cafcass is failing both children of innocent parents and children who are genuinely at risk.

Cafcass is one safeguard in the system that is manifestly failing. Another safeguard is that local authorities cannot remove children without a court order. But the manner in which these court orders are sought means that they are rarely refused (the Government has been unable to give me a single example of a refusal). Parents are not always informed that an order is even being sought, so are not able to defend themselves. Even if they are there, the momentum is unstoppable.

Bill Bache, the indefatigable solicitor who acted for Sally Clark, explained it to me this way. "Court proceedings are initiated within a day or two. The local authority knows the ropes. Most parents, including the brightest and most articulate, are often too distressed and shocked to think straight. They may well turn up unrepresented. The local authority makes its case, often in lurid terms, stressing that the children are in acute danger and they are requesting an immediate interim care order. There is no time sensibly to evaluate the evidence, therefore, no doubt wishing to be safe rather than sorry, the court grants the order. Suddenly the children are gone."

It is impossible to describe the shock, the isolation, that parents feel once their child is gone. Even educated people who can afford a good lawyer struggle to think straight. They feel alone against the system. Judges rely on reports by experts, social workers and guardians, many of whom are used to working together. This can produce a fatal lack of objectivity. I have spoken to some exemplary social workers and judges in the past few years. It is not my intention to demonise them all. But we must be able to spot whether the same individuals are reaching erroneous conclusions over and over again. At the moment any expert, social worker or judge who makes mistakes, goes beyond their brief or is on a crusade against parents is virtually immune from scrutiny. They do not expect that their evidence or their judgments will ever be made public. Remember that Professor Roy Meadow was only uncovered because he gave misleading evidence in the criminal courts, which are open. If family courts remain closed we will never be able to feel sure that justice is being done.

Over the next few days I hope to paint a more detailed picture of the pieces of the secret state, offer some explanations as to why mistakes are made, and to outline some solutions. The Times' interest is more than theoretical: we will continue to challenge various injunctions in the courts. But we also need your help by asking you to write to your MP. We will not give up. Because to sever a child from its family without due cause is licensed state oppression of the worst kind. It is, in fact, child abuse.

Family justice

Why the Government must act

Privacy laws are designed to protect at-risk children. Yet these same laws are cited to prevent local authority childcare professionals, expert witnesses and guardians from being subjected to scrutiny for decisions that can tear families apart.

The system claims that the welfare of children is paramount. But the only way to make the welfare of children paramount is to make childcare professionals properly accountable for their decisions.

The press is allowed to report the workings of the criminal courts, even in rape cases, where victim identities are kept confidential. Yet it is denied access to the family courts that make decisions with far-reaching consequences. In 2005 the Constitutional Affairs Select Committee advised that more transparency was needed and that family courts should be opened to the press in all but exceptional circumstances.

The Government consulted on the proposals, recognising that public confidence was plummeting. But it lost its nerve. The Ministry for Justice has yet to publish the results of a second consultation, which ended last October.

Eight months later the Government cannot even say when it will respond to the consultation.

Family courts: the hidden untouchables

In the second of our special articles, we explain how family courts operate in secrecy

Camilla Cavendish

The Times, 7 July 2008

I wrote yesterday about my gradual realisation that the child protection system is a sort of secret state. Many social workers, psychiatrists and judges are doing their best to help families. But given their power to tear families apart, the lack of accountability is astonishing.

In March 2006 a High Court judge, Mr Justice McFarlane, condemned social workers who had removed a nine-year-old girl from her parents for 14 months in the erroneous belief that her mother was suffering from Munchausen's syndrome by proxy. They had jumped to this conclusion after the mother took the girl to hospital for stomach pains, and a nurse found nothing wrong. They asked magistrates for an emergency protection order to remove the child without telling the parents or seeking any medical opinion. It was granted.

The judge found that every one of the assertions made by the social services team leader was "misleading or incomplete or wrong". He criticised magistrates for granting the order to take the girl. But he did not name the social workers. So we can never know who they are, or whether they are still working. It is a fair bet that none of the people involved has been disciplined.

Frontline social workers are employed by councils, which are theoretically controlled by elected councillors. But in child protection cases, councillors can be kept out of the loop. John Hemming, the Liberal Democrat MP who campaigns on these issues and has also been a Birmingham councillor, says that officials routinely refuse to answer questions. "Even as a councillor and member of the relevant scrutiny committee, they say no, we're not going to tell you anything, because of the secrecy of the family courts." The privacy of the child has become synonymous with the privacy of the professionals.

Parents who want to complain have to go first to the local authority that they are complaining about. Most fear that to do so will entrench the local authority's dislike of them. The few who are brave enough to complain receive a routine response saying that the matter has been investigated internally, and that the local authority is satisfied. Chris Smith, who lost his children to adoption, discovered that the investigator appointed by the local authority was not allowed to see any of the crucial court documentation. When he challenged the council concerned to release key papers under the Data Protection Act, they delayed for so long that the evidence arrived too late for his appeal. Many parents believe that their conversations with social workers have been distorted. But they are denied access to the case notes, even though these can be crucial in the courtroom.

Few parents have heard of the General Social Care Council, which has the power to remove workers from the Social Care Register. Since 2001 it has removed 17 people, mostly for inappropriate relationships with service users. There are 82,000 social workers on the register. Some of these seem to believe that they are above the law.

In February this year, a single mother called Louise Mason was reunited with two of her three children after a five-year battle against social services. It had started when she took her four-week-old baby to hospital. Doctors at first diagnosed a fairly common abdominal tumour. But they sought a second opinion in Belfast, where a doctor suspected that the injury might have been deliberate. Social services and police were called and her children were removed.

It took a year for the police to interview Mason under caution, and another year for her to be tried. During that time her access to her children was tightly curtailed. At worst she was allowed only an hour and a half with them once a month. Eventually a jury unanimously found her not guilty of causing grevious bodily harm. But social workers stuck to their own "guilty" verdict. They pressed on and served adoption papers. It took another two years for her to get two of her children back, with the help of the doctor who had made the original diagnosis. But the middle child had been allowed to see so little of her that he is likely to be adopted rather than returned.

What this case demonstrates is that parents can still lose their children even after being acquitted in the criminal courts. It is impossible to know how common this is. We know about this case only because the High Court judge who heard the appeal ordered that Louise Mason should be named.

It is not only social workers who are unaccountable. The secrecy of the family court system means that there is too little scrutiny of the psychiatrists and paediatricians who give evidence. A small but powerful group of radiologists, for example, believes that certain types of "greenstick" fracture are caused by parents twisting and wrenching a child's limbs - even if there are no bruises, cuts or broken bones. These fractures are often picked up when a child is taken to hospital with an unexplained head injury and given a full skeletal X-ray. One mother who took her baby to hospital with a nosebleed was accused of abuse after an X-ray showed three such fractures. There are now grave doubts about whether these painless fractures are caused by adults at all - yet courts still tend to consider them as absolute proof of abuse.

In 2003 Sally Clark, Trupti Patel and Angela Cannings were all cleared of murdering their babies. Lord Justice Judge declared that no one should go to prison again solely on the basis of expert witness evidence, and the criminal law was changed. But there have been no such changes in the family court system. "Expert" evidence almost always takes precedence over evidence from relatives and people who actually know the family.

The problem is compounded by the fact that judges are also acting in private. Unless they choose to make their judgments public there is no way of scrutinising the quality of those judgments.

Parts of the legal profession are concerned. In March 2005, a seminal report by the Constitutional Affairs Select Committee stated that "a greater degree of transparency is required in the family courts. An obvious move would be to allow the press and public into the family courts under appropriate reporting restrictions". It advised that the restrictions on the discussion of their cases by parents should be removed entirely.

The Government launched a consultation but local authorities, the NSPCC and some family lawyers lobbied successfully against openness, citing the "welfare of the child". In June 2007 Lord Falconer of Thoroton, the Lord Chancellor, stated that a survey of 200 children had shown that many would be anxious about the presence of the press in the family courts. He stated that he wished to concentrate on "improving the information coming out of family courts, rather than on who can go in". This meant giving more information about how the court has reached its decision to the people involved, and encouraging more judges to make their (anonymised) judgments public. A year on, ministers cannot say whether a single shred more information has been forthcoming.

The oldest law of bureaucracies is "first protect ourselves". The need to shed light into dark corners is made all the more pressing by some particularly pernicious allegations that parents find almost impossible to disprove - as I will describe tomorrow.

A Conspiracy of Silence

Allowing the family courts and social services to operate in secret allows miscarriages of justice without the possibility of redress

LEADING ARTICLE

The Times, 7 July 2008

Every parent fears losing their child. Except for those who have hit rock bottom, having a son or daughter taken into care is a desperate experience. The social workers, medical experts and judges who decide to remove children sometimes save lives by doing so; sometimes they ruin them. That is a grave responsibility. It means that the child protection system should be accountable and transparent. Shockingly, it is neither.

As Camilla Cavendish reports in Times2 today, serious miscarriages of justice are occurring behind the closed doors of social services departments and family courts. The area of child protection is described as "a hole inside government", with ministers unable even to say who is responsible. Too often, a "secret state" is at work that seems to assume that parents are guilty, and then obstructs them from establishing their innocence.

Some parents are unable to get copies of the evidence against them, including X-rays. Others are refused permission to call experts in their defence. Many fear that the professionals are distorting evidence and amplifying problems which should be solved by supporting families, rather than by tearing them apart.

It is impossible to know the extent to which miscarriages of justice may be occurring, because the whole system is shrouded in secrecy. Gagging orders on families and draconian reporting restrictions mean that very few cases come to light. Judges can choose to make their judgments public: but few do.

The authorities justify secrecy by arguing that the suffering of children caught in these fraught situations should not be made even worse by publicity. But secrecy also protects incompetence and wrongdoing. It should be quite possible to maintain the anonymity of children while also holding the professionals to account. Rape victims are anonymous in rape cases: that does not prevent police officers making statements in open court, nor the media reporting the evidence in full.

Family courts have a lower standard of proof than criminal courts. Yet they pass effective life sentences. If parents prove their innocence on appeal but their child has been adopted, they will never get that child back.

It is not the intention of this newspaper to demonise social workers, nor expert witnesses, nor judges. It is our intention to expose mistakes, and to create a system which can acknowledge that error is human. Many social workers feel that they can do no right, being criticised for negligence if they fail to spot abuse in time, then accused of being overzealous if parents are found innocent on appeal. That is understandable. They work in fraught situations. They need more support, and oversight. But the minority must not be allowed to act as though they were above the law.

This newspaper recently reported on the case of Louise Mason, whose children were kept from her for two years by social workers, despite her having been exonerated by a jury. Her third child will probably never be returned to her, because he is felt to have bonded so well in foster care.

The Times believes that these are matters of pressing public interest. Many of our readers have already urged us to do more. There is growing suspicion of the authorities which are meant to support families. The only way to quell those suspicions is to let the light in to the family courts.

From today it will be possible to go online (timesonline.co.uk/familycourts) and express support for openness. Please do. We will not be part of what has become, in effect, a conspiracy of silence against children who have no voice.

Family justice: what we can do to protect our children

A ten-point plan to make our courts system fairer

Camilla Cavendish

The Times, 9 July 2008

Over the past three days The Times has set out some of the ways in which it fears the child protection system is being subverted by forces that are largely unaccountable. We believe that the Children Act has unintentionally handed enormous power to local authorities and experts, which some are using arbitrarily. And that secrecy keeps injustices from public view.

Opening up the system sounds easier than it is. Yet there are concerns that it could lead to paediatricians and other experts being vilified and refusing to do child protection work, social workers becoming demoralised and the exposure of families' private troubles. That journalists would not keep confidences. That reports by local papers might inadvertently add to the suffering of children by revealing their identities to people living near by.

These are valid concerns. I know two couples who have adopted children in very difficult circumstances. The natural parents of those children are quite unable to care for them, but they are also vengeful. Those couples and those children should not have to live in fear of being tracked down. They have made me think very carefully about the nuances of this. But I feel that these considerations can no longer outweigh the risk of grave injustices being perpetrated against children. And that we can put safeguards in place that will work.

When the Constitutional Affairs Select Committee heard evidence on this issue three years ago, many of the respondents seemed to assume that media access would inevitably hurt children. That is wrong. In the Court of Appeal almost all family law hearings are in public with reporting restrictions imposed. The press attends family proceedings in magistrates' courts, again with reporting restrictions. The press simply does not identify children when it is illegal to do so. Many of my articles may seem incomplete precisely because I am bending over backwards not to publish information that might identify the child.

The Australian and Canadian family court systems are open and transparent. Children's identities are protected but judgments are public, and so is the evidence on which they are based. That means that justice can be done, and be seen to be done. Their press apparently takes no interest at all in the majority of cases. This would surely be the same here.

The Constitutional Affairs Select Committee took the view that courts should be opened in all but exceptional circumstances. In July 2006, the Government seemed to agree. It published a consultation paper stating that greater openness was required in family court proceedings "so that people can understand, better scrutinise decisions and have greater confidence". It proposed that the media should attend proceedings "on behalf of and for the benefit of the public", with reporting restrictions to keep the parties anonymous. Almost a year later, the Lord Chancellor, Lord Falconer of Thoroton, rowed back, citing a survey of 200 children in which a slender majority had expressed anxiety about letting the media into the family courts. He said that openness would be improved "not by numbers or types of people going in to the courts, but by the amount and quality of information coming out of the courts". A second consultation paper proposed keeping courts closed, but encouraged judges to release anonymised judgments.

That was a tragic loss of nerve. For there is no way that the growing lack of public confidence in the system can be solved by the publication of a bit more information that the authorities decide to let us see. Publishing an anonymised judgment without the evidence will not let ordinary citizens see what is being done in their name. We cannot tell, for example, whether witness X repeatedly goes beyond their remit or offers hearsay evidence. We cannot tell whether local authority B or judge C repeatedly gives X's evidence undue weight. If it was felt too risky to reveal their names, I would suggest that each expert witness could be given a unique code. That would deter the sensationalist hack from malice, but would enable the determined truth-seeker to track the behaviour of individuals over time, and hold them to account.

Many of the children's charities and lawyers who lobby against openness are trying to protect vulnerable people from damaging publicity. It is a tricky balancing act. But the clincher for me is this. One of the most draconian decisions the State makes is to deprive a child of a parent's love and care. Removing a child from its family is not simply a private matter. It is a decision that demands the very highest standards of accountability and transparency.

I believe that wholesale reforms are needed, which can be summed up in ten points:

1. Open family courts to the press in all but exceptional circumstances (as recommended by the Constitutional Affairs Select Committee).

2. Let any parent or carer accused of abuse call any witnesses they need in their defence. At the moment, they are routinely refused permission to do so.

3. Give automatic permission for parents who are refused legal aid to get a lay adviser to help them present their case. This is routinely refused.

4. Remove the restrictions that prevent families from talking about their case (as recommended by the Constitutional Affairs Select Committee).

5. Review the definition of "emotional abuse" across local authorities, to make sure that it cannot become a catch-all for overzealous officials.

6. Provide an automatic right for parents to receive copies of case conference notes and all evidence used against them in court, just as they would in a criminal trial.

7. Create an independent body to oversee the actions of social services, with proper sanctions. If that body is to be the General Social Care Council, make it easier for parents to go directly to that body rather than having to face delays from the local authority.

8. Let children in care waive their right to privacy if they wish to speak out. For gagging children is surely not consistent with promoting their welfare.

9. Restructure CAFCASS, the Family Court Advisory Service, from being an organisation that reports on the parents to the courts to one that actively promotes the parenting needs of children. The primary focus should cease to be assisting the court process. It should be diverting parents away from contested hearings into the making of parenting plans.

10. Review the recent legal aid cut-backs that are deterring lawyers from taking on these complex family cases. It is quite wrong that desperate parents are unable to find a lawyer to help them in their time of need.

Thank you for listening. As Jeremy Bentham said, where there is no publicity, there is no justice. If you support these ideas, please do go online, support our campaign and e-mail your MP.

Family justice: your word against theirs

In the third of our special articles, we look at the pernicious types of allegation that are almost impossible for parents to disprove

Camilla Cavendish

The Times, 9 July 2008

I wrote on Monday about the many desperate parents who have app-roached me after losing their children to social services. One thing that they all have in common is shock at how quickly the system seems to decide against them, and at how doggedly it sticks to that view despite all evidence to the contrary. Some parents find that minor issues are magnified until the conclusions reached are out of all proportion. The opposite also seems to hold true: some children come to terrible harm because the system systematically underestimates the risk to them.

Why does this happen? Eileen Munro, a reader in social policy at the London School of Economics and the author of Effective Child Protection, says that "child protection work inevitably involves uncertainty, ambiguity and fallibility". She believes that it is human nature to form a view based on first impressions, and stick to it. "This has a devastating impact in child protection work," she says, "in that professionals hold on to their beliefs about a family despite new evidence that challenges them. It can be equally harmful whether they are over or underestimating the degree of the risk to the child. They may continue to believe parents are doing well, even though there are successive reports of the child's being distressed or injured. Innocent parents wrongly judged abusive can face the frightening experience of being unable to shake the professionals' conviction, however much counter-evidence they produce."

The risk of groupthink makes it all the more important that decisions are transparent and open to review. We all know of the tragic deaths of children such as Victoria Climbié, who with hindsight should have been saved. We know much less about the tragedies of children wrongly separated from their families, because of the secrecy of the system.

There are several types of allegation that are almost impossible for parents to disprove. One is "emotional abuse". You can see why the category exists. Ill-treatment comes in many forms, not all of which leave visible scars. But in that nebulous phrase lurks the potential for injustice. In the past ten years there has been a 50per cent increase in the number of parents or carers accused of "emotional abuse". It now accounts for 21 per cent of all children registered as needing protection, up from 14 per cent in 1997. Yet the term has no strict definition in British law.

Emotional abuse is not "neglect": that is a separate category. The Department of Health defines it as "persistent emotional ill-treatment ... [that] may involve conveying to children that they are worthless or inadequate ... and may feature age or developmentally inappropriate expectations being placed on children ... Some level of emotional abuse is involved in all types of ill treatment of a child, though it may occur alone."

Local authorities interpret this in different ways. In Nottingham, emotional abuse is "an ingrained pattern of interaction ... which it is essential to observe and understand over time". In Enfield it includes "swearing", "conditional love" or "discriminatory remarks". I have heard anecdotally of councils, including West Sussex and Cambridge, that almost never use the term. There are no statistics to confirm this. But it seems that child protection is as much of a postcode lottery as cancer screening.

Expert medical evidence is also notoriously difficult to disprove, even where there is no circumstantial evidence. Lord Justice Judge (who was named as the next Lord Chief Justice yesterday) has warned against an "over-dogmatic" approach in the criminal courts, when we are "still at the frontiers of knowledge". But it is less clear how family judges should treat syndromes such as Munchausen's syndrome by proxy (MSbP).

Since the discrediting of Professor Sir Roy Meadow, who first defined it, Munchausen's has been relabelled as "fabricated or induced illness". This is a perverse disorder in which an adult invents or deliberately creates a child's illness to draw attention to himself or herself. Even the experts agree that Munchausen's is rare, likely to affect no more than 50 people a year. But campaigners fear that far more people are being accused of it. For the traits of the Munchausen mother are broad enough to cast suspicion on many whose children are genuinely ill. They include a reluctance to leave the sick child's side, familiarity with medical terms and, most devastating, the denial of accus-ations of abuse.

Two years ago, a group of MPs with falsely accused constituents asked the Government how many people nationally were accused of having MSbP. The Government replied that it did not collect such data - even though Department of Health guidelines tell charity workers, nursery nurses, teachers and even pharmacists to look out for the condition.

Last year, social workers in Hexham told a pregnant student at Edinburgh University that she was in danger of developing MSbP when her baby was born, so they were thinking of removing the baby at birth. The student, Fran Lyon, had developed self-harming and eating disorders seven years earlier, after being raped. But these are disorders from which she has fully recovered. The psychiatrist who treated her as a teenager states that she poses no harm to her child. So does another psychiatrist, who knows Lyon through her charity work. The only person who seems to have entertained the idea that she could develop MSbP is a paediatrician who has never met her. But social workers have given his evidence more weight. Lyon fled to Europe last year, unable to trust her own country, and is now in a legal limbo.

To err is human. To refuse to acknowledge that is inhumane. No professional can be right all the time, particularly in this fraught territory. That is why wholesale reforms are needed - as I will explain tomorrow.

Justice can't be done in secret. And here's why

We will always try to twist the evidence to fit our theories. Especially when we are wrong

Daniel Finkelstein

The Times, 9 July 2008

Have you ever heard of "wilding"? Can you remember when you heard of it? I want to refresh your memory.

This week in Times2, my colleague Camilla Cavendish has been telling some terrible stories of children taken from their parents without good reason and adopted against their will, never to be returned. And all in secret. Not a word to be published. I think that the story of wilding will help you to see why the secrecy is a scandal.

On April 19, 1989, a young woman jogging in Central Park, New York, was attacked. That understates it. She was brutally beaten and raped. Her terrible injuries left doctors convinced she would die. Eventually she pulled through, although without a memory of the attack.

The case of the Central Park Jogger became a symbol of a city out of control. The story became even bigger when the first arrests were made. New York police rounded up a gang of young African-Americans who quickly confessed. Apparently they liked to attack strangers, regarding their frenzied assaults as a form of entertainment. Wilding, they called it, and the word became famous.

Now I am going to tell you something you may not know. Certainly I didn't until I stumbled across it a couple of days ago. About ten years after being sentenced for his part in the wilding, Kharey Wise met a man in prison, another New York rapist, called Matias Reyes. And the more Reyes got to think about it the sorrier he felt for his new friend. For Reyes knew something that the police and the courts did not. The wilding story was nonsense. The confessions were coerced, as the young men had claimed for years. How did he know it? Because he, Matias Reyes, had really raped and beaten the Central Park Jogger.

What follows is the shocking bit - shocking but instructive. The moment that Reyes confessed, it was clear that he was indeed guilty. His DNA was linked to the rape, and the chance that the link was mistaken was one in six billion. The wilding teenagers had left no DNA. And, when you came to look at it, their confessions didn't really add up. They weren't consistent with each other or with the facts. The District Attorney concluded that the convictions must be overturned and there can't be much doubt that he was right.

Yet the prosecution lawyer in the original case refused to accept this. She was furious. She stridently opposed the finding of the DA. So did the New York Police Department. They convened a panel that concluded that the police had done nothing wrong and that, even if Reyes was guilty, he may not have acted alone. They concluded, lamely, that the teens must have started the assault with Reyes taking his opportunity later.

Even though the teens were eventually freed, this sort of behaviour is typical. In this country we should know this because we have had the case of Timothy Evans, whose wife and child were found dead at 10 Rillington Place, Notting Hill, West London. Evans was hanged in 1950, found guilty of murdering the child, a crime he blamed on his fellow tenant John Christie.

Then in 1953, other bodies were found at Rillington Place - in the garden and sealed behind wallpaper. Christie was a mass murderer. The evidence that Evans had been executed in error was overwhelming, but the legal Establishment refused to yield to it. There was silence at first. Then there was a review that concluded, preposterously, that he murdered his wife but not the baby. This paved the way to a pardon 15 years after Evans's death. His conviction, obviously wrongful, has never been overturned.

Why does this happen? Why do people refuse to accept what simply has to be true? Social psychologists use a term to describe this behaviour that you may have come across - it is called cognitive dissonance. This is the tension that arises when a person holds two attitudes that are psychologically inconsistent. And it is tension that is hard to live with, tension that simply has to be resolved.

So what do you do? A brilliant new book by Carol Tavris and Elliot Aronson - Mistakes Were Made, but not by Me - explains. You believe that you are a good person, say, yet you know you have done a bad thing. There is dissonance. You resolve it by deciding that the bad thing was not that bad. The worse your behaviour, the harder you will try to twist it around in your head until you can reconcile it with your view of yourself.

It is commonly thought that we have theories and that they are tested by the facts. The opposite is true. We have theories and then we strive mightily to fit the facts into them, ignoring those that don't quite work or reinterpreting them if we have to. The more we have at stake emotionally, the more pressing this task becomes.

Cognitive disssonance explains a great deal. Take Gordon Brown. Some people believe that all the strife, all the difficulties he is encountering may lead him to give up. Cognitive dissonance suggests that the more trouble he is in, the more difficult things get, the harder he will work to convince himself that it is all worthwhile and that he is indispensable. His troubles make him less likely to resign, not more.

Now look at the Central Park Jogger case. People suffered because mistakes were made. The police and the prosecution, believing themselves to be good people doing good work, could not reconcile this suffering with their view of themselves. So they insisted, they had to insist, that the teenagers were guilty. The facts challenged their theory of themselves, so the facts had to be reinterpreted. The Evans case is similar. The legal Establishment regarded itself as dispensing justice and the death of an innocent man didn't fit. It became essential that he not be innocent, whatever the evidence.

When groups - police, medics, politicians, social workers, the Family Court apparatus - get together, convinced of their own righteousness, the facts (like Timothy Evans) can go hang. They are certain that they are right, certain they are just and often, you know, they really are. But when they are not, they will never ever admit it, digging themselves in more and more deeply.

A local authority that has taken your children away can never admit it did so wrongly. And every fact that shows that it did needs to be twisted around until it shows that it didn't. That is what is happening all the time, behind the close doors of our Family Courts, beyond scrutiny.

There's only one way out. That is to allow others, those without a stake in the righteousness of anyone, to shine a light on proceedings. Not to do so is inexcusable. It is an affront to justice and the rule of law.

Europe to begin investigation of secrecy in family courts
by Sam Coates and Camilla Cavendish
The Times Online, 10 July 2008

Britain faces an investigation by Europe into secrecy in family courts, amid growing political pressure to overhaul the system.

The Council of Europe has stepped in after allegations that gagging laws designed to protect the rights of children are allowing miscarriages of justice and children to be removed unnecessarily from their parents.

The Times has been running a series of articles this week about the consequences of the system that keeps reporters and the public out of many family court hearings and obstructs people from seeing evidence against them or obtaining copies of judgments. Opponents of the system say that judges can be too ready to side with social workers and experts who want a child removed but whose evidence is rarely made public.

Family courts in England and Wales hear 400,000 cases a year, mostly divorces and child custody cases. In about 20,000 cases a year, however, local councils apply to remove children from parents on the ground that parents are abusive or neglectful.

The council's investigation was initiated by Paul Rowen, the Liberal Democrat MP who is one of Britain's representatives, and will begin in September. It could involve hearings by a committee that will take evidence and be able to visit courts.

It will come at a critical time for campaigners who are fighting to open up the system. The Government has promised to respond to a long-delayed consultation after the summer.

Three years ago the Constitutional Affairs Select Committee said that greater transparency was required and restrictions on the discussion of their cases by parents should be removed entirely.

Moves to open the courts up were quashed by Lord Falconer of Thoroton in one of his final acts as Lord Chancellor in June 2007. He stated that a survey of 200 children had shown that many would be anxious about the presence of the press in the family courts.

Evidence taken by the Children and Schools Select Committee last month heard how pregnant women who missed antenatal classes were being threatened with referral to social services.

Justice for Families

An enormous response to the articles in The Times highlights widespread concern over the secrecy that shrouds the family courts

Leading Article

The Times, 12 July 2008

It is five days since The Times launched its campaign to open up the family courts and make social services more accountable for the removal of children from their families. The enormous response so far has bolstered our view that this is a vital debate. Many parents, but also lawyers, social workers and members of the medical profession have written in to sound the alarm about different aspects of the child protection system.

Not everyone supports our position. One common criticism was put eloquently by Sir Mark Potter, Britain's most-senior family judge, in The Times yesterday. He argued that the family courts are not "secret", but "private", operating in what he described as "a minefield of complexity and emotion". And that most families desire privacy, because family hearings expose deeply personal details.

This is the same argument that Lord Falconer of Thoroton used last year to explain why the Government rejected the recommendations of the Constitutional Affairs Select Committee for opening the family courts and allowing parents to talk about their cases. This week Bridget Prentice, Minister of Justice, has said that "the right of the public to know what is happening has to be balanced with a child's right to privacy". But the two should not be mutually exclusive. With proper reporting restrictions in place, it is perfectly possible to have accountability and to keep a child's details confidential. That is what happens in Canada and Australia, where the courts are open. It is also the case in the Court of Appeal, where most family hearings are held in public.

There is something very wrong when parents are gagged to "protect" their children, while those same children are routinely pictured and named in adoption magazines. Removing a child from his or her family is not just a private matter. It is a matter for all society. That is why the Council of Europe has taken the extraordinary step this week of launching an investigation into the secrecy of family law in England and Wales.

Sir Mark Potter and many other judges support the Government's proposal that all judgments should be made public in anonymised form, in cases where children are removed. That is a welcome step. But it does not go far enough. Without access to the evidence, it will be impossible to discover whether certain expert witnesses or social workers are making errors repeatedly. The system should meet the very highest standards of accountability, given that its decisions can destroy or save lives.

The Government has committed this week to publishing new proposals after the summer. This is a welcome end to the nine-month limbo since the deadline for its last consultation. But bold proposals are needed to reform a system that is in disarray. These include restructuring Cafcass, the Family Court Advisory Service, to reviewing the cutbacks in legal aid. Parents should have an automatic right to receive copies of the evidence used against them in court, just as they would in a criminal trial. It is outrageous that this point should have to be made at all. A large number of readers have told The Times this week that they have been denied access to papers that they need to mount an appeal. It is a matter of deep concern that parents accused of child abuse have fewer rights than those accused of murder.

Some of those who work in child protection are understandably upset at what they see as an attack on their competence, driven by aggrieved parents who give only one side of the story. But the growing suspicion of the authorities who are meant to support families will not be quelled by continuing to suppress information. We need both sides of the story to be told. That is why The Times will continue to shine as much light as possible on these issues in the coming weeks.

A moving response to our family justice campaign

The Times call for an end to secrecy has produced a huge reaction - except from the man who could change it

by Camilla Cavendish

The Times, 17 July 2008

I am awed by the response to the family justice campaign that The Times launched last week. So many readers have e-mailed their MPs that I am getting calls from all three main parties. Several MPs have also raised their private concerns about how their own local authorities behave. It is uplifting to see democracy in action.

There are chinks of light already. Thoughtful people on all sides of the argument seem to accept that some degree of change is needed. Sir Mark Potter, President of the Family Division, gave broad but qualified support to many of our proposed reforms, although he argues strongly that the courts are private, not secret, and that families want them that way. Bridget Prentice, the Justice Minister, has announced that the Government will finally publish new proposals this autumn.

Many social workers restrained the urge to hurl rotten eggs and supported our call for openness, while saying that the system is not as Kafkaesque as I fear.

Bill McKittrick, a social worker for 35 years and director of Bristol Social Services for ten, wrote to say that openness is a moral imperative in care proceedings where, he tells me, "lawyers get rich, social workers check and check, but children and parents get lost". He says that "groupthink" can easily take hold. "The more people involved in a decision, the more dangerous the decisions are." But he still thinks that mature professionals would get a better press if they gave their side of the story, being honest about the uncertainties involved in decisions, rather than trotting out the mantra of "never apologise, never explain".

Two main arguments have been made against The Times's position. First, that the family courts should not be open to the press because the parents and children involved in cases dread being identified. Sir Mark, the heads of the Children and Family Court Advisory and Support Service (Cafcass), the Royal College of Paediatricians and Child Health and Family Justice Council have all made this point. It is understandable that families don't want the neighbours to know highly personal details.

The same argument was used by Lord Falconer of Thoroton last year to reject the recommendation of the Constitutional Affairs Select Committee, that the family courts should be open and parents no longer gagged. It is prompted by a visceral dislike of the press, which I can partly understand. Yet it is overdone. I see from the inside how concerned the press is to remain within the law. In rape cases and family appeals, reporting restrictions have successfully kept names secret while allowing evidence to be reported.

The halfway house proposed by many, including the Government, is to publish all judgments, but made anonymous. That would be a good step. But without access to the underlying evidence, it will be impossible to discover whether experts or social workers are making repeated errors. The public do not need to name names for justice to be done. But they do need to see the evidence on which people are effectively convicted.

The second criticism is that professionals do their job properly, and we critics do not understand the complexity they have to deal with. The Family Justice Council states that "the courts do not shrink from exposing poor practice by social workers and questionable medical evidence". I cannot agree. In the past few years, Court of Appeal judges have made blistering criticisms of lower courts for relying on shockingly poor statements from social workers and experts. Family court judges can rely heavily on such people, in cases where there is no circumstantial evidence.

It seems Orwellian to ask us to trust people who are not subject to scrutiny to make correct decisions about cases which we are repeatedly told are too complex for us to understand. Years can pass between children being taken into care and a successful appeal. Those are formative years in which children are deprived of their parents, and sometimes adopted before an appeal is even heard.

The Royal College of Paediatricians gives warning that doctors will stop giving evidence for fear of vilification in the media. That very real fear is made worse because so many paediatricians still support Professor Sir Roy Meadow, who went beyond his remit, and gave evidence that led to the jailing of innocent people. If innocent experts do live in fear then that is entirely the media's fault, and we must correct that. But I do not believe that they would have to.

Intriguingly, only one person challenged our view that the system is unaccountable. That was Sir Rodney Brooke, chair of the General Social Care Council. I have seen no evidence that the GSCC has disciplined a single social worker denounced by appeal court judges in the past few years. But I hope to be corrected. Nor did any one of the eminent bodies who wrote to us deny that miscarriages of justice occur. Some of the glib references have made miscarriages of justice sound like a standard occupational hazard. There are 550,000 referrals to social services every year. It makes the Birmingham Six fade by comparison.

Yesterday, Frank Lockyer wrote to point out that the authorities have closed ranks in response to our campaign. "The agencies defend themselves by persisting that things are done as they expect, rather than as they are," he said. Mr Lockyer should know. His daughter was Sally Clark, jailed for killing two of her sons until her conviction was quashed, and who has since died. Mr Lockyer knows that his daughter was exonerated only because she could protest her innocence in public. In the family courts, gagging orders make that impossible. We cannot know how many Sally Clarks have lost their children. The volume of mail on this topic has been hugely welcome. Only one person has remained silent. Jack Straw, the Secretary of State for Justice, holds the power to change the system for the better. It would be good to know what he is going to do about it.

Times wins ruling over secrecy of family court
Rosemary Bennett
The Times, 22 July 2008

Details of private family court proceedings that led to a mother fleeing the country with her son after he was placed in foster care have been disclosed after legal action by The Times.

The highly unusual ruling allows the publication of undisclosed details of the case. The boy's stepfather was sent to prison for 16 months for helping the mother to remove him from care and flee abroad.

She has since had another baby, the couple's first child. The stepfather has been released from prison but is forbidden to contact his wife.

The Times fought to publish more information after an outcry from readers when the case was reported by Camilla Cavendish . She highlighted the perceived secrecy of family courts and the lack of scrutiny of social workers, who have sweeping powers to remove children from their parents. Times readers were particularly outraged that the stepfather served a longer sentence than many muggers.

Sir Mark Potter, the President of the Family Division, dismissed Medway Council's argument that it should not be named publicly in case it led to identification of the child, known as S. With more than 300 children in local authority care in the Kent borough, he said that this was unlikely.

The judge accepted that there was considerable public interest and that reporting a fuller story would "enable the public to form its own view whether the actions of the [Medway] council or the decisions of the court to date have been fairly characterised".

His summary of the care proceedings provides an insight into the secretive family courts, where decisions to remove children from their parents' care are made every day. The Times can report for the first time that social workers became involved shortly before the mother and father split up. In the ensuing care proceedings the mother made claims of domestic violence that were "heavily disputed" by the father. The judge found that, while the mother had exaggerated many claims, the father had on occasion acted "in an aggressive and intimidating manner, which placed S at risk of harm". The mother was found to have a "tendency to play the role of victim".

Judge Cox, the family court judge, concluded that S was "suffering emotional harm due to the conflict between the parents". She ordered that S be taken into foster care until matters improved. There were also concerns about living conditions, with the family home described as "like a building site". At a later hearing the judge said that she was troubled that S was keeping secrets with his mother, who was manipulative.

In a final care order the court ruled that the boy would stay in foster care and his mother was given a list of conditions to meet before he could be returned. These included weekly counselling, a move to secure accommodation and a settled lifestyle. She was also not allowed to discuss with her son the possibility of his returning to her care without social workers' permission. Contact with her son would be reviewed and would depend on her "promotion" of his foster placement. She also had to cooperate with "counselling with S concerning the father's gender identity issues".

A final hearing on the case was due to take place last October. A social workers' report said that there had been no significant improvement in the mother's "insight/approach" towards S. Although the mother had moved house and remarried, the social workers noted that she was still challenging the care proceedings: "Significant improvements are not possible while the mother continues to be of the opinion that much of the previous judgments has been wrong or exaggerated," they wrote.

They concluded that adoption would give S "the best possible opportunity for permanency".

At 4am on September 11 last year, the mother, assisted by M, her new husband, took the child from his foster home and drove to France. When M returned two days later he was arrested and charged with abduction.

John Hemming, a Liberal Democrat MP campaigning for more openness in family courts, said: "I am pleased that Sir Mark has recognised the public interest in people understanding that the reasonings of the family court outweighs the need for the activities of practitioners to be kept secret."

A resolution at the Parliamentary Assembly of the Council of Europe was tabled in October 2008.

http://assembly.coe.int/Main.asp?link=/Documents/WorkingDocs/Doc08/EDOC11742.htmfor full details.

1. The Assembly recognises that the protection of human rights is one of the Council of Europe's core values. It recognises that children are particularly vulnerable and that systems must be in place to protect those children considered "at risk".

2. The Assembly believes, however, that those who are tasked with protecting children need to be accountable for their actions and need to operate in a way which protects the human rights of all the people they are dealing with.

3. The Assembly notes the recent judgment of the European Court of Human Rights, X. v. Croatia (Application No. 11223/04) dated 17 July 2008, which held unanimously that there had been a violation of Article 8 (right to respect for private and family life) on account of the applicant's exclusion from the proceedings which resulted in her daughter being adopted.

4. The Assembly believes that the use of mental incapacity by Croatia to exclude a person from involvement in their children's future is wrong and not only violates Article 6 (right to a fair trial) but also Article 8 (right to family life) and Article 13 (right to an effective remedy).

5. The Assembly notes that in the United Kingdom, the 1989 Children's Act is the main legislation governing child protection and that Cafcass (the Children and Family Court Advisory and Support Service) provides guardians ad litem for children in care cases.

6. The Assembly further notes that since the start of 2008, when Ofsted (Office for Standards in Education) became the regulator for Cafcass, it has issued two reports which have criticised the standards used by Cafcass. It said: "Inspectors could not find evidence about how service managers satisfy themselves that family court advisers are reaching sound conclusions in order to make the right recommendations to courts about children's lives". It found that "most reports contain recommendations to the court that fail to take account of a key principle of the Children's Act that there should be minimum state intervention in family life".

7. The Assembly notes that there are over 100 cases a year in England and Wales in which an organ of the state (the Official Solicitor) displaces a parent in proceedings which may lead to the adoption of their child or children.

8. The Assembly further notes that mothers have had their children removed because they were victims of domestic violence or on the basis of medical evidence for which there had been no second opinion.

9. The Assembly further notes that England habitually gives judgment in family proceedings without the judgment being in public (in conflict with Article 6). This Assembly notes

that there can be an argument for anonymity, but not for the reasoning of the court to be kept secret which means that the court's reasoning is not properly accountable.

10. The Assembly believes that these reports and concerns provide evidence of possible violation by the United Kingdom of Articles 6, 8 and 13.

11. The Assembly notes that Portugal also operates a system of forcible adoption where the parents, having not willingly given up their parental rights, have children forcibly adopted away from them.

12. The Assembly therefore believes that there is sufficient evidence and concern about the operation of family courts in relation to the European Convention on Human Rights in Croatia, Portugal and the United Kingdom to request that an investigation be carried out.

And here are the three Articles in the European Convention on Human Rights in question:

Article 6 – Right to a fair trial

In the determination of his civil rights and obligations or of any criminal charge against him, everyone is entitled to a fair and public hearing within a reasonable time by an independent and impartial tribunal established by law. Judgment shall be pronounced publicly but the press and public may be excluded from all or part of the trial in the interests of morals, public order or national security in a democratic society, where the interests of juveniles or the protection of the private life of the parties so require, or to the extent strictly necessary in the opinion of the court in special circumstances where publicity would prejudice the interests of justice.

Everyone charged with a criminal offence shall be presumed innocent until proved guilty according to law.

Everyone charged with a criminal offence has the following minimum rights:

to be informed promptly, in a language which he understands and in detail, of the nature and cause of the accusation against him;

to have adequate time and facilities for the preparation of his defence;

to defend himself in person or through legal assistance of his own choosing or, if he has not sufficient means to pay for legal assistance, to be given it free when the interests of justice so require;

to examine or have examined witnesses against him and to obtain the attendance and examination of witnesses on his behalf under the same conditions as witnesses against him;

to have the free assistance of an interpreter if he cannot understand or speak the language used in court.

Article 8 – Right to respect for private and family life

Everyone has the right to respect for his private and family life, his home and his correspondence.

There shall be no interference by a public authority with the exercise of this right except such as is in accordance with the law and is necessary in a democratic society in the interests of national security, public safety or the economic well-being of the country, for the prevention of disorder or crime, for the protection of health or morals, or for the protection of the rights and freedoms of others.

Article 13 – Right to an effective remedy

Everyone whose rights and freedoms as set forth in this Convention are violated shall have an effective remedy before a national authority notwithstanding that the violation has been committed by persons acting in an official capacity.

13. RESULTS FOLLOWING CAMPAIGNS BY THE TIMES AND OTHERS

Family courts to be opened up as Jack Straw announces massive shake-up

by Frances Gibb

The Times, 16 Dec 2008

Social workers and local authorities who fail in their duties to families and children will in future be named under radical reforms to open up the family courts.

The move, revealed by Jack Straw, Justice Secretary, in an exclusive interview with The Times, means that in future when social workers or expert witnesses are castigated by judges, they will not have the cover of anonymity.

It follows a series of articles in The Times stretching back three years and highlighting the potential for miscarriages of justice because of the secrecy surrounding family court proceedings.

Mr Straw spoke to The Times as he was preparing to unveil a far-reaching shake-up of the family court system, to make it more transparent.

"Local authorities aren't routinely named at the moment. My view is that ought to be. There should be no restriction on naming social workers or medical experts unless it could lead to the identification of [children] ," he said.

In a second change, Mr Straw announced this afternoon that the media will be able to attend family courts and report on cases as long as they do not name the parties or give out the kind of personal details which allow nosy neighbours to identify them.

People involved in family court proceedings will be able to apply for specific reporting restrictions, Mr Straw said. But he hopes that judges will only rarely accede to such requests. "My hope is that the courts are reluctant to grant these," he said.

Mr Straw will have the support of the senior judiciary. Sir Mark Potter, Britain's most senior family judge, told The Times recently that family courts should be opened to the media to dispel the "myths and inaccuracies" surrounding the system.

The balance had come down "in favour of increased openness by permitting the attendance of the media", subject to protecting the anonymity of children and, "where appropriate, the parties," Sir Mark said.

Mr Straw said that the family courts has been "a closed world". Opening it out would provide a chance that standards would rise and "egregious practices spotted before they become harmful."

Professionals should be prepared to put their reputations on the line in public just as a structural engineer at a planning inquiry does. "People who are professional have to accept that what goes with being professional is the public task," he added

In a third move, parents will be able to disclose information about their case for the purpose of advice and support. Overall, the Justice Secretary believes that the impact of the changes - to take effect from April 1 - will be at local level among local newspapers, with the vast majority of proceedings still unreported.

He paid tribute to The Times for drawing attention to the issue in its campaign which "ensured it landed on my desk." He had also been struck by the levels of secrecy when visiting a Youth Court, where magistrates had a debate about whether to let him in.

"I thought they were being ridiculous. Justice has to be seen to be done."

Family courts: what changed on the long walk to freedom
by Camilla Cavendish
The Times, 16 December 2008

Jack Straw's long-awaited decision to open up proceedings is a welcome one, fuelled by an ever-increasing lobby of which The Times has been at the forefront

Some years ago when he was Home Secretary, Jack Straw wanted to visit a Youth Court in the South of England. It was to prove a salutary lesson in the extent to which the family courts are closed even to a government minister .

Recalling the occasion in an interview with The Times, Mr Straw - now Justice Secretary - said: "The bench had a debate about whether to allow me in. I thought they were being ridiculous. Justice has to be seen to be done. That is regarded as a cliche, but it's actually a very profound point about the operation of the justice system."

As Justice Secretary, he is now in a position to right the balance. In one of the most fundamental reforms to the way the family courts operate, he announced today that from April 1 reporters will be able to attend family court proceedings and report on cases.

The main stipulation is that they do not name the parties or give out the kind of personal details which would allow nosy neighbours to identify them. "It will be open to parties to apply to court for specific reporting restrictions," said Mr Straw. "But my hope is that the courts are reluctant to grant these".

It is a move for which The Times has campaigned vociferously, arguing that keeping the media out of certain courts has led to miscarriages of justice.

The Times has received hundreds of letters from people who have been gagged and powerless to challenge the decisions of social workers and other experts.

For a long time, pleas to open the family courts fell on deaf ears. Questions about how social workers and other experts make decisions, and whether the right children are taken into care - raised most recently by the cases of Shannon Matthews and Baby P - were met with the mantra that family privacy is paramount, and that professionals must remain anonymous. Yet if you are a parent wrongly accused of abusing your child, you do not want the kind of privacy which gags you from discussing your case. If you are a child tortured by a relative under the nose of the state, you do not want the kind of secrecy which protects professionals from scrutiny.

So what has changed?

Talking ahead of his announcement in the House of Commons, Mr Straw credited The Times with bringing the issue to his attention "more graphically than it would otherwise have done".

He said: "You have to deal with shedloads of issues in jobs like this...if something isn't a particular issue at the time, you don't go searching around for it. I commend The Times for running such a professional campaign".

But it is also clear that this is an issue Mr Straw feels passionately about.

"It has been a closed world," he said. "If justice is open, there is a greater chance that standards will rise and that egregious practices may be spotted before they become harmful".

Does he believe there are egregious practices? "I don't know, is the answer. You can't know, because not even I would be able to enter a family court at the moment. The jargon is 'private not secret' - but the public could be forgiven for not making the distinction".

As dramatic in its way as the decision to allow the media in, is the second big change announced by Mr Straw. At the moment it is rare for a judge to even name the local authority, let alone the social workers or the expert witnesses in a case. Court of appeal judges have made stinging criticisms of social workers without saying which council they work for. The media cannot discover which council it is, and elected councillors remain unaware that their own staff have been condemned.

"Local authorities aren't routinely named at the moment" said Straw. "My view is that they ought to be. There should be no restriction on naming social workers or medical experts unless it could lead to the identification of [children]. A structural engineer at a planning enquiry puts his or her professional competence on the line in public. People who are professional have to accept that what goes with being professional is the public task."

I suggested that there would be strong opposition to this move. One of the most powerful lobbies against openness has been from expert witnesses and local authorities. But Mr Straw was prepared for the question. "I know there are arguments in the medical profession, that doctors would be less willing to come forward if they were going to be named, but I happen to think that if you are professional you have to justify your professionalism in public".

What about parents being able to speak out about their cases? It is currently a grey area with some MPs nervous about helping constituents because they are unsure of where the law stands. Mr Straw himself has been involved in trying to help constituents where he wasn't sure where the line was. This will be addressed under his reforms.

"Parents will be able to disclose information for the purpose of advice and support," he said. Did that mean they could go to someone who is not their MP and say 'I need your advice on this?' "Yes. They can pass on the information".

Not everyone will welcome the reforms. Won't the new policy be portrayed as a charter for busybodies, for tabloids wanting salacious details?

Mr Straw was firm. "My view is that the vast majority of proceedings will still go unreported and the major interest will be from local newspapers and I think that is entirely right. It is worth bearing in mind that public law proceedings are paid for by the taxpayer. The media is a proxy for the taxpayer, beside the fact that there is a genuine public interest which the media has to represent, in finding out how the system is operating. I think all these objections would have validity if the parties were going to be named, but because the parties are being protected it is very different".

There is one clear disappointment. A clause in the 2002 Adoption Act means that journalists will not be able to sit in on proceedings if and when a formal application to adopt is made. That is usually the last stage, but some of the most controversial cases are those which end in adoption. Mr Straw is promising primary legislation to overcome this problem. But he will need to remain firm if he is not to be derailed by the parliamentary timetable.

Time running out for one family caught by the family courts
by Alice Fishburn
The Times, 16 Dec 2008

They put the Christmas decorations up a couple of days ago but no one in the Smith family feels much like celebrating. Despite the tinsel draped over their sons' photographs, there are no excited children racing around the flat. Instead, Patrick, 6, and Donald, 2, will be spending the holiday in foster care.

It started with a nosebleed in December 2006. Robert Smith wiped the nose of his stepson Patrick and took him to school. But the teacher spotted some dried blood. When she asked Patrick what had happened, he said "Robert" and made a wiping motion. She went to social services who called the police. That afternoon, Robert was arrested for assault and had to move out of the flat.

"We thought, we'll cooperate, we'll let them do their jobs. It will all get sorted and go away. We knew we'd done nothing wrong." said Robert.

Six months later, a criminal court threw out the charges after the prosecution admitted they had no evidence. But social services wouldn't let Robert move back home.

Two years on, stacks of legal paper under the Christmas tree chronicle the Smith's subsequent struggle with social services in the family courts, where the case is still being heard. Because reporters have until now been unable to cover those proceedings, their story would have remained untold had Robert's parents not read about The Times campaign and alerted the paper to the case. Even so, The Times is unable to report the strength or otherwise of the case against them.

For several months, Robert could only see Donald twice a week under supervision. Tensions with social services rose at home. On one occasion, a row escalated between a case worker and Tara Smith. "She started pressuring me about the whole situation," Tara said, "I put one arm on her to get her out." She pleaded guilty to assault. The judge let her keep her children but ordered that the family be given more support.

Social services did provide some help. Last spring, the Smiths were reunited in an assessment centre with the aim of reintegrating Robert into the family. They thought everything was going well. But after eight weeks, the children were taken into foster care because the parents showed "inconsistent emotional warmth".

They had fifteen minutes to pack and an hour to say goodbye: "I went to pick Donald up and I couldn't stop the tears. I had to put my baby down and run away. I couldn't face it. I had to run away from my child," said Tara.

The Smiths now see their sons for three supervised visits a week. Each lasts an hour. But the worst days are the ones in between visits. "You want to press fast forward on the world for the day," said Robert.

Both parents have lost their jobs and new positions clash with scheduled visit times.

So they sit at home, avoiding the room where their sons slept under Thomas the Tank Engine wallpaper.

"I sometimes feel like I've got no identity," said Tara. "I've always been to work since I left school. And now I haven't got work. I haven't got the children. I've got nothing to live for."

The Times is prevented from identifying the family - their names have been changed in this piece - under separate legislation and that will not change even under Jack Straw's reforms. But they hope that opening up the family courts will aid public understanding about their situation.

Tara has suffered from the stigma around family law. "I'm ashamed, I admit it. I'm ashamed because social services have taken my children away."

Robert believes that greater awareness will help: "People will theorise about things that they cannot get the facts for. When you give them the facts, you take away the mystery."

Robert's parents have launched a complaint about the way social services have handled the proceedings. They also welcome greater transparency in the system: "It's okay to admit you've made a mistake. Just put the child down and step away from the family. If we were all allowed to put this in the paper from day one, social services could look more closely at what was going on in each case."

But for their family, time is running out. Despite positive cognitive behavioural therapy reports, a pre-adoption hearing will take place in the spring.

A tea towel pinned up on the kitchen wall spells out an encouraging: 'Don't Quit'. But the Smiths find it increasingly hard. "Life has been on hold for the last two years. The tape is paused." said Robert.

They hope that Straw's proposals will wind it on enough for them: "This is a step in the right direction, certainly. It's walking, rather than the running that people in our position would like. But everything starts slow. It always has to."

Family courts: case studies
by Fiona Hamilton
The Times, 16 December 2008

The opening up of the family courts will be welcome news for one couple whose case - currently before the Court of Appeal - has been highlighted by The Times after their baby daughter was placed into foster care earlier this year.

But although it means the couple will now be able to discuss their case with the media the reforms do not go far enough for their MP.

Tim Yeo, the Conservative MP for Suffolk South, told The Times that his efforts to help the couple had been thwarted by a system which "prevents natural justice".

Although the couple have given Mr Yeo permission to access information about their case, the authorities have denied his requests and have refused to justify their actions on the grounds of confidentiality.

Mr Yeo said: "They continue to decline to make any information available to me despite authority by the parents.

"They've consistently refused to share their reasons [for placing the child in foster care]. Obviously not publicly, but not even privately with me.

"This makes it very hard for me, as the representative of the parents, to assist them."

The mother first lost custody of her young son to her ex-husband (his biological father), who claimed that she suffered from a condition known as fabricated or induced illness.

When she fell pregnant to her new partner, social services monitored the family. During a conversation with social workers, she explained her fear of losing her newborn daughter by saying that her new partner felt like killing them all if she was also taken away. The couple have no history of violence or abuse. They say that they would not dream of hurting their baby and the remark was merely an attempt to explain the full extent of their agony if she was taken away.

The child has since been taken into foster care. The mother has access to her for just three hours a week and the father has not seen her since. The couple, who have not been given full reasons for the removal, are appealing the supervision order.

Mr Yeo said: "It seems extraordinary that people can have what is a sort of life sentence, in losing their baby daughter, without really knowing what the evidence is against them and without being able to refute it.

"There is this cloak of secrecy in which social services conduct their activities. They would have more rights if they were up on a murder charge."

At 17 years old, Curtis is old enough to move out of home, travel around the countryside for his job and have a girlfriend.

Yet, adult as he is, Curtis is prevented from speaking publicly about his past and the sister that he did not know for much of his childhood, ostensibly for his "protection".

A month before he was born, his 17-month old sister was taken away from his mother and placed into foster care after social services expressed concern about a bruise on the child.

At three-year old his sister was adopted following proceedings in the family court, despite a judge's misgivings, because she had "bonded" with her foster carers after social services denied the mother access. Curtis was only recently reunited with his sister after she tracked down her family.

He approached The Times to tell his story hoping that his case would raise awareness after he found out that social services also tried to place him into foster care despite there being no evidence against his mother.

However, he cannot be named until his 18th birthday and his social services referral sheet, which nearly separated him from his biological mother, cannot be published under restrictions by the Administration of Justice Act.

Curtis told The Times: "It's disgusting. It's my life and I want to talk about it, I want people to know so that maybe this sort of thing can be avoided in the future. It took me ages to get my court documents and even though they're mine, I can't make them public. Social services just get to cover things up and its wrong."

***

Matthew, a working professional in his fifties, was fighting a custody case for several months before he became aware of the damaging allegations against him on his court file.

A supporter of his ex-partner had written the judge a letter in secret making various spurious claims including that Matthew was not to be trusted with his children.

Matthew only became aware of the allegations when he requested other correspondence from his file.

"I was able to reject the allegations and the judge said he wouldn't consider them, but it was highly inappropriate and quite a concern," he said.

"If I hadn't have asked for other information and if this letter hadn't been included with it, I would have never known of its existence."

This blind faith in experts fails family justice

Professionals giving evidence in court are supposed to be independent; too often they are hired guns for local authorities

by Camilla Cavendish

The Times, 9 January 2009

This morning I got an e-mail from Frank Lockyer, the retired police superintendent and father of Sally Clark. His daughter spent three years in jail for murdering two of her sons, during which time she suffered untold torments. She was exonerated later and released, but she never recovered from her treatment at the hands of the British justice system - a system she had once served as a solicitor. She died in 2007.

Mr Lockyer was writing about a recent decision of the Press Complaints Commission to clear me of a complaint made under clause 1 of the Code of Practice (accuracy) by the paediatrician Professor Sir Roy Meadow. He was villified by the media for evidence he gave at Sally Clark's trial and that of Angela Cannings, another mother who was jailed and subsequently released. Professor Meadow had objected to a comment I had made suggesting that he had gone beyond his remit and given evidence that "led to the jailing of innocent people" - partly by presenting statistical evidence of the likelihood of cot death when he was not a statistician.

He felt that this was misleading, for three main reasons. First, he was only one of several witnesses in these cases; second, appeal judges had played down the importance of his statistical evidence in the Clark ruling, and third, we cannot know how much weight the juries actually gave his evidence.

The PCC decided not to uphold the complaint. It took into account that my views were set out in what it felt was an opinion piece and not presented as indisputable fact - and that Professor Meadow had rejected The Times's offer to print a letter from him, setting out his position. It is not an episode I am proud of - it is sobering for any journalist to be accused of inaccuracy. But that he was supported by other paediatricians in bringing the complaint reflects a continuing gulf between the medical professions and the press over what we should expect of expert witnesses.

Mr Lockyer writes that he would never have complained to the General Medical Council about Professor Meadow if he had apologised or admitted that he might have been mistaken. This is a different question from whether he was made a scapegoat when the courts themselves should have been more sceptical. Mr Lockyer wanted accountability, not revenge. He is concerned about what he considers to be the reluctance of so many members of the Royal College of Paediatrics to admit that evidence might sometimes be wrong.

He is not alone. This week I spoke to a Welsh woman whose son has been forced to go on seeing his father although both she and his school fear that dramatic changes in his behaviour are the result of abuse. An expert psychologist has dismissed their concerns by stating - astonishingly - that teaching in Welsh could cause retardation in some children. Despite there being no apparent research to back this up, the court served a penal notice that means that the mother will go to jail if she attempts to protect her son from unsupervised visits by her ex-partner, who she believes is an abuser. Welsh politicians have expressed outrage - Rhodri Morgan, the First Minister, said last month that he "would not dignify that person with the title of 'expert'". But the decision cannot be challenged, even though the expert has refused to indicate what his conclusions were based on.

The worst part of this story is not the expert's "evidence", or the court's apparent acceptance of it. It is that the court has twice denied the mother the chance to call another expert in her defence. This is a common problem if the letters I get from parents are anything to go by.

After overturning Angela Cannings's conviction in 2003, Lord Justice Judge declared that no one should ever go to prison again solely on the basis of expert witness evidence. The criminal law was changed as a result. But in family courts, many decisions are still made on the basis of evidence from psychiatrists, psychologists or doctors, who often take the view that a mother is unstable, sometimes without cross-examination. Too many family courts are being run by experts, rather than judges.

If the courts are not prepared to challenge "expert" evidence, they should surely allow others to do so. In theory, experts are supposed to be independent professionals who have a duty to help the court to come to the right decision. In practice they are often hired guns, paid by local authorities that choose people they know will be a "safe pair of hands" - people they have used time and time again.

In December the Lord Chancellor and Justice Secretary Jack Straw took the heroic decision to open the family courts to the media and to end the gagging of parents who wish to speak out about their cases. In doing so he has struck a huge blow for justice. But blind faith in experts still poses a problem.

The opening up of the family courts will allow the media to scrutinise experts and their evidence - at least when journalists turn up. But although the Straw reforms will let parties disclose court documents to outside experts without a judge's permission, they will still not be able to call those experts in their defence without the court's say-so. Unless defence lawyers are savvy enough to exploit this, there may still be miscarriages of justice.

It is perhaps not surprising that many experts have an inherent tendency to believe that they are right. That is human nature - although you would expect members of the medical professions to be more conscious of scientific complexity and uncertainty. Courts should be more sceptical. If they will not challenge experts, they must let more parents do so.

14. NEWBORN BABIES TAKEN

Hundreds of Social Workers should go to prison for life!!

FORCED ADOPTION IS WICKED!!!

Family Court judges who authorise it are even more wicked, THESE JUDGES ARE CRIMINALS!

Don't believe me? Just read these 6 articles from the *The Sunday Telegraph* and *The Times* and then read on for further useful information.

Adoption increase fails to stop baby deaths
by Ben Leapman
Daily Telegraph, 17 September 2007

A dramatic rise in the number of newborn babies seized by social workers for forced adoption has failed to reduce the murder rate among babies.

Despite the action by social services, intended to protect children at high risk, the number of deaths has actually grown.

Critics claimed that the figures showed that social workers were tearing apart innocent families, while failing to protect babies at the greatest risk.

The concerns will add fresh weight to The Sunday Telegraph's "Stop the Secrecy" campaign for greater openness in Family Courts. At present, judges sit in secret when deciding adoption cases, raising fears that miscarriages of justice go unnoticed.

Earlier this year, the Government abandoned plans to let the media publish anonymised reports on cases. In 1995, when 540 newborns were removed for adoption, there were 17 murders in which the victim was less than a year old. A decade later, in 2005/6, 1,400 were taken, yet the murder total rose to 24.

Liz Davies, senior lecturer in social work at London Metropolitan University, claimed the failures were due to new techniques introduced following the murder of Victoria Climbie.

"Performance targets and the tick-box culture are undermining professional judgement," she said.

In a separate development, ministers announced that 30 English councils shared a payout of £18 million this year for meeting Government targets to increase adoptions.

Critics say the targets give social workers an incentive to take away children who would be better off with their natural parents.

Threat to Take Newborn over Emotional Abuse
by David Harrison
Sunday Telegraph, 26 August 2007

A pregnant woman has been told that her baby will be taken from her at birth because she is deemed capable of "emotional abuse", even though psychiatrists treating her say there is no evidence to suggest that she will harm her child in any way.

Social services' recommendation that the baby should be taken from Fran Lyon, a 22-year-old charity worker who has five A-levels and a degree in neuroscience, was based in part on a letter from a paediatrician she has never met.

Hexham children's services, part of Northumberland County Council, said the decision had been made because Miss Lyon was likely to suffer from Munchausen's Syndrome by proxy, a condition unproven by science in which a mother will make up an illness in her child, or harm it, to draw attention to herself.

Under the plan, a doctor will hand the newborn to a social worker, provided there are no medical complications. Social services' request for an emergency protection order - these are usually granted - will be heard in secret in the family court at Hexham magistrates on the same day.

From then on, anyone discussing the case, including Miss Lyon, will be deemed to be in contempt of the court.

Miss Lyon, from Hexham, who is five months pregnant, is seeking a judicial review of the decision about Molly, as she calls her baby. She described it as "barbaric and draconian", and said it was "scandalous" that social services had not accepted submissions supporting her case.

"The paediatrician has never met me," she said. "He is not a psychiatrist and cannot possibly make assertions about my current or future mental health. Yet his letter was the only one considered in the case conference on August 16 which lasted just 10 minutes."

Northumberland County Council insists that two highly experienced doctors - another consultant paediatrician and a medical consultant - attended the case conference.

The case adds to growing concern, highlighted in a series of articles in The Sunday Telegraph, over a huge rise in the number of babies under a year old being taken from parents. The figure was 2,000 last year, three times the number 10 years ago.

Critics say councils are taking more babies from parents to help them meet adoption "targets".

John Hemming, the Liberal Democrat MP and chairman of the Justice for Families campaign group, said the case showed "exactly what is wrong with public family law".

He added: "There is absolutely no evidence that Fran would harm her child. However, a vague letter from a paediatrician who has never met her has been used in a decision to remove her baby at birth, while evidence from professionals treating her, that she would have no problems has been ignored."

Mr Hemming was concerned that "vague assertions" of Munchausen's Syndrome by proxy - now known as "fabricated and invented illness" - had been used to remove a number of children from parents in the North-East.

Miss Lyon came under scrutiny because she had a mental health problem when she was 16 after being physically and emotionally abused by her father and raped by a stranger.

She suffered eating disorders and self-harm but, after therapy, graduated from Edinburgh University and now works for two mental health charities, Borderline and Personality Plus.

Dr Stella Newrith, a consultant psychiatrist, who treated Miss Lyon for her childhood trauma for a year, wrote to Northumberland social services stating: "There has never been any clinical evidence to suggest that Fran would put herself or others at risk, and there is certainly no evidence to suggest that she would put a child at risk of emotional, physical or sexual harm."

Despite this support, endorsed by other psychiatrists and Miss Lyon's GP, social services based their recommendation partly on a letter from Dr Martin Ward Platt, a consultant paediatrician, who was unable to attend the meeting.

He wrote: "Even in the absence of a psychological assessment, if the professionals were concerned on the evidence available that Miss Holton (as Miss Lyon was briefly known), probably does fabricate or induce illness, there would be no option but the precautionary principle of taking the baby into foster care at birth, pending a post-natal forensic psychological assessment."

Miss Lyon said she was determined to fight the decision. "I know I can be a good mother to Molly. I just want the chance to prove it," she said.

The council said the recommendation would be subject to further assessment and review. "When making such difficult decisions, safeguarding children is our foremost priority," a spokesman said.

• A recording of social workers threatening to take a newborn into care has been removed from the YouTube website after Calderdale Council in West Yorkshire started legal action, claiming the Data Protection Act was breached.

Vanessa Brookes, 34, taped social workers telling her and her husband that they would seek to place the baby, due next month, in care, while admitting there was "no immediate risk to the child."

YouTube Row over Social Services Baby Threat
by Ben Leapman
Sunday Telegraph, 19 August 2007

A heavily pregnant woman is at the centre of an extraordinary legal battle with social workers after she secretly recorded them threatening to take away her newborn baby.

Vanessa Brookes, 34, who is due to give birth early next month, smuggled taping equipment into a meeting with social services officials, fearing they would try to take her baby for forced adoption.

She recorded a social worker telling her and her husband Martin, 41, that even though there was "no immediate risk to your child from yourselves", the council would seek a court order to place the child in foster care.

Mother and baby would be allowed "two or three days" in hospital together, but should not leave the premises until social workers came to remove the infant. In a desperate attempt to keep their baby, the couple have published the recorded conversation on the internet.

Calderdale council, in West Yorkshire, last night accused them of breaching the Data Protection Act by recording its staff without their knowledge or consent. The council said it had begun legal action to have the recording removed from the YouTube website. Mrs Brookes said: "Even puppies and kittens aren't removed from their mothers at birth. Social workers always record everything, so why shouldn't we record them?"

John Hemming, the Liberal Democrat MP and chairman of campaign group Justice for Families, said: "I find it very odd that a newborn baby would be removed when there is not any allegation by the authorities that the child is at risk. Yet this case is not unique. There are many cases in which newborns are removed because of allegations that their mothers may at some later stage 'emotionally abuse' the child."

The case returns the spotlight to claims that social services are being heavy-handed in removing children from their parents, in order to meet Government adoption targets.

The Sunday Telegraph has previously revealed cases of mothers who were not told why their children were taken away, and cases of families whose children were not returned even after the parents had been cleared of wrongdoing. More than 2,000 babies aged under a year were taken for adoption last year, almost triple the level of a decade ago.

Social services took an interest in the Brookes family after Mrs Brookes, who is partially-sighted, was diagnosed with depression and a personality disorder, leading to concerns that her baby might be subjected to "emotional abuse". Neighbours have complained that the couple's household was disorderly, but neither has been accused of abusing or harming a child.

In the recorded meeting, the social worker tells the couple: "It's our intention as a local authority that when your baby is born, we go into court on that same day and ask for an interim court order because we would wish to place your baby with foster carers."

He tells Mrs Brookes: "I would like you and your baby to stay in hospital until the courts have made a decision."

The social worker says the two or three days the mother has with her baby in hospital will allow her to begin breast-feeding and that once the infant is taken away, social services will pick up expressed breast milk from her home and deliver it to the foster carers for bottle-feeding.

The social worker admits to the couple that a back-up plan is being drawn up in case the judge refuses the application for a care order. He says: "What we also have to think about is a child protection plan that looks at you, at home, with your baby. There is no immediate risk to your child from yourselves, that's my understanding from reading documents."

A spokesman for Calderdale council said officials would seek a meeting with Mr and Mrs Brookes "to understand how this information came into the public domain. We are taking action to have this item removed from YouTube. This recording was made without the knowledge or consent of our member of staff.

"The council does not take lightly any recommendation to the court for a child or a baby to be brought into care. The decision whether or not to institute care proceedings is made by social workers who have to consider the best interests of the child."

http://www.familylawweek.co.uk/library.asp?i=2946

The rank hypocrisy of family court judges
by Camilla Cavendish
The Times, 24 May 2007

I was gratified this week to find that an article I wrote in December has been quoted in full by the Court of Appeal. (I only hope there were no typos.) It is flattering that Mr Justice Munby takes The Times seriously. It is of more import that he decided to publish his judgment on the case that I wrote about six months ago. For it is only when judges make their reasoning public that we can start to debate the grounds on which children should be taken into care.

A few long-suffering readers may remember that this peculiar case concerns a woman whose baby was removed by social workers, not because the child came to any harm but because there was a suspicion that her father might have injured a child from his previous marriage. That suspicion was never proven, no charges were ever brought and the child of the earlier marriage was never removed. But a woman who everyone agrees is blameless has lost her only child – for ever – because she is deemed to be besotted with a man who may pose a danger.

As so often in these situations, there are complex allegations and flawed characters. In my view it is questionable whether the father's inability to conceal his loathing of social workers makes him unsuitable for parenthood. Mr Justice Munby has decided on several grounds not to grant an appeal. The case may still go to Strasbourg, but it will be too late: the child will have been adopted.

This couple have become a cause célèbre for campaigners who fear that the Government's drive to get more children adopted is having a perverse effect on some local authorities. For the same local authority to leave a man alone with a child that it thought he had harmed, but to take away another that had not been harmed, does seem bizarre. Until you realise that the child from the first marriage was disabled, and older, and would have been hard to place with an adoptive family. The child from the second marriage was a healthy baby, just the kind of "adoptive commodity" that local authorities find relatively easy to place.

I still believe that ministers were right to want to speed children out of the hell of care. But they have put social services departments in a strange position. We now expect them to combine three contradictory roles: to protect children, to keep families together and to meet adoption targets (which bring financial rewards). Under pressure, in situations that are not clear-cut, those roles are bound to conflict.

What is the evidence? Government figures show a significant jump in the number of babies being taken into care, from 1,600 in 1995 to 2,800 in 2005: a 75 per cent increase in ten years. While there has been an increase across all age groups, it is much, much greater for babies. More 10 to 15-year-olds are removed, but the rate of increase was only 21 per cent.

One possible explanation is that the authorities are now monitoring pregnant women, especially teenagers and substance abusers. But there are also numerous examples of relatives being turned down by local authorities when they offer to take the children of a family member. Some of them may indeed be unsuitable. But the turning-down sometimes seems very peremptory. John Hemming, MP, who follows these issues closely, believes that "the [hard-to-place] children the targets were established to get adopted are not getting adopted; instead a completely new group of children are being taken into care, then adopted". Ministers should be seriously alarmed if a failure to help difficult candidates find homes were being masked by a zealous pursuit of babies.

This case has also brought something else home to me: our hypocrisy about privacy. It is illegal for me to write about most care cases, or to read court papers, even when the parents involved beg me to. I can generally only write when judges go public. Yet I have discovered that even as I was writing about this case last year, painstakingly omitting much of the detail to ensure that no one could identify the child, her picture, real name and age were being published in a national newspaper. Not by a journalist, who would have been in contempt of court. But by an adoption agency, advertising for adopters.

Agencies have to find good homes for needy children. Many do a great job. But for parents who are routinely told that they will be in contempt if they dare to reveal the legal proceedings to anyone outside the court, or even to talk about the child by name, because his or her privacy is paramount, it is staggering to see their children being advertised like pets.

Contempt of court is a serious matter. Last year Harriet Harman, the Minister for Justice, admitted in Parliament that in 2005 "200 people were sent to prison by the Family Courts, which happens in complete privacy and secrecy". Family court judges can send parents to prison for up to six months for contempt. Two hundred people is about four a week. That is far more than the number of suspected terrorists we have locked up without a fair trial. So where are the civil libertarians? One young woman was recently sent to Ashford prison for kidnapping her child back from social workers and trying to flee the country. Others seem to be committed for minor breaches of contact orders. The threat of jail is made time and again, and it is real.

The main justification used for keeping Family Courts secret is to protect the identities of children. It is the argument used to gag parents and the media. How strange that seems when a little girl, whose family struggled to get the right legal advice to keep her, can be paraded around the country.

Every judge in these adoption cases can decide to make their judgment public. Until they do, the pretence of privacy will be nothing but rank hypocrisy.

Guilty of child abuse! (Well, our version.)
by Camilla Cavendish
The Times, 23 August 2007

For a brief time this week, until it was taken down, there was an extraordinary posting on YouTube. It was a covert recording, made by a 34-year-old mother, of her meeting with the social worker who wants to take her next baby into care.

Had it been staged, critics would have called it a caricature. A robotic official orders the sobbing mother to stay in the hospital until his colleagues come to remove her new baby. He refuses her desperate pleas to be monitored with the baby at home. He explains in the tones of a traffic warden the inconvenience of delivering her breast milk. He then lets drop an astonishing admission: that Calderdale Council is pursuing a court order despite there being "no immediate risk to your child from yourselves". Will he say that in court? We will not know, of course, for the court will sit in secret.

Such a chilling drama plays to our deepest fears of state tyranny. There is something wrong with the system. But posting a conversation on YouTube, out of context, is not the way to right it. The council argues that Vanessa Brookes's recording falls foul of the Data Protection Act. Her supporters say that she is a victim of social services and justified in publishing what is essentially her own data. But we do not know whether she is a victim. Who is abusing whom here?

Mrs Brookes's case is not straightforward. She is partially sighted and has suffered bouts of depression. Two of her children have already been adopted. That does not prove that she is an unfit mother - mistakes can be made - but it does explain the council's interest. Equally, I am told that she and her husband have never been accused of harming any child. But this dribble of incomplete facts is fundamentally unenlightening. All it does is illustrate the torturous trade-offs that the system has to make, and our inability to judge those trade-offs because it is illegal to read family court papers.

How should we treat someone like Mrs Brookes, who has troubles enough to worry social services but has not apparently yet harmed a child? She is one of a growing group of people who are categorised as capable of "emotional abuse". You can see why the category exists. Ill-treatment comes in many forms, not just cigarette burns. But in that nebulous phrase lurks the potential for great injustice.

"Emotional abuse" has no strict definition in British law. Yet it now accounts for an astounding 21 per cent of all children registered as needing protection, up from 14 per cent in 1997. Last year 6,700 children were put on the child protection register for emotional abuse, compared with only 2,600 for sexual abuse and 5,100 for physical abuse. Both of the latter two categories have been falling steadily. Meanwhile emotional abuse and "neglect" - which replaced the old notion of "grave concern" in 1989 - have been rising. Both are catch-alls. But emotional abuse is especially vague. It covers children who have not been injured, have not complained, and do not come under "emotional neglect".

The Department of Health defines emotional abuse as "persistent emotional ill-treatment . . . [which] may involve conveying to children that they are worthless or inadequate . . . and may feature age or developmentally inappropriate expectations being placed on children . . . Some level of emotional abuse is involved in all types of ill-treatment of a child, though it may occur alone".

Local authorities have printed their own, wildly differing, interpretations. In Enfield emotional abuse includes "swearing", "conditional love" or "discriminatory remarks". In Nottingham, it is "an ingrained pattern of interaction . . . which it is essential to observe and understand over time". Under that definition, a baby could never be removed at birth. Nottingham also states that emotional abuse should rarely be a cause for removing a child. Meanwhile the NSPCC, the charity that has never knowingly undersold a statistic, states in its briefing on emotional abuse that "18 per cent of children experience humiliation and/or attacks on self-esteem". Should we put them all in care, then?

"You'll know it when you see it - except that you can't see it" is no way to make law. Abuse literature repeatedly states how often parent and child are unaware of the damage done by their relationship patterns. How do we weigh that damage against the trauma of the conveyor belt of foster care? In most such situations, isn't removing a child utterly disproportionate?

Just imagine that some social services departments were crusaders, seeing evil parents everywhere but unable to prove conventional abuse. It is plausible that the number of vague allegations would rise, backed by psychiatrists of a similar mindset who are prepared to enter a "maybe". How else can one explain a 50 per cent rise in emotional abuse cases in ten years? How many of those cases are utterly marginal?

Next, imagine that the rise in these cases had left social workers even more overstretched. They would have less time to monitor children at home and to keep families together. They would also have less time for the hard-core cases. No system can ever protect every child. But the toddler on Haringey's at-risk register who was found dead last week with fractured ribs, a broken back and two missing fingernails was surely more deserving of removal than those at risk of low self-esteem.

So many cases are gut-wrenchingly complex. We need social workers to be properly accountable. We need the family courts to be open. Mrs Brookes is clearly not perfect, but she deserves to have clear grounds for the removal of her child. Right now, it looks as though around 6,000 people stand accused of abuse, or potential abuse, that no lawyer can even define. That is an appalling vista that we must not continue to hide from public view.

The reason for the secrecy in the Family Courts is always touted as the need to protect the children's identity at all costs! Unless of course there is money to be made by 'advertising' them for adoption like pedigree dogs in magazines and newspapers with colour photos, age and first name for easy identification by the neighbours!!

www.adoptionuk.com

Precedent: All mothers have the **LEGAL RIGHT** to breastfeed their babies!

*In the matter of unborn baby M; R (on the application of X and another) v Gloucestershire County Council.

Citation: BLD 160403280; [2003] EWHC 850 (Admin).

Hearing Date: 15 April 2003

Court: Administrative Court.

Judge: Munby J.

Abstract.

"Per curiam. If the state, in the guise of a local authority, seeks to remove a baby from his parents at a time when its case against the parents has not yet even been established, then the very least the state can do is to make generous arrangements for contact, those arrangements being driven by the needs of the family and not stunted by lack of resources. Typically, if this is what the parents want, one will be looking to contact most days of the week and for lengthy periods. Local authorities also had to be sensitive to the wishes of a mother who wants to breast-feed, and should make suitable arrangements to enable her to do so, and not merely to bottle-feed expressed breast milk. Nothing less would meet the imperative demands of the European Convention on Human Rights."...

Published Date

16/04/2003

This case establishes the right of the mother to breastfeed, and is often ignored both by judges and the 'SS' **BECAUSE THE PARENTS ARE NOT AWARE OF THEIR RIGHTS UNDER THIS IMPORTANT CASE.**

Crimes come and crimes go. Homosexual acts were once a crime and now quite rightly they are not. Racial discrimination used not to be illegal and now quite rightly it is a crime. I hope and believe that one day soon it will be a **SERIOUS CRIME** to deprive a newborn baby of contact with a mother of sound mind that has never harmed it. It is not just me (Ian Josephs) a lone individual saying this, I am supported in this view by TV programmes, journalists, MPs, and the above article from that ultra respectable newspaper, *The Times*!

I must repeat that the following extract from a judgement in the House of Lords confirms that alone in Europe the UK **CONTINUES** to allow and encourage the barbaric practice of taking children from loving and desperate parents and giving them to strangers for closed and secret adoptions without parental consent.

House of Lords - Down Lisburn Health and Social Services Trust .

Baroness Hale of Richmond. Judgement

34. There is, so far as the parties to this case are aware, no European jurisprudence questioning the principle of freeing for adoption, or indeed compulsory adoption generally. The United Kingdom is unusual amongst members of the Council of Europe in permitting the total severance of family ties without parental consent. (Professor Triseliotis thought that only Portugal and perhaps one other European country allowed this.) It is, of course, the most draconian interference with family life possible.

CA Doc 1.1 Lord Donaldson MR

Lord Donaldson MR, Re D (A Minor) (Residence Order, 1992) 2 FLR 332, 336. CA

'At the risk of being told by academics hereafter that my views are contrary to well-established authority, I think that there is a rebuttable presumption of fact that the best interests of a baby are best served by being with its mother, and I stress the word 'baby'. When we are moving on to whatever age it may be appropriate to describe the baby as having become a child, different considerations may well apply. But, as far as babies are concerned, the starting-point is, I think, that it should be with its mother.'

At present any mother with a child already in care who gives birth to a new baby almost invariably has that baby snatched at birth by social workers anxious to meet their adoption targets. Changed circumstances are rarely taken into account.

THESE FORCED ADOPTIONS ARE WICKED CRIMES!! All those odious persons involved in these crimes against humanity, the social workers, the 'SS' lawyers, the hired 'experts' and most of all the **RENEGADE COMPLIANT JUDGES** should all serve prison sentences for their crimes just as their predecessors the Nazi judges were condemned at Nuremburg!

15. STOLEN CHILDREN

They're in my life. I love and miss them so much.

Couple who fled to Ireland to keep baby celebrate his first year

by Laura Collins

Mail on Sunday, 27 May 2007

It is the celebration Mark and Nicky Webster feared they would never see - the first birthday of the son they fled England to keep after being branded child abusers by Social Services.

After their first three children were taken into care on the evidence of a single broken leg, the couple decided to escape to Ireland last year while Nicky was heavily pregnant in the hope they would be able to keep their baby.

It was a desperate strategy, but they have now returned to England and, after spending five months under round-the-clock scrutiny in a care facility, they have been allowed to take Brandon back home to Cromer, Norfolk.

The absence of Brandon's two brothers and sister means Tuesday's birthday will be tinged with sadness for Nicky, 26, and Mark, 34.

"Brandon should be surrounded by his big sister and brothers," Nicky said.

"It's always there in the back of our minds, although we do things to take our minds of it. We'll have a birthday cake and of course it's just lovely to have a child in the house, but you can never fully forget. We don't want to forget our other children."

Now, as legal questions are being raised over the speed and wisdom of the irreversible decision to have Brandon's siblings permanently adopted, the Websters are preparing for a final legal battle that would allow them to keep Brandon permanently.

Their nightmare began in October 2003, when their second child sustained unexplained leg fractures.

Although neither of their other children had suffered any injury, Norfolk Social Services were quick to intervene and took all three youngsters into care.

In 2005, following a summary family court hearing and regardless of discrepancies in diagnosis, the decision was taken to have the three children permanently adopted.

A High Court judge has questioned the speed at which the original family court proceedings were conducted.

In an interim hearing in February, Mr Justice Holman admitted: "I can't understand how a case of this seriousness was capable of being disposed of in a day."

The judge added that a "full inquiry" was needed into new evidence brought by an expert witness for the couple, which blew the case "wide open".

Key to this inquiry is the suggestion that the boy's fractures could have been the result of scurvy, caused by vitamin C deficiency due to a naturally occurring intolerance.

The final hearing to decide Brandon's permanent fate will begin at the Royal Courts of Justice on June 25.

The couple's fight to keep their baby was conducted under a shroud of silence until last November, when The Mail on Sunday won a landmark legal case lifting a gagging order restricting Press coverage.

When Nicky and Mark blow out the candle on Brandon's birthday cake this week, there is no doubt what wish they'll be making.

"We just want to have Brandon with us, at home where he belongs," Nicky said. "As far as I'm concerned he's not going anywhere."

But the most damning issue to emerge from a recent court battle over Norfolk County Council's attempt to take the Websters' fourth child was the pressure placed on a care worker to change a positive view about the Websters.

Injustices of this sort are going on all over the country and it will take a lot of effort to get things right. But that just strengthens the resolve of campaigners to keep fighting.

Because it is so important I now **REPEAT** in a slightly different format some of the information already outlined earlier.

As a result of care orders made by secret Family Courts, every year literally hundreds of newborn babies are torn from their loving mother's arms by harsh unfeeling British social workers who then put them out for adoption. It is no excuse to say they were 'following orders'. Any self-respecting social worker should resign rather than obey any order that involves removing a baby from it's mother's loving care and sending it away to be adopted by strangers when no harm has ever been done to that baby by the mother. Alas not one single social worker ordered to snatch a newborn baby at birth has resigned and made any kind of public protest about this barbarism, so all those involved in this revolting activity are at least guilty of criminal indifference to the cruelty in snatching these newborn babies. This draconian practice has already been condemned by the court of human rights.

http://www.nkmr.org/english/p_c_and_s_v_united_kingdom_ver dict.htm

(see paragraphs 133,137,and 138)

133. The Court concludes that the draconian step of removing S. from her mother shortly after birth was not supported by relevant and sufficient reasons and that it cannot be regarded as having been necessary in a democratic society for the purpose of safeguarding S. There has therefore been, in that respect, a breach of the applicant parents' rights under Article 8 of the Convention

http://www.aims.org.uk/journal/vol14no2/statesanctionedkidnap ping.htm

Why does this happen?

In December 2000 *The Guardian* published an urgent demand by Tony Blair made in a white paper that adoption figures be increased 40% by the middle of 2005:

Blair vows to increase number of adoptions
by John Carvel,
The Guardian, 22 December 2000

Tony Blair yesterday promised to achieve a 40% increase in adoptions by 2004-05.

A white paper foreshadowing the biggest shake-up of adoption law for 25 years proposes financial allowances for adoptive parents and a streamlined system to reduce the time children spend in council care.

There would also be a new status of "special guardianship" for children needing a permanent home, but not wanting to sever links with their birth parents.

Ministers said this could be suitable for hundreds of older children who wanted to keep their original family name - and Muslims who have religious and cultural difficulties with full, legal adoption.

Alan Milburn, the health secretary, said: "Children stay in the care system for longer than they should. More than 28,000 children have been in care continuously for more than two years."

He promised national adoption standards setting out what children and parents involved in the adoption process can expect.

Local authorities taking children into care will have to produce a plan for their future within six months. If that involves adoption, a family should be found within a further six months. This would be faster than the average of 16 months before a decision on whether a child should be adopted is made and another seven before the child is placed with an adoptive family.

A task force will tackle poor performance in social services departments and adoption services could be removed from failing authorities.

An adoption register for England and Wales will be drawn up by July to match children with adoptive parents from across the country, in case a local family cannot be found.

People wanting to adopt will gain the right to an independent review if their application is rejected. The government will organise panels to look again at the evidence and tell the relevant adoption agency if it should reconsider.

The white paper said: "No child should be denied loving, adoptive parents solely on the grounds that the child and the parents do not share the same racial or cultural background." Prospective parents "will not be automatically excluded from adoption on grounds of age, health or other factors, except in the case of certain criminal convictions". But there are no plans to change the law which allows only married couples or individuals to adopt. This means that cohabiting couples and homosexual partners will still not be able to adopt together.

After adopting a child, families will have the right to ask for a wide range of support services from the local authority.

They may qualify for a new adoption allowance, including one-off payments for a house extension or larger car, time-limited payments for counselling, or regular payments to cover the cost of visiting birth families.

The government is also proposing 18 weeks of paid adoption leave for one adoptive parent, bringing adoptive parents' rights into line with those of birth mothers with regard to maternity leave.

Mr Milburn promised £66.5m to improve adoption services over the next three years. The money will come from the quality protects programme announced in September. The target is to increase numbers of adoptions from 2,700 this year to at least 3,780 within five years.

Mr Blair, who has given strong personal support to adoption reform, told yesterday how his father, Leo, was fostered when his travelling entertainer parents left him with a couple they met on tour. "In those days there weren't any rules at all. I don't think my grandmother would have passed any tests...But then a framework of rules grew up in a random and ad hoc way. Now is the right time to get back to basics and ask what we want to achieve for children," he said.

Felicity Collier, chief executive of the British Agencies for Adoption and Fostering, said: "We welcome the high profile which is being given to adoption and in particular the personal interest and commitment of the prime minister.

"The biggest problem facing local authorities and adoption agencies is a shortage of families coming forward to adopt. These measures will make a real difference."

Moira Gibb, president of the Association of Directors of Social Services, said its members backed the reforms. The government inquiry "found little evidence of an institutional anti-adoption culture within social work. We have the second highest percentage of children adopted from care in the industrialised world," she said.

Rita Stringfellow, chairman of the Local Government Association's social affairs and health executive, said: "I am delighted that this white paper brings adoption legislation in line with the Children Act and provides a clear duty for health authorities to provide comprehensive post-adoption support services."

Main points

• National target to increase number of adoptions of children in care by 40% over five years;

• councils to decide whether adoption is appropriate within six months and find a family within a further six months;

• a national adoption register to be drawn up by July to match children with parents;

• independent reviews for people rejected as adopters;

• adoption allowances and 18 weeks parental leave for adopters;

• new status of "special guardianship" for children needing a permanent home, but not wanting legal separation from birth parents.

• £66.5m over three years to improve services and support for adoptive families;

• a children's and family court support service to be set up in April to streamline legal procedures.

Children are taken away – but the system can't admit it's wrong
by Cassandra Jardine
Daily Telegraph, 2 August 2004

Social workers who believe that parents have harmed their children say they always act 'in the best interests of the child'. But what happens to those parents who protest – and believe that they can prove – their innocence? In a two-part investigation into the closed world of child protection, Cassandra Jardine hears from families who have suffered at the hands of a system they say is unjust and biased – and uncovers disturbing suggestions that, in one county at least, the council's efforts to meet government adoption targets may be making a bad situation worse.

In room 101 at County Hall in Chelmsford, the Essex adoption managers assembled for their monthly meeting are wreathed in smiles. Under the avuncular leadership of Tony Sharp, county adoption manager, they have much to be proud of. In acknowledgment of its superlative performance during 2002-03, Essex County Council was awarded Beacon status for increasing the number of children adopted, speeding up the process and both recruiting and supporting adoptive parents.

Each child saved from abusive and neglectful parents is a cause for celebration. Some children for whom the adoption teams find new and better homes have been given doughnut burns by being put in scalding baths; others have been emotionally and sexually abused. The faster such children can be moved on to new parents who will give them a second chance, the better.

Essex's adoption statistics are certainly impressive. Four years ago, only 45 children were adopted from care in the county; last year, there were 75; this year, it is hoping the number will reach 100. That will mean fewer children languishing in the care limbo and fewer children becoming too old to be attractive to would-be adopters. It is exactly what the Government hoped for when, in 2000, it called for adoption services to be speeded up and stepped up.

Essex has not just met, but exceeded, the targets agreed with the Government. And, owing to the local authority's foresight in helping adopters cope with their new families, only five per cent of the adoptions they arrange break down, against a national average of 20 per cent.

But there are some outside County Hall who view the Beacon award emblazoned on the local authority's letter paper as an affront. These are parents who believe that a policy designed to prevent children suffering has, in some cases, resulted in a different kind of child abuse. Children, they say, are being taken away from their families for insufficient reason and adopted with such speed that birth parents and relatives are not being given a fair chance to prove that they are capable of looking after them.

Essex is not unique in being the focus of such complaints - you can hear them made against many local authorities - but in that county there is a vocal cluster of parents who, emboldened by one another, are openly expressing their rage and distress. One focus of the campaign is Chris Smith, who runs a website for Pain, Parents Against Injustice. Although he is prevented by legal constraints from discussing his own case, he is adamant that he, and not adopters, should now be caring for his two sons.

The Pain website carries the case of a couple whose baby was taken into care when a bump on his head turned out to be a fractured skull. Although they now believe they can prove that they never harmed their child, they cannot get anyone to listen.

Other cases have come to light. One mother believes she could care for her three children if only her undiagnosed epilepsy had been taken into account. Another woman has moved to Lincolnshire in order to care for her own baby; although her parents and sister were eager to support her, she believes that, in Essex, her child would have been taken into care at birth.

There is a furious couple who went through a court case and five hearings in order to hold on to their child, despite social services being aware of their reasons for thinking that the medical evidence for abuse was unsound. The parents of a child with Asperger's syndrome fear adoption because they are accused of neglecting him by not sending him to school; they argue that he cannot cope. Another mother whose child has been injured - she believes by her partner or a childminder - is frantic because proceedings are under way to take him into care before investigations are complete.

All of these people have similar complaints. They talk of hostile social workers, patchy record keeping, failure to share information, reliance upon experts (psychological as well as medical) whose judgment they question, and Family Courts that are biased against parents and provide no real opportunity for appeal.

Behind it all, they fear that the Government's emphasis on increased and speedier adoption has created a climate in which, once a child has come to the attention of social services, birth parents are disadvantaged. "I feel like a surrogate, who has given birth to a baby for a childless couple," says a woman whose baby was taken into care at the age of six months and is now with adopters.

"I suspect that I wasn't allowed to show I could care for my boys myself, because they are lovely, bright children with no learning or behavioural difficulties and it would be easy to find adopters," says Chris Smith. "Adoption allows the professionals to hang their hook on a noble end game," says another battling father.

The pain these people are suffering is hard to overestimate. Not only have they lost their children, they have also been accused of inadequacy and worse. Depression and suicidal thoughts are common but they are trying to be constructive and to use their distress to highlight flaws in the current system so that others may not suffer as they have done. It is a mark of their desperation that they are prepared to publicise their plight, since the secrecy surrounding the Family Courts, where these cases are heard, means that they risk imprisonment for discussing them, even with their MPs or the Citizens' Advice Bureau.

The time is right for their complaints to be heard. The Adoption and Children Act 2002 comes into force in the autumn of 2005. Some of its measures for speeding up adoption and supporting adopters are already in place but the regulations and guidance are currently out for consultation. By the end of this year, they will be fixed.

Earlier this year, it looked as if there was hope for the thousands of parents whose children have been taken into care and, in some cases, adopted. Following Angela Cannings's successful appeal against imprisonment for causing the death of her children, in January, Harriet Harman, solicitor general, told MPs that if it was unsafe to convict parents under criminal law on the basis of misguided expert evidence, it must also have been wrong to take children away from parents under civil law on the same grounds.

"We will make sure," she said, "...any potential injustices in care proceedings are identified and acted on....We bear in mind the absolute, utmost gravity and seriousness of those whose injustice is not in the hands of the criminal justice system, but as a result of the family justice system."

The following month, however, having listened to the outcry from social services, Margaret Hodge, an Essex MP and Minister for Children, narrowed the scope of review back to the 258 criminal cases in which there had been dispute between medical experts on the cause of a child's death. "It is important nobody over-reacts," said Andrew Cozens, president of the Directors of Social Services. "No child will have been adopted or taken into care solely on the basis of expert witnesses."

Parents' conviction that they have been wronged is hard to reconcile with the social workers' certainty that the procedures they are following are as near perfect as any human agency can be. When I asked Lyndsay Davison, service manager for fostering and adoption, whether she felt that, in Essex, there had been any miscarriages of justice based on medical evidence (widening the question to include civil cases in the Family Courts), she said "No" with complete confidence.

Other managers within the adoption service are equally convinced that justice is being done. "The judge doesn't get it wrong. You've got to trust someone and, if all the work has been done, it can't be wrong," says Pat Howorth, who finds adopters for children who are more difficult to place.

"Providing all the assessments have been done properly, there cannot be a mistake," says Dorothy Henwood, who recruits adoptive families.

Perhaps it is not surprising if the members of the adoption team are not aware of problems: they become involved only once care proceedings are under way. The Child Assessment and Care Management service has the uncomfortable job of taking children into care, assessing parents and developing care plans. But Letitia Collins, service manager for the Braintree area of Essex, is equally convinced that the system is reliable and fair. "There are plenty of checks and balances," she says. "Parents have every opportunity to fight their case."

Often, concern for a child's welfare can turn into a battle between parents and social workers. Whether innocent, guilty or just struggling, parents are afraid when social services become involved in their lives. Bill Bache, Angela Cannings's solicitor, says parents view social services as "the Gestapo" and social workers know it. "Our image is of trendies in sandals who snatch babies," says one Essex child service manager.

It is possible that some of the aggrieved parents who have described their plight to me are, in fact, unsuited to caring for their own children. They don't appear to be chaotic, violent or out of control due to drink or drugs, though some have been through difficult relationships and medical problems that may have made them seem so. It is also possible that there are some poorly trained or officious social workers who wrench children out of their homes on slight grounds, even though those I met in Essex seemed dedicated individuals, motivated by "the best interests of the child".

That phrase, taken from the Children Act of 1989, may be one root of the problem. It has become a mantra for social service departments. Although the Act stressed the importance of keeping families together, the interests of the child have often come to be seen as separate from those of the family. So enshrined is this in current thinking that Earl Howe, opposition health spokesman in the Lords, says: "The Children Bill, now going through Parliament, never once mentions the importance of parents and families. It is all about how the authorities can intervene."

On top of that emphasis on the child came the 2000 White Paper on adoption. This came out of Tony Blair's personal interest in the subject: his father, Leo, was fostered while his entertainer parents were away on tour. He believes that children need the stability of permanent homes and was appalled by the long delays to which children in care were subjected. In 1998, it took 19 months for a care plan for a child to be agreed and a further eight months for the placement; as a result, many children became too old or too disturbed for adoption.

He chaired a Cabinet Committee and commissioned a review of adoption that produced the White Paper, Adoption: a New Approach, calling for "adoption to be maximised" and delays minimised on behalf of the 55,300 in care in 1999, 28,700 of whom had been "languishing in care" for more than two years. Targets were set: a 40 per cent increase in adoption by 2004-05 and 50 per cent by 2005-06. At the time, there were 2,700 adoptions from care per year (almost all of which are contested) - and another 2,000 or so adoptions, mostly by step-parents. Even then, it was the second highest number of children adopted from care - after America - in the Western world. In 2002-03, the number of adoptions reached 3,500.

To speed up proceedings, "parallel planning" has become a legal requirement. Previously, adoption plans could begin only after the court hearing; now, although a child can be prepared for adoption only after the care plan has been agreed (usually in court), adopters are lined up a few weeks after a child comes into care, while attempts are still being made to rehabilitate the child within the family.

"Numbers of children adopted are up because adoption has to be considered for every child," says Jo Willoughby, who manages Essex's post-adoption services. While defending the change, she concedes that: "Birth parents' support organisations would say this new system is very unfair."

Parallel planning prevents children suffering the developmental consequences of hanging around for years in foster care - 40 weeks is now the time within which permanent care plans have to be settled - and, for children of persistently abusive parents, incapable of reform, it is "admirable", according to Earl Howe. But, having spoken to many distressed parents, he finds many aspects worrying.

Planning for adoption at an early stage makes parents feel under threat. They fear that the local authority has a vested interest in seeing adoption through, having spent time and money matching children with prospective adopters. "Parallel planning mustn't influence social services to take children away from their parents," says Tim Loughton, shadow children's minister. "When the Adoption and Children Bill was debated, I was assured that the Government's emphasis was on increasing adoption rates among older problem children, rather than on creating incentives to snatch babies."

Adoption has obvious advantages for local authorities. An adopted child is no longer a drain on the council's resources, unlike a child who is in council care or being monitored on the "at risk" register. It also appeals to local authorities that are keen to avoid accusations of negligence. The inquiry into the case of Victoria Climbie, the eight-year old who died in February 2000 at the hands of abusers who beat her with a bicycle chain and left her tied up in a freezing bathroom, has created a climate of fear in local authority social service departments.

No local authority wants to be the subject of an inquiry, and allegations of abuse have soared from 160,000 in 1997 to 569,000 in 2002. Most children on the "at risk" register remain at home, but 39,000 cases per year go to child protection conference, of which 25,000 go on to full child protection and 3,000 to court for a care order.

The chances of the local authority stepping in depend on where you live. In some areas, fewer than one in 50 are referred to social services; in others, more than one in 10. Essex comes in the middle of the scale and, in the three months to March 31, there was an increase of 10.7 per cent in children given protection. Letitia Collins puts this down to increased drug abuse and better communication between hospitals, schools and social services.

But Rioch Edwards-Brown, who runs the Five Percenters, a support group for parents accused, as she was, of shaking their babies, wonders whether bigger registers are saving children or simply creating suffering. "According to the NSPCC and UNICEF," she says, "the number of children in the UK who die at the hands of adults has remained static at two a week [one of the worst records in the Western world]. And taking children from parents with insufficient reason is doing them the most harm possible." Only now, nine years after her son was returned to her, is she beginning to feel confident of their relationship.

Through the Five Percenters, she has spoken to 2,300 worried parents accused of all manner of abuse. Unexplained injuries lead to children being taken into care, she hears, and doctors often diagnose abuse - or endorse social workers' suspicions - without either examining the child or meeting the family.

Despite the questions raised by the Clark, Cannings and Patel appeals, a small and influential core of doctors appear to share Prof David Southall's assertion that abuse is more prevalent than we, as a society, care to admit. Prof Southall and another eminent paediatrician, Prof Sir Roy Meadow, are soon to come before the General Medical Council but the Royal College of Paediatricians won't revise their views on Shaken Baby syndrome or Munchausen's syndrome by proxy, two of the most controversial diagnoses that have led to children being taken from parents. When a child's illness or injury cannot be explained, doctors don't want to be criticised for inaction if a child is harmed again, so they prefer to err on the safe side - even if a child has had no previous injuries.

Parents report that doctors continue to look for the worst explanation and give opinions outside their specialist knowledge. There are incentives to do so: court appearances can pay £110 an hour, and writing reports is lucrative. "They charge writing time at £80 an hour," says one child protection manager, "so they produce books."

Judges in Family Courts are expected to seek a second medical opinion if the findings are disputed but, in parents' experience (though Essex gives an example to the contrary), doctors tend to operate as a fraternity and back up one another's judgments. Once one doctor has decided an injury is suspicious, it may be hard to find another - in this country at least - who disagrees. "Courts try to persuade both sides to accept one expert," says Earl Howe, "but many experts have a standpoint and, often, families don't know what they are agreeing to."

"It is never just on medical grounds that a child is taken away," says one child service manager. For the local authority's lawyers to agree that there is a case for taking a child into care, there needs to be supporting evidence of bad parenting due to mental or behavioural problems (usually due to alcohol or drugs). These are established in the "core assessment", once a child has been taken into care.

. Some parents feel that such assessments are not carried out with sufficient care. They feel the aim is to prove their guilt, not to seek explanations. A guardian ad litem is appointed by Cafcass (the Children and Family Court Advisory Support Service) as the child's "voice" throughout proceedings, but parents sometimes find that the guardians' probation work or child protection backgrounds lead them to treat parents like offenders.

Guilty parents are, of course, just as likely as innocent ones to say "I didn't do it", but those fighting to get their children back say that, often, their impassioned fights count against them. Passive parents who allow social workers to feel powerful and protective are treated more gently than argumentative ones who view demands for repentance as Maoist. Social workers do not - quite rightly - assume that articulate and rational parents are invariably above reproach and they know they will have a fight on their hands when dealing with such people so, as one said, "we work harder to get the evidence together".

Yet in the same article Moira Gibb who is President of the Association of Directors of Social Services stated that the UK ALREADY has the second highest percentage of children adopted from care in the industrialised world. Many Councils make public service agreements with the government to meet certain targets including increasing adoptions so as to save money spent keeping children in care. Kent for example more than doubled its adoption figures over a 3-year period 2001-2004 and received around £20 million from the government for hitting 10 out of 12 targets set of which increasing adoption figures was target No1.

Most adopters seek BABIES not children so that far from taking children out of care the result was a frantic search by Kent Social Services for babies that could be adopted. More than 3,000 babies under 1 year old every year for the last ten years have been snatched by 'SS' and put into care prior to adoption by strangers. (The figure of 3,000 per year rising to 3,900 per year over a ten-year period comes from the answer to a parliamentary question put by Tim Loughton MP in 2004 to the Minister for children). Most of these were taken from mothers who desperately wanted to keep them but they stood no chance of prevailing against the onslaught of the mighty forces of Social Services...

The demand for newborn babies for adoption used to be satisfied by young girls who had babies out of wedlock. This is no longer a disgrace so that need now has to be satisfied as far as possible by making claims of abuse or neglect against mothers (in their past) that more often than not are false and unsubstantiated and using these as an excuse to take newborn babies away to secret places for adoption by persons who are too ashamed to show their faces to the real parents. These selfish adopters prevent the baby from ever meeting its brothers, sisters, aunts, uncles and grandparents, or even knowing that these relations exist.

Kindness is practically never shown to these mothers and the only abuse to the baby comes from the social workers who deprive it of the bond formed with the mother at birth and prevent it from breast feeding which is the natural way to nourish any baby. The unfortunate mothers however are mostly condemned for life to produce babies not for themselves but to swell the adoption figures for the Social Services.

ONLY IN THE FAMILY COURTS DO VICTIMS (and consequently their children) GET PUNISHED NOT FOR CRIMES THEY HAVE COMMITTED BUT FOR CRIMES THAT SOCIAL SERVICES THINK THEY MIGHT COMMIT IN THE FUTURE!!

Is all this wild talk or can it be proved?

Abuse of contempt
by Nick Cohen
The Observer, 4 December 2005

I know you should not judge by appearances, but 'Mrs B' doesn't look like a child killer. To use old-fashioned language, she is motherly - a plump, rosy-cheeked woman of Kent, whom nature seemed to have created to raise children.

Kent social services soon put a stop to that. In 1999, Mrs B gave birth to a daughter. The child suffered fits that would have baffled previous generations of doctors, but which modern doctors could label with an impressively scientific name. Two concluded that Mrs B was poisoning the girl because she was an attention-seeker suffering from Munchausen's syndrome by proxy. First, they claimed she had fed her tranquillisers. There was no trace of tranquilliser in the child's blood, hair or urine. Then they claimed she had injected her with water from a flower bowl or lavatory. One of Britain's foremost toxicologists said the idea that either could have caused fits was nonsense. The family paediatrician said he found the allegations absurd. The evidence was so feeble the police didn't investigate.

No matter. In 2003, the Family Division of the High Court, sitting in closed session, upheld the decision to take the girl from her mother and send her to live with relatives 200 miles away. Curiously, since the authorities had declared that Mrs B was an insane and depraved woman, the courts allowed her to keep her other two daughters. I don't know how to explain this - maybe it's a miracle - but they survive in rude health.

The Family Division might have been designed to allow miscarriages of justice. Judges need only find the case against parents proven 'on the balance of probabilities' rather than 'beyond reasonable doubt'. Reasonable questioning of their decisions by outsiders is next to impossible because it is a contempt of court to reveal what has gone on.

The formal reason for secrecy is that it prevents the media identifying children - and, undoubtedly, there are circumstances in which they need protecting. When there is an injustice, however, it is in the interests of parents and child for the mother to be able to exercise a free woman's right to make a fuss by going to the papers, local TV station, her councillors and MP.

In normal circumstances, the law would have stymied Mrs B, but she had two strokes of luck. The first was that her solicitor was Sarah Harman.

This case has come close to ruining Harman. The best part of the past 18 months has been the admiring tributes. At the Solicitors' Disciplinary Tribunal last week, clients, judges and fellow solicitors spoke of a lawyer of the highest integrity who 'looks to right injustice wherever she finds it'. People who know her rely on her. After Michael Stone murdered Josie Russell's mother and sister, her father Shaun asked Harman to be Josie's trustee and protect her interests. If you need to smash your way through a brick wall, she is a good lawyer to have holding your coat.

Mrs B was also fortunate that by 2003 politicians were belatedly realising that like many another secret world the Family Division was liable to be swept by pseudo-scientific manias. The spark for their concern was the quashing by the Court of Appeal of the convictions of Sally Clark, Angela Cannings and others allegedly driven mad by Munchausen's. The evidence of Professor Sir Roy Meadow which had sent them down for child killing was revealed to be tosh.

It was not just his cockeyed testimony. The Court of Appeal wisely noticed that doctors were trying to identify illnesses that 'may be unexplained today [but] perfectly well understood tomorrow'. When medieval cartographers did not know what lay beyond the mountains they filled the blank spaces on their maps with 'There be dragons'. Much the same had happened in English law. When no one could explain injuries or illnesses, Meadow and his associates filled the blank spaces with pictures of monstrous women.

Margaret Hodge, the Children's Minister, announced a review that was potentially more explosive than the Court of Appeal's verdicts. Whatever else Angela Cannings and Sally Clark had suffered, their friends and families could at least protest loudly and in public. Hodge was to look at 5,000 Family

Division cases with disputed medical evidence where the courts had taken away children in secret.

Well, thought Sarah Harman, if there's at last going to be a review I want my client's voice heard. She sent details of Mrs B's case to the local MP and to her sister Harriet Harman, the solicitor-general, who passed them to Hodge. Nothing they saw identified Mrs B's daughter. Mrs B also spoke to the Daily Mail and the BBC. Nothing was printed or broadcast which identified the girl.

Closed systems hate daylight. Kent County Council went ape and claimed that Sarah Harman was in contempt of court for talking to politicians and the press. It was far from clear that she was. No other common law democracy imposes such restrictions on child care cases. Even in Scotland, what Sarah Harman had done would not have raised an eyebrow. Kent County Council itself discussed Mrs B with Roy Meadow, even though he was not a witness in the case. If Sarah Harman were guilty of contempt of court, so were its officers, presumably.

Mr Justice Munby heard the argument. On one point all sides agreed: Sarah Harman was slow to disclose what she had done to the court. She had a good excuse. Her doctors had just told her she was suffering from cancer, and she had to endure two bouts of emergency surgery while she was fighting to defend her reputation. You might have forgiven her for being a touch confused. Munby didn't forgive and threw the book at her. She was in contempt of court and had misled the court, he declared. No one had the right to discuss a Family Division case with anyone - not with the Children's Minister or the solicitor-general or their MP.

People talk about judicial activism, but this was judicial totalitarianism. Britain is a parliamentary democracy, but Munby was saying that citizens who brought their grievances to their elected representatives were in contempt of court. Harman had to pay £20,000 in legal costs. The punishments didn't stop there. Last week the Solicitors Disciplinary Tribunal heard Kent County Council's complaint against Sarah Harman and banned her from practising law for three months.

It is an ugly but typical picture of the legal establishment thumping critics when its faults are exposed. The backlash won't work and isn't working. Parliament reacted to Munby's treatment of Sarah Harman by changing the rules and giving citizens the right to discuss injustices. More reform is coming, albeit slowly and timorously. Even Mr Justice Munby told Parliament that he did not think 'the existing rules are necessary'.

The old regime will die, but it is getting its pound of flesh before it goes. Sarah Harman has had her good name blackened and spent so many thousands of pounds defending herself that she has given up counting. I'm not saying all the 5,000 parents who had their children snatched were innocent. But the pathetic and frankly incredible review of their treatment found that in only one case - that's right, just one - did the Family Division get it wrong. Despite the scandal, despite the General Medical Council striking Meadow's name from the medical register, 'Mrs B' and 4,998 others are still being punished as child abusers.

These articles confirm that thousands of children (including hundreds of babies) have been taken via secret courts which imprison parents who dare to complain publicly and which condemn parents on the basis of rumour, gossip and hearsay from witnesses who cannot be cross-examined because they do not go to court. To make matters even worse Margaret Hodge, the former Minister for children admitted in *The Telegraph* that tens of thousands of children have been wrongfully taken from their parents and given for adoption. She stated however that in the children's interests it is better in most cases to leave them where they are. Surely the least she could do in these circumstances would be to end the secrecy and let the birth parents know where their children have gone and by whom they have been adopted? In the name of common humanity please Minister allow parents who have suffered by unjustly losing their children to the State and then to adoption **TO KNOW WHERE THEY ARE**!

Legal aid solicitors never challenge anything the social workers say and hardly ever call the right witnesses to help the parents because they wish to maintain good relations with the Social Services. Ask any legal aid solicitor who specialises in the

Family Court, how many cases they have won against opposition from Social Services so that parents have recovered their children and the answer is usually a big fat ZERO!! Parents cannot complain either by revealing what happened in the secret Family Courts or by naming themselves or their children publicly without risking prison for contempt of the secret court. (Unlike more civilized countries such as Australia, New Zealand, Canada and Ireland where such secrecy in Family Courts does not exist). Social Services however disregard this secrecy that they tell parents is meant to protect the children, when they openly break this secrecy themselves by placing advertisements in adoption magazines such as Adoption UK with large colour photographs and first names plus financial incentives for those willing to adopt the children so advertised!! Imagine the feelings of distraught mothers seeing their beloved children advertised in this fashion and being powerless to recover them, or even to protest publicly themselves!!

The secrecy is also broken when a self-important government minister like David Blunkett is involved, so that when he goes to the Family Court the details of the court proceedings and the names of the children he claims are his are all made very public!! This despite the opposition of the unfortunate husband whose wife he seduced and who only wants to keep his family together.

Mothers are sent to jail and even condemned for murder in the High Court on the basis of unproven crackpot theories put forward by charlatan doctors with no forensic evidence. In the Family Courts parents are often judged to have neglected or even abused their children purely on the balance of probabilities instead of beyond reasonable doubt. Judges nearly always believe social workers to 'probably' be more truthful than parents who therefore have no chance of clearing their names let alone winning their case.

Common sense would indicate that mothers who go to court and who are desperate to rescue their children from care orders and from the Social Services are not usually the type of mothers who abuse or neglect their offspring. That type of mother would hardly ever bother to go to court as she would be glad to be rid of children she did not care for. On this basis, surely most mothers going to court to ask for the return of their loved ones should win with the help of social workers who say that their main job is to keep families together. In fact the opposite is the case, the mothers nearly always lose thanks to the determination of social workers to split up families and make every effort to keep parents and children apart. The sad fact is that children are more than 100 times more likely to be abused in care or worse still in a children's home than if they were left alone to stay with their own sometimes feckless but almost always loving parents.

The terrible truth is that only too often the state equates poverty or illiteracy with inadequate parenting. This results in taking babies and young children from the poor and giving them for adoption to 'the better educated and the better off'. This is **WICKED** and **WRONG, WRONG, WRONG**!!

What about fathers when mothers refuse contact?

This is also wrong and quite simply I believe the partner who does not have custody should normally have the right to receive the children at least during half the school holiday period. There is less room for argument with this system and less disruption for the children. Any parent flouting a Court Order giving access to the other parent should either risk losing custody to the other parent or be liable to prison for contempt until both parents enjoy the access granted by the court. Family allowances should be split and drawn separately in proportion to the access specified.

Older children who are put in foster homes are forbidden to telephone or contact their parents and vice versa by cruel unfeeling social workers even though no judge ever gives such an instruction. Meetings arranged on average 4 times per year are carefully supervised by social workers who harshly forbid parents from discussing their case or even from letting their children know that they have not abandoned them and that they want them back. This censorship takes place even though no judge orders it but the social workers achieve it purely by intimidation and threats.

Very often children are ill treated by the foster parents. Even worse there are frequent examples of sexual abuse by care workers in children's homes. The parents are powerless to complain in public because of gagging orders from the court which are supposed to protect the children by concealing their names and which in fact often leave them open to horrible and vile abuse in the places where they are sent. Children's homes are frequently staffed by paedophiles, and horrific cases of abuse are time and again reported in the national press.

**BEWARE ----- BEWARE ----- BEWARE -----
BEWARE ----- BEWARE ----- BEWARE**

Above all remember the 'number one' golden rule!!! **NEVER, NEVER, NEVER** contact Social Services for help or advice concerning your children because if you do, more often than not they will take your children and have them put into care or worse still get them adopted. Hundreds of angry mothers all over the country have lost their children in this way and can now do nothing about it.

Well good luck to you who are reading this if you are forced to struggle with these horrible and disgusting child snatchers. It is interesting to note that the majority of social workers do not have a happy family life with their own children and that is why they take it out on you. Fight back and fight back hard!!

16. TYPICAL FORCED ADOPTION CASES

Wicked - Wicked - Wicked!

Social Services abuse the babies they should protect by taking them from their mothers and giving them for adoption by strangers.

"Damned if we do and damned if we don't" is the pathetic defensive mantra of the 'SS' child snatchers! This means that they are damned when they **DO** take **BABIES** and children from mothers who cry and plead in vain in the secret Family Courts (press and public are excluded) to keep their **BABIES** since nobody has ever accused these mothers of causing them **PHYSICAL** harm. They are damned when they **DON'T** take children who have massive injuries, cigarette burns and broken bones inflicted on them by parents or 'carers' who wouldn't dream of going to court to try and retain the children as they would be only too pleased to be rid of them!!

MORE THAN 3,000 BABIES PER YEAR EVERY YEAR FOR THE PAST TEN YEARS HAVE BEEN SNATCHED BY 'SS' AND PUT INTO CARE PRIOR TO ADOPTION (The figures for babies put into care over a 10 year period come from the answer to a question put in Parliament to the Minister for Children by Tim Loughton MP in 2004). Any mother who already has a child in care and who gives birth to a new baby **AUTOMATICALLY** has that baby seized at birth by heartless social workers anxious to meet their adoption targets. Changed circumstances are rarely taken into account.

Websters' MP: Stop cash for adoptions

by Laura Collins

Mail on Sunday, 7 July 2007

The MP of a couple who lost three of their children because of a false abuse claim has called for an end to Government adoption targets. Liberal Democrat Norman Lamb said the targets, introduced by Tony Blair, 'provide a perverse incentive', with councils winning cash rewards if a specified number of children are adopted.

Mr Lamb, who also wants family court proceedings to be opened up, has applied for a Commons adjournment debate over the tragedy of Mark and Nicky Webster.

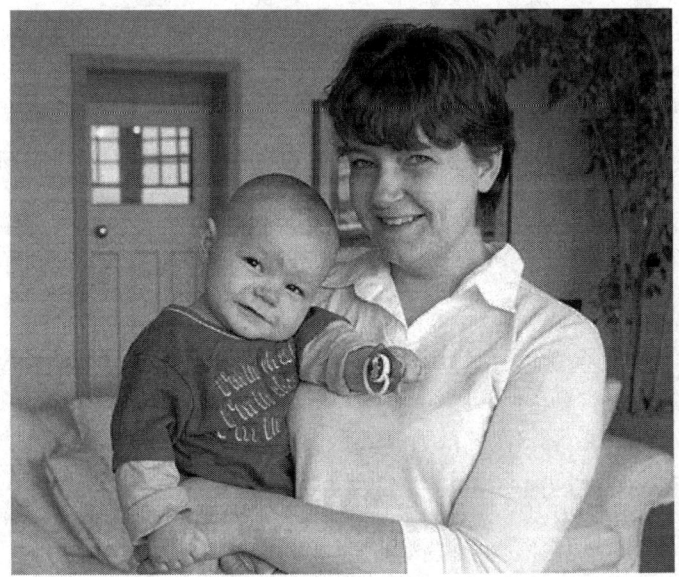

Saved: Nicky with baby Brandon

Their three eldest children were taken from them by Norfolk County Council because one had a fracture that doctors said could only have been caused by physical abuse.

But later, four eminent specialists found that the boy was lactose-intolerant, would not take solids, and was probably suffering from scurvy, which would have made his bones brittle and liable to break.

These experts gave this evidence for Mark, 34, and Nicky, 26, from Cromer, when they won a landmark court fight to keep their fourth child, 13-month-old Brandon.

The Websters are fighting on for the right to have contact with their lost children, who are with separate families, but have been advised that the adoption order is irreversible.

Their story could only be told after The Mail on Sunday and BBC won a ruling allowing the media to report a family court case for the first time.

North Norfolk MP Mr Lamb said: "Theirs was an appalling miscarriage of justice and part of any proper discussion must mean rethinking social services' adoption targets."

The financial incentives were introduced in 2000 in an attempt to see adoptions rise by 50 per cent. The number of babies taken into council care in England before being adopted has risen from 970 in 1996 to 2,120 last year.

Mr Lamb said: "It ought not to be a factor that taking children into adoption means the social services bringing in money from the Government.

"I'm sure that when these annual targets were set, they were done so with the best of intentions.

"But it brings a financial motivation into a process which just should not be influenced in that way."

The Mail on Sunday has learned that a county council, which cannot be named for legal reasons, has won an injunction preventing ITV's Jeremy Kyle Show from featuring a mother whose five children, all under six, are being adopted forcibly.

John Sweeney, an investigative reporter and presenter on the BBC's Real Story, describes reporting on the Family Courts as being as difficult as reporting from Zimbabwe. Of the seven child abuse cases he has covered in the criminal courts over the past few years, all have ended in the quashing of convictions. Some of the defendants - Angela Cannings and Sally Clark - have become household names. But of the five cases he has covered in the Family Courts, all have ended in the parents losing their children for ever. This in itself seems to indicate that when there is a criminal element, the proceedings are consequently public so the parents have a chance to win! The secrecy of the Family Courts, as opposed to the criminal courts, allows compliant establishment judges to make the most outrageous decisions depriving parents of their children, safe from outside scrutiny or criticism. You will probably never know the names of those parents. Their names must be changed and their faces blocked out to 'protect' the children. It is hard to expose miscarriages of justice when the stories are drained of human content.

Delegates at the Millennium Hotel Mayfair London...

Tammy tells her shocking story to the conference:

"In the best interest of the child" that's what the professional's state, but even the professionals and the Family Courts can be wrong as they were in my case.

Let me explain about my birth family, and myself. I am a young adopted adult; I was taken from my mum nearly 17 years ago on a false allegation, I was seven months old and sitting in my bouncing chair, my mum had gone into the kitchen to make me a night feed. I was happily playing with an activity toy, which I dropped on the floor; I leant forward to reach the toy but the chair followed me arid tipped forward falling on top of me. I sustained a bruise on my cheek. And that's where my life was changed forever.

My case was heard within the family court in the years 1989 which lasted all the way to 1992. I was placed with a set of foster carers whom I stayed with for 13 months.

Then one-day social services accused the foster carers of suffering from depression and removed me from their care! I was then placed with three lots of emergency foster carers before being placed with my pre adopters, who then became my parents.

While this was happening to me my mum gave birth to my brother Cameron. One minute after his birth social services (a male) walked into the labour suite and tried to hand a place and safety order in writing to my mum who was laid on the bed with no clothes on and she had not even delivered the placenta. Medical staff asked the social worker to leave on three occasions eventually the social worker left the labour suite, leaving my mum very distressed and losing all her dignity.

My mum and Cameron went home to my grandparents where they resided until the 28th of December 1990. My mum then went to the family court as social services were trying for an interim care order to remove my brother from her care. My mum fought and won full parental rights of Cameron and no further action was taken. All my mum wanted was to fight for me, she attended many Family Courts, which were held in secret and she was not allowed to talk about our case or me to anyone.

Time passed and Cameron reached the age of 21 months old, when the social services actually reached a date for my freeing order, which was in the year of 1992; there were no concerns to Cameron's welfare. She was an excellent mother to him.

The judge who heard my case made his decision on the basis that social services had delayed my case for over two and a half years. On reading his decision to my mum (he stated) "Miss Coulter if I return your daughter home to you, you will be a stranger to her" and on that decision I was freed for adoption and my whole future was completely changed.

Finding out that you are adopted is one of the worst feelings in the world because you feel that all your identity you have known of yourself is a lie; for example your whole childhood and personality.

I found out through photos that my brother was still with my mum and is one and a half years younger than me. This was very upsetting and left me wondering why my mum wanted my brother and not me.

Left with these unanswered questions and feeling very confused; like I did not belong anywhere I wanted to find the truth, and the answers to my questions, the only person who could answer them was my mum.

My decision to find my birth family was not supported in the way in which I would have liked from my adoptive parents. I went about looking for my mum by first of all ringing support after adoption that told me I must wait until I am 18 years of age and would not offer me any help or advice. Which left me more confused and very upset?

In January this year on a Thursday night I received a phone call from my best friend. She told me to go over to her house, as it was very important. I had no idea of what I was to be told. Her laptop was placed on her bed and she told me to read the posting. I was ecstatic as I read the information, which confirmed that my mum was looking for me as much as I was looking for her.

My friend who knew as much as I did about my adoption found the posting when secretly putting my name on Genes Reunited. I found myself emailing her my mobile number as I knew the same information which was written in her posting; which included information that nobody would have known about me.

I waited three and a half hours for the phone call which would change my whole life, and answer all the unanswered questions which had been tormenting me since the age of about 11 when I moved to Comprehensive School where I met many other adopted and fostered children.

Waiting for the phone call was the most exciting and precious time of my life, the hours seemed like weeks. In the next breath I was actually talking to my mum on the phone, we spoke for an hour about everything that we could. We put the phone down and later that evening I rang my mum back and told her I know it was short notice but could we please meet the following morning and she agreed to.

Our meeting was very emotional for the both of us, neither of us spoke we just put our arms around each other and cried together, we held each other very tight and I cant explain how happy I was feeling.

After many secret meetings I decided to tell my adoptive parents about my news, I did not tell them for about two months because I knew what their reaction would be. When I told my mum, as my dad was at work she cried and turned her back on me making me feel very isolated as if I had done something wrong. They never did understand why it was important that I find my birth family nor did they support me at the emotional time. I was keeping in contact via the Internet with my birth family as my mobile phone was confiscated; however they also stopped me from using the Internet to stop any contact, which I was having with my birth family. During this time I was studying for my AS levels which I failed due to all the stress and confusion.

The way my adoptive parents were towards my other life caused a huge conflict in the house making life unbearable at home and at school. I was eventually turned away from my home due to arguments other than my birth parents; this is when I phoned my birth mum, as I had nowhere else to turn. It was too late when I was asked to return to the house I did not want to be treated like a child nor did I want to my feelings to be ignored any longer, so I decided to move in with my birth family.

This brings me to why I am here today, I was a child who was wrongfully removed from the care of my mother and most of all I have had the rights taken away from me to have enjoyed the right to a family life with my natural family.

I would like to say I have had a good upbringing by my adoptive parents and I love them very much, however the complication of my adoption also ruined my relationship with my adoptive parents, as I only wanted to find the truth about my life.

I am publicly speaking today on behalf of children and parents who have also been through the secrecy of family courts and the injustices that have taken place and do still take place and the devastation of what one decision that determines the future of a child can cause to a whole family.

Since I have moved in with my birth family I see the relationship between my mother, brother and sister and cannot help feeling like I have missed out no matter how much I fit in now. We have all bonded very well, I now feel as if I fit in somewhere and feel I can be myself as I have found out who I really am and that my mum never did anything wrong. Over the years Yvonne has been fighting to prove her innocence and that an injustice has taken place. I am very angry and also upset that my mum was treated like a criminal and punished for life on something that she never did, and she had the right to a family life taken away.

Let me explain to you how I am feeling:

• Confused

• Hurt

• Stripped of my identity

• I missed out on a relationship with my brothers and sisters, mum and dad and other close relations

• Exhausted through lies

• I know I am not the only person to have gone through the hell of secrecy in family courts and hope to have expressed the way in which they will feel and are feeling at my age.

Changes that I would like to see happen.

1) For medical evidence used in the courts to not be based on probabilities when determining a child's future, it must be fact.

2) To stop social services making medical diagnoses when not qualified to do so.

3) For social services when conducting assessments to be thorough and not based on self-opinions but facts.

4) For an independent body who is impartial to social services to be brought in when social services are assessing a family and to check they are following all guide lines of social work.

5) More support for families with whatever reason; a low IQ, a mother whom has depression, a parent that has suffered domestic violence and also a parent whom has a disability. More outside agencies should be involved to help put support packages in place to help families stay together and have the right to a family life.

6) Slow integration of a child back with its natural family should be paramount and decisions to take away the child should be the last resort. For example my mum was told she would be a stranger to me if I were returned home to her however my foster parents and my adoptive parents were also strangers.

7) The most important factor of us all being here today is about the secrecy surrounding the family courts and why they should be opened, you have all listened to my story and many of you would have read similar stories to mine in the media. I am of age where I can talk about the detrimental effects that the secrecy of the family courts has caused to me.

Many of the children who have been taken in the past and are still being taken do not have a voice.

The opening of the family courts would make it a fairer, non judgmental and a more impartial system which would help children that are left in the hands of abuser's and would also work by stopping children from being wrongfully removed and injustices from taking place.

Proud Mum Yvonne and daughter Tammy together at last...

So please when considering the opening of the family courts take into account that we are all human and we have feelings and the way in which the courts have been working up to this day has been inhumane in many cases and human rights have been exploited.

The detrimental emotional effects and the separation, has on children torn apart from their birth families, lasts a life time.

Tammy

17. TYPICAL CASE SCENARIOS

These can be separated into the following 9 most frequently occurring categories:

Scenario 1:

Mothers with 'learning difficulties' (meaning a lowish IQ) and/or some physical disability such as being lame or blind, but every capability of looking after a baby especially when aided by a very able and supportive partner.

Usually **all** the children are removed on the grounds that their future development might be prejudiced by their mother's 'problem' and worse still any babies born in future by such mothers are taken away at birth and put out for adoption no matter how hard desperate mothers plead in court to keep their babies. In fact, research has shown that over 50% of parents with learning difficulties have their children snatched by Social Services!

Report backs 'less able' parents
news.bbc.co.uk, 9 May 2006

The report calls for better training of agency officials

Parents with learning difficulties are having their children taken away from them without proper alternatives being considered, a report has said.

Agencies would be better served taking a more positive approach, the Bristol University study suggested.

Parenting classes could be offered in such situations and officials need better training, it said.

If such help was offered, the report said that these parents would not have to lose their children.

Practical help

It is increasingly common for people with learning difficulties to have children.

However, researchers found that in 50% of cases children were being taken from their natural parents.

However, the report's authors believe many of these parents could look after their children perfectly well if they had been offered practical help.

In one case involving a blind mother and her sighted partner the social worker concerned was convicted of perjury and conspiring to pervert the course of justice when caught out lying in her report; however she still won the adoption case and the mother lost her two little girls for ever. The social worker had to resign and was let off with a suspended prison sentence.

Scenario 2:

Mothers who have some sort of record or conviction for violence towards other adults (but not young children) or a partner with a similar record or conviction, even if these events happened many years ago. A parent who was abused whilst in the 'care' of Social Services and now considered too 'emotionally damaged' to keep a baby. A complaint about a noisy argument between parents, or a social worker remembering a disagreement with a parent a long time ago leads to renewed 'SS' involvement......

Decision:

Children are removed and put in care and worse still any newborn baby that arrives is swiftly taken away for adoption by strangers.

Scenario 3:

Mothers with a difficult child with behaviour problems or with stepfathers who resent the children or simply mothers who cannot afford to properly feed and clothe their children due to some sudden glitch or delay in the benefits system or non-payment of maintenance take the rashest step of all. They ask for help and advice from the Social Services!!! Alas 'problems' or 'poverty' are swiftly equated with 'neglect'. Hundreds of mothers up and down the country have made that same fatal error and suffered the same dire consequences. 440 children were removed over a 4-year period simply because the parents had 'a low income' and no other reason!!

Decision:

More often than not children are removed and the oldest are put in care and the youngest are taken for adoption. Any newborn babies are usually seized for adoption by strangers and lost for ever to mothers whose only crime was to ask for help and advice from Social Services.

Lose your children for being too poor
by James Chapman
Daily Mail, 22 August 2005

Social workers faced new accusations of 'child snatching' last night over youngsters taken into care because of poverty.

Campaigners and MPs were appalled by official figures giving low family income as the main reason in 110 cases.

The revelation deepened the row over the 'unjust' removal of youngsters by social services departments. They have already been accused of unfairly targeting parents deemed 'not clever enough'.

Tory spokesman Theresa May, who is calling for an inquiry into adoption policies, said the state should help lift a family out of poverty rather than breaking it up.

Despite the large number of cases, there was no official explanation last night. The Education Department could not say in what circumstances a child would be removed because of family poverty and the secrecy surrounding Family Courts means individual cases cannot be reported.

Campaigners say that setting performance targets for the number of adoptions councils should achieve has created a 'market' in vulnerable children.

Only some 3,000 children are adopted each year and the government has tried to streamline the process. Tony Blair wanted a 40 per cent increase over a five-year period, ending this year.

Official statistics show that there were 61,000 children in care in the year to March, 2004 - an increase of 20 per cent since Labour came to power.

Of those, 38,200 were in care because of abuse or neglect, 6,100 because of 'family dysfunction' 4,900 because of absent parents and 4,200 because their family was in 'acute stress'.

Another 3,500 were removed due to parents' illness or disability, 2,400 because they suffered disability themselves and 1,700 because of 'socially unacceptable behaviour'.

But the main reason in the cases of 110 children was given as 'low income'. Mrs. May said she was concerned that children should be taken into care - even temporarily - because of low income. She said: 'In the 21st century, no child should be taken from their parents simply because of income.

'In a civilised society, with the fourth largest economy, we have a right to expect better than this.

Statistics of Education: Children Looked After in England

More than 75% of care leavers have no academic qualifications of any kind

More than 50% of young people leaving care after 16 years are unemployed

17% of young women leaving care are pregnant or already mothers

10% of 16-17 year old claimants of DSS severe hardship payments have been in care

23% of adult prisoners and 38% of young prisoners have been in care

30% of young single homeless people have been in care

Scenario 4:

Mothers who are extra careful and who take their children to hospital for minor ailments or injuries 'once too often' attract the attention of Social Services who call in their 'old allies' Professors Meadows and Southall who can be relied upon to diagnose 'Munchausen's Syndrome', claiming that the mothers have injured the children themselves to gain attention.

Decision:

Thousands of children have been taken to be put into care and thousands of babies have been given for adoption as a result of this now discredited theory invented by now discredited men. The Minister for children admits that tens of thousands may have been wrongly adopted but claims it is too late to do anything about it now...

Scenario 5:

Once again careful mothers who take children to hospital for minor injuries that turn out to be serious on closer inspection or even fatal after admission.

Decision:

Social Services are alerted and they in turn call in their old friends the Professor/detective Meadows and of course Professor Southall who decided that Sally Clark's husband had murdered her children on the basis of having watched a television programme without ever having examined husband or children!! Meadows had accused the **PREGNANT** wife Sally who was imprisoned for murder and her newborn baby taken for adoption. This took place not in a secret Family Court but in a criminal court so there was widespread publicity. She was later released when it was found that

Meadow's theories and statistics had no scientific basis whatsoever. She and her husband were both exonerated too late to recover the baby that had been adopted. The Family Courts usually attribute even a single unexplained injury to negligence or worse by the parents when it could just as easily have been caused at school or by a family friend or neighbours or simply by accident, with the sad consequence that many children are wrongly deprived of their parents and given out for adoption and the parents themselves are often wrongly imprisoned by criminal courts and only released when it is too late to recover their children from 'forced adoption'.

Scenario 6:

Social Services acting on information from the police or sometimes just from anonymous tip-offs decide that certain children with parents who violently abuse or batter each other or even shouting and arguing parents who are not actually violent at all are suffering from 'emotional abuse'. This is loosely defined as a situation where parents do not bond with their children and who show them no love, but who are either physically violent or who at least shout and criticise each other and their offspring.

Decision:

An allegation of 'emotional abuse' or worse still 'a risk that children might suffer emotional harm in the future' is very difficult for parents to defend against the 'expert psychiatrists' called by the Social Services. The result is usually that **COMPLIANT ESTABLISHMENT JUDGES** authorise that the children are put in care and any new babies born to the mother in question are removed and given for adoption by strangers. This even happens years after a mother has left her abusive partner and established a new relationship with a new non-abusive partner. As a result battered women are afraid to report their plight as if they do they run a very strong risk that they will lose their children! It is no defence to point out that the Royal Family and most of the aristocratic families in Britain should lose their children on the basis of 'emotional neglect' or failure to 'bond' but they of course do not rely on legal aid but can afford top barristers to represent them, and social services tend to avoid anyone with resources like that!

Shattered lives in shadow of abuse

Carol Midgley of The Daily Telegraph tells the harrowing tale of a family that was torn apart by overzealous social workers who suspected the parents of abusing their children

Unsupported: A child separated from his or her parents may suffer irreparable psychological damage

Daily Telegraph, 26 January 2006

Daniel has only hazy memories of the day that his childhood effectively ended. He vaguely recalls, at the age of six, being taken to the head teacher's office at school, of strangers arriving and taking him away in a car. He remembers sitting in a small room as a social worker asked him endless questions, of pleading for his mother but instead being taken that night to a Catholic children's home where they put him in a bath and scrubbed him. He didn't know it then, but he would not return home for another 10 years.

Though the details of these early events are fragmented in his mind, the memory of his tearful bewilderment and desperate longing to go home remains vivid. Today Daniel, a tall, pleasant but anxious young man of 22, is still uncomprehending and very angry. Incredibly, he was forced to live in care between the ages of 6 and 16, torn from his distraught parents, despite a judge ruling that there was no evidence that he was being abused.

But that is not the worst of what happened to his family.

Thanks to the zealousness of a handful of social workers in Rochdale, Lancashire, UK, Daniel's parents, Andrew and Beverley, were wrongly accused of involvement in a Satanic abuse network, a cult that supposedly involved ritualistic sex with minors, the slaughter of animals and the sacrifice of newborn babies. All four of their children were taken from them. Three months later, in June 1990, 12 more children, all friends of Daniel, his sister and the family, were taken from their beds in traumatic morning raids, forced to endure intimate medical examinations and placed in care for months while investigations were conducted. During this time, bizarre though it seems, parents and children were kept apart because social workers suspected that they were communicating secretly with their children via coded signals and gestures.

Andrew and Beverley's other sons, James and Matthew, then 3 and 4, spent seven years in a children's home. Their daughter Julie, then 11, spent five years in care. Andrew and Beverley were allowed to see their children for just an hour a month, monitored by social workers.

Contact with Daniel was reduced gradually from an hour a month to an hour a year. Yet there was never any proof — forensic, medical or otherwise — to support claims of ritual abuse against any of the families.

The "evidence"? It was this: Daniel told his teacher that he was dreaming about ghosts — apparently a mummy and daddy ghost and a baby ghost that died. He was at the time a withdrawn, disturbed child, often hiding under desks and being disruptive. His speech was poor for his age. This, says Beverley, led to him being bullied. The teacher was concerned enough to alert social services.

Scenario 7:

Grandparents are sometimes left to look after the children when the parents die or are incapacitated due to accident, illness, drug or alcohol addiction, or a prison sentence. Often there is rancour within the remaining family structure, and Social Services are called in either for this reason or because social workers in the case of addicted or criminal parents feel that the grandparents must be tarred with the same brush and that in their 60s they are too elderly and old-fashioned to look after young children.

Decision:

As usual the legal aid lawyers agree with Social Services that the children are better off in care and if young enough should be adopted by younger and more respectable strangers. In one well-known case a grandson was taken to male gay foster parents on the orders and recommendation of two married lady social workers who were accorded maximum respect by a Court that followed their suggestions to the letter. Shortly after this these very same ladies who had said the grandparents were not suitable as carers for their grandson, deserted their own husbands and children and proudly set up home together as a lesbian couple. Despite this poor example of family responsibility their advice remained followed and the grandparents lost contact with their grandson for ever.

Scenario 8:

THE WORST CRIME OF ALL!!

A Mother with no criminal record and no problem with drugs or alcohol proudly gives birth to her new baby (very often her first baby!).

That same day (or in some cases a month or two later) two or more social workers, usually accompanied by uniformed police arrive and snatch the baby. Explanations, they tell the distraught mother, will be given later in court!

When the 'SS' apply to the court for an interim care order it will be revealed that though the mother is blameless, nevertheless Social Services have grave suspicions that the father might have a violent past! No matter that he has no criminal record, has never been convicted of violence and usually never even been charged with any crime! No problems with alcohol or drugs, just a distrust of the social workers who kidnapped his child. Such hostility must, they say surely indicate a personality disorder and the need for anger management courses! On top of all this he was perhaps accused of violence in a previous custody or divorce case (like Sir Paul McCartney) or was even suspected of complicity in the death of a previous baby or child but never accused in open court.

Decision:

In vain will the mother plead that she has done nothing wrong. In vain will she plead that she knew nothing of this aspect of her partner's/husband's past but that he is so gentle and kind with her she cannot believe the unproved accusations against him.

This however is quite enough for the wretched judge's decision! You may be innocent he says but the fact that you blindly support your partner/husband (as any married mother swore to do on her wedding day) is enough to show that you will never work properly with the 'professionals' and cannot be trusted with your baby. **SUCH JUDGES COMMIT CRIMES AGAINST HUMANITY AND SHOULD BE THROWN INTO PRISON** like the Nazi judges who were judged in their turn at Nuremburg!

The baby is then given for adoption to strangers and it will probably wonder for the rest of its life why its mother abandoned her child......

These cases are more common than you might think and I am personally helping in one case that has now gone to Strasbourg. The European Court recently condemned the UK practice of taking newborn babies at birth as 'draconian' and fined the UK a large sum!

I am myself appearing as a Mckenzie Friend (a friend to sit by you and help by suggesting questions that you should ask witnesses and making notes of their replies) in a second similar case.

In my opinion social workers who take babies or toddlers in circumstances similar to those are committing crimes against humanity and deserve punishment with a term in prison. One day not too far away I hope and believe that retribution will finally catch up with these heartless criminals!!

For the present however **EVERY COMPLETELY INNOCENT MOTHER IN THE UK IS AT RISK OF HAVING THEIR NEWBORN BABY SNATCHED AT BIRTH BY SOCIAL SERVICES!!!!**

It is enough for some dark secret accusation in the father's past to be unearthed by overzealous social workers! The mother's sin? Choosing the wrong man to father her child even if she knew nothing of disputed incidents in his long distant past!

Scenario 9:

Cruel parents, step-parents, foster parents, or carers in children's homes beat, burn, or sexually abuse the children in their charge. Usually these victims are never believed if they complain and are very often left with broken bones, extensive bruises and burns, and other serious physical damage. If concerned neighbours or relatives persist in complaining a social worker is eventually instructed to visit and inspect.

Decision:

An inexperienced social worker is usually given the unpleasant task of visiting what is usually a very sordid and smelly dwelling to report on the welfare of the children. When this person is met by aggressive and threatening parents or carers who say that the children are 'out' or ill or asleep and not to be disturbed the social worker beats a hasty retreat and promises to call again. Due however to 'pressure of work' this promise is rarely kept and it is only the tragic death of a child that can ever bring these situations out into the light of day. There is little question that if Social Services applied to the Family Courts for care orders in such cases the parents would never bother to go to court let alone oppose the orders.

Councils face abuse trial
Read article here:
http://www.fassit.co.uk/councils_face_abuse_trial.htm

Forced Adoption Case Scenarios: Conclusions

Social services knew of child in danger
by Richard Balls
EDP24 (EASTERN DAILY PRESS), 27 January 2006

A child was allowed to carry on living in squalid and potentially life-threatening conditions - despite social services being aware of the case for nearly four years, the EDP can reveal.

Earlier this month, Nicola Hillier and Jonathan Bush were jailed at Norwich Crown Court after a judge was told of the appalling way in which three children living with the couple were treated.

But it has now emerged that Norfolk social services had been alerted to the situation some four years earlier, when the couple were living with one child at their previous home at Wells.

At one stage a man on the sex offender register was living with them, and neighbours say they repeatedly begged the authorities to intervene as they feared for the toddler's life.

A former next-door neighbour told the EDP that repeated attempts were made to get housing officers and other agencies to intervene and remove the child from the horrifying conditions that confronted visitors, but no firm action was taken.

Neighbours also said the child had to be taken to hospital a number of times, once by air ambulance, after suffering cuts, bruises and other injuries in falls.

Despite the involvement of the authorities over a long period, it was not until around May 2005 - when the couple were living with three small children at a flat on Rye Avenue at Mile Cross, Norwich - that a health worker discovered the 'Dickensian' conditions and a police investigation was launched.

Last night, Norfolk Social Services sought to defend its handling of the case.

Meera Spillett, deputy director of children's services at Norfolk County Council, accepted her department had been involved with the family for several years, but insisted that they had acted when conditions deteriorated despite the support given to the couple.

She said: "We do try and keep family units together but sometimes that is not possible. Considerable support was provided to improve home conditions and to help the carers cope with the demands of children over a long period of time.

"This support included home care, high levels of home visiting, regular assessment and practical help such as making sure the children attended medical appointments.

"In spite of all the support, improvements were not sustained and conditions deteriorated to the point where the decision was made to remove the children for their own protection."

Angry ex-neighbours described how the floors of the council property were covered in human and animal faeces, urine, broken glass and other health hazards while the child crawled around the house, often without clothes.

Police intervened when it emerged that a man lodging with the couple was on the sex offenders register and had not informed the authorities that he had moved to the address.

He was removed from the property at Northfield Crescent, Wells, within weeks of moving in and later appeared in court on a number of charges.

Housing officials at North Norfolk District Council were first alerted to the squalor in which the child was being forced to live after a neighbour saw Hillier discarding soiled nappies in the back garden about four years ago. Social services staff also got involved after the risks being posed to the child were identified.

Neighbours told how;

the child slept on a bed which had been sawn in half and had sharp springs sticking out of it

ambulances were often called after the child sustained cuts, bumps to his head and other injuries the decomposing bodies of guinea pigs were left lying on floors where the child was playing

the child ate from the dog's bowl

human and animal excrement could be seen all over the house, including the bath, as well as broken glass

Hillier and Bush, both, 24, were jailed for nine months after admitting three offences of causing unnecessary suffering over a long period to the youngsters, all under the age of five.

Valerie Roberts, their next-door neighbour in Northfield Crescent, said she was angry when she read about the case and realised the neglect had been allowed to continue after the couple moved to Norwich. She saw with her own eyes the disgusting conditions in which the toddler was living and said it was "a miracle" that he survived.

She said: "The social services went in four years ago and they should have kept tabs on them right the way through. If they were going in and having to change nappies, they must have known.

"I was always on the phone to the local housing department and they could have put a stop to it, but they didn't see anything was wrong.

"That child was crawling around while they were decomposing. Someone babysat in there and said the child was in filth and mess.

"He would run around with nothing on in the freezing cold weather with the windows open. How that child survived I do not know. Many a time he was rushed off in an ambulance after falling downstairs and a helicopter came out once to take him to hospital.

"The child could not speak. If it wanted anything it would scream and we used to hear him [Bush] shouting and yelling. In court they seemed to be making the same excuses for them that they did here, but they were intelligent enough and they had money for cigarettes and his PlayStation. She was a very clever and conniving person."

Norwich Crown Court heard the children were malnourished, wore ill-fitting and filthy clothes and went around in nappies which were so badly soiled they hung around their knees.

One of the boys was so hungry he tried to eat a lump of frozen meat from the freezer, while another picked a cracker out of an overflowing ashtray.

The health worker found that one child had burns to his arm and another had a chipped collarbone and all three were unable to talk properly and resorted to shouting and screaming to get what they wanted. Yet despite the degradation, Bush's security officer uniform was found hanging from the back of a door, freshly washed and ironed.

Jailing them, Judge Peter Jacobs said: "These children were really suffering and at times their lives were sheer hell. The home was not a safe or healthy environment. They were not properly fed, dressed or educated and not kept clean and were exposed frequently to real danger; they were hungry and there was illness, dirt and neglect.

"Conditions have been described as 'Dickensian'. They were seen semi naked in a semi-dark room.

He added: "I accept your inadequacies, but this does not explain the fact you observed their suffering over a long period of time, yet you were both capable of holding down responsible jobs. People who neglect children and cause them suffering will go to prison."

David Williams, head of housing operations for the North Norfolk Housing Trust - the housing department of North Norfolk District Council, said: "We cannot comment on people's personal circumstances. However, I can say that our procedure was then, as it is now, that if our housing officers became concerned about the circumstances in a property, particularly where the welfare of children is an issue, we refer the case to the relevant authorities, like social services or the health service.

"It is not unusual for our tenants to have guests or lodgers and it would rarely, in itself, be cause for us to take immediate or formal action against them."

It follows alas that only those parents and carers in categories 1 to 8 above try in court to keep their children and above all their babies. They are however always destined to lose due to the inertia of legal aid lawyers and partiality of judges who make very sure that in cases involving care orders and adoption the Social Services always, always win! The parents and especially the mothers always, always lose! Parents cannot complain publicly about any injustice they feel they may have suffered in the Family Courts as they and any journalist revealing the slightest detail of those proceedings risk prison for contempt of court.

Secret Family Courts - Contradictions

This secrecy is supposed to protect the children from being stigmatised when in fact it exists to prevent the press and public from knowing about the horrifying injustices that take place in these Family Courts. The proof of this is that every month on a website www.uk-kids.org and in a magazine called "Adoption UK" Social Services all over the country advertise hundreds of children waiting for adoption who are subject to care orders! Incredibly they publish huge colour photographs of these children with first names, birth dates, details of their characters and financial rewards for those who agree to adopt!! Some mothers are bitterly upset to see their children advertised in this fashion. Any person familiar with the family can swiftly identify the children concerned so the only secrecy remaining protects not the children but the judges and social workers!!!

I repeat once again more than 200 MPs think the same as the following Early Day Motion showed!!

EDM 869   WORKING OF THE CHILDREN ACT
200426.10.2005 Source: PIMS

Pickles, Eric

That this House urges the Government to remove the veil of secrecy from the workings of the Children Act 2004; considers that the closed door policy of the Family Courts breeds suspicion and a culture of secrecy which does nothing to instil confidence in those using them, which affects not just the courts but the social services departments of local authorities; and believes that it is possible to preserve the anonymity of children involved in the proceedings without the cumbersome rules which obstruct parents from receiving advice and support, which in particular works to the disadvantage of parents with special learning difficulty.

The only chance of publicity is if criminal charges have been brought as criminal courts are open to press and public. In this way the scandalous 'Munchausen's Syndrome' was eventually exposed for the rubbish that it is by the public freeing of several mothers (on appeal) who had been jailed by courts that had been 'taken in' by this pernicious theory.

Any resistance to the plans of Social Services is exposed as a serious personality disorder and once children are in care, despite opposition in court by the mother, contact with her children is kept to a minimum (telephone calls are usually forbidden). **WORST OF ALL IF ANY WOMAN WITH CHILDREN IN CARE DARES TO HAVE A NEW BABY IT IS USUALLY RUTHLESSLY REMOVED AT BIRTH AND GIVEN TO STRANGERS FOR ADOPTION.** In this way some women are reduced to the level of baby-making machines working to swell the adoption figures of the local council. Changes in circumstances are rarely taken into account. There are no second chances!! The new baby is abruptly deprived of its mother's milk and indeed all contact with mother, brothers, sisters, and grandparents for the rest of its life unless at 18 years old it is lucky enough to overcome all obstacles and be reunited with its real family.

18. PROBLEMS AND REMEDIES

1. **Problem**: Judges who 'play it safe' by going along with Social Services' requests to allow thousands of children to be adopted against the will of parents who have never harmed them.

Remedy: Allow parents in Family Courts to opt for decision by jury as few juries would agree to 'forced adoptions' unless parents were proved to have been physically abusive.

2. **Problem**: Children taken from parents because they are 'at risk' or have suffered 'emotional abuse'. Parents cannot defend themselves against such non-specific accusations. Contact between children in care and parents is usually left to the discretion of Social Services and is often used as a weapon to enforce obedient cooperation. Phone contact is usually forbidden.

Remedy: Social Services should only be allowed to take children who have actually suffered significant physical damage through the fault of their parents (established by a criminal conviction) such as broken bones, cigarette burns, sexual abuse, malnutrition, drug or alcohol addiction. Contact arrangements should be specified in court for children in care and phone contact should always be allowed unless there are exceptional circumstances.

3. **Problem**: Newborn babies are taken from mothers because they have already had children taken into care and they are thus prevented from making a fresh start in life.

Remedy: As 2 above. Unless a mother has harmed her baby physically it should never be removed at birth and deprived of breast feeding.

4. **Problem**: Family Courts are secret and parents and the press are forbidden to publish names and details of injustices even at the request of the parents concerned. Hearsay evidence that cannot be questioned properly and the absence of the children themselves from the court make it difficult for parents to present their cases effectively.

Remedy: Family Courts should be open to press and public but names should not be revealed. Nevertheless, parents should be allowed to waive their anonymity (in the same way as victims in rape cases) and go to the press openly if they feel their children have been unjustly taken from them. Hearsay evidence should **NEVER** be admitted in the Family Courts and children should come to give evidence in court if the parents so request.

Local authorities should not be allowed to anticipate the decisions of the courts by 'advertising' in magazines and on the internet, photos and descriptions of children who are still under interim or full care orders but who have not yet been freed for adoption.

WHO PROFITS FROM THE ADOPTION RACKET?

- Local Authorities (stars, beacon status, and financial rewards under public service agreements).

- Very highly-paid 'professionals' presume to 'assess' the parenting skills of distraught mothers who have had their children taken into care (around £3,000 per 2-3 hour session).

- 'Legal aid lawyers' (a case in the Family Courts costs an average of £70,000 per day so total legal costs of over £500,000 for one case are not unusual!).

- Therapists, psychiatrists and counsellors who are paid around £3,000 for a few hours work eagerly predict that parents might 'emotionally abuse' their children at some time in the future.

- Tame medical experts somehow always side with Social Services against the parents (they also receive around £3,000 for one afternoon session plus a report).

- Foster parents (up to £400 per week per child plus allowances for Christmas and holidays).

- Special schools charging up to £7,000 per week per child (as shown on TV's Channel 4).

- Adoption and fostering agencies charging up to £18,000 per placement.

Some statistics from an article in *The Evening Standard* make for some startling and horrifying reading. It seems that not all are suffering in the adoption & fostering system in the UK.

One adoption agency, Foster Care Associates in 2003 showed the following:

- £56 Million Annual Turnover

- 8 Directors paid themselves £2.2 Million in fees

- The same Directors also paid themselves a staggering average of £285,000 each in pre-tax profits.

- Judges safely immune from any criticism that might adversely affect their careers in the secret Family Courts (eventual promotion is likely as long as they side with Social Services).

- Middle-aged professional types whose careers have taken priority over childbearing (until too late) seize the opportunity with the help of Social Services to take free of charge the (preferably white European) babies and young children of those in society who for one reason or another are too weak to defend themselves effectively.

- Lastly of course the social workers themselves whose promotion and career prospects depend on achieving adoption targets and working to perpetuate the system.

The merciless forces of the State combine to organise and support a system of 'forced adoption' that the weaker elements of society are helpless to resist. Huge sums of money are at stake in this pernicious industry where the commodity is 'children'.

I believe that future generations will look back in horror at the activities of our Social Services in much the same way that we now regard the appalling treatment of poor children working long hours down coalmines and up chimneys in Victorian England. At least however even in those days the unfortunate children were usually left with their own families.....

Millionaire Baby Brokers
Firms cash in on shortage of foster homes
by Robert Mendick,
London Evening Standard, 2 October 2005

LONDON: Private agencies are making millions of pounds out of a critical shortage of foster homes for children. Firms are charging councils on average £800 per child per week, an EVENING STANDARD investigation revealed.

This amounts to £41,600 a year to find suitable homes for the most vulnerable children in society.

One head of social services said: "It is cheaper to send the children to Eton."

London councils are so desperate to hold on to their foster parents that two are offering them free loft conversions - worth up to £30,000 - so they can take in more children. Britain's largest independent agency Foster Care Associates had a £56mn turnover in 2003, the last year for which accounts are available.

Its eight directors - seven of them social workers who set up the company 10 years ago - paid themselves total fees of more than £2.2mn as well as sharing pre-tax profits of almost £900,000.

The directors awarded themselves on average £285,000 each - about 10 times the annual salary of a social worker.

There is an estimated shortage of 10,000 foster carers across the UK. This has driven up the prices charged by the 150 or so independent agencies.

It costs councils between £300 and £400 a week to place children with their own approved foster carers but they cannot meet the demand and have to turn to outside agencies. More difficult children can cost as much as £1,500 per week to place in foster homes.

The problem is especially acute in London, where out of 11,500 fostered children up to one-third are found homes through independent agencies. Many of them are 'dumped' in outlying towns around the capital. A total of 60,000 children are fostered nationally.

A spokesman at the department for education said: "We know there are too many children being placed outside of authorities. We commissioned a report last year looking at how we can reduce that number."

Out of the 11,500 fostered children in London, half of them are teenagers, about 3,000 aged eight to 12 and 2,500 aged under eight.

Children are typically being sent from London boroughs to Kent, miles from their schools and friends. Some 330 problem children from London are being fostered in the Margate area.

This has prompted the Kent child protection committee to compile a report, sent to ministers, warning the town is now at a 'tipping point' and branding the situation 'explosive'.

Paul Fallon, director of social services at Barnet council and spokesman for all London's social services directors, said: "Every penny we spend on one child is a penny we can't spend on another child. If I place a child with Barnet it is £400. But it costs me about double that to place a child in an independent placement.

"It is a sellers' market and that will impact on prices. We are stuck. It is cheaper to send children to Eton."

He estimated that in Barnet about 30 to 40 children - about 10% of the number needing foster care - are unaccompanied child refugees. They have helped to swell numbers of children needing placements, putting added pressure on social services.

A spokeswoman for Richmond council, where private places at £900 cost three times as much as council places, said: "In emergencies we will negotiate with another borough for a temporary foster place, but that's very rare."

The crisis has prompted Barnet council and Hammersmith and Fulham to offer grants of up to £30,000 to foster parents to build loft conversions to house more children. A spokeswoman for Hammersmith and Fulham said the outlay would pay itself back within one to two years even if it creates just one extra fostering place.

Defenders of private agencies point out councils often do not factor hidden staffing costs - such as administration and on-call social workers - into their weekly fees. Private agencies also point out they are often called upon to find placements for the most difficult children. They point out they also provide round-the-clock social worker support as well as educational support and therapy. Not all agencies are profit-making with fostering services carried out by charities such as Barnardo's and NCH.

Marcelle Ibbetson, service development manager at NCH, which also typically charges £800 a week, said: "We don't think local authorities have properly costed the real cost of foster care. Their behind the scenes costs are hidden. What we provide is private placements at the specialist end of the market."

None of the directors of Foster Care Associates was available for comment. But in an interview last year Sally Melbourne, FCA's director for the Yorkshire and Lincolnshire region, said: "The majority of the fee we charge local authorities goes to the carer and on the welfare of the child. We are a business but we make very little profit, last year we made 5% profit."

A spokesman for the company added: "The company specialises in children that are difficult to place. That is not necessarily behaviourally difficult children but it could be kids with five siblings that need to be kept together or from the ethnic minorities that needs to be placed in their own community. We offer a complete support structure including therapy and education, which is why the costing may look more expensive."

19. WHY DO THEY DO IT?

"Surely", I can hear you say, "British Justice is the finest in the world and I just cannot believe things are as bad as all that" and then you add "social workers take up that profession because they want to help people, so how can I believe they turn into the sort of monsters you portray? Why on earth would they do the sort of things you say they do?" Well, if your child has a tragic accident, do not expect comfort or sympathy from Social Services! Expect instead a merciless attack and the removal of your other children!

A **DEVASTATED** couple (see below) had a child taken away by social workers as their 20-month-old son lay dying in hospital. Tyler Black, who had fallen into the family pond 24 hours earlier, died the day after the other youngster was removed. The coroner attributed no blame and sympathised with the parents for what he described as a tragic accident with **NO** suspicious circumstances. The social workers however still refused to restore the surviving child to the grieving parents!

Couple see child taken away as son in pond fall lay dying
by Ben Clerkin
The Daily Mail, 23 November 2006

A DEVASTATED couple had a child taken away by social workers as their 20-month-old son lay dying in hospital. Tyler Black, who had fallen into the family pond 24 hours earlier, died the day after the other youngster was removed.

Yesterday, a coroner ruled that the toddler's death was an accident.

Now his parents, Caren and Adrian Black, are pleading to be reunited with the child who they can see only twice a week.

The tragedy happened in July. Moments before he fell into the pond, Tyler had woken from a nap and was playing happily at the family home in Bicester, Oxfordshire.

When his 30-year-old mother realised he was missing, she checked the garden as it was a hot day and the back door of the house had been left open. There she found her son's lifeless body floating in their 3ft deep koi carp pond. Giving evidence at the inquest, Mrs Black said: 'I could not see him from the back door; I went straight to the pond.'

He was taken by ambulance to the John Radcliffe Hospital in Oxford where doctors battled for two days to save him.

Detectives, who had been asked to investigate by social workers, found no suspicious circumstances and yesterday a coroner ruled that Tyler's death had been nothing more than an accident. Through tears, Mrs Black said after the inquest into her son's death that she felt she had lost more than one child when Tyler died.

'Social services marched in and the child was taken away before our son died.

'There was not even any chance to say goodbye to Tyler.' Mr Black, a 34-year-old mechanic, said he hoped the coroner's verdict would force social services to reconsider.

'I've said all along that it was at lent. They tried to say there's a risk of neglect but the children had anything they wanted. 'And I'm going to make sure the authority knows I'm not going to back off.

Recording an accident verdict, Oxfordshire coroner Nicholas Gardiner said: 'This was a tragic but not suspicious incident.'

Detective Sergeant Christopher Whitwell told the inquest in Oxford that his investigation of the death had not found anything suspicious. 'The matter was brought to our attention by the child protection team in Banbury,' he said. 'But it was an unexplained death and we would have been involved as a matter of course.'

Emma Boulter, a neighbour, helped Mrs Black attempt to resuscitate Tyler after she heard the distraught mother's screams in the garden.

During the inquest, she said: 'I could see some sort of green slime coming out of his mouth and there was some sort of yellow mucus coming out of his eyes, which were shut.'

Seconds later, Mr Black came running up the garden path after his wife had fetched him from a nearby pub.

He told the inquest through tears: 'I was only in the pub not even a couple of minutes when Caren came in crying and screaming. 'She was very, very distressed. She was screaming Tyler, Tyler, Tyler. It just did not enter into my mind that this could have happened.

'So I ran in through the back gate and through the back door. Our neighbour was clutching hold of Tyler who, by this time was quite grey, a bluey-purply colour.'

Both of Tyler's parents broke down as they gave evidence to the inquest into the death of their son who they called a 'cheeky little monkey'.

A spokesman for Oxfordshire social services refused to comment.

Mother wins fight to get her baby back
By Shan Ross
The Scotsman, 15 June 2006

Corellie Bonhomme now happily reunited with her daughter Fifi after the sheriff's ruling

- Social workers condemned after newly born child was taken from mother

- Woman was in last stages of giving birth

- Sheriff rules social workers action as 'wrong'

A SHERIFF has condemned social workers who removed a newborn baby from her mother only minutes after the child's umbilical cord was cut.

Two social workers and two sheriff officers entered the birthing suite as Corellie Bonhomme went into the final stages of labour. Immediately after her daughter, Fifi, was born, they took her away after obtaining a sheriff's order giving them permission to take custody.

Key quotes

He said Ms Bonhomme's long-running dispute with social workers in Camden had led to the authorities in Scotland taking the baby into care unnecessarily. He also criticised the way Fifi was taken.

Commenting on the incident in the birthing suite, Sheriff Ross said: "Fifi was removed very soon after birth. It was not clear to me why that was necessary. She was in hospital in the secure care of the staff there. There was no evidence that Ms Bonhomme was intending to leave precipitately."

He also questioned Dumfries and Galloway Council for basing the Child Protection Order on "extremely contentious" English proceedings.

Mother

"I was in the throes of labour, quite dilated and about to deliver. My back was bent backwards, the head was sticking out and I was just about to push the rest of the body out. I raised my head and saw two men and two women walk into the birthing room." - Corellie Bonhomme

Motivation

In common with the majority of civil servants, social workers feel that 'the State knows best'. They have gradually convinced themselves that huge numbers of single mothers or parents who have been abused while 'in care' or by their partners, or who have learning difficulties, a low income or a lack of routine just do not have the requisite parenting skills! A dirty and untidy house, a disorganised way of life, or even simply a hostile attitude to social workers is usually enough for them to remove children from their parents. Often without consulting medical opinion they conclude that a parent has inflicted an injury that could just as easily have been a routine accident, or worse still, they have accused thousands of mothers of deliberately causing injuries to their children to gain attention for themselves! They believe that it is in the interests of these children to place them for long-term foster care or adoption with families better equipped to fulfil the children's material and/or intellectual needs! The result is that large numbers of largely healthy and happy children have been abruptly removed from their homes and transferred to the care of complete strangers!

"And what about Victoria Climbie?", I hear you cry, "and other children who have been brutalised or even killed by their parents?" Well, Victoria was not with parents, **SHE WAS IN THE CARE OF SOCIAL SERVICES**!! They allowed her to stay with 'carers'. Victoria was covered from head to foot with bruises, cigarette burns and had obviously broken bones. No medical qualifications were needed to prove the sort of brutality she had certainly endured. She was however callously left to die in agony, maybe because social workers consider that children who have been physically or sexually abused are not really as suitable for fostering or adoption as those from poor but happy homes. These social workers prefer the easy risk-free routes so they tend to avoid the dangers of being assaulted by the brutal type of parent and pass on to easier targets! In any case the sort of mother who comes weeping into court to beg for the return of her children is not usually the type of person who would physically injure her child or allow others to hurt it. Cruel parents who physically mistreat their children almost never come to the family court and would rarely oppose any plans for fostering or adoption if any were made.

"Surely" you say, "A conscientious social worker who found after all that there was no good reason to remove a child would then leave it where it was?" Well, have you ever heard local government officials admit that they have made a mistake? Not often I'm sure! And that is where the trouble begins....not with the error but with the cover-up and the determination not to lose face and to be proved right in the end. The initial assessment must always be proved right whether favourable to parents or not and only evidence favourable to that initial conclusion is noted. Anything unfavourable to 'SS' conclusions is usually discarded. The call by Tony Blair to increase adoption figures and the setting of adoption targets by local authorities has further exacerbated the situation as social workers are motivated more by achieving adoption targets than by helping families to stay together. With these targets in view social workers tend to come to a swift opinion of the parents they visit and if that opinion is unfavourable they try very hard to maintain that opinion against all opposition. To this end they collect all the evidence they can to support that opinion, discarding any evidence that tends to criticise or undermine it.

Parents who resist are usually labelled 'in denial', 'suffering from personality disorder', or even 'paranoiacs'! The worst sin the parents can commit is to persist in asserting their innocence! The 'Social Service thought police' supported by the Family Court judges usually insist on 'confession' before any question of restoring the children or even arranging regular contact can be considered. The same process is seen in the Family Courts if parents fight to retain their children. Social workers, keen above all to be vindicated, fight to win their case so that the welfare of the child is often lost in the overwhelming desire to **WIN** at all costs!

Social workers always try to escape responsibility by saying 'the courts decide so it's not up to us', but of course the judges rarely refuse care orders or adoption placements when Social Services request them. They treat social workers like police whose word is always to be preferred to the parents' if there is a conflict. Judges have publicly admitted that usually they 'go along with Social Services' as the 'safest option' but probably it is really because they feel that to refuse would be taking a risk for which they could be crucified in the press if disaster followed! **THESE COWARDLY FAMILY COURT JUDGES ARE THE REAL VILLAINS!** Many Family Court judges should themselves be punished. **THESE RENEGADE ESTABLISHMENT JUDGES**

SHOULD BE SENT TO PRISON for authorising the snatching of newborn babies at birth from mothers who have never harmed them but who chose 'the wrong man' to father their babies! A jury would in most cases come to conclusions and consequently verdicts quite opposite to those of the judges as they would be for the most part very reluctant to remove children for such hazy concepts as 'emotional abuse' or worse still 'risk of future emotional abuse' and there would of course be no risk of a comeback for a jury if a single mistake was made.

All over the world there are famines, random killings and genocides. Unfortunately in this country there are hundreds of cases of child abuse by parents but also by fosterers, social workers and paedophiles working in children's homes!

Foster carers abused young boys
BBC News at bbc.co.uk/news, 22 May 2006

A gay couple have been warned they face lengthy prison sentences after being found guilty of sexually abusing young boys placed in their foster care.

Ian Wathey, 40, and his partner Craig Faunch, 32, were found guilty at Leeds Crown Court of a series of sex offences against the boys.

The couple, of Slides Road, Pontefract, were approved as foster carers in 2003, the court heard.

Judge Sally Cahill remanded them in custody while they await sentencing.

The judge asked for pre-sentence reports to be drawn up and warned Wathey and Faunch they were "facing a substantial period in custody".

Indecent photos

The men were using the boys for their own sexual gratification within months of being approved as carers by Wakefield Council, the court heard.

They were found guilty of the charges following a two-week trial.

Faunch was convicted of two charges of making indecent photos of a child. The court was told that he used a camcorder to film two naked eight-year-old boys in the shower.

He was also found guilty of five counts of sexual activity with a 14-year-old boy.

Wathey was found guilty of four charges of sexual activity with a 14-year-old boy. He was also convicted of encouraging a child to watch sexual activity.

Wathey was cleared of two charges of sexual activity with a child by the jury.

'Bizarre allegations'

The court was told neither had been in trouble with the police before and were approved as foster carers after checks and training.

Defence barristers had claimed the allegations were "bizarre", "incredible" and unfounded.

The court was told the couple had taken a photo of a boy in their care while he was urinating.

Social workers decided the men had been "naive and silly" for taking the photo after hearing their explanation that they had used the picture to embarrass the boys into closing the toilet door, which they kept failing to do.

The victim whose complaint triggered the police inquiry gave evidence via a video link. Describing the abuse, he said: "It hurt. Afterwards, I said 'Pack it in now,' and then I went to bed.

"I was gutted. I didn't want anything to do with anyone else. All I could do was sit there and cry."

'Lessons learned'

Wakefield Council's Service Director for Children in Need, Kitty Ferris, said the safety of children in the council's care was its first priority.

She said: "Mr Faunch and Mr Wathey have not been permitted to care for children in their capacity as foster carers since the allegations were made, in line with council policy.

"The council has now terminated their approval as foster carers.

"Although correct procedures were carried out at every stage, the service has reviewed its internal procedures to identify what lessons should be learned.

"Checks are in place for foster placements including unannounced home visits and the council is regularly inspected by the Commission for Social Care Inspection.

"The council has offered support, where appropriate, to children who have been affected by this case."

Friendly neighbours who had lived peacefully side by side for years in Kosovo and in Bosnia suddenly turned on each other savagely, slaughtering babies and young children. It is a sad fact that seemingly normal, decent people can very often be persuaded or tempted to perform extremely cruel and horrific deeds. It should not therefore be too hard to understand that the desire of social workers (who are certainly no exception) to be proved right, more often than not outweighs the welfare of the child. The secrecy of the Family Courts and the gagging of aggrieved parents who are unable to protest to the media when they lose their children combine to facilitate wins in court for Social Services and losses for parents!

In Spain, France, Italy and most of the countries in Western Europe children are only forcibly separated from their parents when they suffer extreme physical violence or sexual abuse. Professionals from European counties are horrified when they see social workers and secret courts in England taking young children and worse still newborn babies for such spurious reasons as 'risk of emotional harm'. This concept just does not exist on the continent. Children simply cannot be removed from their parents unless a crime has been committed. Separating children from their parents for past behaviour in different circumstances many years ago is considered a violation of the Human Rights of both child and parent. The UK was condemned by the European Court in the case of p, c and s for actions considered 'draconian' and the UK was fined. Unfortunately the UK Family Courts still largely ignore human rights and parents are strongly advised to consider pursuing their cases in the European Court when all else fails.

There is of course also the money racket that really oils the wheels of the 'SS' adoption and fostering machine and all the official figures and government statistics supporting claims made in this chapter plus other details of these horrors can be found in my **CASHING IN** chapter.

150 years ago very young children worked in factories and went up chimneys. We look back in horror nowadays and wonder how our great grandfathers let such things happen. I believe that future generations in the UK will take a similar view when reading about the Family Courts of this era in Britain. Nevertheless such things did happen in Victorian Britain and the horrors in the Family Courts that you read about in the papers are equally true at the present time.

Extreme power can corrupt even the nicest people and it is no exaggeration to say that in many ways social workers certainly have more power over selected individuals than any government minister! Social workers can and do get emergency protection orders on the flimsiest pretexts (suspicion of devil worship for instance!) and on allegations against parents that frequently have no foundation. No evidence need be presented as simple allegations by social workers or anonymous 'referrals' are nearly always sufficient. Conveniently, there seems to be no penalty if subsequently the allegations against parents (who must be absent and are not allowed to defend themselves at this stage) prove malicious and false.

Judge Condemns Council Staff
by Steve Doughty
Daily Mail, 18 March 2006

Social workers 'took girl from her family on a whim'

SOCIAL workers took a nine-year-old girl away from her family for more than a year on a whim, a High Court judge said yesterday.

They embellished facts, told untruths and misled a court after deciding to take the girl into care on the spur of the moment, according to a judge.

Social workers decided the child's mother suffered from Munchausen's Syndrome by Proxy - a condition which is said to make a parent wish to harm their child, Mr. Justice McFarlane's Judgement revealed.

They did not consult a doctor about their assumption until the girl had been living in council care for three months.

He said he suspected one social worker of a 'malevolent and unprofessional motive' and said the attitude of the council bosses who defended her and her colleagues was 'astounding'.

The judgment said that shortly before the girl was taken from her parents for 14 months, a council meeting on the case had noted: 'home and care good. Mother and child have good relationship. Detrimental to move.'

Sometimes the Social Services behave so outrageously that it is too much for even the most 'SS tolerant' of judges in the Family Court. However, the clearly wronged parents in a case like the recent one portrayed above still took a year to retrieve their daughter and nobody was prosecuted for perjury or held in contempt for misleading the court!

Once the order is granted the social workers can demand a police escort to break into the parents house (often in the middle of the night) to drag the children away without giving any reason for their actions! Alas, once the children have gone and are 'twin tracked' for fostering and adoption it can be very hard indeed for parents to retrieve them. No politicians have powers like these and it is just human nature that powers this great will be abused and used to achieve the social workers' target objectives rather than the reunification of the family and the welfare of the child.

The only way to improve the present situation is to bring in some or most of the reforms suggested here and similarly on the *Fassit* web site (www.fassit.co.uk).

Only in the **SECRET** Family Courts are punishments (losing their children to long-term foster care or worse still adoption by strangers) imposed on persons (parents) who have neither committed a crime nor even been accused of committing any crime! **THERE IS NO OTHER CASE IN UK LAW WHERE THIS CAN HAPPEN**!

Social workers themselves are sometimes convicted criminals as *The Daily Mirror* found out and exposed in the following article!!

EXCLUSIVE: ANTI-SOCIAL WORKERS....

Hundreds of criminals apply for care jobs

by Tom Pettifor

Daily Mirror, 20 May 2006

HUNDREDS of would-be social workers have serious criminal convictions.

Official figures list 375 fully qualified social workers being considered for official registration as having records for high or medium-risk offences.

They include murder, robbery, sex crimes, theft, drug dealing, possessing hard drugs, grievous bodily harm, domestic violence, fraud and serious driving offences.

The General Social Care Council - the social workers' regulatory body - could not say last night how many are actually in a job.

A spokesman said: "There's a good likelihood they may still be working but their employers may have put them on other duties."

The convictions were discovered when the GSCC began compiling the first social care register in April 2003, when all fully qualified social workers were required to reveal any criminal history.

It is not known how many were working at the time or if bosses already knew of their convictions.

They can work despite having very serious convictions if deemed suitable by bosses and registered.

GSCC chief executive Lynne Berry said: "People need to know social workers can be trusted.

"We look especially hard at medium to high-risk offences and need to be assured they are safe to be registered."

A GSCC statement added: "Where there is a recommendation to refuse registration or grant it with conditions, it is considered by an independent committee."

The GSCC defines high-risk offenders as "likely to pose a risk to safety and wellbeing" of clients.

Medium-risk offenders, guilty of drink driving or other serious motoring offences, theft or drug crimes, "may" pose a risk.

The GSCC said it believed most were medium risk but admitted: "A large percentage were things like assault, grievous bodily harm, drugs, public order offences, some sex offences and robbery."

Two criminals were allowed on the register with conditions.

One committed murder nearly 25 years ago but it was decided he was fully rehabilitated.

The other committed "a range of offences" nearly 20 years ago.

The GSCC rejected 105 applications - two for criminal records.

One man was convicted of four indecent assaults on a child, the other of assault and drink driving.

I repeat **THAT SOCIAL WORKERS** (who may sometimes be criminals themselves) **REMOVE CHILDREN** for compulsory adoption **FROM PARENTS WHO HAVE NOT BEEN ACCUSED OF ANY CRIME**!!! What about the judges? Don't they have to agree? Yes they do and almost inevitably (as they have admitted publicly) they take the 'safe route' and usually 'go along with Social Services'.

They justify this with the help of so-called 'experts' and 'professionals' who make complicated forecasts and who 'predict' (gypsy fashion!) that something bad might happen in the future. This so-called 'risk' is enough to separate parents and children **FOR LIFE**!! Hard to believe that such things happen in Britain today isn't it? Yet there are an average of 600 cases every year held in strictly secret Family Courts where the judge tells a distraught mother (or father) that she is being 'unreasonable' in withholding her consent to the adoption of her newborn baby or young child by complete and unknown strangers! The unfortunate children are then 'lost' for good. Yes, this really does happen and it is a national disgrace!!

Forced adoption is wicked! Forced adoption is like capital punishment, it is irreversible!

THESE FORCED ADOPTIONS ARE WICKED CRIMES!! All those odious persons involved in these crimes against humanity, the social workers, the 'SS' lawyers, the hired 'experts' and even the compliant judges should all serve prison sentences for their crimes just as their predecessors the Nazi judges were condemned at Nuremburg!

Abuse is a crime and wilful neglect is a crime but 'putting a child (or even more absurdly a newborn baby) at risk of future 'emotional abuse' is not a crime yet it is still one of the most frequent reasons given by the Family Courts for taking children into care and eventually 'forced adoptions' (adoptions that are actively opposed by a parent or parents in person and in court). Parents cannot defend themselves against the dire predictions made 'crystal ball fashion' by highly paid 'experts'. These so-called 'professional' judgements are made on an entirely subjective basis and no matter what the parents say the 'experts' are nearly always believed in preference to mothers or fathers. Any expert who sides with the parents is usually quietly ignored and discarded, soon to be replaced by an expert with views that accord with Social Services. The result is that the unfortunate children and even more unfortunate babies are doomed to long-term fostering or forced adoption despite the despairing but hopeless opposition of the distraught parents.

I must repeat again that an average of more than 600 forced adoptions (with no step-parents involved) take place every year. 600 bitterly-contested court cases where weeping parents plead in vain to at least keep contact with their beloved children. There are double that number that take place 'uncontested' because the parents are too distraught to do so or because their lawyers advise them to 'go along with Social Services' and on no account to fight or resist them and then 'everything will be all right!' These children are then condemned to spend the rest of their lives wondering who their real parents are and why they were so callously abandoned!

20. STATISTICS

Forced adoption should be abolished NOW!!

In answer to a parliamentary question (March 21st 2005) the Minister for Children admitted that 6643 children over a 10-year period had been adopted by force against the will of mothers pleading in court to keep their children. These figures do **NOT** include any cases where step-parents were involved and exact adoption statistics are available from the following tables.

Contested Adoptions

Tim Loughton: To ask the Secretary of State for Education and Skills how many contested adoptions have taken place in each of the last 10 years. [222035]

Mr. Lammy: I have been asked to reply.

21 Mar 2005: Column 563W

The number of contested adoptions that have taken place in each of the last 10 years are contained in the following table.

	Step-parents (9)		Other		Total	
	Contested	Uncontested	Contested	Uncontested	Contested	Uncontested
1995	491	2,388	733	1,707	1,224	4,095
1996	362	2,384	518	1,700	880	4,084
1997	272	1,780	555	1,542	827	3,322
1997	237	1,556	477	1,377	714	2,933
1997	211	1,332	716	1,617	927	2,949
2000	167	1,193	651	1,992	818	3,185
2001	141	1,055	653	2,329	794	3,384
2002	109	827	725	2,212	834	3,039
2003	129	840	938	2,489	1,067	3,329
2004	104	767	677	2,583	781	3,350

(9) Step-parent adoption occurs where the step-parent applies to formally adopt the child or children of their spouse and assumes parental responsibility to the exclusion of the other birth parent. Contested step-parent adoption cases arise where the non-resident birth parent does not consent to the adoption

EXTRACT FROM "NATIONAL STATISTICS"

Between 1994 to 2004 there were steady decreases in the proportions of children who were aged 5 to 14 who were adopted, and a significant increase in the proportion adopted who were aged 1 to 4. In 2004, 49 per cent of children adopted were in this age group compared with 26 per cent in 1994, while 13 per cent of adopted children in 2004 were aged 10 to 14 compared with 23 per cent ten years earlier.

The sad fact is that social workers rarely 'target' the violent type of parent who tortures, burns and breaks a child's bones. Too often a nervous social worker retreats hastily and sometimes leaves the child to die. Such violent parents practically never come to court to reclaim their surviving children so the Family Courts hold no terrors for them. Parents in the Family Court nowadays are those whose poverty is only too often equated with neglect, or those judged on an entirely subjective basis to have emotionally neglected or abused their children. In my opinion children can far better bear emotional abuse (if this really exists as a serious factor) than the trauma of being separated from the family they know and being given for long-term foster care or worse still, for adoption by complete strangers.

340 children were removed over a 3-year period simply because the parents had 'a low income' and no other reason!

KEY POINTS from the latest DCSF Figures

http://www.dcsf.gov.uk/rsgateway/DB/SFR/s000810/SFR23-2008Textv1oct.pdf

Children looked after at 31 March 2008 - Tables A1 to A5

• There were 59,500 children looked after at 31 March 2008, 1 per cent fewer than last year's figure of 60,000 and a decrease of 3 per cent compared to 2004 (61,200).

• Overall, the main reason why social services first engaged with these children looked after was because of abuse or neglect (62 per cent). This percentage has changed little over the past 5 years.

• Most children looked after at 31 March 2008 were of White British origin (74 per cent). Their number and percentage has decreased over the last 5 years from 46,300 (76 per cent) in 2004 to 43,900 (74 per cent) in 2008. The breakdown by the different ethnic groups has remained similar since 2004.

• At 31 March 2008, 37,200 children were looked after under a care order which represents 63 per cent of all legal statuses. This is a decrease of 4 per cent from last year's figure of 38,600 and a decrease of 6 per cent from 2004 (39,700). 6 per cent of children were looked after under a placement order.

• 42,300 children looked after at 31 March 2008 were in a foster placement (71 per cent). This is an increase of 1 per cent on the previous year's figure of 42,100 and an increase of 3 per cent from 2004 (41,200).

Unaccompanied Asylum Seeking Children (UASC) – Table A4

• There were 3,500 UASC who were looked after at 31 March 2008, this is an increase of around 100 children compared to the figure for 2007.

• In 2008 the percentage of UASC children of Black African origin decreased by 7 percentage points to 24 per cent, whilst the percentage of UASC children of any other Asian background increased by 7 percentage points to 31 per cent.

Mothers aged 12 and over – Table A5

• There were 280 mothers aged 12 and over who were looked after at 31 March 2008, a decrease of 20 per cent from the previous year's figure of 360 and a decrease of 5 per cent from the 2005 figure.

Children who started to be looked after during the year ending 31 March 2008 – Tables C1 to C3

• There were 23,000 children who started to be looked after during the year ending 31 March 2008, a decrease of 4 per cent from the previous year's figure of 24,000 and a decrease of 8 per cent from the 2003-04 figure of 25,000.

• During the year ending 31 March 2008, 38 per cent of children who started to be looked after were aged between 10 and 15 years old. This figure has decreased over the past 5 years.

• The percentage of children who started to be looked after in the year ending 31 March 2008 who were white British has decreased over the last 5 years from 71 per cent in 2003-04 to 66 per cent in 2007-08.

Children who ceased to be looked after during the year ending 31 March 2008 – Tables D1 to D3

• There were 24,100 children who ceased to be looked after during the year ending 31 March 2008, a decrease of 3 per cent from the previous year's figure of 25,000 and a decrease of 6 per cent from the 2003-04 figure of 25,700.

• The percentage of children who ceased to be looked after aged between 5 and 9 years old decreased over the last 4 years from 17 per cent in 2003-04 to 13 per cent in 2007-08. There was a similar drop in the 10 to 15 age category where the percentage dropped from 30 per cent in 2003-04 to 24 per cent in 2007-08. However, the percentage of children who ceased to be looked after aged 16 and over increased over the past 5 years from 27 per cent in 2003-04 to 34 per cent in 2007-08.

• The proportion of children of white British ethnic origin who ceased to be looked after decreased from 74 per cent in 2004 to 68 per cent in 2007-08 whereas the proportions of children from other Asian backgrounds and of African ethnic origin have increased from 1 per cent in 2003-04 to 3 per cent in 2007-08 and from 4 per cent in 2003-04 to 6 per cent in 2007-08 respectively.

• In the year ending 31 March 2008, most children who ceased to be looked after had a foster placement as their final placement (12,600). This represents 52 per cent of all final placements.

Mothers aged 12 and over who ceased to be looked after – Table D3

• There were 340 mothers aged 12 and over who ceased to be looked after during the year ending 31 March 2008, an increase of 3 per cent from the previous year's figure of 330.

Children looked after who were adopted during the year ending 31 March 2008 – Tables E1 and E2

• 3,200 children looked after were adopted during the year ending 31 March 2008. This represents a 5 per cent decrease from the previous year's figure of 3,300 and a 16 per cent decrease from the 2003-04 figure of 3,800.

• The number of children looked after who were under 1 year old at adoption decreased over the last 5 years from 220 in 2003-04 to 120 in 2007-08.

• The percentage of children looked after who were adopted that were of white ethnic origin decreased over the past 5 years from 86 per cent in 2003-04 to 83 per cent in 2007-08, whereas the percentage of mixed ethnic origin children looked after who were adopted increased over the same period from 9 per cent in 2003-04 to 11 per cent in 2007-08.

• Before being adopted in 2007-08, 9 per cent of children were looked after under a freed for adoption final legal status, 23 per cent were looked after under a care order and 61 per cent were looked after under a placement order.

• The average duration of the final period of care that children looked after had before being adopted in 2007-08 was 2 years and 7 months. This has changed little over the past 5 years.

Adopters of children looked after who were adopted in the year ending 31 March 2008 – Table E2

• 91 per cent of children looked after who were adopted in 2007-08 were adopted by two people (2,900). Most adopters were married (84 per cent), 5 per cent of adopters were an unmarried couple (different gender), 2 per cent of adopters were an unmarried couple (same gender) and 1 per cent of adopters were civil partners.

• 9 per cent of children looked after who were adopted in 2007-08 were adopted by a single adopter. Of these single adopters, 99 per cent were female.

• This is the second year this information has been collected. The percentage of children looked after who were adopted by two people have remained the same at 91% as have the percentage of adopters who were married at 84%.

Children who ceased to be looked after aged 16 years and over during the year ending 31 March 2008 – Table F1

• The number of children aged 16 years and over who ceased to be looked after during the year ending 31 March increased from 6,900 in 2003-04 to 8,300 in 2007-08.

• 61 per cent of these children ceased to be looked after on their 18th birthday, 24 per cent ceased to be looked after aged 16 years.

• The percentage of children aged 16 and over who ceased to be looked after during the year ending 31 March of white British ethnic origin decreased from 71 per cent to 62 per cent over the last 5 years whereas the percentage of those from other Asian backgrounds and of African ethnic origin increased respectively from 1 per cent in 2003-04 to 5 per cent in 2007-08 and from 6 per cent in

• Before ceasing to be looked after during the year ending 31 March 2008, 3,200 children aged 16 and over were in a foster placement (39 per cent), 2,100 in secure units, children's homes and hostels (25 per cent) and 1,900 were placed in the community (23 per cent).

• In 2007-08, 47 per cent of these children had at least 1 GSCE or GNVQ (3,900) and 7 per cent of the 8,300 children obtained at least 5 GCSEs at grade A* to C.

Children now aged 19 years who were looked after on 1 April 2005 then aged 16 years – Table G1

• The number of children now aged 19 years who were looked after on 1 April 2005 then aged 16 years increased from 5,100 in 2004 to 5,800 in 2008.

• Over the past 5 years, the percentage of children now aged 19 years who were in education other than higher education increased from 18 per cent to 28 per cent. The number for those who were in training or employment increased from 1,600 to 1,800 between 2004 and 2008. The number for those who were not in touch with the local authorities decreased from 15 per cent to 6 per cent over the last 5 year's.

• Most children now aged 19 years who were looked after at 16 years were accommodated in independent living. This percentage has remained fairly stable over the last 5 year's.

Children aged under 16 years who have been looked after continuously for at least two and a half years – Table H1

• 67 per cent of children aged under 16 years who have been looked after continuously for at least two and a half years were in the same placement for at least two years, or were placed for adoption.

This relates to the Public Service Agreement (PSA) target which is to narrow the gap in educational achievement between looked after children and that of their peers, and improve their educational support and the stability of their lives so that by 2008, 80 per cent of children under 16 who have been looked after for two and a half years or more will have been living in the same placement for at least two years, or are placed for adoption.

Figures from Department for Children, Schools and Families. SSDA903 return.

	Year ending 31 March in which adopted												
	1995	1996	1997	1998	1999	2000	2001	2002	2003	2004	2005	2006	
All Children1,2,3,4	540	510	520	690	720	920	1,000	1,200	1,300	1,300	1,400	1,300	
Age when first taken into care													
0 to 7 days	370	340	350	430	530	670	730	790	920	880	920	920	149%
8 to 14 days	100	100	100	130	90	180	160	200	210	230	240	220	120%
15 to 21 days	40	30	40	70	70	40	90	90	80	100	110	100	150%
22 to 30 days	30	30	30	50	30	30	60	70	90	70	100	100	233%

Children looked after who were adopted during years ending 31 March 1995 to 2006 and their ages when they were first started to be looked after1,2,3,4,5													
England	Year ending 31 March in which adopted												
	1995	1996	1997	1998	1999	2000	2001	2002	2003	2004	2005	2006	Growth 1995-2006
All Children 1,2	2,000	1,900	1,900	2,200	2,100	2,700	3,100	3,400	3,500	3,800	3,800	3,700	
Age when first taken into care													
Under 1 month	540	510	520	690	720	920	1,000	1,200	1,300	1,300	1,400	1,300	141%
From 1 months to under 2 months	80	90	80	100	140	130	150	210	160	170	160	190	138%
From 2 months to under 3 months	70	80	60	70	90	100	110	90	130	120	120	120	71%
From 3 months to under 4 months	60	50	40	70	60	70	80	80	100	80	90	80	33%
From 4 months to under 5 months	40	50	50	70	70	50	90	90	90	70	70	80	100%
From 5 months to under 6 months	30	40	30	60	30	50	70	40	90	70	70	50	67%
From 6 months to under 9 months	70	80	90	120	110	170	160	150	130	170	150	160	129%
From 9 months to under 1 year	60	70	70	130	80	110	150	150	130	130	140	140	133%
Babies (under 1 year)	950	970	940	1,310	1,300	1,600	1,810	2,010	2,130	2,110	2,200	2,120	123%
From 1 years to under 2 years	260	230	240	250	250	370	450	500	430	470	470	460	77%
From 2 years to under 3 years	230	200	180	220	180	250	280	380	370	390	380	340	48%
From 3 years to under 4 years	170	170	140	140	120	180	210	230	270	310	290	260	53%
From 4 years to under 5 years	140	110	100	120	80	120	130	140	160	200	200	210	50%
From 5 years to under 6 years	80	80	100	50	80	80	70	100	80	150	120	120	50%
From 6 years to under 7 years	60	50	60	40	30	50	40	60	60	80	80	70	17%
From 7 years to under 8 years	50	50	30	10	20	20	10	30	30	40	40	40	-20%
From 8 years to under 9 years	20	20	20	20	-	10	10	-	10	20	10	-	
From 9 years to under 10 years	20	20	10	10	-	0	10	10	10	10	10	-	
10 years and over	30	10	20	10	0	10	10	-	10	20	10	10	-67%

21. LOVE

'**LOVE**' is not a term that is politically correct, so it is very rarely mentioned in the parental assessments and judicial pronouncements that decide the children's fate. 'Bonding' is the preferred term employed by social workers for a 'parent and child relationship' and this portrayal can just as easily be applied to members of the Welsh rugby team! Bonding really is not at all the same thing as 'love' (especially the love of a child for its mother) which should surely be the most determining factor of all when deciding the future of a newborn baby or young child.

The **LOVE** of a child for a parent (or grandparent) and vice versa ought to (but rarely does) outweigh the so-called disadvantages of grandparents too old at 60, or parents with learning disabilities, an ancient history of petty crime, extreme poverty, a dirty house, or a long ago cured addiction. **LOVE** just does not count when weeping and highly emotional mothers plead in court for the return of their children yet **IT SHOULD**!! It certainly **SHOULD**!! Instead such parents frequently get accused in court of an 'emotional instability' that further demonstrates their unfitness as parents! Unfortunately the 'professionals' (who by definition are those people who make money when parents have their children taken by Social Services) make decisive 'parenting assessments' and consider resistance to fostering or adoption 'non-co-operation' and failure to 'confess' to allegedly bad parenting 'a retreat into denial' and as for 'hostility and distrust' of the social workers who take the children, that is either a 'personality disorder' or 'paranoia'! This despite articles appearing regularly in the quality press expressing exceptionally strong criticism of social workers, Family Courts, hired experts and the adoption/fostering system as a whole.

http://www.parliament.the-stationery-office.co.uk/pa/cm200304/cmhansrd/vo040311/text/40311w24.htm.

Foster carers to get more money
BBC News online, www.news.bbc.co.uk
Tuesday, 21 June 2005

The council hopes the new allowance will cut long-term costs.

Foster carers in a Berkshire borough are to be offered a bigger allowance in a bid to encourage more volunteers. Foster parents in Slough will receive £400 a week for each child, an increase from the current maximum of £137.

Team members from the Slough Family Placement Service will be on hand to tell people more about fostering at a launch in the Town Square on Sunday. The launch will feature face painting, a balloon release and an appearance from a David Beckham lookalike. The council hopes the increased allowance will save money in the long term by reducing the need to use fostering agencies.

Jane Tomlinson, head of education and children's services at the council, said: "Fostering offers great challenges and great rewards. Even if you've never thought about it before, why not come down on 2 July to find out more?"

The former Minister for Children admitted that local authorities were set 'adoption targets' and it is a fact that many local authorities like Kent were awarded large monetary rewards (£21 million for hitting 10 out of 12 targets; adoption increase being target number one) via public service agreements. One result of all this has been to strongly motivate social workers to procure children suitable for adoption even if this means splitting up the very families they are meant to support and protect!

More than half the adoptions 'from care' in the UK are contested by parents vainly fighting to keep the children they love, but government research papers admit that the courts very rarely decide in favour of the birth parents. The same papers also admit that only too often the needs of the children are forgotten in the struggle to meet 'adoption targets'.

IMPORTANT EXTRACT FROM OFFICIAL GOVERNMENT PAPERS:
http://www.local.odpm.gov.uk/research/beacyr3/adoption/07.htm

Courts At least half of current adoptions are contested although the contest seldom goes in favour of the birth parents. This inevitably causes delays and, indeed, delays may not necessarily be a bad thing if the issues are very complex. Court-based delays may also be caused by lack of available court time, or the courts requiring further re-unification attempts.

Councils A lack of clear policies integrating adoption into the overall children's plan. Budgetary constraints limiting the availability of post adoption services and allowances. There was also concern paradoxically that the needs of children may be overlooked in the struggle to meet targets. The more rural councils will struggle to run regular preparation courses to meet the assessment targets, even when co-operating with other agencies.

Once Social Services have decided a child should be taken into care or freed for adoption any resistance from the mother or father is considered as 'non cooperation'. Social workers then use just about any means and often go to almost any lengths to win their case without regard to changing circumstances or anything else but achieving yet another court victory. Perhaps the worst effect of these changes has been to encourage social workers to perpetrate what I at any rate, consider the appalling crime of taking newborn babies away from mothers at birth!! Certainly adopters prefer to take babies rather than children, making it much easier to hit adoption targets if enough babies are 'collected' In practice any woman with a child already in care who dares to give birth again risks the arrival of a grim po-faced social worker who will callously take the baby away with a view to getting it adopted by strangers. A mother for example who lost a child to 'care' because she failed to protect it from a violent father cannot make a fresh start with a new partner. Usually she becomes a baby-making machine for 'the adopters' as every baby she has subsequently is taken at birth and given to strangers for adoption!

The judge in the Family Court will inevitably sweep away the mother's objections to any projected adoption on the grounds that 'her consent to the adoption is being unreasonably withheld!!' How any judge can say a mother is being 'unreasonable' because she does not want her baby adopted by strangers is beyond me but that is what they do! This practice was roundly condemned as 'draconian' by the European Court Of Human Rights but the decision came too late for the distraught mother whose child had already been adopted by strangers. This happens regularly even when the new birth happens several years later than the original order and when circumstances have often changed for the better but are rarely taken into consideration. This typically happened in the case of P C and S v United Kingdom

http://www.nkmr.org/english/p_c_and_s_v_united_kingdom_ver dict.htm
(see paragraphs 133,137,and 138)

PARAGRAPH 133. "The Court concludes that the draconian step of removing S. from her mother shortly after birth was not supported by relevant and sufficient reasons and that it cannot be regarded as having been necessary in a democratic society for the purpose of safeguarding S. There has therefore been, in that respect, a breach of the applicant parents' rights under Article 8 of the Convention."

These unfortunate mothers are in effect turned into baby-making machines to meet the 'adoption targets' whilst older children often languish in 'special children's homes' where they are frequently subjected to the most horrific abuse by the paedophiles who so eagerly seek and obtain employment in such places. Typical recent examples of widespread abuse in 'children's homes' or false accusations of mass parental abuse occurred in Leicestershire, Staffordshire, Wales, Cheshire, Merseyside, Hackney, Islington, Orkney, Cleveland, Rochdale, Bishop's Auckland, and Ayrshire.

Lives ruined in secret Thousands
by Nick Cohen
The Observer, 25 January 2004

The story of a couple I had better just call Mr and Mrs A is just one of thousands in the greatest miscarriage of justice of our times. The As lived in the West Country and had four children. The first died. The second was fine. The third died. By the time the mother was pregnant with the fourth, the local social services had decided to act. It's easy to write: 'The baby was taken from her at birth.'

It's harder to imagine feeling a child grow inside you, going through the agonies of labour and then - at a click of a bureaucrat's fingers - seeing your baby snatched away. The expert opinion of Professor Sir Roy Meadow and his disciples had been sought, and they had concluded that the mother was killing her babies.

There was no trial; she didn't have the opportunity to demand that the terrible accusations against her be proved beyond reasonable doubt. Instead, a judge sitting in his chambers decided that, 'on the balance of probabilities', she was a killer. The interests of her surviving children must come first, and they must be taken into care. Unsurprisingly, given the loss of all her children, the mother's mind and marriage fell apart. She and her husband divorced, and he became the obvious candidate to bring up the children.

But there was a catch that the organisers of the Salem witch trials would have applauded. His solicitor, David Sterrett, explained that it wasn't enough for the witch to be condemned without trial. Her husband had to join the denigration of his ex-wife and say that she was a murderer. He didn't believe that for a moment and refused to go along with Meadow. His failure to accept the omniscience of the great man was intolerable. He was deemed unfit to look after his own children and has spent so many years in courts fighting for the right to visit them that his lawyer says he is broke and suffering from 'litigation fatigue'.

The couple might have gone to their local paper for help. They had a sensational story. Their children were to be taken because a professor was claiming the mother was suffering from an exotic condition, Munchausen's syndrome by proxy, which propelled her to kill her children as a means of gaining attention.

Perhaps one reporter in the West Country wouldn't have got very far, but the cumulative effect of reporters on papers around Britain covering the Munchausen mania would have warned the authorities that something akin to a medieval witch craze was sweeping the country. Pressure groups and politicians would have had some hard facts to get their teeth into and the few doctors prepared to break the omertà of the medical profession and dish the dirt on colleagues would have been mobilised.

As it was, Prof Meadow was deferred to for years. The scale of the injustice he contributed to makes the false convictions of the Birmingham Six and Guildford Four look like trivial technical problems. Lord Goldsmith, the Attorney-General, said last week that 258 convictions for murder, infanticide and manslaughter will be reviewed as a matter of urgency.

They are merely an appetiser. Beyond the homicide convictions are the people such as Mr and Mrs A, who have had their children taken into care because they are presumed on the 'balance of probabilities' to be murderers or the aiders and abetters of murder, but have never had the chance to clear their names in court.

Margaret Hodge, the Children's Minister, said that 'thousands or even tens of thousands' of children may have been taken from their parents over the past 15 years because of Meadow's theories. Neither she nor anyone else could be certain because the mass seizure of children took place in camera. There was never a hope of the public being alerted and Meadow being stopped before he caused too much misery. The grotesque snatching of thousands of children was an operation conducted under conditions of the strictest secrecy. Anyone who blew the whistle on the proceedings of the family courts faced prosecution for contempt.

The maxim 'the interests of the child come first' is seductive. Who but a brute could disagree with it? Who would want the interests of the child to come second or third, or not be considered at all? But like many other sweet platitudes, it can lead to monstrous consequences. The supposed interests of the child dictate that mothers can be treated as murderers on 'the balance of probabilities' rather than because they have been found guilty beyond reasonable doubt. If Meadow or one of his clique said that Munchausen's by proxy was probable, then that was enough. The supposed interests of the child also dictated that the courts must destroy families without public scrutiny because publicity would lead to the child being 'stigmatised'.

Yet its clearly not in the interests of the child for the courts to allow him or her to be taken from a loving and innocent mother. The interests being placed first here were the interests of Meadow and Family Court judges who have got away with destroying the lives of largely working-class women for more than a decade, secure in the knowledge that their crackpot theories would never be exposed or tested.

During the years of Meadow's ascendancy, the family courts resembled a secret society. Because there were no outside checks, Munchausen's by proxy became a theory that explained all inexplicable infant deaths. If a baby was fighting fit before dying, then Meadow would say that was proof that a Munchausen mother had smothered the child to attract attention. If a baby was ill before dying, then Meadow would say that was also proof that a Munchausen mother had smothered the child to attract attention.

Munchausen's was an incredible concept in crime fighting: whatever the circumstances, it could damn the guilty woman. It was only when the Court of Appeal spoilt everything by deciding that, while there was no evidence of smothering, there was plenty of evidence that the children were suffering from genetic disorders to such an extent that the universal efficacy of Munchausen's was questioned.

Secrecy allowed incompetence and mania to flourish, as it has done for 20 years. It is not too great an exaggeration to say that families have been forced into a legal world whose practices and assumptions are closer to those of a tyranny than a democracy.

It is a modern phenomenon. In the late 1980s, Iain Walker, a journalist on the Daily Mail, noticed that there was an explosion in the number of injunctions banning inquires about the state's treatment of children. In most cases, no one in his newsroom had the faintest idea who the children were or why the authorities thought reporters might be interested in them. But the injunctions kept dropping out of the fax machine. Disquieted by the assault on freedom of speech, Walker took a sabbatical at Oxford University and published an investigation into the closed world of the Family Courts. As ever, the interests of children came a poor second to the interests in covering up the rank failures of the bureaucracy.

The popularity of gagging orders began after the murder in 1987 of Jasmine Beckford, the Victoria Climbié of her day. Her brutal stepfather was free to kill her in the most revolting manner, even though she was on the at-risk register of Brent council in north London.

The council faced intense media criticism as journalists talked to Jasmine's brothers and sisters about its many failings. The courts agreed to a request from a desperate council that Jasmine's siblings should not be identified, and killed the story.

Brent's success in stopping unwelcome questions encouraged others to go further. Until the exposure of Meadow, the most shocking abuse of state power in family law had been perpetrated by social workers, who had fallen for the theories of American born-again Christians that rings of Satanists routinely abused then ritually sacrificed children in the covens of devil-worshippers. When Rochdale council was caught up in the witch craze, the courts happily granted an injunction that not only prevented the identification of the children involved, but also 'the solicitation or publication of any information about the circumstances of or the reason for those proceedings'.

Nothing could be done to investigate the actions of the social workers, who were eventually proved to be the dupes of hysterics. Even councillors were banned from speaking up for their constituents. As Walker said, Britain was coming perilously close to the 'pre-censorship of totalitarian regimes'.

Margaret Hodge and Helena Kennedy QC are investigating what can be done to clear up the wrecked lives that Meadow has left behind him. A modest first step would be that blundering theorists should not be protected by legal secrecy. If the authorities believe there is evidence to justify taking a child into care, they should present it in open court. If the judge thinks the child should not be named, that would be up to him or her, but the evidence should be tested in public.

After the Meadow disaster, it is time to return to the basic principle that justice is done in the light.

22. URGENT CONCLUSIONS

As I said earlier:

1. There really are **SECRET COURTS** in the UK

2. These courts take children from loving parents who have committed no crime

3. These parents lose their children forever to adoption by strangers

4. Parents are **GAGGED** and regularly sent to prison in secret proceedings if they reveal what went on in court

5. Establishment judges make decisions to take thousands of babies for risk of possible future emotional abuse

6. No jury would take babies from mothers because some expert made predictions of their future behaviour

7. Criminals facing 6+ months in prison can demand a jury; parents losing their children for life cannot

8. Pregnant mothers with no criminal records or disabilities are told their babies will be taken at birth!

9. Local authorities are rewarded by central government for reaching 'adoption targets' hence adoption is prioritised

10. Fosterers get up to £400 per week per child, special schools up to £7000 per week, adoption agencies, experts and lawyers all cash in lavishly!

So what to do?

- Stop the secrecy and the gagging of parents

- Stop adoptions of children for emotional abuse or for 'risk'

- Stop judges deciding cases of long-term fostering or adoption, and give juries the final decision

- Stop excessive rewards for those who live off the misery caused by this wicked system!

This would be a very very good start!

23. USEFUL QUOTES

1. 'It should, surely, be a crime to remove a newborn baby from a mother who has never harmed it.'

Camilla Cavendish, The Times, Dec 26 2006

2. 'Last year something like 200 people were sent to prison by the family courts, which happens in complete privacy and secrecy.'

Harriet Harman (Minister of State, Department of Constitutional Affairs) statement in Parliament

3. "Emotional abuse' has no strict definition in British law. Yet it now accounts for an astounding 21 per cent of all children registered as needing protection, up from 14 per cent in 1997. Last year 6,700 children were put on the child protection register for emotional abuse, compared with only 2,600 for sexual abuse and 5,100 for physical abuse.'

Camilla Cavendish, The Times, Aug 23 2007

4. 'Family courts are refusing to tell mothers why their babies are being taken away and put up for forced adoption.'

Ben Leapman Sunday Telegraph, Aug 2007

5. 'After a host of miscarriages of justice based on discredited expert witnesses, calls are growing for radical reform of their use in court'

Lois Rogers, The Sunday Times, Nov 18, 2007

6. Tim Loughton: 'To ask the Secretary of State for Children, Schools and Families which local authorities have received payments from central Government for achieving adoption target levels; and how much each received in each of the last three years.' [151067]

John Healey: I have been asked to reply:

'30 local authorities have been rewarded for successfully achieving adoption targets in their local public service agreements (LPSA).'

7. 'There is, so far as the parties to this case are aware, no European jurisprudence questioning the principle of freeing for adoption, or indeed compulsory adoption generally. The United Kingdom is unusual amongst members of the Council of Europe in permitting the total severance of family ties without parental consent.'

House of Lords - Down Lisburn Health and Social Services Trust.

Baroness Hale of Richmond. Judgement

8. 'Councils are paying up to £6,000 a week to place children with extreme and complex needs in "one-person children's homes" without any proof that this will help them. '

Lucy Ward, The Guardian, Mar 28 2007

9. 'Kafkaesque children's courts sitting in private are playing God with the families that come before them. They sound like a chilling legacy from the bad old days of the Soviet Union — secret courts that have taken thousands of children from their families and put them into foster homes or farmed them out for adoption.'

Stuart Wavell, The Sunday Times, July 6 2003

10. 'LONDON: Private agencies are making millions of pounds out of a critical shortage of foster homes for children. Firms are charging councils on average £800 per child per week.'

The Evening Standard, Oct 2 2005

These following reforms would stop most of the present injustices.

1. Abolish the Family Court secrecy that gags parents who wish to complain.

2. Abolish 'emotional harm' and 'risk' as justifications for putting children into care.

3. Abolish 'forced adoption' if a parent opposes an adoption in court.

4. Abolish decisions by Family Court judges to take babies and young children into care (let juries decide).

5. Abolish the power of Social Services to regulate and control contact between parents and children, to censor their conversation or to restrict phone calls. The court must control the frequency of contacts.

6. Abolish the restriction preventing a lay advisor from presenting a case for parents refused legal aid.

7. Abolish hearsay evidence in Family Courts and require witnesses to stick to facts without 'speculation'.

8. Abolish the removal of children for non life threatening forms of neglect such as absences from school or insanitary dwellings unless a written warning has been served and the situation has not been remedied.

Re K D [1998] 1 AC p. 812 letter B

Lord Templeman stated;

"The best person to bring up a child is the natural parent. It matters not whether the parent is wise or foolish, rich or poor, educated or illiterate, provided the child's moral and physical health are not endangered. Public authorities cannot improve on nature."

And so say all of us!!

ACKNOWLEDGMENTS

Grateful acknowledgement is made to the following sources for permission to reproduce material in this book:

BBC News at bbc.co.uk/news, 'Can children in care avoid prison?' *BBC News*, 15 May 2002, ©2002 BBC.

BBC News at bbc.co.uk/news, (2007), 'Foster carers abused young boys"', *BBC News*, 22 May 2006, ©2006 BBC.

BBC News at bbc.co.uk/news, 'System "failing children in care"', *BBC News*, 23 Aug 2006, ©2006 BBC.

BBC News at bbc.co.uk/news, 'Babies "removed to meet targets"', Brian Wheeler, *BBC News*, 26 Jan 2007, ©2007 BBC.

Daily Mail, 'Lose your children for being too poor', James Chapman, *Daily Mail*, 22 Aug 2005, ©2005 Associated Newspapers Ltd.

Daily Mail 'The minister for child betrayal', *Daily Mail*, 12 Nov 2003, ©2003 Associated Newspapers Ltd.

Daily Mail 'Judge condemns council staff', Steve Doughty, *Daily Mail*, 18 Mar 2006, ©2006 Associated Newspapers Ltd.

Daily Mail '60,000 children in care "betrayed" as three out of four fail at school', *Daily Mail,* 18 Sep 2006, ©2006 Associated Newspapers Ltd.

Daily Mail 'Couple see child taken away as son in pond fall lay dying', Ben Clerkin, *Daily Mail*, 23 Nov 2006, ©2006 Associated Newspapers Ltd.

Daily Mail 'Parents win right to keep fourth child - but to fight for the other three', Laura Collins, *Daily Mail*, 1 Jul 2007, ©2007 Associated Newspapers Ltd.

Daily Mail 'Councils making millions in incentives after snatching record numbers of babies for adoption' Sue Reid, *Daily Mail,* 2 Jul 2007, ©2007 Associated Newspapers Ltd.

Daily Mail 'My baby will be taken from me the moment it's born', Helen Weathers, *Daily Mail*, 6 Sep 2007, ©2007 Associated Newspapers Ltd.

Daily Mail 'Baby 'snatched' from mother minutes after birth is ordered back into foster care', David Wilkes, *Daily Mail*, 2 Feb 2008 ©2008 Associated Newspapers Ltd.

Daily Mail 'Jailed: The man who helped his wife flee abroad as social workers threatened to take their baby', Fiona Barton, *Daily Mail*, 7 Feb 2008, ©2008 Associated Newspapers Ltd.

Daily Mail 'My baby had cancer but social workers falsely accused me of child abuse and took all three of my children', Sue Reid, *Daily Mail*, 22 Feb 2008, ©2008 Associated Newspapers Ltd.

Daily Mail 'How social workers took away our children for 11 months without a shred of evidence', Sue Reid, *Daily Mail*, 9 May 2008, ©2008 Associated Newspapers Ltd.

Daily Mail 'Back to Barristers 'exploiting misery' as fees in family law cases rise 25% in 5 years', *Daily Mail*, 19 Jun 2008, ©2008 Associated Newspapers Ltd.

Daily Mail 'Boy, 5, forced into adoption with gay couple pleads: 'We want to stay with our gran and grandad"', Jonathan Brocklebank and Michael Seamark, *Daily Mail*, 29 Jan 2009, ©2009 Associated Newspapers Ltd.

Daily Mail, 'Social services Stasi should hang their heads in shame', Amanda Platell, *Daily Mail*, 29 Jan 2009, ©2009 Associated Newspapers Ltd.

Daily Mirror 'EXCLUSIVE: ANTI-SOCIAL WORKERS....Hundreds of criminals apply for care jobs' Tom Pettifor, *Daily Mirror,* 20 May 2006, ©2006 Daily Mirror/Mirrorpix.

The Daily Telegraph, 'Shaming" policy on adoption attacked', Nicole Martin, *Daily Telegraph*, 19 Jun 2001, ©2001 Daily Telegraph.

The Daily Telegraph, 'Children are taken away - but the system can't admit it's wrong', Cassandra Jardine, *Daily Telegraph*, 02 August 2004, ©2004 Daily Telegraph.

The Daily Telegraph Magazine 'Parents champion', Cassandra Jardine, *Daily Telegraph Magazine*, 11 Feb 2006, ©2006 Daily Telegraph.

The Daily Telegraph 'Gay foster parents abused young boys', Nigel Bunyan, *The Daily Telegraph,* 23 May 2006, ©2006 Daily Telegraph.

The Daily Telegraph 'Shattered lives in shadow of abuse', Carol Midgley, *The Daily Telegraph*, 26 Jan 2006, ©2006 Daily Telegraph.

The Daily Telegraph 'Adoption increases fails to stop baby deaths', Ben Leapman, *Daily Telegraph*, 17 Sep 2007, ©2007 Daily Telegraph.

The Daily Telegraph '7 children may be buried at Jersey care home', Caroline Gammell, *Daily Telegraph*, 26 Feb 2008, ©2008 Daily Telegraph.

The Daily Telegraph 'Telegraph View: Child abuse won't be overcome until we define what it is. Ed Balls will fail unless he gives guidance on what social workers should be doing', *Daily Telegraph*, 10 Jan 2009, ©2009 Daily Telegraph.

Eastern Daily Press, 'Social services knew of child in danger', Richard Balls, *EDP24 (Eastern Daily Press)*, 27 Jan 2006, ©2006 Eastern Daily Press, Norfolk.

The Guardian 'Blair vows to increase number of adoptions', John Carvel, *The Guardian*, 22 Dec 2000, ©2000 Guardian News and Media Ltd.

The Guardian, Council must pay £500,000 for wrongly taking girl into care', Clare Dyer, *The Guardian*, 17 Mar 2006, ©2006 Guardian News and Media Ltd.

The Guardian 'Concern over vulnerable children placed in isolating care homes', Lucy Ward, *The Guardian*, 28 Mar 2007, ©2007 Guardian News and Media Ltd.

The Guardian 'Unfit to be a mother? In the 60s, many women were forced to give up their illegitimate babies. Everyone now agrees that was a shocking practice', *The Guardian*, 15 Jan 2008, ©2008 Guardian News and Media Ltd.

The Independent 'The neglect that reduces girls to a life on the streets', Maxine Frith *The Independent*, 14 Dec 2006, ©2006 The Independent.

London Evening Standard 'Millionaire baby brokers firms cash in on shortage of foster homes', *London Evening Standard*, 2 October 2005, ©2005 Associated Newspapers Ltd.

Mail on Sunday 'Care home girl abused by 25 men in 2 years' Jo Knowsley and Eileen Fairweather, *Mail on Sunday,* 27 Aug 2006, ©2006 Associated Newspapers Ltd.

Mail on Sunday 'Couple who fled to Ireland keep baby celebrate his first year', Laura Collins, *Daily Mail*, 27 May 2007, ©2007 Associated Newspapers Ltd.

Mail on Sunday, 'Websters' MP: stop cash for adoptions', Laura Collins, *Mail on Sunday*, 07 Jul 2007, ©2007 Associated Newspapers Ltd.

The Observer 'Abuse of contempt' Nick Cohen, *The Observer*, 4 Dec 2005, ©2005 Guardian News and Media Ltd.

The Scotsman 'Mother wins fight to get her baby back', Shan Ross, *Scotsman*, 15 June 2006, ©2006 The Scotsman.

The Scotsman 'Council let known paedophile become foster parent', Patrick Barnham and Raymond Hainey, *The Scotsman*, 9 Mar 2007, ©2007 Patrick Barnham and Raymond Hainey.

South Wales Echo 'Scandal of children's homes abuse payouts', Moira Sharkey and Phillip Nifield, *South Wales Echo,* 2 Oct 2006, ©2006 South Wales Echo www.icWales.co.uk.

The Sunday Telegraph 'YouTube row over social services baby threat', Ben Leapman, *Sunday Telegraph*, 19 Aug 2007, ©2007 Sunday Telegraph.

The Sunday Telegraph 'Threat to take newborn over emotional abuse', David Harrison, *Sunday Telegraph*, 26 Aug 2007, ©2007 Sunday Telegraph.

The Sunday Telegraph 'Courts won't reveal rulings in adoption cases', Ben Leapman, *Sunday Telegraph*, 8 Aug 2007, ©2007 Sunday Telegraph.

The Sunday Telegraph 'MP bids to lift secrecy in family courts', Ben Leapman and Andrew Alderson, *Sunday Telegraph,* 7 July 2007, ©2007 Sunday Telegraph.

The Sunday Times 'The expert as judge and jury', *The Sunday Times*, 18 Nov 2007, ©2007 Times Newspapers Ltd.

The Sunday Times 'Secret courts that steal our children', Stuart Wavell, *Sunday Times,* 6 Jul 2003, ©2003 Times Newspapers Ltd.

The Sunday Times 'Harman's sister attacks Hodge over child cases', Sian Griffiths, *The Sunday Times*, 04 Dec 2005, ©2005 Times Newspapers Ltd.

The Times 'How can this happen here?' Simon Barnes, *The Times*, 18 May 2006, ©2006 Times Newspapers Ltd.

The Times 'Blind justice without a name', Camilla Cavendish, *The Times*, 19 Oct 2006, ©2006 Times Newspapers Ltd.

The Times 'Family courts are the B-side of the law', Camilla Cavendish, *The Times*, 26 Dec 2006, ©2006 Times Newspapers Ltd.

The Times 'Children's single-place homes can charge £6,000 per week', Rosemary Bennett, *The Times*, 28 Mar 2007, ©2007 Times Newspapers Ltd.

The Times 'The forces of secrecy are prevailing', Camilla Cavendish, *The Times*, 29 Mar 2007, ©2007 Times Newspapers Ltd.

The Times 'The rank hypocrisy of family court judges', Camilla Cavendish, *The Times*, 24 May 2007, ©2007 Times Newspapers Ltd.

The Times 'Guilty of child abuse! (Well, our version.)', Camilla Cavendish, *The Times*, 23 Aug 2007, ©2007 Times Newspapers Ltd.

The Times 'British justice: a family ruined: A chilling example of our secret State where a mother and child are forced into hiding' Camilla Cavendish, *The Times*, 21 Feb, 2008, ©2008 Times Newspapers Ltd.

The Sunday Telegraph 'The unnatural justice of secret family courts', Leader Article, *The Sunday Telegraph*, 26 Aug 2007, ©2007 Sunday Telegraph.

The Times 'Free the 'Grandfather One: Is it really in the public interest that a grandparent is jailed for not avoiding his grandson? Camilla Cavendish, *The Times*, 13 Dec 2007, ©2007 Times Newspapers Ltd.

The Times 'Judges condemn 'foul play' on adoptions', Rosemary Bennett, *The Times*, 2 May 2008, ©2008 Times Newspapers Ltd.

The Times 'The Bar Council, which represents nearly 15,000 barristers in England and Wales, will announce its proposals in a paper before an all-party meeting of MPs tomorrow', *The Times*, 19 June 2008, ©2008 Times Newspapers Ltd.

The Times 'A secret state is operating in which families are being torn apart', Camilla Cavendish, *The Times*, 20 Oct 2008, ©2008 Times Newspapers Ltd.

The Times 'Family courts to be opened up as Jack Straw announces massive shake-up', Frances Gibb, *The Times*, Dec 16 2008, ©2008 Times Newspapers Ltd.

The Times 'Family courts: what changed on the long walk to freedom', Camilla Cavendish, *The Times*, 16 Dec 2008, ©2008 Times Newspapers Ltd.

The Times 'Time running out for one family caught by the family courts', Alice Fishburn, *The Times*, 16 Dec 2008, ©2008 Times Newspapers Ltd.

The Times 'Family courts: case studies', Fiona Hamilton, *The Times*, 16 Dec 2008, ©2008 Times Newspapers Ltd.

The Times 'This blind faith in experts fails family justice professionals giving evidence in court are supposed to be independent; too often they are hired guns for local authorities', Camilla Cavendish, *The Times*, 9 Jan 2009, ©2009 Times Newspapers Ltd.

All material from Parliamentary Information Management Services (PIMS), Hansard, Office of Public Sector Information (IPSO) and Judicial Communications Office (JCO) are © Crown Copyright and reproduced with kind permission.

Thanks also to David Ayres for his help in putting this book together.